ECONOMICS OF HEALTH CARE

PRAEGER STUDIES IN GRANTS ECONOMICS

General Editors:
Kenneth E. Boulding
Janos Horvath

ECONOMICS OF HEALTH CARE

edited by
Jacques van der Gaag
William B. Neenan
Theodore Tsukahara, Jr.

PRAEGER SPECIAL STUDIES • PRAEGER SCIENTIFIC

Library of Congress Cataloging in Publication Data

Main entry under title:

Economics of health care.

    (Praeger studies in grants economics)
    Includes bibliographies.
    1. Medical policy—United States. 2. Medical
economics—United States. I. Gaag, J. van der.
II. Neenan, William B., 1929-   III. Tsukahara,
Theodore. IV. Series.
RA395.A3E27   362.1′0973   82-3699
ISBN 0-03-061501-1   AACR2

Published in 1982 by Praeger Publishers
CBS Educational and Professional Publishing
a Division of CBS Inc.
521 Fifth Avenue, New York, New York 10175, U.S.A.

Printed in the United States of America

CONTRIBUTORS

Ralph L. Andreano
Professor of Economics
University of Wisconsin-Madison

Ronald B. Conners
St. Luke's Roosevelt Hospital Center
New York

Margaret A. Cooke
Service Fellow
National Center for Health Statistics
Maryland

Jay P. Crozier
Research Assistant
The Maxwell School
Syracuse University

William Der
Research Associate
Human Resources Research Center
University of Southern California

Richard L. Ernst
Research Associate
Human Resources Research Center
University of Southern California

Susan Feigenbaum
Assistant Professor of Economics
Claremont McKenna College
Claremont Graduate School

Paul J. Gertler
Graduate Student
University of Wisconsin-Madison

Paul B. Ginsburg
Deputy Assistant Director for
Income Security and Wealth
Congressional Budget Office
U.S. Congress

Nancy T. Greenspan
Chief, Economic and Long Range Studies Branch
Health Care Financing Administration
U.S. Department of Health and Human Services

Michael Grossman
Professor of Economics
City University of New York
Director, Division of Health Economics
National Bureau of Economic Research

Joel W. Hay
Assistant Professor
Department of Behavioral Sciences
and Community Health
University of Connecticut Health Center

Evelien M. Hooijmans
Research Associate
Center for Research in Public Economics
Leiden University

Steven Jacobowitz
Assistant Professor of Economics
C. W. Post Center
Long Island University

Stephen H. Long
Associate Professor of Economics
The Maxwell School
Syracuse University

M. Susan Marquis
Economist
The Rand Corporation

Catherine McLaughlin
Assistant Professor of Economics
Tufts University

Rita Ricardo-Campbell
Senior Fellow
Hoover Institution
Stanford University

Sherwin Rosen
Professor of Economics
University of Chicago
Research Associate
National Bureau of Economic Research

Anne A. Scitovsky
Palo Alto Medical Research Foundation
Health Policy Program
School of Medicine
University of California

Paul Taubman
Professor of Economics
University of Pennsylvania
Research Associate
National Bureau of Economic Research

Robert M. Veatch
Professor of Medical Ethics
Kennedy Institute of Ethics
Georgetown University

Wynand P. M. M. van de Ven
Research Associate
Center for Research in Public Economics
Leiden University

Ronald J. Vogel
Director
Division of Economic Analysis
Health Care Financing Administration
U.S. Department of Health and Human Services

Barbara L. Wolfe
Associate Professor
Departments of Economics and Preventive Medicine
Institute for Research on Poverty
University of Wisconsin-Madison

Donald E. Yett
Director, Human Resources Research Center
Professor of Economics
University of Southern California

FOREWORD

In responding to queries about ecodynamic phenomena, Kenneth Boulding reflected that more often than not the process of development is good, but the ensuing hugeness is bad. This philosophical insight helps when contemplating the current controversies surrounding the health care industry. Yet, is it not irreverent even to intimate the notion that the growth of health care could be pathological? To such a provocative question the answer will vary depending on the test employed, such as, size, proportions, burdens, beneficiaries, and resilience within the system.

The researcher may approach the differentiating of health care provisions by observing whether they are purchased by private individuals or by public agencies. The private purchase is a market transaction (quid pro quo), while the publicly financed purchases entail sizable welfare components even though insurance for private risk pooling is also a market transaction. But the very presence of any welfare grant component changes the characteristic of a transaction with respect to such dominant social targets as equity, efficiency, growth, and stability.

That the present volume amounts to a successful diagnosis of the health care industry is attributable to two things. First, the authors are leading authorities in health economics who make creative use of the state of the art and masterfully advance knowledge in the chapters contributed. Second, in the design of the book the editors have imaginatively adapted grants economics, a conceptual framework uniquely befitting to the task.

This book is one of the Grants Economics Series preceded and succeeded by a dozen other volumes that deal with the financial system, higher education, income distribution, regulatory impacts, foreign aid, industrial concentration, etc. Since grants economics is the organizing notion of these endeavors, a sketch of it is offered herein as orientation to the unfolding material.[1]

Grants economics, defined simply, identifies the size and traces the leverage of grants elements as they interface with exchange elements in all kinds of economic processes. Grant describes the unmatched transaction where the net worth of one party—the grantor—diminishes, while the net worth of the other party—the grantee—increases. Deviating from the norm of exchanging equal values, such transactions contain certain grant elements. Beyond the clearly visible explicit grant—gift, aid, and unilateral transfer—there exists a vast network of implicit grants in the private as well as public sectors of the economy. The visible explicit grants are only the tip of the iceberg while the much larger amorphic bulk of implicit grants remains hidden and therefore often escapes attention.

Much of the initial work in grants economics has dealt with the issues of the urbanized economy, income distribution and redistribution as these affect efficiency and equity, the tax-expenditure structure, externalities in the environment, intrafamily and intergenerational granting. The international economy is a major field of inquiry. The inflation-unemployment dilemma is explained through institutional rigidities which generate implicit grants to those who restrain potential supply. In the macroeconomy a grant dollar spent tends to generate more production and income than an exchange dollar because the granting is often conditioned on complementary exchange transactions. A recurrent theme is that grants economics is a major instrument by which people and institutions hope to change the world for the better. As a network of policy instruments, the grants economy represents the heart of political economy, because routinely it is by pulling the levers of positive and negative subventions that the political system intervenes smoothly into the economic system.

Notwithstanding its versatility, the grants economy is subject to perverse effects. Just as the theory of market failures acknowledges that exchange economy cannot achieve certain types of economic ends, the pathologies of the grants economy call for diagnosis. Far from remedying all distortions brought about by the market process, it is a political irony that regulations and subventions have often exacerbated the problem. Indeed, grant economics could make a unique contribution to the regulatory reform through sorting out good grants and bad grants, i.e., those which achieve socially desirable goals from those with perverse effects.

The future is likely to witness that in health care delivery some perplexing problems will become demystified by realizing that the remedy for occasional market failures is not necessarily an uncritical reliance on the grants economy. Rather it will be an iterative search for the optimum blend of market transactions and grant transactions. The analytical techniques and the normative guides of grants economics will offer the key to scrutinizing as well as answering such pertinent questions as: (1) who pays the bill; (2) how do the institutional arrangements translate into economic initiatives; (3) how do distributive equity and allocative efficiency reinforce or erode each other?

Because these very questions represent the leitmotif of the ensuing chapters, I foresee the book not only as a sought-after policy guide but also as an agenda for research.

Janos Horvath

NOTE

[1]This sketch draws on: Janos Horvath, "Grants Economics" in Encyclopedia of Economics, ed. Douglas Greenwald (New York: McGraw-Hill, 1982), pp. 458–460. For a general exposition: Kenneth E. Boulding, A Preface to Grants Economics: The Economy of Love and Fear (New York: Praeger, 1981). The currently evolving books in grants economics are published in Praeger's Grants Economics Series.

CONTENTS

PART 4
HEALTH AND PUBLIC POLICY

PART 5
SELECTED ISSUES

INTRODUCTION

In 1980, the American people spent $247 billion, or $1,067 per person, on medical care. For this amount they bought the products and services of one of the most sophisticated health-care industries in the world. The growth of that industry during the past decades has been enormous. For instance, in 1970 4.3 million workers were employed in the health-care industry. In 1979 the number had increased to 6.7 million, a rise of 55 percent. In the same period the total U.S. work force increased only 23 percent. As a portion of gross national product, total expenditures on health care increased from 4.4 percent in 1950 to 9.4 percent in 1980.

In any other industry such growth would be considered a sign of vitality. In most industrialized western nations, however, the high growth rate and the size of the health-care industry are observed with increasing concern. It is remarkable that, in spite of a wide variety in the organization of the health-care system, all industrialized western countries have experienced similar growth patterns in their health-care industries. As a result, West Germany in 1975 spent 9.4 percent of its GNP on health care, the United States 8.6 percent, Sweden 8.5 percent, and The Netherlands 8.1 percent.

Certain similar underlying causes of this growth of the health industry can be identified. First, demographic changes increased the population share of high users of medical care. This trend will continue and become even more important in the near future as the percentage of very old people (75 years and over) will increase at a faster rate than any other age group in the population. The consequences for the health industry are enormous. For instance, an increase of 54 percent in nursing home use has been estimated from now until the year 2000, as a result of demographic shifts alone. By the year 2030 the increase will be as high as 135 percent.

Second, an increasing part of the health-care bill is being paid by public or private "third parties." In the United States during 1980, only one-third of the health care bill was paid directly by the consumers, whereas in 1965 more than 50 percent was paid directly. Third, the development of medical knowledge and technology has dramatically affected costs of medical care. The fact that many health distortions that used to be fatal can now be cured, or at least treated, has significantly contributed to the industry's growth.

None of these trends can be considered socially undesirable. The demographic shifts are to a large extent beyond our control, and the fact that people live longer cannot, by itself, be a reason for concern. Increased insurance coverage reflects the preferences of the population. Few can object to progress in medical knowledge and technology.

Why then is the development of the health-care industry often referred to as a "health care crisis"? Why do public officials propose an increasing number of drastic measures to cure this crisis? These measures range from a completely government-run national health services system to increased copayments by the consumers and more competition among providers.

The reason, we think, is not so much the growth of the industry per se, but rather the perception that the industry suffers from excess capacity and lack of incentives to produce its goods and services in an economically efficient way. Thus, developments that have increased access to medical care, such as greater insurance coverage, more hospitals, nursing homes, and physicians, have, at the same time, reduced many economic incentives that moderate the consumption of medical services and serve to improve efficiency in the production of those services.

Consequently, it is widely perceived that, even if total health-care expenditures cannot be reduced, the product bought for the current outlays can be significantly improved. Alternatively, if the right economic incentives were in place, the same quantity and quality of health care presently consumed could be provided for less money. Of special concern is the lack of evidence that increased health-care spending improves health status and longevity. Comparing West Germany and the United States, for instance, shows that they rank numbers one and two in health-care spending but are only numbers ten and nine, respectively, on a mortality scale that compares ten industrialized countries. Of course, factors other than expenditures on medical care play a dominant role here.

This volume contains economic analyses aimed at enhancing our understanding of the health-care system. Included are studies focusing on health outcomes of public programs and policies and on variables other than the consumption of medical care that have an impact on health (the chapters by Rosen and Taubman, Grossman and Jacobowitz, and Hooymans and van de Ven). These studies provide information pertinent to the question of how to allocate scarce resources among medical care and all other goods and services.

Other chapters address the question of how to raise and spend the money for medical care efficiently and equitably. Long, Cooke, and Crozier, and Marquis study the distributional impacts of alternative ways of financing medical care. Scitovsky studies the effect of alternative reimbursement systems on utilization rates, and Wolfe examines the question of whether public policy has been successful in achieving equality in consumption levels of medical care among children with various socioeconomic backgrounds. Ginsburg, Greenspan, and Vogel investigate structural demand shifts after the introduction of Medicare in 1966.

A number of chapters deal with the behavior of one or more actors within the health-care system. Yett, Der, Ernst, and Hay present a model of physician behavior, Gertler and Andreano present a model of the nursing home industry, and Feigenbaum examines the performance of nonprofit charities.

Though these studies all deal with a different part of the health-care system, their common message is loud and clear: all actors in the health-care system, nonprofit charities included, react to changes in the economic incentives they face. Consequently, any set of policy measures aimed at improving efficiency or reducing cost in one part of the system must be scrutinized for its possible effects on the entire system. The lack of success of past government measures to curtail medical care expenditures might be attributed to our lack of understanding of the interactions within the system and between the health-care system and the rest of the economy.

Three of the studies included in this volume evaluate the performance of the health-care industry. Conners explains the quantity and quality of changes in hospital labor. McLaughlin studies the impact of unions on a hospital's wage structure, and Ricardo-Campbell studies the effects of government regulation on the drug industry. Emphasizing the need to include nonhealth benefits and nonhealth costs when regulating the marketing of new drugs, the author widens the base on which policy should be made.

All the studies mentioned above are written by economists. Dealing with the familiar problem of how to apportion limited resources, they address the question of how to produce medical care efficiently and how to distribute medical care in an equitable way.

Choices have to be made—choices that imply value judgments. Veatch's introductory chapter to this volume deals with these implicit value judgments. He alerts us to the ethical dimensions that must be considered when structuring the health-care system. By explicitly identifying the ethical dimensions of the distribution of health care, he provides economists and policymakers with the background needed to evaluate with sensitivity the issues of health-care provision and financing.

Jacques van der Gaag
William B. Neenan
Theodore Tsukahara, Jr.

ECONOMICS OF
HEALTH CARE

PART I
Ethics, Risk-Taking, and Public Policy

1

ETHICAL DIMENSIONS OF THE
DISTRIBUTION OF HEALTH CARE

Robert M. Veatch

The issues of health economics are increasingly intertwined
with ethical and other value questions in health planning. While on the
one hand there are some who maintain that economics can and should
be entirely a descriptive science, increasingly it is being realized
that the description of economic relationships alone leaves the economist studying health policy issues with many unanswered questions.
Some maintain that a value-free economics is itself an impossibility
since the very theoretical structure of any scientific discipline contains within it value premises.

Even those who reject this critique of a value-free economics
recognize that some of the most important and interesting questions
in health planning require moving beyond the description of economic
relationships to the making of value judgments about what the health-
care system should look like, what kinds of health-care interventions
deserve priority, and what counts as an appropriate distribution of
resources in a society. If a volume on health economics fails to examine explicitly the ethical and other value dimensions, it will, therefore, overlook some of the most significant questions of the field.
This first chapter will outline some of the most critical points of
intersection between economics and ethics in health-care delivery.

RELATIONSHIP OF HEALTH TO WELL-BEING

It is not obvious to everyone why the planners and health economists should be interested in the distribution of health care. Some,
such as Charles Fried,[1] argue that what people might more reasonably
be concerned about is the distribution of well-being. Some people
choose to use their resources investing in other basic goods, such as
food, clothing, shelter, or recreation. Because of that investment
strategy, they may not be as healthy as others. According to this

view, this should not be a matter of great social or moral concern. Health is merely one component of the aggregate well-being of individuals and does not in itself merit isolated attention as a matter of social policy.

In one sense these critics are certainly correct. Health planning cannot be isolated totally from the other dimensions of social policy. Yet a case can be made for focusing more directly on the distribution of health care. Often the task of the health planner is to determine the most appropriate use of a fixed health budget. It has been left to others to deal with the largest scale macroallocational questions. If it has been determined by a legislature or some other social policy decision-making mechanism that a fair proportion of resources devoted to health care is, say, 10 percent of the gross national product, then the health planner's task is to divide up that 10 percent in the most appropriate way. If there is such a division of labor, the distribution of health care becomes a critical issue, albeit one subordinated to the initial resource allocation decisions.

Others have argued that there is a more fundamental reason why we should be interested specifically in the distribution of health care. They claim that there is something unique about health and about interventions to maintain and restore health. Health care, according to this view, is fundamentally different from beer and panty hose; it is not a matter of satisfaction of individual desires but something to which individuals have a fundamental claim by right.

The existence of a right to health care is controversial.[2] We must distinguish between a legal right to health care and a moral right. Whether there is such a right as a matter of law depends on the jurisdiction. Within the United States, certain rights claims have been made, especially for individuals in special groups, such as veterans, public employees, and wards of the state. Moreover, courts have found that hospitals and other health institutions receiving public funding have an obligation to deliver certain kinds of care to those who are otherwise unable to obtain it.[3] By statutory law, individuals are increasingly being given a legal right to health care through Medicare- and Medicaid-type programs. Beyond that, it is not clear whether the case can be made for a constitutional right to health-care services.

Health planners are likely to be interested not only in the question of what the current state of the law is but also in what the law ought to be and what social policy ought to be. Thus they may want to know whether there is an ethical claim to a right to health care and if so, to what kind of care. It seems clear that there cannot be an unlimited right to all conceivable kinds of health care that anyone may desire. That would include apparently frivolous services such as face-lifts, as well as deviant and unorthodox therapies, such as megavitamin treatment for cancer and faith healing. It is clear, however, that it will be impossible to establish a public policy related to health care without some judgment about the ethical and other normative priorities for the distribution of health care.

We are still left with the question of why a society might acknowledge a right to health care in a way that is any different from other basic goods. Some argue that for many kinds of basic goods the need of each individual is approximately equal; within a certain narrow range, each of us needs the same amount of food, clothing, and shelter. Variations in consumption really depend largely on matters of individual preference. There are other basic goods, however, for which it appears that the need is not distributed evenly. Two obvious examples are education and health care. If health care services were distributed evenly, either certain constitutionally healthy individuals would have to have more care than they need or less healthy individuals would have considerably less care than they need. Some have, therefore, concluded that even if we ought to focus generally on the distribution of well-being, permitting individuals to use a generalized medium such as money to trade various goods in order to maximize their personal well-being, that strategy would not work for health care. Therefore, as a matter of social policy there must be some judgment about how health care ought to be distributed. This chapter proceeds on the assumption that there is reason for health economists to be interested in the distribution of health care.

THE NOTIONS OF EQUITY AND EQUALITY

The central issues of distribution are often addressed in welfare economics under the rubric of equity or equality. These notions are themselves complex; they are closely related to what philosophers refer to as justice or sometimes as fairness. [4] It is clearly an open question whether what is equitable or fair or just is total equality. Moreover, the concept of equality is itself ambiguous. Distributing one kind of good equally may turn out to distribute something else very unequally. For example, distributing health-care resources equally to each person will distribute health very unequally. For purposes of this chapter we will focus on the distribution of health-care resources—physicians, nurses, budgets for funding health programs, clinic facilities, and the like.

For distributing health-care resources, just as for distributing any other goods in a society, a number of competing theories have been put forward to account for what is a fair or equitable distribution. These various accounts focus on individual effort, personal ability, need, usefulness to the society, or proportionality. Sometimes the concept of justice is expanded to include consideration of previous harms done to others. This notion of "compensatory justice" will be addressed briefly at the end of the chapter.

To make matters more confusing, sometimes the term justice is used in a much broader, more inclusive way. Aristotle, in the fifth book of the Nicomachean Ethics,[5] distinguishes between what he calls complete justice and partial justice. By complete justice he means complete virtue or excellence. Sometimes justice is simply a synonym for doing the right thing. That is not the way the term is used, however, in debates over equity and distribution. Contemporary accounts discussing justice in health care refer to the term in a much narrower sense, what Aristotle called fairness in distribution.[6] Thus, it is possible that there are right-making characteristics of actions other than whether the action is fair. One might, for example, be concerned about whether it is an example of honesty, preservation of autonomy, production of good consequences, or fidelity. Thus, if we use the term justice in this narrow sense we could say of health-care policy, that it is not a particularly fair or just one but nevertheless produces good consequences or preserves individual freedom. Depending on one's normative ethical theory, one might even say that because of these other characteristics the health policy is the most appropriate one, even the right one, in the moral sense of the term. Of course if justice in the sense of equity or fairness turns out always to be the decisive moral characteristic, it would be impossible to reach such a conclusion.

To make matters more complicated, those working in medical ethics quickly discover that the traditional, professionally articulated codes of medical ethics have virtually nothing to say about how health-care resources are distributed. The Hippocratic oath, for instance, pledges physicians to apply measures for the benefit of the sick according to their abilities or judgment without any explicit instructions on how the benefits to the sick are to be distributed.[7] Should a physician have more than one patient and there is a critical need for services, the Hippocratic tradition gives no guidance. Should national health-care planners have perceived more need than their budgetary resources will fulfill, traditional professionally articulated ethics gives no guidance. Since 1957 the principles of ethics of the American Medical Association have included an explicit pledge that physicians should use their talents to serve the community as well as the individual. This has remained controversial. Even with the acknowledgment of a community focus in medicine, however, there is still no guidance on how competing claims of the community might be addressed.

There is another, more subtle problem with these codes of ethics articulated by professional groups such as physicians. Even if such a group has addressed this question directly, it is not clear why economists, health planners, members of legislative bodies, or anyone else in the society should find such a professional consensus determinative of social policy. Members of these groups will have to address directly the ethical and other values of questions in planning health-care distributions.

THEORIES OF EQUITABLE DISTRIBUTION

The enterprise of health planning thus necessarily deals with ethical questions, especially questions of equity or justice. Several major normative answers present themselves. While no single health-care plan is likely to reflect any one of the following theoretical positions completely, economists and others participating in the debate over health-care planning are likely to find themselves taking predominantly one or another of these positions.

Libertarianism and Pareto Optimality

One dominant position is what is sometimes called the entitlement theory. It is the view expressed by those grounded in the philosophical position of libertarianism. The most sophisticated contemporary philosophical defense of this view is articulated by Harvard philosopher Robert Nozick in his volume Anarchy, State, and Utopia.[8] It is a theory about personal property rooted in the views of John Locke and other political philosophers, emphasizing a doctrine of private property and individual rights. The core of the position is that one is entitled to what one possesses, provided it was acquired justly.[9] Goods are acquired justly if they are obtained by just acquisition or transfer, that is, from appropriation of goods not previously possessed by gift or by exchange. The state's role is simply to protect against unjust appropriation. Nozick makes clear that such a theory provides no definite pattern of distribution at all. There is no end state or end result that will be definitively fair.[10] Rather, individuals will buy, sell, bargain, trade, or exchange until they have improved their lot to the maximum extent possible, based upon their own preference functions. Whatever results will be viewed as fair, that is, fair in the sense that there has been no unjust appropriation or transfer of goods.

The implications for health economics are substantial. The attack by physician Robert Sade on the notion of the right to health care illustrates one physician's interpretation of their implications.[11] According to Sade, physicians as individuals are entitled to what they possess or create for themselves. They have no primordial obligation to patients unless they adopt a position of charity or unless they have willfully contracted to provide services for the patient. [12]

More generally, an entitlement theory gives no moral weight to the fact that some are unfortunate in the natural lottery. [13] It is simply a matter of fate that some are born with a healthy constitution while others are plagued with chronic medical problems. There is a sharp contrast between what is unfortunate and what is unfair. [14]

In economics the concern for Pareto optimality can most easily be accounted for under the entitlement or libertarian theory of distribution. Each member of a society is seen as a rational agent striving with self-interest to maximize his or her position. Social exchange will take place as long as everyone has something to gain. There is no independent moral obligation to sacrifice one's own welfare for the welfare of another. When one contributes to the health care of another, it is out of a sense that that simultaneously promotes one's own interest, at least in some subtle way.

There are real problems with the entitlement or libertarian theory as well as with the notion of Pareto optimality as it is applied to health policy. First there are empirical problems. It has been argued that no one in contemporary society has attained anything by appropriating it as a good not previously possessed, and no one has received goods that over many previous generations have been consistently transferred justly. [15] At some point in the past, unfair advantage was taken through slavery or its equivalent.

Moreover, many possessions are really received in trust as public, social goods. For physicians, education is acquired through public support. They incur an obligation in exchange for the benefits of their education and the monopoly practice of medicine. For health institutions, public funding generates a similar kind of involvement. The knowledge used in the practice of medicine is publicly generated and transmitted. It is not available for private possession.

More fundamentally, even if one could appropriate from the state of nature, this position would not, according to the critics of the entitlement theory, be an adequate account of a fair distribution of health-care resources. The world is not ours to possess, according to the critics. The libertarians never provide an adequate justification for this view. Either critical components belong to the community as a whole or, if they ever belong temporarily to individuals, their entitlement does not extend perpetually in the face of the need of others. In short, critics say there is no unlimited right of personal property. Certain patterns of outcome are morally preferable, especially in a sphere such as health care, in which outcomes are so largely independent of individual control.

If the entitlement theory and the economic principles entailed in it are unacceptable, one or another of the patterned theories of equitable distribution may have to be substituted.

Utilitarianism and Cost/Benefit Analysis

A second interpretation of what would count as a fair and just distribution of health care is one often favored by health planners and economists. It is based on the distributional principles of the utilitarianism of Jeremy Bentham[16] and John Stuart Mill.[17] Holders of the utilitarian interpretation say that when we cannot buy every service everyone would like, we should calculate the benefits and costs of alternative courses of action and choose either the plan that maximizes the benefit-cost ratio or the one that maximizes the net benefits over costs. The goal, according to the classical utilitarians, is to produce the greatest good for the greatest number. The correct distribution of a good such as health care, according to the utilitarians, is determined by looking at the consequences.

In that sense it is similar to the ethic of the Hippocratic tradition that focuses on benefits and harm to the patient. Utilitarians, however, refuse to limit their attention to isolated individuals such as a single patient. In doing so they overcome a deficiency of the Hippocratic ethic: it is silent on problems of resource allocation. They also overcome the difficulties suggested in the libertarian approach in that utilitarians are able to envision a pattern of distribution that is the most appropriate one.

Cost/benefit analysis and systems analysis, in their most common forms, usually incorporate the ethical presumptions of utilitarianism. Both are theoretical works attempting to apply cost/benefit analysis to the health-care delivery system[18] and specific applications of cost/benefit analysis to problems of health policy.[19] They attempt to measure the efficiency or value of a potential health-care innovation by examining the aggregate costs in comparison with the aggregate benefits of alternative policy innovations. Cost/effectiveness analysis[20] narrows the analytical problem by comparing the costs of what appear to be alternative ways of achieving a predetermined objective. Although they appear to be alternative ways of achieving a single predetermined objective, there will always necessarily be differences in the approaches being compared even if those differences do not affect aggregate consequences. There may be, for example, differences in the way benefits are distributed. It must remain an open question whether those differences are morally relevant. Whether the analyst is engaged in cost/benefit or cost/effectiveness analysis, however, the utilitarian presupposition is made: that aggregate net benefit is critical in determining policy.

There are also serious problems with the utilitarian approach. First, there are likely to be problems with accounting. The most important benefits and harms may be subtle and nonquantifiable. It is difficult, for instance, to quantify pain and suffering or the value of the loss of a loved one. It is difficult to determine the numerical value of the destruction of a principle held dear by society. In the health-care sphere it is notoriously difficult to compare benefits and harms. It is widely recognized that a simple comparison of economic costs will be inadequate unless other subtle social, psychological, moral, and spiritual costs are also taken into account when comparing alternative policies.

It is equally difficult to quantify benefits. Some cost/benefit analyses have focused exclusively on changes in mortality rates or on length of survival. Yet patients make clear that other values are important as well, including the value of decreased morbidity and freedom from pain and suffering. Early efforts to calculate the monetary value of life, for example, the human capital approaches of Rice and her colleagues,[21] have sometimes been interpreted to imply that the value of an innovation can be determined by measuring the dollars added to the gross national product, implying that health-care innovations that on balance add years of gainfully employed life expectancy to males are more valuable than those adding to females; that innovations targeted on whites are more valuable than those targeting on other racial groups; and that those for retirees are virtually worthless. Clearly other benefits of potential innovations must be considered, and it must be determined whether actual existing income patterns have any moral relevance whatsoever when the value of health-care programs is determined.

Any cost/benefit analysis that attempts to aggregate benefits of alternative health-care innovations will have to answer the question of how these disparate, apparently nonquantifiable benefits are related. Users of such a strategy will also have to determine whether the goal is to concentrate on present benefits or future benefits. They will have to determine how to take into account benefits to future generations and whether or not it is morally necessary to do so.[22] For example, if benefits to all future generations are taken into account, health planning may be heavily skewed toward research and development as opposed to therapeutic interventions to treat the presently sick, yet if they are ignored, research as well as resource preservation may be undervalued. It may not be sufficient to calculate discount rates based upon present preference systems because some who may have a legitimate claim on future resources may not presently be able to express preferences.

In spite of the fact that there are serious methodological and empirical problems in quantifying costs and benefits, cogent defense of the possibility of at least approximating such quantification has been offered.[23] While human capital approaches to the calculation of the value of life have been found wanting for their failure to take into account values other than productive labor, other strategies, such as willingness-to-pay formulas and calculation of quality adjusted life years, seem to take into account many additional values.[24] Defenders of these approaches argue that at least rough approximations are made routinely in one's life, when benefits and harms of alternative courses are compared. As long as one continues to acknowledge the lack of precision, some of these problems of quantification can, therefore, be surmounted.

A second kind of objection cuts more deeply. This is that the utilitarian interpretation of the principle of justice and its application in cost/benefit and cost/effectiveness analyses fails to take into account the distributions of benefits and harms. To be sure, relatively unequal distributions are likely to have a disutility of their own because of decreasing marginal utility of resources. John Stuart Mill recognized this in the fifth chapter of Utilitarianism,[25] when he argued that justice can be understood as a requirement derivative from the general principle of utility.

Critics of Mill do not find this adequate. They are concerned about cases in which an unequal distribution of benefits and harms will produce a greater good in aggregate. They argue that, at least hypothetically, there must be cases in which unequal distribution of benefits and harms will produce a greater good in aggregate. They argue that, at least hypothetically, there must be cases in which unequal distributions will maximize utility. In such cases they claim that the matter is not necessarily settled in favor of the inequality. The distribution of benefits and harms per se may be morally relevant. It may be important, for example, that some small group of persons receives substantial harm, while another larger group is helped somewhat by a policy innovation. It may be important beyond the obvious possibility that the disutility of the substantial harm may be very great even though the number of people hurt is small. Critics of the utilitarian interpretation of the distributive principle claim that it matters morally who is harmed and who is helped, or at least it may matter. Defenders of the entitlement interpretation at least recognize this. Critics say there is no particular reason why society should be interested in the total aggregate amount of good per se. They argue that at least this should not be decisive and claim that other matters may be relevant morally, such as whether promises are kept, whether a policy protects the rights of individuals, and whether people are treated fairly.

Anyone who uses the utilitarian assumption in cost/benefit analyses, cost/effectiveness analyses, or related health-care planning must be prepared to defend the assumption that the only goal that is legitimate in health planning is maximization of the aggregate net benefit. That is an assumption that is rejected by many people. It is rejected by libertarians and defenders of Pareto optimality. They claim that it is wrong to deprive another of resources, even if it will increase the aggregate amount of good to do so. It is also rejected by those who defend more emphasis on distribution on the basis of need. It is to those interpretations that we must now turn.

Rawlsianism and Maximin Analysis

Another major tradition for interpreting the principle of equity or justice as it is applied to health care focuses on the needs of various individuals in the society. Marxist, socialist, and many welfare economics theorists as well as many contemporary philosophers and political scientists working on the theory of justice have come to reject both the libertarian and utilitarian interpretations of the principle. One group, influenced by the theoretical work of the contemporary philosopher, John Rawls, have opted for a <u>maximin</u> interpretation of the principle of justice.[26] Defenders of this view say that the goal of a health policy or any other social welfare program should not be to maximize aggregate net benefit or average outcome, but to maximize the position of certain least well-off members of the society. The Rawlsian analysis is presented at a highly abstract level, so that its implications for the economics of health planning are not obvious. Certain followers of Rawls, especially Ronald Green, the ethicist at Dartmouth, have, however, extended the Rawlsian analysis to the health-care sphere.[27]

Rawls articulates two principles of justice that he claims would be agreed to by reasonable people taking the moral point of view. First he claims that "each person is to have an equal right to the most extensive total system of equal basic liberty compatible with a similar system of liberty for all."[28] He goes on to argue that reasonable people subject to constraints he outlines would agree that, once equality of liberty is assured, social and economic inequalities are to be arranged so that they are for the benefit of the least advantaged.

Critics of the maximin interpretation attack from both right and left. Some insist that it is more rational to follow the libertarian or utilitarian approaches, permitting free bargaining among individuals to determine distribution[29] or striving for the arrangement that will maximize aggregate utility.[30] Others are criticizing from the left, arguing that the maximin formula may, in fact, permit unjustifiable inequalities in the distribution of health care.[31]

These critics argue that, although often it would be the case that one can improve the lot of the least well-off by concentrating a resource on members of the least well-off groups (because of decreasing marginal utility of resources), that is not always the case. In some situations, they claim, it might be more efficient to improve the lot of the least well-off by concentrating resources on certain elites who have the ability to benefit the least well-off if properly motivated.

The question that separates the defenders of the maximin position from these critics is whether or not it should be considered fair, just, or equitable to increase the differences that exist among members of the society in order to benefit the least well-off. Defenders of the maximin interpretation of the principle of justice say that it would be fair. Its critics reject this conclusion; they say that it might be prudent to increase inequalities in such circumstances but that it cannot be labeled as fair or just. Some would go so far as to say that on balance it might be the right thing to do because of other moral considerations, such as freedom or efficiency (these arguments will be discussed below). Some insist that the consent of the least well-off may be an additional necessary condition. They claim, however, that it simply cannot accord with our sense of justice that inequality should be increased, even if the net result is an improvement in the lot of the least well-off group (as well as the elite). The maximin interpretation justifies a trickle-down approach to distribution, thus justifying substantial rewards for those with creativity, medical skill, or administrative ability. However, this defense of the trickle-down theory has been criticized.

Egalitarianism and Distributional Analysis

Some argue that when equity or fairness is appealed to as one of the moral criteria for the evaluation of health-care policy alternatives, the goal should be to equalize individual net benefits, or at least opportunities for such benefits. Brian Barry, for example, argues that people in Rawls' original position might not always conclude that it is just or fair to permit inequalities as long as they redound to the benefit of the least well-off.[32] In some cases individuals might consider that the fair thing to do is to strive for a greater equality.

Holders of this position will have to determine whether the goal is that everyone should end up over a lifetime with the same amount of net benefit or whether the goal of public policy should be to try to equalize the benefit at a fixed period in time. The choice between the alternatives would have great implications, for example, in choosing between giving priority to a person who has had a long, healthy, happy life but currently suffers greatly from a terminal illness and another person who is relatively healthy and happy at the moment but who has led a miserable existence in poverty.

In either case, this more egalitarian interpretation of the

requirements of justice envisions some people who will have very high benefits counterbalanced with large amounts of disutility in their lives, while others might have smaller amounts of both benefit and harm. According to this egalitarian view, the goal is to strive for equality of net outcome. The principle is one that disregards aggregate amounts of benefit as well as average amounts.

Insofar as this principle is applied directly to health care rather than to larger questions of social equity, health planners accepting this interpretation would strive for a plan that distributes health care in order to give everyone an equal chance to be healthy.[33] The focus would not be on free exchange among individuals regardless of the consequences, as would be the case with the libertarians. It would not be on the aggregate net utility of alternative courses, as would be the case with the utilitarians. It would not even be on the impact of alternative policies on least well-off groups, as would be the case with the Rawlsians. Rather, the focus would be more directly on matters of distribution.

The dominant statistic for the egalitarian is the statistic that measures distribution, such as the standard deviation. The goal insofar as justice is concerned for the egalitarian is to opt for the alternative that will minimize the standard deviation in the distribution of the benefits. Thus, the egalitarian argues for having the health planner program his computer to calculate distributional measures rather than or in addition to aggregate benefit measures.

Two kinds of criticisms have been offered against the egalitarian position. First, some see no reason why we should strive for equality, especially in situations where equality violated liberty, failed to produce maximum aggregate utility, or failed to benefit least well-off groups. Both Rawls and Nozick have argued that the only adequate psychological account for opting for the egalitarian interpretation is one rooted in the emotion of envy. It is the view that if I cannot have something, others should not have it either.[34] Historically, however, many of the most articulate defenses of the egalitarian interpretation have come from those who are well endowed rather than those who are in a position to be envious. It may reflect a sense of sympathy for those who do not have equal resources. It expresses a basic identification with others in the moral community, an affirmation of a fundamental equality, something that is morally at least as basic as the preservation of liberty or the promotion of aggregate good consequences.

A second criticism of the egalitarian position is one based on the claim that the outcome of that position is not only totally unacceptable but actually makes continued existence impossible. The critics point out that the most equal society in the world would be one where all had their health status reduced to that of the sickest person. It seems obvious that that cannot be the moral principle upon which to build a health policy. Whether or not this is an insurmountable problem for the egalitarians will depend upon how they relate the claims based on the principle of justice to the other ethical principles that might impinge upon health planning. It will, therefore, be necessary to examine these other ethical principles to see how they relate to the evaluation of health policies based exclusively on the principle of justice.

OTHER ETHICAL CONSIDERATIONS IN DISTRIBUTION

When health planners are assessing the ethical and other evaluative dimensions of health policies, they may want to take into account questions other than the fairness or equity of the policies. For example, if an elderly population has been promised lifetime medical services under an insurance plan, a health proposal that abandons that commitment breaks a promise made and would be subject to the criticism that it has violated the obligation to keep promises. According to many accounts, this duty to keep promises cannot be reduced to the good consequences of keeping them. A health plan that incorporated some deception or dishonesty would be subject to the criticism that it violates the principle of veracity or truth telling. Virtually all ethical theories incorporate the principles of promise keeping and veracity. Some, such as Kantian and other deontological theories, have viewed these as independent right-making characteristics. Others, such as the version of utilitarianism known as rule utilitarianism, incorporate them as principles derived from some more basic moral obligation, such as the promotion of good consequences.[35]

While these considerations are in principle relevant to the assessment of the distribution of health care, it will normally be the case that alternative health policy proposals will not differ markedly as to the extent to which promises are broken or deceptions are incorporated. Three other important normative considerations, however, do often impact more directly upon the evaluation of health policy alternatives. Depending on one's ethical theory, they might provide some moral pull that counterbalances the implications of the various interpretations of the principle of justice or equity. These are the duties to promote beneficence, respect autonomy, and provide compensation for previous wrongs done to others.

Beneficence

A most obvious concern of economists and health planners is that the health-care delivery system efficiently restore, maintain, and improve the health status of the members of the society. That goal is so obvious that it is often taken for granted. In fact, it is often considered the only legitimate goal for a health plan.

Any evaluation of alternative health programs that evaluates good outcomes in terms of reductions in mortality, morbidity, loss from the labor force, or any other aggregate measure of health status is an evaluation striving to promote good or avoid evil insofar as the good and evil are within the sphere of health. Beneficence is the term often used to denote the normative principle that there is an obligation to promote the good in a society. But those who have begun making the case for the principle of equity interpreted as a concern about a patterned distribution of benefits on other than utilitarian grounds have made a strong case, that beneficence cannot totally dominate the evaluation of health policies. To the extent these critics are right, any evaluation that focuses exclusively on aggregate health and disease measures such as morbidity and mortality statistics has to be called into question. Critics claim that many other moral principles, including honesty, promise keeping, and equity, have a legitimate place in the evaluation.

Still, even if the critics of an exclusively consequentialist evaluation are correct, many would claim that the principle of utility must play some role in the evaluation of health policies. For example, it seems obvious that even the egalitarian would agree that a population with everybody equal at a low level of health is not as acceptable as a population with everyong equal at a higher level. Virtually everyone agrees that beneficence is a relevant characteristic, and most would concede that it is morally relevant. The question is one of how utility relates to the other right-making characteristics, such as equity.

Of course, if the principle of justice is one that is merely derived from beneficence or utility, as the utilitarians have claimed, then the problem is solved. It is solved, however, at the expense of generating objections that many have found to be insurmountable.

Any health policy analysis will have to incorporate some answer to the question of the proper relationship between beneficence and the other right-making principles.[36] It is literally impossible to decide which distribution of health care is the most acceptable without some conclusion on this basic normative ethical issue. In addition to the already discussed solutions that reduce the principle of justice to considerations of beneficence or completely eliminate concern for beneficence by focusing exclusively on equality of outcome, several alternatives are available to answer this basic question.

One strategy is to view the concerns of beneficence and equity as equally weighty. In that case, the policy analysis would have to include a balancing, at least an intuitive mental balancing, of the two concerns. The best distribution of health care would be one that concerns itself with producing efficiently good consequences but also concerns itself with distributional questions independent of the consequences, giving these variables equal weight.

Relatively little work has been done on the mathematics of such comparisons. What would be needed would be a set of statistics that expresses both aggregate outcome and distributional characteristics in units common to alternative health plans being compared. An aggregate measure such as the mean or aggregate increase in life expectancy divided by the standard deviation in the distribution of the increase in life expectancies might be a mathematical approximation for this kind of balancing.

Another approach sees the nonconsequentialist claims, such as those for equity and honesty, as having a priority over simple concerns for aggregate benefits. In the traditional language of Western political philosophy, the rights of individuals take priority over the production of good social consequences. For holders of this view, one solution that still permits the incorporation of some concern for beneficence is to give priority to distributional considerations so that, for example, those who are least well-off have a rights claim based on Rawlsian or egalitarian interpretations of the principle of justice. Beneficence might still function as a tie breaker when two alternatives are equal in their distributional impact. Alternatively, it might be held that bearers of a claim of justice are entitled to waive the exercise of their right. The net effect would be that certain least well-off groups have a rights claim to the health-care resources needed to be as healthy as other people, but at their own option they might waive the claim to equality of outcome in cases in which it serves their own interests. This would explain why society might give special consideration to rewarding elites in those cases in which the least well-off favor such a reward system.

Regardless of which of the many possible interpretations for the relationship between beneficence and equity are chosen, some understanding will have to be incorporated into any full policy planning procedure. Even if the economist chooses the traditional course of providing only background data for policymakers, it will be up to the economist to point out the variety of data that are available, not only measures of aggregate impact and averaging statistics, but also measures of distribution such as standard deviation. In addition, data might be available on the distribution of the preference system for alternative health policies. All of these data may be critical for those who are making the actual policy decisions.

The Principle of Autonomy

A second additional principle beyond justice or equity that will have to be taken into account in evaluating the distribution of health care is the principle of autonomy. It will not be sufficient to examine the aggregate social consequences and the equity of the distribution of those consequences. It may be that two competing candidates for health policies differ substantially in the extent to which autonomy for providers and consumers of health care is preserved. The system of liberal political philosophy of the West has given great emphasis to the principle of autonomy. It is quite likely that, other things being equal, the health-care system that maximizes autonomy will be considered morally the most appropriate system. In fact, the libertarian interpretation of the principle of justice elevates concern for preservation of autonomy to such a point that it is the only consideration.

One increasingly important ethical dimension in evaluating health-care policy alternatives that is closely linked to the principle of autonomy is the problem of what ought to be done about apparently voluntary behavior and life-style choices that have harmful effects on health. It is becoming increasingly clear that life-style choices have an important impact on health status.[37] In some cases if efficient production of improved health were the only concern, the policy of intervening to change health-related behavior, by coercion if necessary, might have much to recommend it. To the extent that least well-off groups are also at high risk for the detrimental effects of these life-style choices, they would also benefit disproportionately from the interventions.

Two criticisms of this strategy of health promotion are now being offered. One group attacks the empirical premises. Crawford,[38] Guttmacher,[39] Dan Beauchamp,[40] and others are claiming that what is thought to be a voluntarily chosen life-style pattern is, in reality, a response to social structural forces such as racial, gender, age, ethnic, and socioeconomic discrimination. To focus on individual behavior is, therefore, "blaming the victim."

Others, while conceding that these factors affect health status, still accept that, in principle, some behaviors that affect health can be voluntary. They argue, however, that if autonomy is an important value, individuals should be permitted to choose those life-styles. The policy implications are significant. They are especially significant if planners conclude that these considerations should affect what counts as a fair distribution of health-care resources. Some have argued that, if voluntary behavior affects health status while at the same time autonomy is a fundamental value for the society, society should not have to bear the costs of the health care that results from the behavior either. This has led to proposals to require those who engage in such behavior to buy special insurance, pay "health fees" designed to cover the cost of extra medical needs, or enter separate risk pools. Some have even argued that, in rare cases such as situations in which limited health resources are available, it might be necessary to assign access priorities to those needing scarce medical skills and resources for reasons unrelated to voluntary choices on their own part. [41]

The result is that the principle of autonomy combined with empirical assumptions about what behavior is truly voluntary will have a critical impact on the analysis and evaluation of health-care distribution. Different kinds of data may be needed and different weights may be given to the data, depending upon how one evaluates the ethical principle of autonomy and how one relates autonomy to other principles.

While most refuse to give autonomy absolute priority, they find that it must at least compete with other ethical concerns, including beneficence and justice. The problem is then, once again, one of deciding how the claims of autonomy relate to other morally weighty considerations.

One strategy is to view the principle of autonomy as coequal with the other principles such as beneficence and justice. In evaluating health policy alternatives, then, the impacts on the autonomy of individuals would be put on the scales as a coequal weight, together with the other considerations. It cannot be denied that autonomy or freedom is a very fundamental concern in liberal society. Many, including those who evaluate ethical options in terms of the rights of individuals, give autonomy a special place. While they may not give it absolute priority, it is, in all but the most extreme circumstances, seen as being more critical than the mere production of good consequences. That same tradition, however, is less likely to place autonomy in a rank order of priority when it is compared with concerns for justice or equity. The tradition of American political philosophy consistently links liberty and justice as coequal concerns. Citizens are not only endowed with rights but created equal.

If the absolute ranking of one principle as highest priority is unacceptable and the balancing of them as coequal is also unacceptable, one other alternative might be considered: the nonconsequentialist principles such as liberty and justice might be considered coequal to be balanced against one another. In aggregate, however, they might take priority over the production of good consequences. That would explain our notion that individuals are the bearers of entitlement and liberty rights that cannot be defeated by the mere appeal to consequences. Rights claims rooted in these inherent right-making characteristics such as liberty, justice, honesty, and promise keeping "trump" claims based on utility (or claims based on efficiency, which is essentially a utilitarian concern). When they conflict among themselves they necessarily are balanced as coequal principles, but in aggregate they would take priority over beneficence.[42]

This does not mean that beneficence (the efficient production of net good consequences) would play no role in the ethics of public policies related to health care. It would become dominant when no other ethical principles are at stake or where they are equally counterbalanced. Moreover, if individuals are bearers of certain rights rooted in these first priority principles, they might also be permitted to waive those rights in cases where, to them, production of good consequences was more important. Utility then becomes a second-order consideration when the bearers of the rights take it upon themselves to waive their rights claims temporarily.

Regardless of which strategy is chosen, those who evaluate the distribution of health care will have to have some formula for taking into account the claims of the principle of autonomy just as they take into account beneficence and justice. The relationship among these principles will be decisive in the policy analysis as well as in determining what kinds of economic data are relevant to the analysis.

Compensation for Previous Wrongs

One final consideration will be relevant in evaluating the ethical dimensions of the distribution of health care. The problem is that of determining whether previous wrongs done by a society to certain groups within the society have any bearing on how health care should presently be distributed. If two groups in a society, let us say a racial minority and a group of genetically afflicted infants, are due to be equally poorly off and equally in need of health-care interventions, but one group is poorly off because of the previous oppression of the society whereas the other group is in its disadvantaged position through no previous wrongs of the society, should that variation have any bearing on deciding the priorities for distributing health care between the two groups? If we use the Rawlsian methodology, we might ask whether rational contractors operating under the constraints Rawls imposes might accept the principle that previous social wrongs deserve compensation over and above the claims of others who are equally poorly off but who have not been previously harmed. If such a principle is accepted, this would justify targeting health programs for least well-off groups who have previously been oppressed.

Even those who accept in principle some notion of compensation for previous social harms may be concerned that such a targeting for oppressed groups may create a special class of health care that eventually would be viewed as separate and inferior or stigmatizing. Thus, even if in principle targeting for such groups is ethically justified, there may be pragmatic reasons why members of such groups may prefer to receive their health care within the mainstream of medical services, rather than being singled out for special treatment.

CONCLUSION

It is possible that some of these ethical dimensions in the distribution of health care can be discounted, at least for some phases of policy analysis. Some may conclude, for example, that the claim of previously wronged groups for health care derives from the fact that they are in need or from the fact that great good can be done efficiently by targeting for those groups rather than from the fact that they have been wronged per se. Economists and other health-care policy analysts, however, must at least be aware of the principles and their impacts. Some of those consuming the analyst's work and many of those impacted by it are likely to hold each of these principles dear. It is impossible to reach policy conclusions without at least considering whether the claims based on these principles—the principles of equity, beneficence, autonomy, and reparation for previous harm— are relevant and, if so, what priority they have in relating to claims based on other principles.

These ethical principles are crucial not only for the normative evaluation of what health-care plan ought to be adopted and what distribution is appropriate. If that were their only impact, economists might retreat to the defense that they are only providing the data for planners and policy evaluators and legislators. Answers to the questions raised by the basic ethical principles, however, also determine which data are to be gathered, which observations reported to the consumers of the economist's services, and which statistical manipulations performed on the data. It makes no sense to calculate only mean health mortality and morbidity statistics or cost/benefit ratios if policy should be made on the basis of the distributional effects of policy alternatives.

It may make no difference as a matter of policy that it is more cost efficient to lower morbidity by treating injuries sustained as a result of voluntarily chosen behavior rather than those resulting from the wrongs of previous social policies. If ethical considerations assign priority on some other basis, data may be produced needlessly.

Unfortunately, the consumers of the health economist's services may not themselves be aware that different data are needed depending upon the ethical evaluation of the alternatives. They may not themselves realize that health-care plans may be defended or rejected on grounds other than efficiency and cost/benefit considerations. When that happens, it may be up to the economist to initiate the ethical as well as the economic analysis.

NOTES

1. Charles Fried, Right and Wrong (Cambridge, Mass.: Harvard University Press, 1978), p. 127.
2. William T. Blackstone, "On Health Care as a Legal Right: Philosophical Justifications, Political Activity, and Adequate Health Care," Georgia Law Review 10 (Winter 1976): pp. 391–418; Edward V. Sparer, "The Legal Right to Health Care: Public Policy and Equal Access," Hastings Center Report 6 (October 1976): pp. 39–47.
3. Sparer, "The Legal Right to Health Care," pp. 40–43.
4. John Rawls, "Justice as Fairness," The Philosophical Review 67 (April 1958): pp. 164-94.
5. Aristotle, Nicomachean Ethics, trans. Martin Ostwald (Indianapolis: Bobbs-Merrill, 1962), pp. 111-17.
6. Ibid., p. 118.
7. Ludwig Edelstein, Ancient Medicine: Selected Papers of Ludwig Edelstein (Baltimore: Johns Hopkins University Press, 1967), p. 6.
8. Robert Nozick, Anarchy, State, and Utopia (New York: Basic Books, 1974).
9. Ibid., pp. 150-53.
10. Ibid., pp. 155-64.
11. Robert M. Sade, "Medical Care as a Right: A Refutation," New England Journal of Medicine 285 (1971): 1288-92; see also his "Concept of Rights: Philosophy and Application to Health Care," Linacre Quarterly (November 1979): 330–44.
12. Sade, "Medical Care as a Right."
13. Nozick, Anarchy, pp. 235-38.
14. Ibid.
15. Laurence B. McCullough, "Medical Ethics, History of: Introduction to the Contemporary Period in Europe and the Americas," in Encyclopedia of Bioethics, vol. 3, ed. Warren T. Reich (New York: The Free Press, 1978), pp. 975-76.
16. Jeremy Bentham, An Introduction to the Principles of Morals and Legislation (New York: Hofner, 1948 [1789]).
17. John Stuart Mill, Utilitarianism, ed. Samuel Gorovitz (Indianapolis: Bobbs-Merrill, 1971).
18. Elizabeth B. Drew, "HEW Grapples with PPBS," Public Interest 4 (Summer 1966): 102-15; R. Zeckhauser and Donald S. Shepard, "Where Now for Saving Lives?" Law and Contemporary Problems 40 (Autumn 1976): 5–45. Cf. Michael S. Baram, "Cost-Benefit Analyses: An Inadequate Basis for Health, Safety, and Environmental Regulatory Decision-Making," Ecology Law Quar-

terly 8 (1980): 473-531; Vincent Taylor, "How Much is Good Health Worth?" Policy Sciences 1 (1970): 49-72.

19. William B. Stason and Milton C. Weinstein, "Allocation of Resources to Manage Hypertension," New England Journal of Medicine 296 (1977): 732-39; Stephen C. Schoenbaum et al., "Benefit-Cost Analysis of Rubella Vaccination Policy," New England Journal of Medicine 294 (1976): 306-10; Brandon S. Centerwall and Michael H. Criqui, "Prevention of the Wernicke-Korsakoff Syndrome," New England Journal of Medicine 299 (1978): 285-89.

20. Donald S. Shepard and Mark S. Thompson, "First Principles of Cost-Effectiveness Analysis in Health," Public Health Reports 94 (1979): 535-43; Milton C. Weinstein and William B. Stason, "Foundations of Cost-Effectiveness Analysis for Health and Medical Practices," New England Journal of Medicine 296 (1977): 716-21; Jane Sisk Willems et al., "Cost Effectiveness of Vaccination Against Pneumococcal Pneumonia," New England Journal of Medicine 303 (1980): 553-59.

21. Dorothy P. Rice, "Estimating the Cost of Illness," Health Economics Series No. 6. U.S. Department of Health, Education, and Welfare, PHS Publ. No. 947-6, May, 1966; Dorothy P. Rice and Barbara S. Cooper, "The Economic Value of Human Life," American Journal of Public Health 57 (1967): 1954-56.

22. Martin Golding, "Obligations to Future Generations," The Monist 56 (1972): 85-99; Daniel Callahan, "What Obligations Do We Have to Future Generations?" American Ecclesiastical Review 164 (1971): 265-80.

23. Tom L. Beauchamp, "Utilitarianism and Cost/Benefit Analysis: A Reply to MacIntyre," in Ethical Theory and Business, ed. Tom L. Beauchamp and Norman E. Bowie (Englewood Cliffs, N.J.: Prentice-Hall, 1979), pp. 276-82.

24. T. C. Schelling, "The Life You Save May Be Your Own," in Problems in Public Expenditure Analysis, ed. S. B. Chase, Jr. (Washington, D.C.: Brookings Institution, 1968); R. Zeckhauser and Donald S. Shepard, "Where Now for Saving Lives?" Law and Contemporary Problems 40 (Autumn 1976): 5-45.

25. John Stuart Mill, Utilitarianism, pp. 42-57.

26. John Rawls, A Theory of Justice, pp. 79-80, 302.

27. Ronald Green, "Health Care and Justice in Contract Theory Perspective," in Ethics and Health Policy, ed. Robert M. Veatch and Roy Branson (Cambridge, Mass.: Ballinger, 1976), p. 112.

28. John Rawls, A Theory of Justice (Oxford: Clarendon Press, 1973), pp. 302-542.

29. Charles Fried, "Equality and Rights in Medical Care," The Hastings Center Report 6 (October 1976): 33.

30. Robert L. Cunningham, "Justice: Efficiency or Fairness?" Personalist 52 (1971): 253-81.
31. Brian Barry, "The Liberal Theory of Justice: A Critical Examination of the Principle Doctrines" in A Theory of Justice, by John Rawls, p. 109; Robert M. Veatch, A Theory of Medical Ethics (New York: Basic Books, 1981), pp. 263-69.
32. Brian Barry, "The Liberal Theory of Justice," p. 109.
33. Robert M. Veatch, "What Is a 'Just' Health Care Delivery?" in Ethics and Health Policy, ed. Robert M. Veatch and Roy Branson, pp. 127-53.
34. Nozick, Anarchy, p. 239; Rawls, A Theory of Justice, pp. 538-39.
35. John Rawls, "Two Concepts of Rules," The Philosophical Review 44 (1955): 3-32.
36. Arthur M. Okun, Equality and Efficiency: The Big Tradeoff (Washington, D.C.: Brookings Institution, 1975).
37. Nedra B. Belloc and Lester Breslow, "Relationship of Physical Status, Health and Health Practices," Preventive Medicine 1 (1972): 409-21.
38. Robert Crawford, "You are Dangerous to Your Health," Social Policy 8 (1978): 11-20.
39. Sally Guttmacher, "On the National Commission: A Puritan Critique of Consensus Ethics," The Hastings Center Report 9 (1979): 22-27.
40. Dan Beauchamp, "Alcoholism as Blaming the Alcoholic," International Journal of Addiction 11 (1976): 41-52.
41. Robert M. Veatch, "Voluntary Risks to Health: The Ethical Issues," Journal of the American Medical Association 243 (1980): 50-55.
42. Robert M. Veatch, A Theory of Medical Ethics, pp. 303-5.

2

RISK BENEFIT/COST BENEFIT: IMPROVING GOVERNMENT REGULATION OF APPROVAL OF NEW DRUGS

Rita Ricardo-Campbell

This chapter presents the reasons for and a method of using economic data from controlled, prospective clinical trials to widen the data base on which the government regulates the marketing of new drugs. The potential of economics to make more inclusive the data on which the assessment of the societal benefits and societal costs of new drugs is made is being ignored worldwide. Cost/benefit analysis can use a unitary measure to add economic data derived from controlled, prospective trials of a drug, while risk/benefit analysis is limited to use of the clinical, nonadditive biological data from such trials. Questions can be inserted in the clinical protocol, and the answers will provide information from which estimates can be made of the direct medical costs and the indirect costs of a disease and its treatment.

Cost/benefit analysis can derive a net benefit or loss from the use of a new drug in the subset of the population in the trials. If that population subset is not unique, the trial results of benefit or cost may be generalized to the population at risk. Because the measures of biological functions (such as blood pressure, sugar in the urine, etc.) cannot be added, the overall biological assessment of the drug's net benefit or loss is in part subjective. It is influenced by two subjective assessments: the patient's self-perceived well-being and the clinical investigator's evaluation of that assessment with reference to the nonadditive, biological data about the patient. The latter data may consist of several variables, and the weights assigned to their importance usually vary among clinical investigators.

Cost/benefit analysis weighs all the pros and cons of a given action; in this instance, approval of a drug. Risk/benefit analysis weighs only the pros and cons that affect health, usually measured in terms of biological tests and extended days of life. Both techniques are seeking better measures of the quality of the extended days of life that medical intervention can convey.

This chapter compares and contrasts risk/benefit with cost/benefit analysis. An understanding of the two approaches is important because of the continuing public controversy surrounding the role of economic analysis in governmental decisions to ban potentially carcinogenic pesticides, other environmental pollutants, food additives under the Delaney Amendment, and to approve or disapprove new drugs for marketing. "The absence of explicit statutory rules for risk and benefit assessment has led to a situation where each substance is considered separately, and widely disparate outcomes are influenced more by adversary emotions than by real values."[1] If the U.S. Congress revokes the Delaney Amendment, which requires the removal from the marketplace of any food additive that is found to induce (when ingested) any trace of cancer, no matter how small, in animal or man, cost/benefit analysis rather than risk/benefit analysis would be the more relevant analytical technique to assess the net benefit of the food additive.[2]

Far-reaching new legislation has been proposed in the United States that would permit the Food and Drug Administration (FDA), under its aegis, to approve the marketing of new drugs and to regulate the experimental and statistical design of research trials to test a new drug.[3] However, the proposed legislation does not address the increasing acceptance of cost/benefit analysis by both clinical physicians and policymakers in decisions about drugs and medical devices and by policymakers about the allocation of scarce resources for maximum health in society.[4] Some believe that "given current concern about the economy-wide allocation of scarce resources, a study of the costs and benefits of each new procedure and associated technologies should be undertaken prior to commitment of public monies to pay for them."[5] This position is being advocated especially in the United Kingdom, where tax revenues pay all or most of the medical costs.[6]

RISK/BENEFIT ANALYSIS

The current practice in the United States, under the FDA's approval or nonapproval process to permit marketing of a new drug, is to emphasize the individual's health risk and use a partial risk/

benefit analysis for a statistical, nonidentifiable individual on the basis of which risks and benefits for society are implied. Nonhealth benefits as well as nonhealth costs are ignored, primarily because they are difficult to quantify. How the jump from the individual to society is made is not explained.

Among the unknowns in the data are part of the biological data on which both risk/benefit and cost/benefit analyses depend. Techniques have been developed to handle some of the uncertainties, but neither risk/benefit nor cost/benefit analysis removes the uncertainties stemming from the unknown distribution and level of probabilities of risk, the lack of data about the natural course of a disease, and patients' preferences.

Comparative risk assessment of different medical interventions coupled with cost-effective rankings is beginning to be used, especially by third-party payers in the United States who reimburse costs of the use of medical devices. To use this technique to choose among alternative drugs rather than among an array of quite different procedures would place a high premium on the relative efficacy of a drug. The variation in costs among drugs is less than the variation between the immediate costs of surgery and no surgery coupled with medical management and the use of drugs. The comparative risk assessment technique is not risk/benefit analysis or cost/benefit analysis but, rather, it is used to select the most cost-effective means to attain a given goal. It has the advantage that because it does not assign monetary values to the benefits, it is more acceptable to many people. However, unless such values are assigned, with all the faults in so doing (discussed later in this chapter), it is difficult to compare alternative medical interventions. The measure most commonly used in risk assessment, and increasingly in risk/benefit analysis, is quality adjusted life years (QUALY).

Risk/benefit analysis is rarely precisely defined. For example, "it formalizes and quantifies the sorts of ideas and discussions that already take place in a less formal manner in the political and regulatory process . . . the analytic process is inherently subjective and constrained by limitations of human judgment and ingenuity,"[7] or "such policies are based on some kind of risk-benefit equation whose elements are usually concealed or poorly articulated."[8] Government decisions are made to minimize the possibility of severe adverse risks that are rare and may not actually occur. The FDA's understandable avoidance of unfavorable publicity is predicated on the unknown probability of a rare, severe, and adverse occurrence from use of a newly approved drug. A severe, adverse risk is a rare risk because the early drug trials that expose animals and humans, Phases I and II, would otherwise have revealed it. The history of drug trials substantiates this. If the risk is only one in one million, it could take one million or even more persons exposed for that side effect to appear. However, the first person exposed may experience the severe risk, even death. Government regulators understandably fear the early occurrence of severe harm to several persons. Postmarket surveillance can reduce the incidence of this risk but cannot eliminate it.

Nonapproval of a new drug until its safety and efficacy are assured is not without substantial costs to society, including the cost of loss of life and continuing low level of health because the new drug is not available. The regulator's refusal to look at total costs—including those that follow from unavailability of a relatively safe, therapeutic, life-saving drug or a drug that improves productivity and the quality of life of some otherwise ill persons—deprives U.S. society for a period of time, sometimes years, of the benefits of that new knowledge. This is a cost to society.

> The use of the term "risk-benefit" rather than "cost-benefit" seems to equate biological "risks" with all the "costs" incurred and to define "benefits" as only "good" benefits uncorrected for any negative benefits or losses. Thus, society's costs are underestimated in "risk-benefit" decisions.[9]

Not all scientists or lawyers recognize this. For example, note the following:

> Where benefits are underweighted or risk overweighted, the result may be a decision that bars or postpones a benefit; but this means only that society is deprived of an opportunity for improvement. On the other hand, the opposite approach may expose society to actual injury. It is not difficult, therefore, to find justification for an overweighting of risk relative to benefit.[10]

"Benefits" and "risks," not "benefits" and the more inclusive concept "costs," are the government's balance sheet headings for drug assessment. The methodology appears to be invariant whether decisions are made concerning the individual or society.

From the biological data of controlled clinical, double-blind trials[11] required for approval or disapproval of new drugs,[12] the government estimates an individual's probability of potential health benefit and risk from the use of a new drug. This data base usually does not include: (1) the patients' preferences, especially with respect to the difficult-to-measure subjective benefits and costs included in the term "quality of life"; (2) the most relevant population group at

risk to a disease; (3) the losses of those individuals who would benefit from the new drug and thus avoid ill health and the costs of medical treatment and even premature death; and (4) the disability and
income losses associated with ill health. If lives are "saved," the
method does not include future costs of this nature that eventually
will be incurred by the saved life. However, these "saved lives" as
a group would presumably contribute through work, paid or in the
household, more to society than their future health resource costs.

The redistributive effect of denying benefits to relatively many
unknown persons in order to avoid a potential loss from an adverse
effect suffered by a few persons whose identity would be known and
publicized is hidden. Yet there may be subsets of patients who will
benefit from a new drug even when there is no statistically significant
difference between the typical end points of an already available drug
and a new drug. These population subsets may be revealed through
economic data on income losses as well as through biological data.
"An important area of research concerns detection of subsets of
patients who benefit from some of the treatments even when overall
there may be no statistically significant difference in the treatments."[13] A significant statistical difference may not be a significant
biological difference.

A SPECIFIC CASE*

The well-publicized U.S. delay in the approval of sodium
valproate until February 28, 1978 (initial approval, France, 1967),
a drug effective in controlling multiple epileptic seizures in a small
subset of epilepsy patients, illustrates the greater emphasis on an
identifiable, rare risk as compared with a potentially larger net
societal benefit. On July 7, 1977, NBC described on national tele-
vision the "need" for approval. Eight more broadcasts followed. The
Congressional Epilepsy Commission (in August 1977) and the FDA's
Neurologic Drugs Advisory Committee (on October 12, 1977) recom-
mended approval. The new drug application included 200 favorable
medical literature citations, 30 on clinical trials, 5 of which were
controlled, double-blind clinical trials. Risk/benefit analysis, as
applied by the FDA, requires clinical data from two acceptable, controlled, double-blind clinical studies to prove safety and efficacy.[14]
The FDA questioned the acceptability of all but one study.

---

*This section was included at the suggestion of one of the mem-
bers of the Program Committee of the World Congress of Health Economics at Leyden University, The Netherlands.

The FDA's "soon to be announced" approval was reported by the Washington Post on February 25, 1978, four days after that newspaper published a lead story identifying a youngster who had 100 seizures a day and 11 days after a meeting of the Neurologic Drugs Advisory Committee had ended without any public statement about FDA's intent. The number of persons with 12 or more seizures annually is about 300,000 persons in the United States.[15] The severity of the disease and the potential number of persons who might be helped appear to have been undervalued in the FDA's apparent sole reliance on proof from two controlled trials. The unknown probability of an individual's incurring liver damage was evaluated against the individual's probability of biological benefit from relief of seizures. Exactly how the societal evaluation was made in this risk/benefit analysis is unknown.

Cost/benefit analysis would have isolated the loss to some individuals in society stemming from nonapproval of that drug. Adults with uncontrolled seizures cannot work or, in most states, drive a car. Children with seizures cannot be educated, and they become potentially unproductive members of society. Their parents' abilities to live normal lives are impaired. Dollar values could have been placed on many of these items. These indirect costs are incomplete because of omission of the sizable psychic costs of enduring such a disease and the emotional distress of persons caring for individuals with this disease. A benefit could be estimated by comparing the costs restrospectively before and after the estimated relief from the new drug, with correction for adverse effects. Ideally, the prospective, controlled clinical trials might have elicited data to estimate some of these costs.

Individuals differ in their willingness to bear voluntary risk to their health and in their biological responses to a drug. In cases of terminal disease where death is judged to be imminent, a low probability of an anticipated benefit to health may be assessed as worth the risk of a high probability of incurring a severe adverse effect. This is because the record of alternative, existing treatments makes some patients believe that they have "little to lose."

An individual's "risks" and "benefits" are sometimes being balanced impersonally by U.S. government regulators who never even see the ill individual rather than personally by the individual and his physician, who can take into account that individual's unique biological characteristics and preferences.

An acting director of a division of the FDA's Bureau of Drugs writes that

"compassionate INDs" [investigational new drugs] . . .
[have] been a generally accepted (though unwritten) policy

for some time. As any NDA [new drug application] nears approval and the public becomes aware of the promising new drug, there are usually many requests to obtain the drug prior to marketing. In certain cases, such as patients unresponsive to other drugs, it is difficult if not impossible to refuse. Other examples are in cases of a patient having taken a drug in a foreign country and now residing in the United States, or patients with diseases for which there is no known treatment, although the drug may not have been shown to be safe and effective. An individual benefit/risk decision is made on a case by case basis.[16]

The risks and benefits of drugs or medical procedures are usually not expressed in a common measure, and this makes it impossible to subtract from the benefits the costs of the risks resulting from the medical intervention. There is no common unit of measure to compare the risks and the benefits, such as inches or dollars, although the number of days of life of a given quality can conceptually be used in some instances. Benefits from drugs are often described by various nonadditive, biological measures: changes in blood pressure or changes in the amount of sugar in the urine.

An individual's probability of a severe adverse effect on health is usually expressed as one in several thousands exposed to some irreversible damage or even death. This probability is compared to the individual's anticipated medical benefits. Both risks and benefits can be expressed in terms of fewer or more days of life of a given quality if the adverse effect hastens death or the disease being treated shortens life. It may also be possible, when death is not involved, to express risks and benefits in a common measure, such as bed disability days. Development of the probabilities and common measures of quality of health is needed for risk/benefit analysis as well as for cost/benefit analysis. If the biological data are combined to estimate an overall improvement in quality of health and/or extension of the number of days of life of a given quality, the different variables will be weighted in a subjective fashion.[17]

Risk-benefit analyses derived from controlled randomized trials are being increasingly attacked because the number of subjects in the trials is often too small for regulations to be based on their results. This is especially true for negative trials; that is, those that find no statistically significant deviation in outcome between a new drug and an existing treatment. Out of 71 such trials, 67 had a 10 percent or more probability of missing an actual 25 percent therapeutic improvement and "with the same risk, 50 of the trials could have missed a 50 percent improvement."[18] Because the FDA requires two randomized, controlled double-blind trials to fulfill their requirement of "substantial evidence," the policy implications of these false negatives in risk/ benefit analysis are very serious.

In both risk/benefit and cost/benefit analyses, there may be statistical errors, poor deductive reasoning, and an unawareness of the costs of the patient's anxiety. "Once a new element of risk is announced, it provides individuals with something to think and worry about."[19] The exclusion of all items that are not directly health related in risk/benefit analysis ignores consumer preferences and assumes that everyone is adverse in the same degree to risks to their health. Data indicate that the daily smoking of a given number of cigarettes over a given period of time decreases, on the average, the probability of life by x number of days. Smoking, under certain genetic and environmental conditions, may be a causal factor in new disease and makes worse a preexisting disease, possibly in the asymptomatic stage. Why, then, do persons smoke? Medical risk/benefit analysis does not answer this question.

COST/BENEFIT ANALYSIS

A cost/benefit analysis uses the sum of all the benefits minus all the costs resulting from the use of a new drug. This yields a net benefit or loss measure that can be used in ranking various treatment regimens to achieve a given goal. Some might prefer to express these data in terms of a ratio rather than subtracting the benefits from the costs. Because there is no upper bound or limit to the costs, this is technically incorrect.[20] However, if no market price of a drug exists and there is a sole purchaser or monopoly buyer, such as a government, an upper bound or budget restraint could then exist. "In the general case, it is the benefit-minus-cost difference not the benefit-over-cost ratio that should usually control action."[21]

Items identified for costing in assessing the value of a drug include medical procedures, tests, hospital days, physician visits, drugs, etc., while the indirect items include the loss of time from paid work, from work in the household, and the psychic or nontangible costs of anxiety and pain. Reducing all these costs and benefits to a common monetary unit requires quantification of some items that are difficult to measure. Thus, "shadow prices" are used for hard-to-measure variables. A common shadow price is the price of an individual's hourly pay on a job. It ideally includes the hourly value of fringe benefits, such as premiums paid by the employer for health and life insurance. The dollar value of work lost because of illness and its treatment acts as only a partial shadow price of psychic costs and benefits. Pain, nausea, and anxiety each have a cost (and their relief, a benefit) above the loss of earnings.

It is easier to rank the various components of the quality of life by preference or in sequence than to assign them numerical weights and combine them into a single index.[22] Both techniques have been used in attempting to assess the values of health benefits from medical interventions for persons who do not work because of preference, disabling illness, or age. Measures of changes in social functioning and in moods or outlook on life are also used. Among several functional scales are the Barthel Index, the Sickness Impact Profile, and the Pulses Functional Profiles that can be used to obtain cardinal comparisons.[23]

Because time spent on household activities and in leisure also has value, an arbitrary amount may be added to the basic value of the time lost from work. The more persons in a household, the more value has the nonmarket labor of the person who runs the household. The costs of drugs, their numbers, and the strength needed to relieve pain can act as shadow prices for some nontangible items. The most difficult nontangible item to quantify is probably the reassurance or relief from the anxiety that a suspected illness might exist. What is the value to a person suffering from severe chronic headaches to be assured by a brain scan that he does not have a brain tumor? Less dramatically, many common tests, x-rays, and physical examinations act to relieve anxiety, as may also a brief, physician office visit.

The prices of medical care are often higher than their true resource cost because of pricing practices by hospitals, government regulations, and third-party payments that inflate medical care prices above their resource costs. This problem can be ignored in initial cost/benefit studies, or an arbitrary corrective factor can be used.

Many practicing physicians have recognized the subjective component of benefits and costs that are traditionally encompassed by the economic term "utility."[24] The individual patient's assessment of the anticipated benefit and the anticipated costs, including risks from a new drug or medical procedure, can be theoretically included by the economist if interview data from fully informed individuals about their preferences for a new treatment and its existing closest substitute are available. To inform patients fully about the probabilities of adverse effects and outcomes is time-consuming. Many physicians argue that most patients do not want the information and, moreover, will not understand it. The hypothesis that a sufficient number of persons, those "at the margin," will not understand the risks and benefits written in clear (nonmedical) language, needs testing.

Dollar estimates of psychic costs and benefits are contained within insurance valuations and awards by the courts. Insurance and judicial awards act only as benchmarks, not as precise valuations of pain from loss of life or limb.

Physicians and patients usually dislike using monetary units or any numerical measure to describe costs of pain or benefits of relief from pain, or especially the value of life. Despite this, decision analysis as used by the economist is being recognized as useful in making clinical decisions. An example of the numerical ordering of an individual's benefits translated into monetary terms follows:

> If restoration of normal health were given a utility value of 100 units and if death following a prolonged painful illness were given a utility value of 0 units, a dollar expenditure of $5000 might be assigned 20 or 30 units, an anaphylactic reaction to a drug might be assigned 10 units, and improvement of health to the point where the individual could return to work on a part-time basis might be assigned 60 or 65 units.[25]

Cost/benefit analysis has some of the same defects as risk/benefit analysis. If both techniques use data from clinical trials, then whatever defects the trials have, such as too few subjects, apply to both techniques. Additionally, more work on how best to measure the elusive costs and benefits implied by the term "quality of life" is needed. Quality of life measurements that modify the quantity of life outcomes may change an individual's treatment preference.

Although the estimates of costs and benefits in a cost/benefit analysis do not cover fully gains or losses, their use permits ordered thinking and an indication of the upper and lower bounds of a potential net benefit or loss. In the process of doing a cost/benefit analysis, gaps in information and the assumptions are revealed. The redistribution of health benefits is indicated, and the economists' concern is "not traditional myopic preoccupation with the GNP,"[26] but the traditional analysis of externalities as developed by A. C. Pigou in his Economics of Welfare, first published in 1920. Cost/benefit analysis includes second-order effects.

The end result of some untreated diseases is a decrease in life expectancy. The patient's current value of more days of life at some future date, such as ten years hence, is usually discounted because the days occur in the future. Future income is discounted because if it were available currently, it could earn interest. Days of life after retirement are in a similar sense considered less valuable than before retirement. An arbitrary factor can be added to include an amount to approximate the value of nonmaterial activities and pleasures. Because of the deterioration of human capital due to age, there is a decline in value of life as one ages. Not all persons will agree with the above.

Those who do not, usually prefer to value added days of life on the basis of responses to questions about how many dollars, or other monetary unit, one would be willing to pay to increase the specific probability of an increase in life expectancy. This latter method is theoretically superior to a solely discounted stream of earnings valuation because there is no falloff to zero value for days of life upon retirement. Empirical data to support the willingness-to-pay approach are not consistent. "As a person's survival chances decrease, his willingness to pay increases at an increasing rate."[27]

Other approaches to evaluate life are to use a discounted value of future consumption by nonworkers or to compare premiums for riskier jobs to less risky jobs requiring equal skill. Combination approaches that list different valuations over a range of values are also used. It is generally accepted that the value of life is greater than the value of a person's future stream of discounted earnings.

Individuals will differ about the precise valuations because, regardless of the method used, assumptions are made and value judgments must be employed. Further, there "is no testable relationship between the willingness-to-pay and the human capital approaches to placing a value on the loss of a human life."[28] In 1980, $300,000-$500,000 has been the dollar range used by some economists for the value of one life. The amount is greater than the average person's discounted lifetime earnings. Some government regulators generally place much higher values (several million dollars) on lives saved by government regulation. John P. O'Neill, of the Occupational Safety and Health Administration (OSHA), explains that "we do not use a cost-benefit analysis . . . We're not making a balance, we're making a judgment."[29] Cost/benefit analysis is broader than risk/benefit analysis because risks are only a part of the total costs. Costs also include the direct costs of medical care and the indirect costs of the value of the loss of paid work and unpaid work because of a disease and its treatment. Benefits include others than health benefits. These nonhealth benefits are difficult to quantify, but progress in this area is being made.

Those who object to any cost/benefit approach to allocation usually do so because they prefer distribution of medical care to be egalitarian, that is, not influenced by the market or nonmarket productivity of individuals or by their willingness to pay. To carry over this value judgment to whether cost/benefit analysis may better assess a drug's worth than risk/benefit analysis is inappropriate. Although the measure of the benefit may depend in part on the earnings of individuals in the trials, the ultimate distribution of the benefit from a drug in society has no relationship to how the drug's benefit was initially measured.

PROPOSED METHOD*

A conservative economic measure of the net value of a new drug that may cure or substantially alleviate a disease can be derived by comparing two groups of randomly selected persons, each ill with a given disease, one group being treated with a new drug and the other group not. The nontreated or control group may receive a placebo or an existing available treatment for the disease.

The difference in the arithmetic means of the total of direct and indirect costs of the treated (including the costs of the adverse effects, if any) and the control group is tested for significance. If the new drug is more effective than the placebo or an existing drug used as a control, the new or test drug group will have significantly lower average costs per unit of time than the control group.

The indirect costs or value of hours of work that are lost because of the disease and its treatment can be obtained from individual patients at pretreatment and over the given time period of the controlled drug trials. The indirect costs of medical care for the disease can be derived from the clinical trial data, which record utilization of hospital days, medical procedures, tests, drugs, and physician visits. The utilization rates are adjusted for the higher number of mandated procedures and physician visits in a controlled trial than those that would normally occur. Additionally, indirect and direct costs are similarly computed since any adverse effects from the drug may be sufficiently severe to cause a loss of work time and/or medical treatment.

When the double-blind of the clinical trial is broken, the indirect costs (value of hours of work lost) and the direct (medical) costs per person per given unit of time are computed in two ways: (1) using only the observed data and (2) using the adjusted medical utilization data and the observed time lost from work data. This is done for each group, the control and the treated. The computation using only the observed data acts merely as a reference point. The artificial constraints in the long-run cimetidine trials, which is the first attempt to derive a net economic benefit from such trials, clearly illustrate the difficulty of using only observed data. The trial protocol mandated endoscopy[30] at six months and twelve months. Patients with a history

---

*Very early, William M. Wardell, M.D., Ph.D., of the University of Rochester Medical Center, was involved in the development of this method, and SmithKline Corporation is testing the method in their long term cimetidine studies. Roger J. Crossley, M.D., of SmithKline, William Wardell, and I have been jointly evolving the application of this method in these trials.

of peptic ulcer disease but without ulcer symptoms are unlikely to undergo this expensive (about $350) and unpleasant procedure in normal medical practice. Patients in any controlled trial will have scheduled office visits and tests more frequently than in everyday medical practice. This is because subjects in a trial must be kept under frequent medical supervision in case an adverse effect develops or individuals in the untreated group develop serious, life-threatening symptoms from the untreated disease. Because the trial utilization data distort actual medical practice, the data are restructured using the consensus of a panel of expert physicians about the usual clinical handling of patients classified by the severity of their symptoms and/ or disease. Each person in the controlled trials is classified into one of the severity of disease categories and his or her utilization of physician visits, medical procedures, and tests follows the expert panel's consensus, modified by the actual use of hospital days. Alternatively, published consensuses about the usual treatment for a typical case of the disease can be used. This is less satisfactory because no distinction based on the severity of a patient's disease can be made except when hospital days are used by previously ambulatory patients. Although modes of medical practice differ among regions in the United States as well as among countries, agreement about preferable clinical management within a narrow range can be expected.

The prices of the medical procedures, tests, x-rays, and physician visits may possibly be obtained directly from the clinical investigators conducting the trials or from published sources. Hospital rates per diem are much higher in metropolitan than in rural areas, but they are fairly easy to obtain. The pharmaceutical company can provide prices of drugs. Physicians who are board-certified specialists charge more than the general practitioner for the same procedure. Otherwise, quality differences are ignored.

Because it is difficult to correct for quality, and unexplained differentials exist, it is more desirable to have the actual prices charged for initial office visit, return office visit, and medical procedures such as x-rays, blood tests, and any special procedures.

A viable alternative in the United States is to use pricing data supplied by the fiscal intermediaries under Medicare or the usual, customary, reasonable (UCR) charge that Medicare reimburses. These data are available under the Freedom of Information Act in the United States. The average actual prices in the marketplace as supplied by the clinical investigators would probably be higher than the UCR charge. However, medical prices in the United States are higher than the true resource costs, and the UCR charges can act as an arbitrary correction for this. If the data are used eventually to extrapolate a net societal benefit, a percentage of the reported charges, such as the ratio of the average of UCR-Medicare charges to the average of all pricing in the geographic areas where the clinical trials are conducted, would be desirable.

Indirect costs of time lost from work can be obtained from an economic assessment data sheet of questions inserted into the biological protocol. Clinical investigators are hesitant about asking questions that may be construed to invade the privacy, especially about economic matters, of the patient. Some physicians may be reluctant even to ask the patient his or her occupation, although the disease for which this approach is being tested is a peptic ulcer and many patients believe that a peptic ulcer can be the result of on-the-job stress. Because of this reluctance, the only question in the short-run cimetidine trials that sought economic data was: "time lost from work due to ulcer disease during the previous week."

In the long-run trial, the clinicians were willing to ask a patient (as part of the patient's history at the first visit) his or her occupation, in what industry, and the number of hours lost from work because of ulcer disease or its treatment during the week prior to a physician visit. Also asked was whether the patient had changed jobs. An attempt was made to ascertain the level of the new job in relationship to the previous job.

The major measure of the indirect costs used was the value of the time lost from work. This loss can be costed in two ways: first, by using the clinical data about sex, age, geographic area, occupation, and industry with the detailed Bureau of Labor Statistics (BLS) Occupational Wage Rate Series, and secondly, by using the BLS Series of average annual earnings now available by sex and five-year age groupings. The analysis can compare the results from both sets of data. If the end point is to find a net economic benefit of a new drug to the person in the trials, the first approach is better. If the end point of the analysis is a potential benefit for all persons in the population who have medical indications of the disease and if the individuals in the trials do not differ either from these or from the population as a whole in ways other than by sex and age, then the second approach may be theoretically better and simpler and permits more easily sensitivity analysis to changes in variables.

Reservations about the use of the second approach exist. An older person on the average earns more than a younger person up to a given age, but the peak-earnings age differs by occupation. The more education an occupation requires, the later the age of the earnings peak. High mobility of workers coupled with seniority rules weakens age as a good proxy for experience and thus earnings.

In this very early stage of developing a method with the primary end point of measuring a net economic benefit from a new drug, probably both approaches should be used and compared. However, both approaches depend on loss of market earnings and can be criticized for leaving out imputed, nonmarket earnings in the household. Several economists and the U.S. government have estimated the value of a housewife's time when there are two or more persons in the household. Additionally, the BLS has computed with great care a factor to account for average fringe benefits (1.126). The BLS has computed dollar values of imputed household income separately for males and females by five-year age groupings.[31] These valuations can be incorporated into the analysis.

A major assumption is that patient-reported absences from work that are claimed due to illness are actually because of illness. This is not always the case. Workers should be fairly accurate, however, when reporting illness to a clinical physician who is not connected with their employers. In clinical trials, there are usually no company physicians and, in the United States, no requirements of a physician's signature to receive pay or cash sickness benefits. Data on hours worked are more accurate than days worked because many persons, such as professionals, who are not paid an hourly rate are likely to come in late and/or leave early when ill rather than miss a whole day of work. The BLS data show that in May 1978, "managers and administrators, except farm," had 1.4 percent of total work time lost because of illness and injury, and this was the lowest rate among all occupations, which averaged 2.3 percent.[32]

The relationship between absence from work and severity and type of illness obviously differs among different persons, depending on the individual worker's circumstances. Size of earnings, how pleasant remaining at home might be, how well a person likes the paid work, whether the worker has high opportunity costs of unpaid time, how the homemaker values her share of household labor, whether sick leave is paid or unpaid, and other independent variables affect the decision of whether or not to work. In cases of asymptomatic disease, such as hypertension, there is some evidence that merely labeling a person as ill will decrease his or her work hours.[33] There are few, if any, studies that use regression analysis or similar quantitative techniques to explore to what degree these many variables, in addition to health status, may influence working hours of individuals.

If there were a decline in the "work ethic" in the United States, then sickness might be used as an excuse for absence from work when no sickness exists. However, recent data from the Bureau of Labor Statistics for full-time, nonfarm wage and salary workers show no increase in the percentage of scheduled weekly hours lost for any reason: 3.5 percent in 1973 and 1978, and for weekly hours lost because of illness and injury, 2.4 percent in 1973 and 2.3 percent in 1978.

Because there is no national sickness benefits program, it is reasonable to expect that a stronger work ethic exists in the United

States as compared with that of the United Kingdom or in other countries that do have such a program. In 1972 and 1973 "in West Germany, 11 percent of scheduled work-time was lost; in Holland, 10
percent, and in Italy, 15 percent, as compared with 3.5 percent in
the United States. Nonetheless, paid sick leave accounted for about
1 percent of total compensation paid by U.S. employers in 1976, a
cost equivalent to six cents for every hour paid."[34] There is no
estimate of a drop in productivity of those who continue to work when
ill. Persons who are paid by the number of units they produce ("paid
by the piece") could provide some indication of on-the-job loss of
productivity because of illness.

If clinical trial data were used to estimate the potential net
benefit of the drug to the larger population of persons suffering from
the disease, then a correction might be made for the implicit assumption that the workers in the trial can always find full employment.

Omitted from the cost/benefit analysis are the psychic costs of
pain and anxiety and the psychic benefits from their relief. The philosophy of cost/benefit analysis is not limited only "to economic analysis since the scope of the cost-benefit study conducted in prospective
clinical trials could include psychological or sociological evaluation
leading to an assessment of quality of life."[35]

If the cost/benefit approach were used in an ideal fashion rather
than as a first time adjunct to a biological, traditional, controlled
clinical trial, the economic data base derived from the trials could
be improved. Questions about sick pay while out of work because of
illness and the size of the households of women patients could be included. Additionally, data on hours lost from work because of illness
for the weeks other than the week prior to visiting a physician could
be sought.

In clinical trials, patients do not visit a physician each week,
and therefore, to ask for hours lost only during the week prior to a
physician visit means that the work experience in some weeks is
omitted from the data base. Although the recall of how one feels is
believed by many physicians not to be accurate for more than one week,
it is possible that the recall of how many hours of work one missed
may be accurate for a longer period of time. Recall on loss of work
can, if patients agree, be checked against employer records. In some
controlled trials, a symptoms diary is kept by the patients in the trial.
It would be a simple matter to include in such a diary a weekly question about the number of scheduled hours lost from work because of
illness or its treatment during the preceding week.

In long-run trials the problem is greater because as the trial
continues, the time interval between the physician visits increases,
up to three months in the case of the cimetidine trials. It may be
possible to construct an econometric model using the biological vari-

ables obtained from the trial data to yield an estimate of the total time lost during the whole treatment period. A major problem of this method is that it makes it impossible to compare meaningfully the net economic measure of benefit with the traditional, controlled clinical trial's overall measure of "global efficacy." This is because both rest on the same variables.

Global efficacy is a subjective measure on two counts: (1) the patients at the end of the trial indicate (either by checking descriptors or indicators along a scaled line) their self-assessment of general well-being, and (2) the clinical investigator may also, depending on the protocol used in the trial, make a similar assessment that may stand alone or modify the patient's assessment. It would be enlightening to compare the net economic benefit measure, derived by "combining and condensing the multivariate clinical response to a drug into univariate economic (monetary) terms . . . with the traditional clinical measure of 'global efficacy,' and serve as a first step in developing a methodology to evaluate the comprehensive impact of a drug."[36]

NOTES

1. Gio Batta Gori, "The Regulation of Carcinogenic Hazards," Science 208 (April 1980): 256.
2. Rita Ricardo-Campbell, Food Safety Regulation: Limitation and Uses of Cost-Benefit Analysis (Washington, D.C.: AEI-Hoover Institution, 1974).
3. U.S. Department of Health, Education, and Welfare, Federal Drug Administration, News Release, pub. no. 79-27 (October 11, 1979); and Investigational and New Drug Regulations, rev., concept document (Washington, D.C.: Government Printing Office, 1979).
4. John P. Bunker, Benjamin A. Barnes, and Frederick Mostehev, eds., Costs, Risks, and Benefits of Surgery (London: Oxford University Press, 1977). However, the confusion in the medical literature, as indicated by the very title of this book, does not clearly state that risks are part of total costs. Among additional writings that support the basics of the thesis presented are Milton C. Weinstein and William B. Stason, "Foundations of Cost-Effective Analysis for Health and Medical Practices," New England Journal of Medicine 296, no. 13 (March 1977): 716-21; M. J. Orloff et al., "Contributions of Surgical Research to Health Care, 1945-1970: Report of the Research Subcommittee of the Study on Surgical Services for the United States," offprint, n.p., n.d.; and Marshall J. Orloff, "Contributions of Research

in Surgical Technology to Health Care," in R. H. Egdahl and P. M. Gertman, eds., Technology and the Quality of Health Care (Aspen, Colo.: Aspen Systems Corp., 1978), pp. 71-103.

5. John B. Reiss, Fred Hellinger, and John Burkhardt, "Issues in the Cost and Regulation of New Medical Technologies and Procedures: Heart Transplants as a Case Study," Paper presented at the Conference on Critical Issues in Medical Technology, Boston, Mass., April 1980, p. 1.

6. Mary-Ann Rozbicki, "Rationing British Health Care: The Cost/Benefit Approach," case study, U.S. Department of State, Executive Seminar in National and International Affairs, Twentieth Session (1977-78), p. 18. Also, John C. Goodman, National Health Care in Great Britain (Texas: Fisher Institute, 1980); and Louise Russell, Technology in Hospitals: Medical Advances and Their Diffusion (Washington, D.C.: Brookings Institution, 1979).

7. Paul Slovic, Statement to the U.S. Congress, Joint Hearings of the House Subcommittee on Science, Research, and Technology and the Senate Subcommittee on Science, Technology, and Space, Risk/Benefit Analysis in the Legislative Process (July 24-25, 1979), p. 178.

8. Samuel S. Epstein, The Politics of Cancer, rev. ed. (New York: Doubleday, Anchor Press, 1979), p. 465.

9. Ricardo-Campbell, Food Safety Regulation, p. 19.

10. Harold P. Green, "The Risk-Benefit Calculus in Safety Determination," George Washington Law Review 43, no. 3 (March 1975): 807.

11. A double-blind trial is one in which neither the patient nor the investigating physician knows what treatment is being given to any one patient. In a double-blind, controlled trial, some patients will be given the test medication and others in the control group will be given a placebo or an already available medication that is accepted as an effective treatment of the disease. The double-blind is not broken until all the data are collected in order to avoid any subjective interpretation by the physician. Selection for each group is "random." One group receives the test drug and the control group(s) (placebo and/or available treatment) receives medication that appears identical to the test drug. A placebo control is used in order to subtract from the observed effect of the test drug the "placebo effect" that has been proven clinically to occur apart from the observed effect of the test drug. An existing treatment control may be used where investigators believe that a placebo, or sugar pill, is unethical to give anyone because there is already available a drug that is accepted as effective to treat the disease.

If there is a lack of data to support the belief that an existing treatment is effective, a placebo control is preferred.

12. Exceptions may occur in those cases where ethical considerations overrule the use of a control group of persons who receive a "placebo," not a drug, such as in clinical tests of oral contraceptives.

13. David P. Byar et al., "Randomized Clinical Trials," New England Journal of Medicine 295 (July 1976): 79.

14. The FDA's interpretation of "substantial evidence" is not in the governing statute.

15. It is estimated that there are about 300,000 persons who have uncontrolled seizures at least once a month. Richard L. Masland, M.D., Executive Director, Commission for the Control of Epilepsy and Its Consequences, Department of Health, Education, and Welfare, No. 77-185, Workshop on Antiepileptic Drug Development (Washington, D.C.: Government Printing Office, 1977), p. 55.

16. Ronald Kartzinel, M.D., Acting Director, Division of Neuropharmacological Drug Products, Department of Health, Education, and Welfare, Federal Drug Administration, letter to author, dated September 6, 1977.

17. A. J. Culyer, "Need, Values, and Health Status Measurement," in A. J. Culyer and K. G. Wright, eds., Economic Aspects of Health Services (London: Martin Robertson, 1978), pp. 9-31.

18. Jennie A. Freeman et al., "The Importance of Beta: The Type II Error and Sample Size in the Design and Interpretation of the Randomized Control Trial," New England Journal of Medicine 299 (September 1978): 690.

19. Richard Zeckhauser, "Procedures for Valuing Lives," Public Policy 23, no. 4 (Fall 1975): 442.

20. David E. Bell, Ralph L. Keeney, and Howard Raiffa, eds., Conflicting Objectives in Decisions, series 1 (New York: Wiley, 1977), p. 254.

21. Ibid.

22. Culyer, "Need, Values and Health Status Measurement," pp. 17-23.

23. Dorothy P. Rice and Thomas A. Hodgson, "Social and Economic Implications of Cancer in the United States," Paper presented to the Expert Committee on Cancer Statistics, the World Health Organization, and the International Agency for Research on Cancer at Madrid, Spain, June 20-26, 1978, pp. 5-6.

24. L. B. Scheiner and K. L. Melmon, "The Utility Function of Antihypertensive Therapy," Annals of the New York Academy of Sciences 304 (1978): 114.

25. Jerome P. Kassirer, "The Principles of Clinical Decision Making:

An Introduction to Decision Analysis," Yale Journal of Biology and Medicine 49, no. 2 (May 1976): 155.

26. Epstein, Politics of Cancer, p. 315.

27. Joanne Linnerooth, "The Value of Human Life: A Review of the Models," Economic Inquiry 17 (January 1979): 57.

28. Ibid., p. 72.

29. As quoted in "Can Government Place a Value on Saving a Human Life?" National Journal, February 17, 1979, p. 254.

30. A visual examination of the duodenum (site of the peptic ulcer) or other body cavity by insertion through the mouth of a flexible, narrow, lighted tube.

31. Lynn C. Pringer and Aviva Berk, Costs of Illness and Disease, Fiscal Year 1975 (Washington, D.C.: Georgetown University, 1977), prepared for the National Institutes of Health, January 4, 1977, U.S. Department of Commerce, National Technical Information Service, pub. no. PB-280298, pp. 82, 87–88.

32. U.S. Bureau of Labor Statistics, Press Release, 79-174 (March 12, 1979).

33. R. B. Haynes et al., "Increased Absenteeism from Work after Detection and Labeling of Hypertensive Patients," New England Journal of Medicine 299, no. 14 (October 5, 1978): 741–44.

34. Daniel E. Taylor, "Absence from Work Measuring the Hours Lost, May 1978," Monthly Labor Review, August 1979, p. 49.

35. Rita Ricardo-Campbell, Martin M. Eisman, William M. Wardell, and Roger Crossley, "Preliminary Methodology for Controlled Cost-Benefit Study of Drug Impact: The Effect of Cimetidine on Days of Work Lost in a Short-Term Trial in Duodenal Ulcer," Journal of Clinical Gastroenterology 2 (March 1980): 41.

36. Ibid., p. 37.

3

PUBLIC POLICIES AND
CHILD HEALTH CARE UTILIZATION:
HAS EQUALITY BEEN ACHIEVED?

Barbara L. Wolfe

The health of children is an important determinant of their future
well-being. It is also important to society, in that it can be thought of
as a form of human capital. Good health, in childhood and after, is
likely to be related to higher income and more choice in the use of
leisure time than is poor health. Poor health is likely to limit job
opportunities and to increase the potential need for transfers. Beyond
market effects, health may influence the probability of marriage and
the characteristics of one's future mate, further influencing income.
Some types of poor health may affect the health of others through
various public health externalities; for instance, a contagious disease
such as German measles causes birth defects. This may require government intervention.

Thus, from several perspectives—the desire to create equality of
economic opportunity, the effort to control externalities, and the need
to increase productivity—there is reason for government to intervene
and to seek ways to influence children's health status. Education, nutrition, and medical care for pregnant women are all possible strategies for influencing a child's health status. Perhaps the most direct
path, however, is through the medical care system affecting the level
or type of services received by children, especially those who would
otherwise receive too little care.

This research was supported in part by funds granted to the
Institute for Research on Poverty at the University of Wisconsin-
Madison by the Department of Health and Human Services, pursuant to
the provisions of the Economic Opportunity Act of 1964. The author
would like to thank Margaret Helming for her able research assistance.

Programs to provide medical care to children other than the Maternal and Child Health Act (1935) are relatively recent. They include the Neighborhood Health Center (NHC) program (a 1965 Office of Economic Opportunity program) and Medicaid (a 1965 Title XIX program under the Social Security Act). Medicaid is by far the largest program. It is primarily a financing program that is made available on the basis of low income; generally, eligibility for welfare also qualifies an individual for Medicaid, and in 28 states, this includes low-income families with two parents (AFDC-U). In 17 states, all children in families with incomes below AFDC eligibility are covered, and in 28 states, there are medical "spend-down" provisions, by which families that expend a certain amount of their incomes on medical care thereafter become eligible for Medicaid.

But do these programs go far enough to create equal utilization? We will evaluate this question, using data from an area that has extensive Medicaid coverage and a relatively well-developed Neighborhood Health Center system, which is encouraged by a major university medical school. In this case, our question goes further. Given a situation where medical care programs are generously funded and readily available, do there remain differences in the utilization of medical care for children?

Clearly, the demand for children's medical care is tied to child health. Children who are well need less care than children who are ill; thus, we will be careful to control for health status. However, since medical problems are reported by the parents, bias may exist in that poorly educated parents may not recognize a medical problem or may be less able to afford care for it and, therefore, may not report it. We do not deal with this bias except by controlling for parent education.

The variables we emphasize are income, time constraints, availability, and the role of insurance—particularly the differences between those with private insurance and those with Medicaid. All these are factors that enable a person to obtain medical care. The emphasis here is on "enabling" rather than on "need" or "taste" factors.

The underlying model is

$$U = \gamma X + \beta H + \gamma T + \epsilon$$

where U = a vector of utilization variables,
X = a vector of enabling variables,
H = a vector of health or need variables,
T = a vector of taste or predisposing variables,
γ, β, γ = corresponding coefficients, and
ϵ = a vector of error terms.

There are several utilization variables; the first is whether or not a child received medical care in the past year. It is considered as recursive to the rest of the utilization measures and is estimated in logit form, using the entire sample. The next measure, which is made conditional on some visit or visits, is number of visits during the 12-month period. The remaining measures, percentages of visits to specific types of providers, cover visits to private practitioners, health centers or clinics, hospital outpatient clinics, hospital emergency rooms, and school infirmaries. This approach allows us to separate visits that are parent initiated from follow-up visits initiated by, or at least reflecting, provider recommendations that may alter responses to the explanatory variables.

This emphasis on alternative providers is introduced because of the view that public policies may have led to dual quality care, that is, better care for those who have private insurance or who can afford to pay the asking price. Unfortunately, few attempts have been made to measure the quality of care in the most important sense, its effect on health status. We have generally adopted prevailing views about the quality of providers that emphasize factors such as continuity of care, experience, and turnover. These imply that private practitioners will be ranked highest and emergency rooms lowest; clinics and health centers fall in between. School infirmaries are not included in the ranking, since services there are likely to be limited to screening programs, some of which may be required by law (for example, hearing tests).

To get some sense of the patterns of utilization of private practitioners, and especially whether the patterns differed among neighborhoods, a regression was run using census tracts as the unit of observation and using certain census tract information (U. S. Bureau of the Census 1972). The percentage of children using private providers in each tract was made the dependent variable. The results suggest that income, race, and availability all make a difference.

Percentage whose regular provider is a private physician:	−.004% black (2.83)
	+.06 median income (7.20)
	+.06 GPs & pediatricians/1000 (2.17)
	+.01 distance to clinic (2.24)
	+.01 distance to hospital (1.14)

$$R^2 = .54$$

$$N = 155$$

(t statistics are in parentheses.)

Regarding race, children living in areas with a high percentage of black persons are less likely than those in white neighborhoods to see a private provider; the maximum difference within Rochester neighborhoods is 38 percent.

Regarding income, children in areas with higher median incomes are more likely than those in areas with low incomes to see a private provider: the income range would imply a maximum difference of 101 percent.

Going from one extreme to the other in the availability of general practitioners and pediatricians, we see an increase of 36 percent in the probability of using a private provider; the range of clinic distances suggests an increase of up to 41 percent in the probability of using a private practitioner if the nearest clinic is far enough away to take 41 minutes travel time.

What all of this suggests is some rather systematic patterns of use in which those who should be considered "disadvantaged," in the sense that they live in poorer areas with fewer medical care providers, are less likely than the advantaged to use private practitioners. Our microstudy, controlling for need and for other enabling and predisposing factors, will further explore this pattern, but first the data base will be described.

DESCRIPTION OF THE DATA AND THE LOCATION

The data used in this study came from the Rochester Community Child Health Survey, part of a long-term multidisciplinary research project that was begun in the mid-1960s in Rochester, Monroe County, New York, and was aimed at gaining a better understanding of child health and community health services. A sequence of surveys was conducted between 1966 and 1975. The 1975 survey is the basis for the empirical work in this paper. The general plan for the 1975 survey was to obtain a 1 percent sample of families in Monroe County with children under 18 years of age and to interview or gather information on all children and adults in the families. The families were interviewed from March to December, 1975, and data were collected on 3,116 individuals, of whom 1,107 were children, aged 1 to 11. Only 75 percent of these children are used in this analysis, since: (1) only children living with their mothers were included, and (2) individuals who reported days during the last two weeks when "they were not able to carry on as normal because of illness or injury" were not asked about illness or use of medical care during the preceding 12 months. Their data during the preceding 12 months are not comparable to those for the rest of the sample, and therefore, they are excluded.

The 1974 population of the community was 706.9 thousand. In 1970, the population was 92 percent white; 9.1 percent of the total population was under 5 years of age; 19.8 percent was 5 to 14 years of age. The average per capita income was $3,821, the average household income, $15,455; 16.9 percent of families and unrelated individuals had incomes under $3,000, and another 8.3 percent had incomes in the $3,000 to $4,999 range. In 1975, there were 31,288 on AFDC, or 41.3 per 1,000.

Providers

There are seven acute-care hospitals in Monroe County, with an average bed ratio of 3.42 per 1,000, which is below the nationwide average but probably well above the ratio needed. All hospitals have emergency rooms, 3 hospitals have full pediatric outpatient services, and there are 7 neighborhood health centers and a number of well-child clinics. The physician/population ratio is 1.77/1,000, which is above the national average. There is one medical school and a number of nursing schools in the county. Fewer than 10 percent of the physicians are in general practice; nearly 8 percent are pediatricians. The pediatricians are reportedly very busy, and there is a suggestion of maldistribution away from the inner city and outer suburban areas. In 1974, outpatient visits totaled 105,252 per 100,000 population, a 6 percent decrease in outpatient visits from 1973. There were a similar number of inpatient days per 100,000 population—102,995; this was a 1 percent decrease from 1973.

Nationwide, most people use private practitioners (in group or solo practice) as their regular medical care providers, and Rochester is no exception. Among children aged 1 to 11 in the sample, 79 percent used private practitioners. Nearly 10 percent used neighborhood health centers or other clinics, and approximately 2 percent used hospitals. The average income level was highest for those who used private practitioners—$18,176—and lowest for those using hospital-based facilities. Users of the neighborhood health centers had an average income of $9,858.

Those with Medicaid coverage followed the same sort of pattern; those with the lowest incomes used hospitals, the next group used health centers or clinics, and the highest-income group used private practitioners.

Insurance Coverage

Nationwide, we are not sure of the number of persons covered by insurance, though it has been estimated that 18 to 26 million persons do not have hospital insurance, the most common form of insurance. We do, however, have data on the expenditures covered by insurance and on the number of policies. In 1977, nearly 70 percent of the funds spent for personal health care involved a third-party payee (Gibson and Fisher 1978), government programs accounted for 40 percent, and private health insurance paid for nearly 27.6 percent. The percentages differed by type of expenditure and were highest for hospital care (94.1 percent of all hospital expenditures were covered by insurance, and 37 percent by private insurance).

Among the sample of children 1 to 11 (N = 810), 82.4 percent were covered under some form of private health insurance, 9.6 percent were covered by Medicaid, nearly 6 percent were covered through a Health Maintenance Organization (HMO) type arrangement, and 2.3 percent had no insurance coverage.

The average income of the families with different types of coverage followed the expected pattern: those with private insurance lived in families with the highest average family incomes—$17,802; children covered under Medicaid lived in families with the lowest average income—$5,610. Those without coverage came from families with the next lowest average income—$13,370; this can be thought of as the "squeezed" group. Those with HMO coverage fell in between, with an average family income of $15,054. The general pattern is similar for the adults in the sample.

All children in families eligible for AFDC (in New York State that includes families with unemployed fathers) were covered under Medicaid. Children in families with incomes above the AFDC level were eligible if their family income fell below this line after deducting medical expenses (under the "spend-down" provision). Inpatient and outpatient hospital care, physicians' services, early and periodic screening, diagnosis, and treatment, including laboratory and x-ray tests, were covered for children and individuals under 21.

In 1970, 55 percent of children in poverty under 21, nationwide, were Medicaid recipients. In New York State, the percentage was 168 percent of the children in poverty, the highest figure for any state, but this was down to 92.5 percent in 1974. Payment per child recipient in 1974 was $174 nationally and $326 in New York (Davis and Schoen 1978, p. 68). The ratio of payments in large urban counties (including Monroe) to New York City was .84. Children represented nearly 50 percent of the recipients but received less than 20 percent of the funds.

As suggested earlier, insurance is viewed as an enabling factor; it reduces the price of care. However, insurance coverage is itself voluntary. Presumably, its purchase depends upon expected medical care expenditures and the price of insurance. Medicaid is somewhat different, in that coverage depends upon meeting certain eligibility criteria.

We estimated the probability of insurance coverage and viewed it as recursive to the utilization results. In general, we expected higher income to be positively associated with private insurance purchase and working mothers also to be associated positively, since that offers another chance to purchase group insurance; we also expected older (and larger) families to be more likely than younger and smaller ones to purchase insurance. Better education may also lead to more insurance purchases, perhaps reflecting a longer time horizon. Finally, we would expect both the nonwhite race and the receipt of welfare or child support to be negatively associated.

A number of the results are as expected in the private insurance equation reported in Table 3.1. These include income, welfare, race, working mothers, age, and education. In fact, the only surprise is the sign of family size. Perhaps, however, this reflects the greater demand on resources made by larger families. The negative sign may suggest that income should be in equivalence terms. In any case, the elasticity is small; the only elasticities above .05 are mother's education and family income.

The HMO results are uninteresting. The only significant variable is mother's age, suggesting that older families are less likely to use HMOs. The number in the sample is small, and perhaps represents availability more than socioeconomic factors.

The Medicaid equation is of greater interest. Income is entered as a linear spline around eligibility.[1] The equation weakly suggests that those with the lowest incomes are most likely to have Medicaid coverage. Those with incomes between welfare and medical assistance show a flat relationship, while beyond the income levels that define eligibility, the probability may decline. Households that receive welfare or child support are more likely to have Medicaid coverage than those with working mothers (perhaps because of the greater availability to the latter of private insurance). Single-parent households are more likely to have Medicaid coverage than are two-parent ones.

Thus, it appears that income and price (as measured by working and by eligibility factors) are important determinants. Expected use, as measured by the numbers likely to use care, is less important.

Neighborhood Health Centers

In 1976, there were approximately 125 health centers operating in the United States, serving some 1.5 million persons. Over a third

TABLE 3.1. Logit Results: Probability of Having Different Types of Insurance

Variables	Private Insurance ($\bar{x} = .91; \sigma^2 = .08$)		HMO ($\bar{x} = .07; \sigma^2 = .06$)		Medicaid ($\bar{x} = .06; \sigma^2 = .06$)		Mean
	coef. asym. t	elasticity	coef. asym. t	elasticity	coef. asym. t	elasticity	
Log family income	1.88 (4.91)*	.20	-.15 (0.34)	-.69	1.71 (2.99)*	.26	.15
Receive welfare on child support	-1.76 (4.38)*	-.01	-1.08 (1.62)	-.15	.40 (0.73)	.05	.12
Nonwhite	-.25 (0.49)	-.00	-.92 (1.53)	-.11	-1.95 (2.87)*	-.41	.21
Mother works full-time	2.70 (4.11)*	.01	.34 (0.79)	.07	-1.89 (2.07)*	-.37	.20
Mother works part-time	1.05 (1.69)	.004	.42 (1.01)	.08			
Mother's occupation	.00 (.09)	.00	-.03 (1.37)	-1.52			49.3
Father's occupation	-.02 (1.19)	-.02	-.01 (0.67)	-.59			49.3
Not married	-2.24 (2.11)*	-.01	-.03 (0.03)	-.00	1.91 (3.17)*	.23	.12
Mother's education	.24 (2.77)*	.06	-.11 (1.19)	-1.31			12.7
Mother's age	.06 (2.35)*	.04	-.06 (2.48)*	-2.07			35.8
Number of siblings	-.21 (1.93)*	-.01	.18 (1.30)	.43	.43 (1.45)	1.08	2.54
Income spline (00's)							
Family income					-.03 (.58)	-4.83	168.6
(Income-pub. asst., 0)					.04 (.24)	4.69	
(Income-med. asst., 0)					-.05 (.43)	5.95	
Constant	-9.33 (3.41)		3.31 (1.52)		-1.93 (1.63)		
X²	214		23		211		

N = 675

*Significant at the 5% level.
Note: The unit of analysis is the household.

of the patients were children. Persons below the poverty line were treated without cost; those above it paid.

In Rochester, a special clinic was set up in a hospital in 1964, but distance and difficulty of access (to reach it two bus changes were required) limited its success. There was little health care available in the neighborhood itself—only 2 family doctors for approximately 25,000 persons (Haggerty, Roghmann, and Pless 1975, p. 223). Now a neighborhood health center, set up in 1968, serves individuals in the seventh ward, a poor black ghetto. It has evening hours and a 24 hour on-call system. The NHC tries to attract recent graduates from the University of Rochester to its staff. In pediatrics and family medicine, it has been successful.

Although a number of studies (Davis and Schoen 1978, pp. 180-85) have tried to show that the quality of these separate facilities is equal to that of other providers, one problem reducing quality is the high turnover of professional personnel. On other quality dimensions, the Rochester data used in this study suggest that physicians in health centers: (1) rank below physicians in private practice, though above those in hospital clinics, in terms of the ranking of medical schools attended; (2) are younger and less experienced than other practitioners; (3) are more likely to be board-certified; but (4) are less likely to be specialists or affiliated with a hospital.

EMPIRICAL RESULTS ON UTILIZATION

We turn now to the subject of primary concern: utilization of medical care. We stress enabling variables and certain predisposing factors. The variables included are: income, insurance coverage by type, race and median tract income, attitude toward reasonable costs and convenient hours, parents' time and number of children in household, availability measures, mother's education, whether the child has a regular M.D., parents' utilization, and routine checks. Need factors, such as various measures of health status, age, sex, and age of mother at birth, are controlled. Thus, if utilization were equalized by the existence of these programs, we would expect income, race, and availability measures to be insignificant. The effects of family size and parents' time are less clear. Some parents may prefer larger families (quantity) while others prefer to invest more in each child (quality) (Becker and Lewis 1973). If so, more children may be associated with lower utilization. Parents who work or are single parents have less time with their children. A negative sign may indicate the more severe time constraint or lack of flexible provider hours. Alternatively, parents who have more time may substitute

TABLE 3.2. Logit Results: Probability of Having Seen a Provider
During Last 12 Months

Variables	Coef.	Asymptotic t	Elasticity	$\bar{x}$	σ
Enabling factors					
Family income (Y) in 000s	-.07	1.2	-.14	16.46	7.96
Max (Y - 1.5 Pov. Line, 0)	.05	0.8	.04		
Median income—census tract	.09	1.9*	.14	13.28	3.26
Nonwhite (dummy variable)	-.04	0.1	.00	.15	.36
Insured (dummy variable)	-.00	0.0	-.00	.97	.15
Parent's time	-.00	0.1	-.00	112.13	23.84
Number of siblings	-.28	2.9*	-.11	3.01	1.23
Drs./population	-.19	-1.4	-.00	.17	.66
Distance to clinic	.01	0.8	.02	11.59	9.03
Need factors					
Ill	.61	2.2*	.02	.19	.39
Accident	.64	1.0	.00	.04	.19
Hospitalizations	1.47	1.7	.02	.09	.18
Predisposing factors					
Age	-.16	4.3*	-.14	6.73	2.93
Mother's education	.05	1.0	.07	12.54	2.66
Average parent's use	-.00	0.1	-.00	2.28	2.54
Reas. cost (dummy)	-.06	0.2	-.01	.71	.45
Conv. hours (dummy)	-.18	0.9	-.01	.59	.49
Constant	2.74	2.4			
X^2	75.5				
N	810				

*Significant at the 5% level.

their own time for medical care. If this is so, the combined result
may show no effect, but underlying differences may remain.

Mother's education may also follow a pattern likely to show
insignificant results. Mothers with more education may be more efficient at producing any given level of health (a negative association)
but may also demand more care or be better able to judge when to go
to a provider. Thus, an insignificant result here may still hide important differences.

We began our analyses of utilization by asking whether a child
received medical care over the past 12 months. This question is
separated from frequency to allow us to analyze visits that were
patient initiated, or in the case of children, parent initiated, from
follow-up visits that may have been provider initiated (Newhouse and
Phelps 1976, p. 275) or have reflected provider recommendations that
could alter responses to the explanatory variables. Table 3.2 presents
regression results on an equation run to "explain" whether or not a
child saw a provider over a 12-month interval.[2]

Only a few of the factors of greatest interest (Enabling factors) appear related to the probability that a child saw a provider. These include median income in the area of a child's residence and number of siblings. Family size has a negative association, perhaps because of additional financial or time constraints, or perhaps because parents eventually learn from experience how to manage children's health problems. The positive association with tract median income may be cause for greater concern; it may represent availability of medical care, discrimination by providers, or community norms. In its larger statistical associations it may better represent permanent family income, signifying a maintenance of income differentials in the use of medical care.

The need factors, where significant, indeed suggest that those with greater need, as measured by their health status, are more likely to receive care. Among predisposing factors, age follows the expected pattern—more care at youngest ages, then a leveling off. Greater parental use of medical care does not appear to be associated with greater probability of use by their children.[3] Thus, there are differences in care related to constraints.

For those with any visits, we next analyzed the total number of medical care visits. The results are presented in Table 3.3. These provider visits appear to be only minimally affected by the factors of greatest interest—income, race, mother's education, income level of the community and, interestingly, insurance coverage. This suggests that among children aged 1 to 11, level of utilization is primarily explained by other factors, such as health and age.

Perhaps surprisingly, there appears to be no independent association between utilization of care and insurance of any type. This is confirmed in other model specifications in which "no insurance" is the included insurance variable and in specifications interacting income and insurance. In a simple cross-tabulation, the number of visits appears somewhat associated with income; the greatest average number is for those with incomes 1.5 times the poverty line and the lowest for those 1 to 1.5 times the poverty line, but the differences are small—2.4 compared with 2.7.

The findings on number of children suggest increased utilization until there are three children and then less use. Again, this may indicate either economies of scale (gains in home production) or substitution of quantity for quality.

The finding on availability of doctors[4] suggests that greater availability is, to some extent, associated with greater utilization. It is not clear if this is because an existing demand can be met now or whether it represents supplier-induced demand. The result does suggest some inequality.

TABLE 3.3. Medical Care Utilization Results[a]

Variables[b]	Total No. Visits	Private Office Visit (%)	Health Center or Clinic (%)	Emergency Room (%)	Outpatient (%)	School (%)
Enabling variables						
Family income (Y) in 000s	.03 (0.5)	-.03 (3.2)*	.02 (3.0)*	.002 (0.4)	-.01 (2.9)*	.02 (4.2)*
Max (Y-1.5 Pov. Line, 0)	-.01 (0.2)	.03 (3.2)*	-.02 (2.8)*	-.003 (0.5)	.01 (2.9)*	-.02 (4.4)*
Median income—census tract	-.00 (0.7)	.02 (3.3)*	-.02 (4.2)*	-.003 (2.4)*	.003 (1.2)	.001 (0.4)
Nonwhite (dummy variable)	.04 (0.7)	-.32 (6.8)*	.32 (8.2)*	-.02 (0.9)	.01 (0.1)	.01 (0.4)
Insurance dummies						
Private	.20 (0.6)	.14 (2.3)*	-.11 (2.2)*	.04 (1.1)	-.02 (0.7)	-.04 (1.5)
Medicaid	.08 (0.2)	-.25 (3.0)*	.17 (2.4)*	.04 (0.8)	.07 (1.5)	-.02 (0.6)
HMO	-.18 (0.4)	-.10 (1.5)	.20 (3.7)*	-.09 (2.4)*	.003 (0.1)	-.01 (0.4)
Reas. cost (dummy)	-.30 (0.7)	-.19 (2.7)*	.14 (2.5)*	.05 (1.4)	-.03 (0.8)	.02 (0.4)
RC x Priv. or no insurance	-.09 (0.2)	.15 (2.0)*	-.13 (2.0)*	-.05 (1.2)	.04 (1.0)	-.01 (0.4)
Convenient hours	.28 (1.9)	.02 (0.9)	.01 (0.3)	-.01 (0.6)	-.03 (2.0)*	.004 (0.4)
Parents' time	-.00 (1.2)	.001 (2.5)*	-.001 (1.3)	.00 (0.0)	-.001 (0.4)	-.001 (2.6)*
Number of siblings	.50 (1.7)	.05 (1.0)	-.02 (0.6)	-.01 (0.3)	.05 (1.9)*	-.06 (2.7)*
(Number of siblings)^2	-.08 (1.8)	-.01 (1.0)	.003 (0.4)	.002 (0.6)	-.004 (1.1)	.01 (2.2)*
Availability						
Drs./population	.18 (1.6)	.01 (0.6)	-.01 (0.8)	.01 (1.2)	-.01 (0.9)	-.002 (0.2)
Distance to clinic	.00 (0.1)	-.01 (1.0)				

	2.64	.74	.13	.06	.04	.03
Distance to HMO		.00 (1.4)	-.001 (0.6)	-.002 (2.1)*	-.001 (1.4)	.002 (2.2)*
Distance to hospital		-.00 (0.1)	.00 (0.1)	.0004 (0.3)	.001 (0.9)	-.001 (1.3)
Predisposing						
Routine check	-.28 (1.2)	.06 (1.6)	-.003 (0.1)	-.08 (3.4)*	-.01 (0.3)	.02 (1.2)
Mother's education	-.01 (0.3)	.01 (1.5)	.001 (0.2)	-.001 (0.4)	-.005 (1.6)	-.003 (1.2)
Aver. parent's visit	.04 (1.5)	-.02 (3.3)*	.01 (1.3)	.01 (2.8)*	-.002 (0.8)	.005 (2.0)*
No regular M.D.	-.27 (0.4)	-.18 (1.7)	-.21 (2.4)*	.57 (9.6)*	-.09 (1.7)	-.89 (1.8)
R^2	.33	.50	.43	.29	.15	.11
N	682	682	682	682	682	682

[a]Equation also includes need variables, a constant, and certain additional predisposing variables; see Table 3.4 for these results.

[b]Means for the dependent variables in order are: 2.64; .74; .13; .06; .04; .03.

*Significant at the 5% level.

Note: t-statistics in parentheses.

TABLE 3.4. Further Utilization Results: Independent Variables Not Shown in Table 3.3

Variables	Total Visits	Private Office Visit (%)	Health Center or Clinic (%)	Emergency Room (%)	Outpatient (%)	School (%)
Need variables						
Ill	.40 (2.8)	-.01 (0.3)	.03 (1.4)	-.04 (2.5)*	.03 (1.7)	-.01 (0.7)
Accident	-.10 (0.3)	-.13 (2.1)*	-.09 (1.7)	.28 (8.0)*	-.03 (1.0)	-.03 (1.2)
Hospitalizations	1.24 (3.3)*	.04 (0.6)	-.05 (0.9)	-.05 (1.4)	.04 (1.1)	.02 (0.8)
Days ill	.09 (13.9)*	-.001 (1.3)	.001 (1.3)	-.00 (0.5)	.001 (1.6)	-.00 (0.6)
Predisposing variables						
Age	-.56 (5.2)*	.02 (1.0)	.002 (0.1)	-.005 (0.5)	-.01 (1.1)	-.005 (0.6)
Age^2	.03 (3.9)*	-.002 (1.3)	-.00 (0.1)	.00 (0.5)	.001 (0.8)	.001 (1.4)
Female	.05 (0.3)	.01 (0.6)	.002 (0.1)	-.04 (2.7)*	.01 (0.6)	.01 (1.2)
Low mother's age	-.08 (0.3)	-.06 (1.2)	-.06 (1.5)	.04 (1.4)	.11 (4.3)*	-.03 (1.2)
Unhappy family	-.38 (1.5)	-.04 (0.9)	.08 (2.4)*	.01 (0.5)	-.01 (0.6)	-.04 (2.2)*
Children share provider	.30 (1.3)	.05 (1.4)	.02 (0.5)	-.03 (1.5)	-.02 (0.9)	-.02 (12)
Constant	3.26	.32	.23	.19	.17	.09

*Significant at the 5% level.
Note: t–statistics in parentheses.

In general, there is little cause for alarm in these findings. The findings on use or nonuse provide more cause for concern and appear to reflect mainly differences in income level and family size.

PATTERNS OF UTILIZATION

There are five types of providers used by children in the sample: private practitioners, health centers or clinics,[5] hospital outpatient clinics, emergency rooms, and school infirmaries. The last accounts for a very small percentage. As suggested earlier, by traditional standards, private practitioners are rated highest in terms of quality and emergency rooms are rated lowest (except for accidents). (The difficulty with health centers and clinics is primarily lack of continuity and, possibly, less experienced doctors.)

In the analysis, the percentage of total annual visits using each type of provider is related to the probability of using each particular type of practice. Since the independent variables are the same in each equation, the system is estimated using single-equation OLS. (This gives the same results as estimating the system as a whole. The coefficients, added across, sum to zero, except for the constant and rounding errors.) Most visits, 74 percent, are to private providers; 13 percent of visits are to health centers or clinics; 6 percent are to emergency rooms; 4 percent are to outpatient clinics, and nearly 3 percent are to school infirmaries.

Insurance Coverage

Children whose parents have private insurance appear more likely to be taken to private practitioners and less likely to use health centers or clinics than those without insurance. This may reflect personal choice for private practitioners. The lower probability of using health centers or clinics may reflect special payment features of these practices.

Children covered under Medicaid are most likely to use health centers or clinics, least likely to use private practitioners, and somewhat more likely to use hospital outpatient clinics than non-Medicaid children. Those covered through an HMO-type arrangement are most likely to use such centers and least likely to use emergency rooms or private practitioners.

There is nearly a 40 percent difference in the probability that children in families with private insurance and those with Medicaid will use private practitioners. Since we noted clear associations between income and the probability of private insurance, this differential pattern suggests continued inequality in medical care utilization.

Income

Although the income findings are significant, they are small and cancel out at 1.5 times the poverty line. They do indicate that, among the lowest-income groups, controlling for insurance, race, median-tract income, availability, need, and other factors, there is a high probability that those with the lowest income (up to 1.5 times the poverty line) will see private practitioners or use outpatient clinics or schools. The findings for median-tract income, which might be considered a measure of permanent income, suggest that children in higher-income families are likely to use private practitioners. These children are less likely to use health centers or clinics or emergency rooms. This suggests that income has not been "neutralized" through public programs, but that families who live in higher-income areas take their children to private practitioners. Alternatively, this pattern may reflect provider location or neighborhood norms.[6] Any one of these might be reason for our wishing to reappraise both the provision of care and public policies in this area.

Race

White children are more likely than nonwhite ones to use private practitioners; nonwhite children are likely to use health centers or clinics. This difference remains after controlling for insurance, including Medicaid, income, tract income, family size, need, and other predisposing factors. In fact, the largest single coefficients are for race (-.32 for private office visits). This is a significant difference and is confirmed by cross-tabulation results: 85 percent of whites with incomes above 1.5 times the poverty line use private practitioners, but only 32 percent of nonwhites in this income category do so; 33 percent of whites with incomes below the poverty line use private practitioners, but only 8 percent of nonwhites with similarly low incomes do so. All of these results give reason to believe that utilization patterns remain unequal.

Parents' Time

Two-parent households and those with a nonworking parent generally have more time available to spend with the children than do households with single and working parents. Does this affect utilization? There is some evidence here that it does: children of parents with "more time" available are somewhat more likely to see a private practitioner. The effect is small: a 40-hour increment of available time would be associated with a .04 increase in the probability of seeing a private provider. Having a parent who did not work might add another .04 or .08 increase.

Families with more children have greater demands on their resources of both time and money than those with fewer children. The results suggest little effect on patterns of utilization: there is some increase in the probability that they will use hospital outpatient facilities, and they are somewhat less likely to use school infirmaries.

Availability and Attitudes toward Cost

A priori, we expected availability to influence utilization. Our results do not substantiate this. One explanation is that we are dealing with one county only, whereas availability appropriately applies to a broad geographical area (though quality is not necessarily homogeneous), and physicians are about equally accessible throughout the area. Another is that the doctor/population ratio, though limited to pediatricians and general practitioners, includes doctors at health centers, clinics, and hospitals. These latter tend to be in the poorer areas, though they provide care to a broad population group and so may overstate physician/population ratio in these areas. Thus, the ratio of private practitioners to population might be a better measure than the one used here.

In general, distance shows little effect; however, there is a very small increase in the probability that school facilities will be used if the mileage to an HMO is further. There is also a very slight (and inexplicable) negative relationship for emergency rooms. The coefficients are small: 20 additional miles reduces the probability of using an emergency room by .04, or 4 percent.

Certain families respond that reasonable cost is an important consideration in selecting medical care. Does this influence their behavior? First of all, such individuals are more likely than those who do not worry about cost to take their children to a health center or clinic and less likely to take them to a private practitioner. The coefficients are quite large, confirming that cost is an important determining factor for them.

This cost variable is made to interact with one designed to measure whether the family pays first-dollar costs. The proxy for this second variable is lack of HMO or Medicaid coverage; that is, the family has no insurance or has private insurance. These families who care about cost and do not have first-dollar coverage appear to have less response in terms of their children's utilization patterns: a small reduction (-.04) in the probability of using private practitioners compared with families with similar insurance but without such concerns and no effect on the use of health centers or clinics. This suggests that this combination of characteristics has its major impact on type of coverage—a theory to be explored in the future.

Certain families place value on convenient hours in selecting a provider. The only influence of this variable on patterns of utilization in this study is to decrease slightly their probability of using hospital outpatient clinics, a response that may reflect either the clinics' hours of operation or the waiting time in such clinics.

Mother's Education

There is some indication that mothers with more education are more likely than less educated ones to take their children to private practitioners and less likely to take them to hospital outpatient clinics (although the results are not significant). This would be consistent with a perception that private practice offers better care.

SUMMARY AND CONCLUSIONS

Children who may be considered disadvantaged, those in lower-income areas who are nonwhite and whose parents have less time available, tend to use private practitioners far less than do whites from higher-income areas. Coverage by Medicaid further reduces the probability of using private practitioners. These parents may choose to use alternative care, or the results may reflect the location of private practitioners away from nonwhite or low-income areas and financial limitations in Medicaid that discourage private practitioners from taking Medicaid patients. Whatever the cause, these findings suggest that public policies have not been entirely successful in equalizing medical care utilization by children.

The provision of financial resources through the Medicaid system and the availability of alternative types of care have not achieved an equal level or quality of medical care utilization among children in the Rochester area. This is so even though the community has extensive benefits and a large program committed to pediatrics and is probably a community in which greater efforts have been made to equalize care than in many others.

In terms of the probability of a visit or number of visits, much equality has been achieved. However, children whose families live in areas (as defined by census tracts) that have higher incomes are more likely to get medical care, and children with more siblings are less likely to be taken to the doctor. Both of these are causes for concern. Race and family income do not appear to generate significant differences in the amount of utilization among users, a finding that reaffirms that equality in certain dimensions has been achieved.

Sharper differences are suggested when we examine patterns of utilization, however. White children in high-income areas from families with a parent at home and with private insurance are more likely than other children to see a private practitioner. (This result is somewhat similar to that in Davis and Reynolds 1976, where blacks were found to use less ambulatory care than whites.) If continuity and/or experience of practitioners are used as indicators of quality, this pattern suggests that high-income white children get higher quality care than low-income black and other disadvantaged children. This result may stem from Medicaid's payment system, the availability of providers, or other forms of discrimination.

Removing financial constraints is only one part of providing access to care: location of care, ease and cost of transportation, hours of practice, and information about when to go and about quality of care are not included in the current policy package. Yet they are important in determining patterns of use and affect utilization patterns.

GLOSSARY

Letters in parentheses following standard deviations
are keys to sample size.

Enabling variables:

Family Income: Total annual family income; $\bar{x}$ = \$16,860, σ = \$7,810 (A), $\bar{x}$ = \$16,460, σ = \$7,960 (B).

Max (Income − 1.5 Poverty Line, 0): Linear spline with corner at family income minus 1.5 times the matched poverty line (by size and headship).

Max (Income − Pub. Asst., 0): Linear spline with corner at family income minus the public assistance income limit, matched by family size.

Max (Income − Med. Asst., 0): Linear spline with corner at family income minus the medical assistance income limit, matched by family size.

Log Family Income: Log of total annual family income; $\bar{x}$ = 5.00, σ = .57 (A).

Receive Welfare or Child Support: Dummy variable, 1 = family received welfare or child support, 0 = no such income; $\bar{x} = .15$, $\sigma = .36$ (A).

Median Income—Census Tract: Median 1969 family income for the family's census tract; $\bar{x} = \$13,280$, $\sigma = \$3,260$ (B).

Nonwhite: Dummy variable, 1 = nonwhite, 0 = white; $\bar{x} = .12$, $\sigma = .33$ (A), $\bar{x} = .15$, $\sigma = .36$ (B).

Private insurance: Dummy variable, 1 = family coverage through Blue Cross, Blue Shield, or other private plans, 0 = no family coverage through those plans; $\bar{x} = .91$, $\sigma = .29$ (A). $\bar{x} = .89$, $\sigma = .32$ (C).

Medicaid: Dummy variable, 1 = family coverage through Medicaid or public welfare, 0 = no such coverage, $\bar{x} = .06$, $\sigma = .24$ (A), $\bar{x} = .09$, $\sigma = .29$ (C).

HMO: Dummy variable, 1 = family coverage through an HMO, 0 = no such coverage; $\bar{x} = .07$, $\sigma = .25$ (A), $\bar{x} = .06$, $\sigma = .24$ (C).

Insured: Dummy variable, 1 = family coverage through private insurance, Medicaid or welfare, or an HMO, 0 = no family coverage. $\bar{x} = .98$, $\sigma = .15$ (B).

Reas. Cost: Dummy variable, 1 = reasonable fees rated "very important" in choice of provider, 0 = any other rating; $\bar{x} = .71$, $\sigma = .45$ (B).

Reas. Cost x Priv. or No Insurance: Interaction of Reas. Cost and a dummy variable for which 1 = private insurance or no insurance, 0 = Medicaid or HMO coverage.

Conv. Hours: Dummy variable, 1 = convient hours rated "very important" in choice of provider, 0 = any other rating; $\bar{x} = .59$, $\sigma = .49$ (B).

Parent's Time: For each parent present, 84 hours less 40 if parent works full time, or less 20 if parent works part time, is in school, etc. $\bar{x} = 112.13$, $\sigma = 23.84$ (B).

M full-time: Dummy variable, 1 = mother works full-time, 0 = mother does not work full-time; $x = .21$, $\sigma = .41$ (A).

M part-time: Dummy variable, 1 = mother works part-time, 0 = mother does not work part-time; $\bar{x} = .20$, $\sigma = 1.23$ (B).

N children: number of children under 18 in the family; $\bar{x} = 2.84$, $\sigma = 1.14$ (C).

Not married: Dummy variable, 1 = not currently married (only mother present), 0 = both parents present; $\bar{x} = .12$, $\sigma = .33$ (A).

Availability Variables:

Drs./Population: Number of G.P.s and pediatricians per pop. in family's neighborhood, $\bar{x} = .17$, $\sigma = .66$ (B).

Distance to clinic: Driving time in minutes between the family's neighborhood and that of the nearest clinic; $\bar{x} = 11.59$, $\sigma = 9.03$ (B).

Distance to HMO: Driving time in minutes between the family's neighborhood and that of the nearest HMO; $\bar{x} = 11.87$, $\sigma = 8.67$ (C).

Distance to Hospital: Driving time in minutes between the family's neighborhood and that of the nearest hospital; $\bar{x} = 11.65$, $\sigma = 6.12$ (C).

Need Variables:

Ill: Dummy variable, 1 = child has or has had serious or chronic illness; 0 = no such illness, $\bar{x} = .19$, $\sigma = .39$ (B).

Accident: Dummy variable, 1 = child's last illness caused by an accident; 0 = last illness not accident related; $\bar{x} = .04$, $\sigma = .35$ (B).

Hospitalizations: Number of hospitalizations before the 12-month study period; $\bar{x} = .09$, $\sigma = .18$ (B).

Days Ill: Number of days child was ill in previous 12 months; $\bar{x} = 6.34$, $\sigma = 11.30$ (C).

Predisposing Variables:

Age: Age of child; $\bar{x} = 6.93$, $\sigma = 2.93$ (B).

Female: Dummy variable, 1 = female, 0 = male; $\bar{x} = .49$, $\sigma = .50$ (C).

M age: Mother's age; $\bar{x} = 35.79$, $\sigma = 8.12$ (A).

Low Mother's Age: Dummy variable, 1 = mother's age - child's age < 20, 0 = mother's age - child's age $\geq$20; $\bar{x} = .06$, $\sigma = .24$ (C).

Mother's education: Years of school completed; $\bar{x} = 12.65$, $\sigma = 2.57$ (A), $\bar{x} = 12.54$, $\sigma = 2.66$ (B).

M Occ: Ratings of mother's occupation based on Bogue Index; high values = high prestige occupation; $\bar{x} = 49.29$, $\sigma = 7.65$ (A).

F. Occ: Rating of father's occupation; $\bar{x} = 49.20$, $\sigma = 21.49$ (A).

Average Parents' Use: Average number of physicians visits of parents in last 12 months; $\bar{x} = 2.28$, $\sigma = 2.54$ (B).

Routine check: Dummy variable, 1 = at least one family member's last physician visit was for a routine check; $\bar{x} = .89$, $\sigma = .31$ (C).

No regular M.D.: Dummy variable, 1 = child has no regular provider, 0 = child has one or more regular providers; $\bar{x} = .15$, $\sigma = .12$ (C).

Unhappy family = Dummy variable based on a composite of three family and marital happiness variables; 1 = respondent answered negatively on at least one variable; $\bar{x} = .09$, $\sigma = .29$ (C).

Children Share Provider: Dummy variable, 1 = all children under
17 have same provider (including cases of one-child families);
0 = children go to different providers; $\bar{x}$ = .87, σ = .34 (C).

Keys to samples for which means and standard deviations are given:

A: N = 675 (one observation per family)

B: N = 810 (all children, ages 1-11)

C: N = 682 (all children with at least one provider visit in
the previous 12 months)

NOTES

1. See Menchik 1977, for eligibility criteria in New York.
2. Logit analysis is used since the dependent variable only takes on
one of two values: one, if the child saw a physician; zero, otherwise. While this maximum likelihood formulation is desired in
such cases since it constrains the probability to be between zero
and one, there are certain disadvantages including, in general,
a greater restriction on the number of variables included.
3. This variable may represent attitudes or physician-induced
demand.
4. Distance and weighting of availability by neighborhood proximity
was done using proximity information from Roghman and Zastowny
1979, and provider location and specialty information from the
1976 U.S. Physicians' References Listing.
5. Data-collection procedures unfortunately limit our ability to
differentiate between neighborhood health centers and HMO-type
clinics.
6. The doctor/population ratio measures all general practitioners
in an area. This includes those practicing in health centers and
clinics.

REFERENCES

Becker, G. S., and Lewis, H. G. 1973. "On the Interaction Between
the Quantity and Quality of Children." Journal of Political Economy, 81, 2.

Davis, K., and Reynolds, R. 1976. "The Impact of Medicare and
Medicaid on Access to Medical Care." In The Role of Health Insurance in the Health Services Sector. New York: National Bureau
of Economic Research, pp. 391-425.

Davis, K., and Schoen, C. 1978. Health and the War on Poverty. Washington, D.C.: Brookings Institution, pp. 391–425.

Gibson, R. M., and Fisher, C. R. 1978. "National Health Expenditures, Fiscal Year 1977." Social Security Bulletin, July, pp. 3-20.

Haggerty, R. J., Roghmann, K. J., and Pless, I. B. 1975. Child Health and the Community. New York: Wiley.

Menchik, M. D. 1977. Hospital Use under Medicaid in New York City. New York: Rand Institute, R-1995 NYC.

Newhouse, J. P., and Phelps, C. E. 1976. "New Estimates of Price and Income Elasticities of Medical Care Services." In The Role of Health Insurance in the Health Services Sector. New York: National Bureau of Economic Research.

Roghmann, K. J., and Zastowny, T. R. 1979. "Proximity as a Factor in the Selection of Health Care Providers: Emergency Room Visits Compared to Obstetric Admissions and Abortions." Social Science and Medicine, 130, pp. 61-69.

U.S., Bureau of the Census. 1972. Census of Population and Housing: 1970, Census tracts. Final report PHC (1)—176 Rochester, N.Y., SMSA. Washington, D.C.

Wolfe, B. L. 1980. "Children's Utilization of Medical Care." Medical Care, December 1980, pp. 1196-1207.

1976 U.S. Physicians' References Listing. 1976. Clifton, N.J.: Fisher-Stevens.

PART II

Distributive Impacts of Health Policy

4

INCOME REDISTRIBUTION UNDER NATIONAL HEALTH INSURANCE FINANCING ALTERNATIVES

Stephen H. Long
Margaret A. Cooke
Jay P. Crozier

The purpose of this chapter is to examine the potential for income redistribution under various methods of national health insurance financing. While the chapter is cast in terms of "national health insurance," its conclusions are equally applicable to any large scale changes in health-care financing, regardless of whether or not they are introduced under the rubric of national health insurance (NHI). For example, recent proposals to substitute general revenues for current Medicare payroll tax financing are readily analyzed, using the framework introduced here.

The chapter begins by briefly distinguishing between the transfers from healthy to sick present under any health insurance scheme and the income transfers through publicly financed health care that are the subject of this chapter. The second section outlines the current private and public sector mechanisms of health-care finance in the United States and the distribution of their burdens by income class. Next, the alternative sources of NHI finance are examined, with special attention paid to the income redistributions that would follow from greater reliance on each source. Other effects of financing are mentioned in the fourth section, which is followed by a short

An earlier version of this paper was prepared for the Secretary's National Advisory Committee on National Health Insurance, Department of Health, Education, and Welfare, January 1978. The authors gratefully acknowledge extensive computer programming assistance from Robert Bart, Robert Cohen, and Mark Miller and helpful comments from Karen Davis, Irwin Garfinkel, and Janet Johnson. The opinions are the authors' alone and should not be attributed to any of the above organizations or persons.

conclusion. The microsimulation techniques used to estimate the burdens from the various financing sources are described in an Appendix.

TWO FORMS OF REDISTRIBUTION
UNDER HEALTH INSURANCE

The market for health insurance arises because of certain peculiarities in the patterns of family medical expenditures. While some medical expenditures can be considered normal and are, therefore, anticipated beforehand, most very large expenditures are the result of events that cannot be predicted. As a consequence, uninsured families confronted with such expenditures are at risk either financially or medically, in the first sense because such expenditures can only be met with great financial hardships, or in the second, because they might not be met at all, effectively preventing access to the required care. While there is considerable uncertainty about the expenditures for an individual family, there is much less uncertainty about the average for a large group of families. Many families, therefore, find it desirable to confront this more certain average via the payment of insurance premiums than to continue to self-insure.

The uniform premium payment required of all families within the insured group will reflect the average expenses incurred plus the insurer's administrative costs and profit margin (if any). The premium is therefore unrelated, per se, to the income level of each family within the group and accordingly implies no relationship between income level and the probability of illness. The premium payment constitutes the market price of the insurance coverage and, like the prices of other market goods and services, is one deemed fair by both buyer and seller. Of course during any given time period some families will consume medical services whose cost is greater (less) than the cost of the premium and will thus be financially better (worse) off than they would have been in the absence of coverage. Thus, unlike other market goods and services, the purchase and use of insurance coverage implies significant after-the-fact transfers of income; specifically, transfers from the healthy to the sick.

The dominant American device for the purchase of health insurance has been the employer group. While families can, as some do, purchase individual policies outside of such groups, the cost of such insurance is very high relative to the coverage provided because of high insurer administrative costs. Moreover, for high-risk groups, insurance coverage may not be available at all because of adverse selection. Taken together, these facts effectively exclude certain groups from the insurance market—notably, the retired elderly, the unemployed and unemployable (for example, the severely handicapped), and, of course, the poor. In the absence of a nonmarket mechanism, such groups would remain uninsured and thus at risk either financially or medically (Arrow 1963). The passage of Medicaid and Medicare and the continuing efforts at passage of various NHI plans reflect the social desire to use the public sector to provide coverage to groups effectively denied coverage by the private market sector. Because these groups are generally of low income and taxpayers are of relatively higher income, public sector coverage will implicitly entail significant transfers of a second type; namely, transfers among families at various income levels. Accordingly, one of the key issues raised by any NHI plan is the degree to which its specified financing sources, that is, the sources of funds raised to reimburse providers of health care to the plan's eligibles, would affect such transfers.

A financing source is commonly referred to as progressive if its burden, expressed as a percent of family income, rises as family income rises, proportional if its burden remains constant, and regressive if its burden falls. The final burdens of various NHI proposals on families at different income levels can differ dramatically, depending on the mix of financing sources specified by each. It is important to understand from the outset, however, that any statement about the progressivity, proportionality, or regressivity of the burden of any NHI plan is meaningful only when compared with the burden imposed by the current system. Accordingly, this examination of NHI financing issues begins with a close look at the sources used to finance the current system of health care.

FINANCING HEALTH EXPENDITURES: THE CURRENT SYSTEM

In 1978 national health expenditures totaled $192.4 billion or 9.1 percent of GNP, compared with $12.7 billion or 4.5 percent of GNP in 1950 (Gibson 1979). The dramatic rise in this aggregate reflects growth in population and per capita utilization, greater "intensity" (that is, greater use of labor and capital per unit of output), and inflation, for which rates have been higher in the health sector than in the rest of the economy. For the foreseeable future at least, these forces will continue to act in the same direction and, as a consequence, spending on health care will continue to rise in both absolute and relative terms, even in the absence of an NHI plan.

Behind the aggregate expenditures lie important and changing patterns in their composition. Expenditures on health care may be classified either by use, that is by the kinds of medical services purchased, or by source, that is by the financing sources used to

TABLE 4.1. Personal Health Care Expenditures, 1978
(billions of dollars)

	Total	Hospital Care	Physicians' Services	Dentists' Services	Other Professional Services	Drugs	Eyeglasses and Appliances	Nursing Home Care	Other Health Services
TOTAL	167.9	76.0	35.3	13.3	4.3	15.1	3.9	15.8	4.3
Direct patient payments	55.3	7.5	12.0	10.2	2.2	12.7	3.5	7.2	*
Private insurance	45.4	26.7	13.8	2.5	1.0	1.1	*	.1	*
Medicare	24.9	18.3	5.5	*	*	*	.2	.4	.1
Medicaid	18.4	6.9	2.1	.4	.4	1.1	*	7.2	.2
Other public programs	21.8	15.8	1.8	.1	.2	.2	.1	.7	2.9
Philanthropy, industry	2.2	.8	*	*	*	*	*	.1	1.2

*Less than 50 million.
Source: Gibson (1979).

reimburse health-care providers. Both classifications are displayed simultaneously in Table 4.1 for personal health expenditures in 1978, which do not include expenditures for administration, research, and construction. Hospital care (both inpatient and outpatient) accounted for $76 billion and nursing home care for $16 billion, for a total of $92 billion, or 55 percent of the total on institutionally related care. Physicians' services amounted to $35 billion, about one-fifth of the total, while those of dentists and other professionals accounted for another 10 percent of personal health expenditures. Finally, $19 billion, or 11 percent, was spent on drugs, eyeglasses, and appliances. Historically, the most striking trend has been the tremendous growth of institutionally related care; in 1950 it accounted for less than one-third of the total expenditures but by 1978 it accounted for over one-half.

Even more marked changes have occurred in financing sources. Third-party payments, that is reimbursements made either by private insurance companies or government programs, accounted for almost two-thirds of the 1978 total, compared with less than one-fifth in 1950. Private insurance, which contributes mainly to inpatient hospital care and physician services, accounted for a rapidly increasing percentage of the total during the period 1950-65, by the end of which it accounted for about one-fourth the total (a fraction that has remained more or less constant in recent years). Since 1965, most of the rapid increase in third-party payments is attributable to government programs, largely because of the passage and subsequent rapid growth of the Medicare and Medicaid programs. Medicare primarily finances inpatient hospital care and physicians' services. The greatest dollar amounts paid by Medicaid go to nursing homes, hospitals, physicians, and drugs, in that order. Other public programs finance hospital care, both inpatient and outpatient, physicians' services, and other health services. Additionally, the tax codes in 1978 provided another $10 billion in subsidies to individuals via tax exclusions and deductions allowed for employer group and individual insurance premiums and certain out-of-pocket expenses (Steuerle and Hoffman 1979). If this amount is included in the government share, that share rises from 39 percent to 45 percent.

Direct patient payments, which have declined in relative importance since 1950, were $55 billion, almost one-third of the 1978 total. Such payments accounted for major portions of almost all types of care but particularly for physician, dental, and other professional services, drugs, eyeglasses and appliances, and nursing home care.

Age is a major variable in the use of health services. For example, as shown in Table 4.2, though the elderly comprised only 11 percent of the population, they accounted for $49 billion (29 percent) of all personal health expenditures made in 1978. This is in

TABLE 4.2. Personal Health Care Expenditures by Age Group
and Source of Finance, 1978
(billions of dollars)*

	Total	Under 65	65 and Over
TOTAL	168 (100%)	119 (100%)	49 (100%)
Direct payments	55 (33%)	41 (35%)	14 (29%)
Third-party payments	113 (67%)	78 (66%)	35 (71%)
Private insurance	48 (28%)	44 (37%)	3 (7%)
Government	65 (39%)	34 (28%)	32 (64%)

*Percentages are the share of total expenditure on behalf of
each age group that were represented by each financing source.
Private insurance includes amounts spent by philanthropy and
industry.

Source: The percentages above were calculated by Fisher
(1980) for 1977. We have applied them to the 1978 expenditures from
Table 4.1 to produce the dollar estimates above.

contrast with persons under age 19 who, although they comprised
31 percent of the population, generated only 12 percent of total spending. Perhaps even more striking is the age breakdown by source of
payment, public sources paying for 64 percent of the expenses incurred by the aged, compared with less than 30 percent of public
payments for the remainder of the population. This difference is
mostly attributable to the Medicare program, which is the largest
single publicly financed health-care program, and which, with some
exceptions, largely benefits the elderly population.

Just as current financing sources vary in importance across
different kinds of health care and across different age-groups, so
too do their burdens vary across families at different income levels.

Direct Patient Payments

Survey data on direct patient payments by family income and
by type of service in 1975 are shown in Table 4.3. Out-of-pocket
payments to hospitals actually fell in absolute terms as income levels
rose, due to better insurance coverage for higher-income families.
Payments to physicians, to dentists, and for optical needs rose as
income rose, reflecting the desirability of these services as financial

TABLE 4.3. Direct Patient Payments per Person, 1975

Family Income	Hospital	Physician	Dental	Prescription Drugs	Optical	Other Health	Total	Per Capita Total as a Percent of Family Income*
All Persons	$30	$63	$41	$31	$15	$6	$186	1.2%
Less than $3,000	60	59	18	31	12	5	185	9.2
$3,000–4,999	47	66	21	45	12	8	199	5.0
$5,000–6,999	36	59	29	33	12	7	176	2.9
$7,000–9,999	33	68	30	35	12	5	183	2.2
$10,000–14,999	30	61	40	28	13	4	176	1.4
$15,000–24,999	21	58	51	27	16	6	179	0.9
$25,000 and up	20	78	75	34	23	5	235	0.8

*Calculated using the midpoint of each interval and $2,000 and $30,000 for the end classes.
Source: USDHEW, National Center for Health Statistics (1978).

constraints were relaxed. Out-of-pocket costs are incurred by individuals who either possess no insurance coverage for a particular service or whose policies contain deductible, coinsurance, or co-payment provisions. The final column of Table 4.3 shows total direct payments as a percentage of income and clearly indicates the regressivity of this financing source. (Recall from Table 4.2 that one-third of all current health expenditures are financed by direct patient payments.)

Private Insurance

Since 1950 the number of persons enrolled in private health insurance plans has more than doubled. For 1977 it is estimated that 168 million persons, or over 75 percent of the population, had some coverage for hospital care and a majority had some protection against the cost of physicians' services, surgical care, and prescribed drugs (Carroll and Arnett 1979).

Most of the growth of private insurance has been in employee group plans, where both the number of workers covered and the extent of coverage have grown rapidly. The number of wage and salary workers (excluding dependents) with hospital coverage grew from 24 million in 1950 to 58 million in 1975. Even more striking are the expansions in types of coverage over this same period. The growth

TABLE 4.4. Extent of Employer Contributions toward Family Health Insurance Policies Carried through a Work Group or Union (percent)

Extent of Contribution	1953	1963	1970	1977
Employer pays all	10	27	39	66
Employer pays part	49	52	53	32
Employer pays none	41	21	8	2

Sources: Figures for 1953, 1963, and 1970 are from Andersen (1975) and are based on surveys of the civilian, noninstitutionalized population. The 1977 data, from Battelle Human Affairs Research Centers (1980), are based on a survey of firms, weighted by employment, and are not strictly comparable to the earlier data.

TABLE 4.5. Group Health Insurance Coverage of Full-Time Wage and Salary Workers by Industry, 1976

Industry	Full-Time Workers (millions)	Percent Covered by Group Health Insurance*
TOTAL	81.3	75
Agriculture, forestry, and fishing	3.6	33
Mining	.7	88
Construction	5.4	63
Manufacturing	20.6	87
Transportation, communications, and utilities	5.5	85
Wholesale trade	3.7	80
Retail trade	11.3	62
Finance, insurance, and real estate	4.6	82
Services	21.0	73
Government	5.0	87

*Includes both employer-group and union health insurance plans.

Source: Authors' tabulations of 1976 Survey of Income and Education (U.S. Department of Commerce, 1978).

in surgical coverage was from 18 to 57 million workers, while the comparable figures for other medical coverage indicated a rise from 8 to 56 million workers covered. Yet by 1975, only 30 million workers were covered for major medical expenses, leaving considerable room for further expansion (Yohalem 1977).

Employers have contributed an increasing share of the expanding total cost of group health insurance premiums, as shown in Table 4.4. For example, while in 1953 only 10 percent of employer-employee group policies were fully paid by the employer, the comparable figure in 1977 was 66 percent. However, the general expansion in employer group coverage and in employer contributions for coverage has not been even across industries (Table 4.5). Group health insurance coverage is especially common in highly unionized industries, such as mining and manufacturing, and for government employees (nearly nine of every ten workers have some form of coverage). In contrast, industries characterized by the presence of many small firms and seasonal or part-time employment are much less

TABLE 4.6. Group Health Insurance Coverage of
Full-Time Wage and Salary Workers
by Family Income, 1976

Family Income Quintile (in ascending order)*	Percent Covered
All Families	75
1	30
2	56
3	75
4	83
5	85

*In this and all subsequent tables reporting amounts by family income quintiles, the lowest 20% of the families ranked by total family income from all sources is assigned to quintile 1, and each successive 20% of the families is assigned to the next quintile, culminating in the 20% of all families with the highest income grouped in quintile 5.

Source: Authors' tabulations of 1976 Survey of Income and Education (U.S. Department of Commerce, 1978).

likely to offer group health insurance plans. Hence, the odds that a full-time worker is insured range from just over three in five for construction and retail trade down to one in three for agriculture, forestry, and fisheries.

Group health insurance is currently distributed disproportionately toward workers from families at or above the median family income. Table 4.6 shows that, while 75 percent of full-time workers had some form of group coverage for medical expenditures, only 30 percent of the full-time workers from families in the lowest 20 percent of the income distribution were covered.

It is generally agreed by economists that, as with payroll taxes, the employer portion of the insurance premium is ultimately borne by the employee in lower wages (Mitchell and Phelps 1976). Thus, the burdens of premium financing fall upon the covered families, whether they pay the premium directly or receive some or all of it as an employee benefit. The data in Table 4.5 suggest that the rate of employee group health insurance coverage rises rapidly, moving from low-income to middle-income families, and then rises slowly at higher-income levels. It seems likely that premiums vary directly with income, as well. While ideal data are unavailable, it appears that the existing pattern of premium financing may be progressive in early income ranges but is clearly regressive from the middle through higher income ranges where, in spite of any rising dollar magnitude of premiums with income, the proportion of income consumed by health insurance premiums falls. Thus, current private insurance, which finances about one-quarter of U.S. healthcare expenditures, tends to be a regressive financing mechanism over most of the income range.

Government Expenditures on Health

Table 4.7 shows the financing sources for federal, state, and local health programs and tax expenditures and their costs in 1978. Medicare, which provides health insurance for the elderly and disabled, and Medicaid, the joint federal-state program that reimburses health care provided to the eligible poor, account for nearly 60 percent of all public expenditures on health care. Other federal health service delivery programs include those offered by the Department of Defense, the Veteran's Administration, the Indian Health Service, and the Public Health Service, as well as many special programs such as maternal/child care, family planning, and disease prevention/ control. In addition, the federal government offers three subsidies for health-care expenditures through the personal income tax. Since all three can reduce income tax liabilities, they may be thought of as equivalent to direct expenditures; hence they are commonly termed tax expenditures. They are: (1) the deduction for one-half of individually paid insurance premiums, up to a maximum of $150, (2) the exclusion from taxable income of the employer's share of employer-group private insurance premiums, and (3) the deduction of expenditures for prescription drugs exceeding one percent of adjusted gross income and other out-of-pocket medical expenses exceeding three percent of adjusted gross income. Provisions (1) and (2) encourage the purchase of private health insurance. The last provision serves as a catastrophic insurance plan of sorts (Mitchell and Vogel 1975), the "deductibles" of which are proportional to adjusted gross income according to the above percentages and the "coinsurance rates" of which (equal to one minus the marginal income tax rate) decline with income. These tax expenditures are not trivial. In 1978 their magnitude was nearly equal to that of the entire federal portion of the Medicaid program. Moreover, while most public spending on health is targeted to the aged or low-income population, recent studies have shown that the bulk of tax expenditures benefit middle- and high-income families. Such families itemize their deductions more frequently, purchase greater health insurance, and face higher marginal income tax rates than other families (Steuerle and Hoffman 1979).

With the exception of a small premium-financed portion of Medicare and the state portions of Medicaid, all of the above government expenditures are financed from federal tax sources. State portions of the Medicaid program vary according to state per capita income levels, ranging from 22 percent to a current maximum of 50 percent. Other state and local health programs include the Worker's Compensation Program, financed via employer premiums, and general hospital/medical care, child health services, and public health activities, all financed via the general revenues of these governments.

Estimates of the ultimate financial burden on families in various income classes of the combined federal, state, and local government health expenditures are shown in Table 4.8. The average

TABLE 4.7. Government Health Expenditures, 1978

Program	Financing Sources	Billions of Dollars
TOTAL		74.9
Federal		
Medicare	Payroll taxes, federal general revenues, premiums, interest on trust fund	24.9
Medicaid	Federal general revenues	10.2
Tax expenditures	Foregone federal general revenues	9.9
Other federal programs	Federal general revenues	11.4
State and Local:		
Medicaid	State general revenues	8.1
Other state and local programs	Employer premiums, state and local general revenues	10.4

Sources: All figures are from Gibson (1978) with the exception of tax expenditures, which are from Steuerle and Hoffman (1979).

TABLE 4.8. Burden of All Government Health Expenditures by Family Income Quintiles, 1978*

Family Income Quintile (in ascending order)	Average Burden per Family	Burden as a Percent of Family Income
All Families	$960	5.24
1	165	4.61
2	427	4.68
3	746	4.89
4	1,158	5.06
5	2,301	5.64

*Estimates are based upon the 1978 government health expenditures in Table 4.6. The family income distribution for computing quintiles and the number of families are based upon the 1976 Survey of Income and Education. However, in calculating the burden as a percent of family income, the SIE incomes were projected to 1978 by the actual rate of growth of U.S. personal income over the period.
Source: Authors' calculations. See Appendix.

burden over all families in 1978 was $960, or about 5.24 percent of family income. Because of the important role of federal general revenues, the publicly financed portion of the current health-care system imposes progressive financing burdens (note the rising percents by quintile in Table 4.8). This progressivity is in marked contrast to the regressive burdens imposed by privately financed health insurance premiums and direct patient payments.

ALTERNATIVE NHI FINANCING SOURCES

The numerous proposals to modify the current system of financing health care in the United States have generally gone under the heading, national health insurance. Several sources that summarize the provisions of these proposals and analyze their effects along various dimensions are available, so the NHI proposals will not be reviewed here. For example, Waldman (1976) summarizes the features of 18 bills pending before the 94th Congress. Davis (1975) analyzes some of the major alternatives in considerably more detail. Long and Palmer (1981) evaluate four general approaches to reforming health-care finance from an income-testing perspective. Finally, the features of a competition-oriented plan are introduced by Enthoven (1980).

Abstracting from the detailed provisions of any particular NHI plan, a set of generic financing sources can be identified. These alternative sources are either those currently not being tapped at all or those that would acquire greater relative importance in the total financing package with the passage of an NHI plan. This section discusses the following generic sources of NHI financing: (1) federal general revenues, including the personal income tax, the corporation income tax, and various excises and other receipts; (2) payroll taxes; (3) earmarked excise taxes on "unhealthy" goods or activities; (4) repeal of current tax expenditures; (5) mandated premiums; (6) state and local taxes; and (7) direct patient payments.

To illustrate the degree of redistribution inherent in several generic alternatives, we have estimated their final burdens on families, using a modified version of the Transfer Income Model simulation software with the 1976 Survey of Income and Education. (The details of our procedures are described in the Appendix.) Since the current revenues from these sources vary greatly in their magnitudes, the estimates presented here have been standardized to yield $10 billion in revenue from each financing source. This facilitates comparisons of burdens per family and percentages of income taxed, in order to evaluate the relative degrees of redistribution implied by the alternatives. All estimates are displayed for quintiles of the distribution of total family income. The calculations provided here can be used, singly or in combination, to estimate the income redistributions inherent in a wide variety of NHI financing packages that vary in magnitude and composition. Our methodology owes a substantial intellectual debt to that developed by Mitchell and Schwartz (1976) to examine the distributive implications of four prototypical NHI plans being considered in the mid-1970s. Their estimates, however, are limited to burdens on a hypothetical family of four persons with a single full-time worker. Among the potential advantages of our methodology are: (1) household survey data allow rich detail on the relative importance of different income sources at various points across the income distribution; (2) we are able to account for part-time and part-year work, as well as multi-worker families, in calculating premium and payroll tax burdens; and (3) our data provide detail on varying family size and composition over the income distribution that is especially important in calculating personal income tax burdens.

The burdens of various alternatives on families will depend on: (1) the composition of family income at different income levels, and (2) the kinds of income on which the ultimate burdens fall, that is, the actual incidence of each financing source. Table 4.9 shows the kinds of income received by families at different income levels.

TABLE 4.9. Sources of Family Income, 1975

Family Income Quintile (in ascending order)	Wages and Salaries (%)	Self-Employment Income (%)	Property Income* (%)	Transfer Income (%)	Other Income (%)
All Families	74.8	5.2	8.5	9.5	2.4
1	30.2	0	6.6	58.7	4.9
2	57.8	3.2	8.8	26.1	4.8
3	75.8	3.6	7.3	10.6	3.3
4	82.5	3.8	6.1	5.8	2.2
5	77.8	7.5	10.4	3.2	1.3

*Property Income includes 35% of total farm and 20% of total nonfarm self-employment income. Also included is 33% of private and government pension income (remaining pension income is shown in the "Other Income" column). These percentages reflect U.S. Treasury (1975) estimates regarding the proportions of these incomes representing returns to capital.

Source: Authors' tabulations of 1976 Survey of Income and Education.

Transfer income (for example, social security payments, AFDC, SSI), which is nontaxable, is a very large portion of total income at very low income levels but declines to trivial proportions at middle or higher income levels. Most of this decline is traceable to wage income, which constitutes the bulk of family income at middle-income levels, but begins to decline in relative importance thereafter. Property income is concentrated among the lower-income aged and those at very high income levels, and self-employment income gradually increases with increasing family income. Because of these differences, even a financing source that imposes a proportional burden on a particular kind of income will not result in a proportional burden across all income classes.

Federal Taxes

Any NHI proposal will require a significant amount of federal tax revenue to finance benefits for, at minimum, the low-income and aged populations. Before discussing each tax source, it is helpful

TABLE 4.10. Shares of Major Tax Sources in Total Federal
Revenues, 1950-1980

Tax Source(s)	1950 (%)	1960 (%)	1970 (%)	1980 (%)	1980 Dollar Amount (billions)
TOTAL	100.0	100.0	100.0	100.0	608
Personal tax and nontax items	39	45	47	46	280
Corporate profits tax accruals	31	23	18	15	77
Indirect business tax and nontax accruals	18	14	10	7	53
Contributions for social insurance	12	18	25	32	198

Source: U.S. Office of Management and Budget (1981).

to review the trends in federal tax receipts over the past 30 years.
Table 4.10 shows the relative importance of major federal revenue
sources at 10-year intervals over this period. The corporate income
tax and excise taxes have declined in relative importance over the
period, while personal taxes (primarily the personal income tax),
have remained relatively stable. The dramatic change has been the
sharp increases in payroll tax-financed contributions to social insurance programs. Thus, a reading of the data indicates that the federal
government is increasingly relying on the personal income tax and
the payroll tax as its principal revenue-raising instruments.

Federal General Revenues

The general revenues of the federal government, that is, those
that are not earmarked for particular purposes, consist of receipts
from the corporate and personal income taxes, some excise taxes,
estate and gift taxes, customs duties, and other miscellaneous taxes.
If general revenues were used to finance NHI, it is difficult to know
precisely how the present tax base and rate structure would be
altered to raise the required additional revenue. In the absence of
this knowledge, the effects produced by the current rate structures,
income definitions, and mix of taxes are calculated.

The burden of the personal income tax is generally assumed to fall on those individuals upon whom the tax is levied. Table 4.11 shows in Columns 1 and 4, for each $10 billion of revenue, the average income taxes and the percent of income paid by families in various income quintiles in 1975. As indicated by the percentages of family income, this tax clearly imposes a progressive burden, not only because of its progressive rate structure but, just as importantly, because of its imposition of liabilities against all forms of income excepting transfer payments. Figure 4.1 displays the simulated personal income tax burdens geometrically, plotting the percent of income taxed against the level of family income. The rising percentage burdens, as family income rises, similarly illustrate the progressive nature of this revenue source.

There is less agreement among economists regarding the ultimate burden of the corporation income tax. Some have argued that the burden is shifted forward to consumers in the form of higher prices; others, that the burden is shifted backward to labor in the form of lower wages. But the view that seems to be most common is that the burden of the corporate tax ultimately falls on owners of all property, corporate and noncorporate, in the form of a new, but lower, equilibrium rate of return. On this assumption, the calculated burden of a $10 billion tax (shown in Columns 2 and 5 of Table 4.11) is slightly regressive in low-income ranges but progressive thereafter; this is a reflection of the "u-shaped" distribution of property income shown in Table 4.9.

Finally, by combining the burdens of the personal income tax, the corporation income tax, and the other general revenue sources in proportion to their recent shares, Columns 3 and 6 of Table 4.11 display the burden of $10 billion of general revenue financing. This burden is distinctively progressive. For example, families in the highest quintile pay over 40 times as much as those in the lowest quintile, bearing a burden 3.5 times the percent of total income paid by the lowest income group.

Many NHI plans would rely upon additional federal general revenue financing or upon earmarked contributions from a particular tax, most commonly the personal income tax (Waldman 1976). Considering the regressivity of current private insurance premiums and direct patient payments, it is clear that the choice of greater general revenue financing for NHI would be a choice for income redistribution as well as for an alternative health-care financing source. A move toward greater reliance on general revenue financing should also improve horizontal equity. That is, viewed in terms of the burdens imposed on families at the same income level, the income tax is regarded as fairer than others because of its provisions for personal exemptions and allowable deductions for certain expenses judged to be

TABLE 4.11. Burden of Raising $10 Billion via Federal General Revenues by Family Income Quintile*

Family Income Quintile (in ascending order)	1 Average Personal Income Tax per Family	2 Average Corporation Income Tax per Family	3 Average General Revenues per Family	4 Personal Income Tax as Percent of Income	5 Corporation Income Tax as Percent of Income	6 General Revenues as Percent of Income
All Families	$128	$128	$128	.95	.95	.95
1	1	20	9	.05	.74	.35
2	23	66	39	.34	.99	.58
3	75	91	83	.67	.82	.74
4	151	114	144	.90	.68	.86
5	391	349	364	1.30	1.16	1.21

*Federal general revenues have been simulated using the following incidence assumptions: personal income taxes are borne by payers, corporation income taxes are borne in proportion to all forms of property income, and excise and other taxes fall in proportion to disposable income.

Source: Authors' calculations. See Appendix.

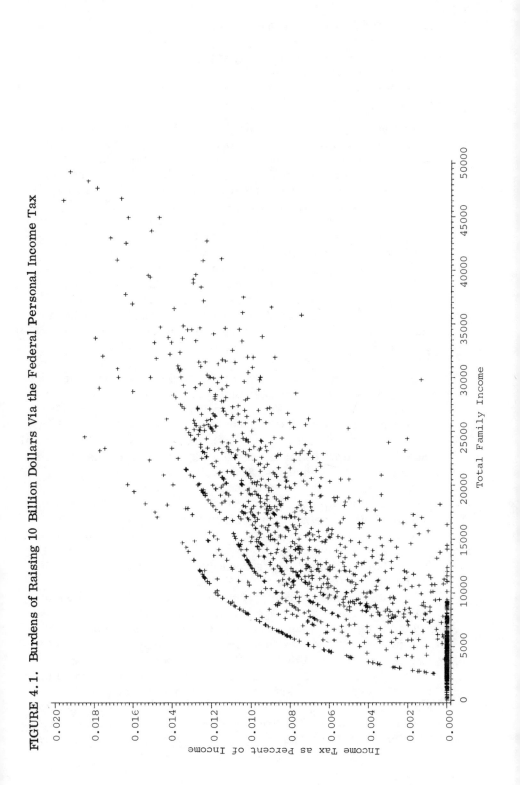

FIGURE 4.1. Burdens of Raising 10 Billion Dollars Via the Federal Personal Income Tax

especially burdensome (including at present, large medical expenses and private insurance premium payments).

Payroll Taxes

The current federal OASDI/HI payroll tax, which finances Medicare Part A (hospital insurance) as well as the Social Security and Disability Insurance programs, is a proportional tax on wages up to the taxable wage ceiling. At present all employed persons are liable except federal (and some state and local) civilian employees, self-employed persons earning less than $400 a year, and domestic and farm workers earning less than a specified amount from a single employer. In the past, it has been relatively easy to raise the level of payroll taxes since they have not constituted the major tax liability confronting most families. Moreover, because they are earmarked taxes (as they would be under various NHI plans), the relationship between taxes paid and tangible benefits surrounds them with the politically appealing aura of insurance premiums, in keeping with the tradition of private employer-group insurance plans. On the other hand, certain demographic trends, notably the aging of the population and declining birth rates, have required constant upward adjustments in both the tax rate and ceiling. For example, the combined employer-employee tax rate and taxable wage ceiling have increased, respectively, from 3 percent and $3,000 in 1950, to 7.25 percent and $4,800 in 1965, and to 13.3 percent and $29,700 in 1981. Currently, the OASDI/HI tax raises 70 percent as much revenue as the personal income tax and is the largest tax liability confronting millions of low- and middle-income families. The political pros and cons of additional payroll tax financing are reflected in many recent NHI proposals, which would rely partly, but not wholly, on such taxes, usually in combination with general revenues (Waldman 1976). A recent example of a payroll tax proposed by another name, presumably to avoid the political liabilities of suggesting a payroll tax increase, is the "earnings-related premium" of the Kennedy NHI proposal introduced in the late 1970s.

It is generally agreed that most, if not all, of the burden of payroll taxation falls on wage earners, irrespective of the way in which the tax rate is nominally divided between the employer and the employee. On this assumption, the burden of raising $10 billion in revenues via the 1975 OASDI/HI tax has been calculated in Table 4.12 and is displayed in Figure 4.2. It is clear from this table that the tax is highly progressive in the lower-income ranges. For example, the percentage of family income taxed nearly doubles, from .44 to .84, when moving from the first to the second quintile. This is primarily because transfer payments, which are a major source

TABLE 4.12. Burden of Raising $10 Billion via Payroll Taxes
by Family Income Quintile*

Family Income Quintile (in ascending order)	Average Payroll Tax per Family	Payroll Tax as a Percent of Income
All Families	$128	.95
1	12	.44
2	56	.84
3	122	1.09
4	188	1.12
5	261	.87

*Based on the 1975 OASDI/HI and Railroad Retirement Payroll
Taxes and the 1975 income distribution. Calculations assume that
full burdens of employer and employee portions fall on employees.
Source: Authors' calculations. See Appendix.

of income for low-income families, escape payroll as well as income
taxation. The burdens reach a maximum in the third and fourth quintiles but become regressive thereafter, not only because of the taxable wage ceiling, but because of the increasing importance of self-
employment income, which is taxed at a lower rate, and property
income, which escapes the tax altogether.

The payroll tax performs poorly in terms of horizontal equity
because of the absence of any provisions for personal exemptions
and deductions and because of its unequal treatment of different kinds
of income. Additionally, because the tax filing unit is the individual
worker rather than the family, the tax can discriminate against multi-
earner families. In general, this will be the case if two or more
workers within a family earn wages that individually are less than
the taxable wage ceiling but collectively are greater. These characteristics account for the wide scattering of points seen in Figure 4.2.
Points below the cluster marked AB, extending to the ceiling wage
of $14,100, are the burdens of families receiving at least some trans-
fer, property, or self-employment income. (The few points above
this cluster represent families with taxable wages and with losses
in, for example, rental or self-employment income categories such
that the effective payroll tax rate on net family income exceeds the
statutory rate.) The observations above and beyond the cluster of
points labeled BC, forming a hyperbola from the ceiling wage downward and to the right, represent the burdens on multi-earner families

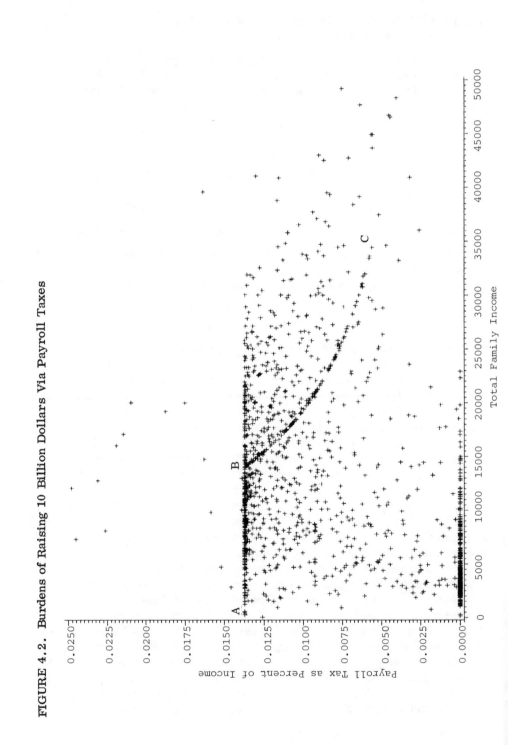

FIGURE 4.2. Burdens of Raising 10 Billion Dollars Via Payroll Taxes

whose wage levels subject them to horizontal inequity from the payroll tax.

While we have been using the current OASDI/HI tax as the prototypical example of payroll taxes, alternative forms are possible. Many recent NHI proposals have specified different rates and ceilings and, in one instance, a different filing unit (the household rather than the wage earner). These changes could alter the burdens of payroll taxation but only within inherent limits. If the aim is to reduce the regressivity of the tax, the ceiling could be eliminated and the tax rate on self-employment income could be made equal to that faced by the rest of the employed population. These measures could temper, but never eliminate, the regressivity generated at higher-income levels because, by its very nature, a payroll tax fails to impose liabilities against property incomes, and as such, could never completely substitute for general revenue financing. Low-income workers could be relieved of tax burdens by introducing a progressive tax-rate structure, or a taxable wage "floor," below which wages would be exempt. Such measures, however, would seriously erode the tax base and require increasing the burdens imposed on other workers and thus, in turn, aggravate the regressivity generated in the higher-income ranges. An alternative solution would be to offer income tax credits to offset payroll tax payments. This, of course, would amount to a thinly disguised form of general revenue financing.

Special Excise Taxes

There are a number of consumable goods and activities that lead to poorer health or at least increase the probability of poorer health. Examples include cigarette smoking, chronic consumption of alcohol, carrying of firearms, exposure to occupational safety and health hazards, and reckless driving. In practice it would be difficult to design taxes that would reduce the level of health-impairing activities, and accordingly, any special excise taxes used as NHI financing sources would probably take the form of levies on certain consumption goods. An argument can be made for such taxation on both efficiency and equity grounds. To the extent that the demands for the taxed goods are elastic, consumption will decrease, leading to improvements in health that might not have been achievable even by consumption of medical resources at very high levels. Since NHI implies some form of collective financing, the excise taxes could be thought of as surtaxes on individuals who, because of their continued consumption of the taxed goods, are likely to receive a greater than average share of NHI benefits.

Rather than consider the whole range of possible special excise taxes, the focus here will be on levies against cigarettes, which are

TABLE 4.13. Burden of Raising $10 Billion via an Excise Tax on Cigarettes by Family Income Quintile

Family Income Quintile (in ascending order)	Average Excise Tax per Family	Excise Tax as a Percent of Income
All Families	$128	.95
1	72	2.72
2	104	1.56
3	136	1.21
4	146	.87
5	182	.61

Source: Authors' calculations. See Appendix.

currently subject to both federal and state excise taxation. The federal excise tax on cigarettes is eight cents per pack, unchanged since 1951. Most states have also imposed substantial excise taxes on cigarettes. The combined federal and state tax revenues from cigarettes were nearly $6 billion in 1976. To suggest some crude orders of magnitude, an increase in the federal tax by twelve cents per pack might raise over $3 billion; an increase by twenty cents, which implies roughly a 30 percent increase in total price, would raise about $5 billion. Proposals to use such taxes to finance health-care expenditures have gained support as evidence linking smoking to poor health has accumulated and become increasingly well publicized, particularly since the release of the 1964 Surgeon General's Report on Cigarette Smoking.

Table 4.13 and Figure 4.3 illustrate the burdens on families at various income levels of raising $10 billion from an excise tax on cigarettes. The tax simulated here is a simple ad valorem tax which, since cigarette prices per unit do not vary greatly, approximates a uniform unit tax on cigarettes. Available data do not allow us to simulate more complex taxes, such as a levy on tar and nicotine content (Harris 1980). (While $10 billion is, perhaps, an unrealistic yield from a cigarette tax alone, it is more reasonable as a yield from cigarettes and alcohol combined. Moreover, the $10 billion figure facilitates comparisons across the various financing sources.) While absolute levels of taxation rise moderately from the first to the fifth quintile in Table 4.13, the positive income elasticity of demand is not nearly sufficient to make this special consumption tax even proportional to income (note the declining proportion of income

FIGURE 4.3. Burdens of Raising 10 Billion Dollars Via an Excise Tax on Cigarettes

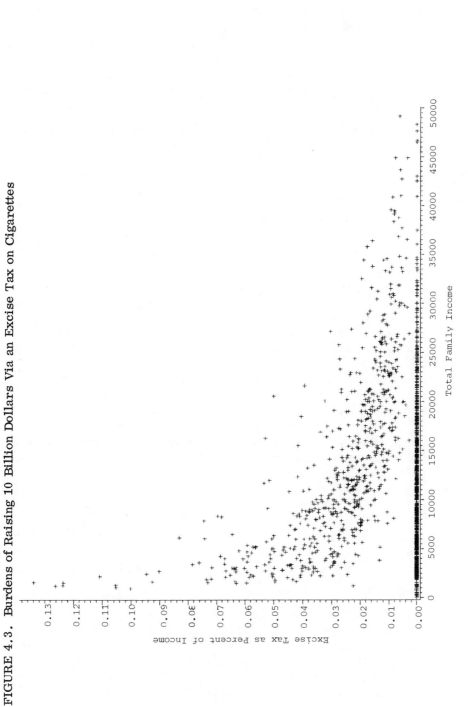

taxed as income rises in Figure 4.3). Yet the regressivity of special excise taxes is not as compelling an argument against them as it is when made against other regressive financing sources. First, there are the efficiency and equity rationales cited above. Second, there is an element of voluntarism that is absent from other taxes. The payment of excise taxes on cigarettes, as an example of an unhealthy commodity, would be confined to individuals who, in the face of well-publicized health risks, have made the conscious choice to continue smoking.

Current Tax Expenditures

Repeal of the current medical tax expenditures would, under most circumstances, increase personal income tax receipts and can, therefore, be viewed as an NHI financing source. For example, Enthoven's (1980) plan depends critically upon this approach, both to correct the present tax-induced relative price advantage of health benefits at the margin and as a major source of financing to offset tax losses from his proposed tax credits and vouchers. We do not present estimates of the redistributive effects of this financing source here, due to a lack of suitable microdata on the value of employer premium payments. However, the direct impact on current coverage would be decidedly progressive, owing to the following factors: (1) the rising coverage rates by income (see Table 4.6), (2) rising marginal tax rates by income (Figure 4.1 is suggestive of this point), and (3) the likelihood that employer shares of the total premium rise with worker income (though we have no direct evidence on this point).

The total amount of extra revenue raised by the repeal of tax expenditures will depend on the structure of a particular NHI plan. Current law treats the employer's share of group private insurance premiums as it does any other nontaxable "fringe" benefit. Elimination of this exclusion would raise varying amounts of revenue, depending on the incremental increase in coverage provided to the employed population and the source used to finance such coverage. A plan specifying mandated premiums would actually increase revenues more than estimates of the current subsidy suggest, to the extent that greater coverage would increase the total employer premium shares to be taxed (Mitchell and Phelps 1976). On the other hand, whether payroll tax financing would generate the same result depends on the treatment of the required employer payments. At present, such payments made under the OASDI/HI payroll tax are, in effect, excluded from the taxable income base. If this treatment continued in the context of NHI payroll tax financing, personal income tax revenues might actually decline to the extent that the required employer tax contributions exceeded the current total of employer premium shares.

Any NHI plan that reduces direct patient payments below the current level would generate additional income tax revenues because of the accompanying reduction in itemized medical expense deductions. Elimination of such deductions would, of course, magnify this effect, but a good argument can be made for their retention if only because even the most comprehensive NHI plans would either not, or only partially, include certain kinds of services in their benefit packages. For these services, notably dentistry, out-of-hospital drugs, and long-term care, allowable deductions could continue to serve as a catastrophic insurance plan of sorts.

Other Financing Sources

While the sheer magnitude of current health-care expenditures immediately recommends federal tax financing of NHI, other possibilities are feasible and have been specified by many recent proposals. These possibilities are often referred to as "off-budget" financing sources, because their use under an NHI plan would not result in increases in the size of the federal budget.

Mandated Premiums

Some recent proposals would extend insurance coverage by compelling the purchase of private insurance by employer groups that currently are not covered at all or whose coverage does not meet the minimum standard specified by the particular proposal. In some cases, the minimum standard would require a "catastrophic only" benefit package; that is, a benefit package that would include a very large annual deductible, below which the insured would have to pay full cost. An arrangement by which the federal government compels certain private purchases would certainly be nothing new and is analogous, as an example, to current federal legislation that, in effect, requires the purchase of a minimum amount of automotive safety and pollution control equipment. As with payroll taxes, the political appeal of mandated premiums lies in the fact that they would be tied to employment and would be in keeping with the tradition of employer-group private insurance plans.

Because of the element of compulsion involved, the premium payments can properly be viewed and analyzed as taxes. Again, as with payroll taxes, the burdens of mandated premiums are generally assumed to fall on wage earners irrespective of the way in which the premium cost is nominally divided between the employer and the employee (Mitchell and Phelps 1976). Because the minimum standard of coverage varies enormously from one NHI proposal to the next, we have used as our prototypical example a universal plan under

TABLE 4.14. Burden of Raising $10 Billion via a Mandated
Employer-Employee Insurance Premium
by Family Income Quintile

Family Income Quintile (in ascending order)	Average Premium Payments per Family	Premium Payment as a Percent of Income
All Families	$128	.95
1	24	.90
2	90	1.34
3	137	1.22
4	170	1.01
5	220	.73

*Calculations assume premium burdens fall entirely on em-
ployees. In 1975, a premium of $122 per worker would have been
required to raise $10 billion in revenues.
    Source: Authors' calculations. See Appendix.

which all employed workers would be required to pay an annual
premium. (Since most plans would exempt students and those who
work less than 25 hours per week, our simulations do not charge
premiums to wage and salary workers earning less than $2,000 per
year, as a proxy for these exempt groups.) In 1975, such a plan
would have required a premium payment of about $122 per worker
for each $10 billion in revenue raised. The average burdens imposed
by our example on families at different income levels, displayed in
Table 4.14, range from $24 to $220 as we move from the lowest to
the highest quintile of the income distribution. The marked regressivity of this financing source is shown vividly in Figure 4.4, where
the clusters of observations represent single, dual, and higher orders
of multi-earner families. Mandated premiums would expand on the
current system of voluntary employer-group insurance plans, rein-
forcing and increasing the regressive burdens discussed above by
imposing premiums on employers of lower-income workers not
presently covered or with below-standard coverage. The extreme
burdens on low-income workers suggest some of the same relief
mechanisms discussed previously in connection with payroll taxation.
Income tax deductions or refundable tax credits could be granted
such workers. Again, however, these subsidies would amount to
thinly disguised forms of general revenue financing.

FIGURE 4.4. Burdens of Raising 10 Billion Dollars Via a Mandated Employer-Employee Insurance Premium

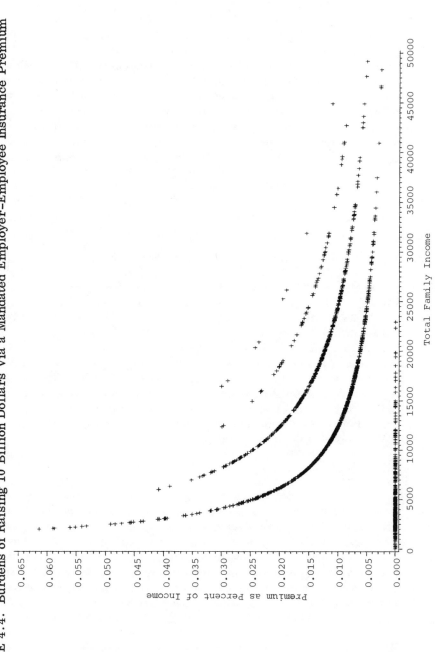

State and Local Taxes

As shown in Table 4.7, state and local expenditures represent a significant proportion of current government health expenditures. Moreover, budget proposals being made in the early 1980s suggest some pressure for health-care financing reform that would shift fiscal and administrative responsibilities for many health programs from the federal to the state and local levels. Currently, state contributions to the Medicaid program account for the largest single portion of such expenditures, followed by state and locally run hospitals, public health activities, Workers' Compensation programs, and medical public assistance, in that order. The tax packages used to finance these programs impose a net burden that is roughly proportional to income (Pechman and Okner 1974), although some taxes taken alone are quite regressive. Detailed assessment of their burdens is complex because, at the state level alone, there are fifty different tax packages, each in turn an amalgam of sales, excise, property, and income taxes. The burden on an individual family will, therefore, depend on its place of residence as well as on its income level. Due to these complexities, we have not attempted to simulate the burdens of a typical state and local tax package here. In any event, most NHI proposals would either retain the role played by such taxes by leaving unaltered the current Medicaid program or reduce that role by federalizing the program. The incremental reduction (if any) in state and local financing could be more than offset, however, if the NHI plan in question encouraged (or required) states to contribute to some uncovered benefit area such as long-term care. Under such an arrangement the designers of NHI would have little control over the precise nature of the burdens imposed by the additional state and local expenditures.

Direct Patient Payments

As made under the current system, direct patient payments impose highly regressive burdens, although this need not be the case under an NHI plan, particularly if such payments were income tested, as explained below. While such payments could be used as devices for moving NHI costs off the federal budget, it is clear by now that there are other potential financing sources that could serve the same purpose. The real case for or against direct patient payments lies in their effects on access and in their perceived ability to control expenditures, issues discussed in the next section.

OTHER NHI FINANCING ISSUES

The array of potential revenue-raising instruments would allow designers of an NHI plan to custom tailor the financing burden to practically any agreed-upon standard of equity. Unfortunately, a consensus as to what constitutes equity in health-care financing is as illusive as a consensus on equity in general. Further complicating the design of an NHI plan is the fact that the financing package will, often in conflicting ways, have implications for other issues of importance in the debate.

Control of Costs

In the context of rapidly rising health-care costs, no NHI plan will be implemented unless it contains convincing mechanisms for cost control. By cost control, we mean the methods used to allocate scarce resources in a way that would ideally eliminate expenditures for "unnecessary" care, as well as those methods used to control per unit input costs.

There is general agreement that, under the current system of public and private insurance, considerable health resources are being devoted to the provision of care that does not result in improvements in health justifying their social costs. Performing unnecessary surgical procedures is one of the more well-publicized examples. Beyond this consensus, however, lie fundamentally opposed views on the best way to discipline consumption decisions, reflecting their proponents' opinions about the relevance of traditional market theory to the health-care sector.

One view holds that medical markets are not fundamentally different from others and that, accordingly, the best hope for rationing health-care resources lies in use of the price system via inclusion of direct patient payments in the financing package. Consumers wishing to translate their perceived medical "needs" into consumption of health-care resources will confront financial constraints, consisting of any prices faced at the point of consumption and any time and transportation costs required by the provision of care. Tax and premium financing will impose dollar burdens on consumers, but such burdens will be felt as fixed costs that are invariant with respect to an individual's level of consumption. At the margin, consumers will have an incentive to weigh the cost against the benefit of an additional unit of care only to the extent that direct patient payment provisions require out-of-pocket expenditures.

When included in the financing package, direct patient payments are usually income tested as a concession to the access goal (discussed below), an agreement whereby the severity of the deductible or co-insurance provisions are directly related to the income level of each beneficiary. Ideally, direct patient payments would vary across different types of services to encourage substitution out of more costly forms of care toward less costly alternatives (for example, from inpatient to outpatient care or from curative to preventive care).

Other analysts believe that medical markets possess certain peculiarities that erode the ability of price signals to generate effective rationing. This view is based on the observation that the demands for many services are relatively price inelastic and that many consumption decisions are "supply induced," that is, they are made by providers rather than consumers of health care. In this view, the best hope for effective rationing lies in the use of exclusive tax financing, with its inherent potential for a centrally administered "top-down" budgeting mechanism, similar in principle to that used by Great Britain's National Health Service. Moreover, it has been observed that one potential difficulty with direct patient payments is that eligibles may elect to purchase supplementary private insurance to "fill in" the deductible and coinsurance provisions. An example of such behavior is the widespread private supplementation practiced by Medicare beneficiaries, which leads to substantial increases in demand for services (Link, Long, and Settle 1980). Unless such options are effectively outlawed, and it is difficult to see how that could be accomplished, an NHI plan that attempts to effectively ration by eliminating "first-dollar" coverage in the beginning may not succeed in doing so in the end.

Successful control over input costs will rest on the ability of the plan to restrain rapidly rising reimbursement rates without at the same time reducing the supply of inputs. Preservation of the current dual reimbursement system via combined tax and premium financing would limit government control to the tax-financed segment. Experience under the Medicaid program has shown that attempts to exercise even this limited "leverage" often reduces access for eligibles whose care is tax financed, as providers show preferences to treat patients under the less constrained private reimbursement system (Sloan, Mitchell, and Cromwell 1978). These experiences have led to a more general complaint against such financing, namely, that eligibility is tied to the source of payment, creating in effect a "two-class" health-care system, in which those eligible for tax-financed care experience the stigma that often falls on welfare recipients.

At present, much of the control over input supply rests with states, whose legislatures control the licensing of physicians, nurses, and other health personnel, and (in some cases) restrict otherwise redundant hospital purchases of expensive, high-technology equipment. Since legislatures tend to guard their powers zealously, it is difficult to conceive of circumstances under which Congress could successfully co-opt such powers. Retention of at least some state and local taxation in the NHI financing package would provide the incentive for these legislatures to use their powers to regulate labor and capital inputs so as to restrain rising costs.

Access to Care

It is commonly agreed that NHI should promote all persons' access to acceptable quality health care, regardless of income, age, race, or place of residence. However, operational specifications of plans to achieve this goal differ greatly. At one extreme, the most conservative plans would confine the provision of tax-financed care to low-income and elderly groups but limit the government's obligation to the employed population by merely requiring, via mandated premiums, purchases of private insurance up to a specified standard of coverage. At the other extreme, the most generous NHI plans would provide fully tax-financed care to all, reflecting the view that access to comprehensive care is every citizen's "right." While both approaches would expand insurance coverage beyond current levels, any NHI plan that relies partly on financing sources that are tied to employment, that is, on mandated premiums and (in some cases) payroll taxes, could create "cracks" in coverage through which would fall part-time employees, workers between jobs, the unemployed, and those outside the labor force, unless special provisions were made for their inclusion. Another difficulty with combined tax and mandated premium financing is that, in preserving the current dual reimbursement system, it would (as now) limit the government's "leverage" over providers, including their location decisions. Present unequal geographic distributions of health-care resources are a reflection of traditional consumption patterns. Those persons living in areas where per capita resources are below the average are among those traditionally denied access to care and, accordingly, such individuals would still confront often prohibitive time and transportation costs even in the absence of price constraints faced at the point of consumption. A centrally administered reimbursement system could be manipulated to provide incentives to health-care providers to locate in resource-scarce areas.

On- versus Off-Budget Costs

An issue that is of great political significance is the amount of total NHI costs that will be added to the federal budget. To separate the substance from the symbolism of this issue, it is important to consider the nature of costs attributable to establishing an NHI plan. Any net increase or decrease in total health expenditures induced by an NHI plan will depend on its impact on access to care on the one hand, and its ability to control expenditures on the other. Unlike the experiences of other industrial countries that have adopted NHI in previous decades, any NHI plan legislated in the United States will be implemented against an already extensive backdrop of third-party payment mechanisms. (Recall from Table 4.2 that such payments already account for more than two-thirds of current expenditures.) Much of the ability of the price system to constrain expenditures has already been eroded. As a consequence, the largest share of total national health expenditures incurred under an NHI plan would have been incurred in its absence. Any net increases or decreases will be small, relative to existing expenditures that will simply be transferred from patients, private insurance, and current government programs to the NHI payment mechanism. Department of Health and Human Services' actuaries estimate that nearly 90 percent of the total costs of an NHI plan involve such transfers. Thus, an NHI plan financed exclusively from federal tax sources could transfer to the federal budget an amount in excess of $100 billion, even in the absence of any concomitant changes in the quantities, prices, types, locations, and recipients of health care. The magnitude of this figure in combination with growing concern over increases in federal spending, particularly the explosive increases for social programs that have occurred since the 1960s, will provide a political advantage to NHI plans that rely heavily on off-budget financing.

Impacts on Employment

As stated earlier, there is general agreement that the burdens imposed by payroll taxes and mandated premiums fall on wage earners, no matter how these taxes on labor are nominally divided between employers and employees. Thus, NHI plans that rely on these sources would tend to reduce the nominal wages received by workers or, in the context of an inflation-prone economy, reduce the rate at which such wages rise. Employers paying wages at or near the minimum wage level, however, would be legally prevented from shifting the costs of their nominal premium or tax contributions to their employees and would have an incentive to substitute capital or more skilled labor for minimum wage labor. In the short run, at least, both financing sources could generate substantial unemployment among current low-wage earners, but of the two, mandated premiums would produce the greater effect because the employer's nominal contribution would amount to a fixed tax per worker, invariant to the worker's wage level. Additionally, unemployment would be felt unevenly across different sectors because average wage levels tend to vary systematically by industry, as do the levels and extent of existing employer coverage (see Tables 4.4 and 4.5). Mitchell and Phelps (1976) and Emery, Long, and Mutti (1979) have estimated substantial short-run unemployment effects from mandated premiums.

Technically, the above incidence assumption is equivalent to the assumption that payroll or premium financing would not reduce the amount of labor supplied to markets. The situation with respect to other tax sources is less clear, however. The sheer magnitude of income, excise, or state and local taxes required to even partially finance an NHI plan makes any possible work disincentives an important consideration.

Role of the Private Insurance Industry

The size of the private insurance industry makes it a force to be reckoned with in the NHI debate. (Recall from Table 4.1 that in 1978 private premiums alone financed over $45 billion of health services. Moreover, the industry served as a fiscal intermediary for the Medicare program and many state Medicaid programs.) A mandated premium financing approach would enhance its role by, in effect, creating a "captive" market for its services. On the other hand, exclusive tax financing would reduce its role to, at best, an administrative one, much like the role it currently plays under the Medicare and Medicaid programs.

Stability of Revenue Sources

Most plans include financing sources, the revenues of which are earmarked for NHI. However, changes in the economy, such as varying levels of inflation and employment, will lead to instability in annual revenues from these sources. The projected short-run deficit in the OAS Trust Fund in the early- to mid-1980s is an example of this phenomenon. Financing packages should: (1) be balanced by sources that vary in opposite directions, (2) include a reserve fund to cushion short-run revenue fluctuations, or (3) depend upon supplemental Congressional appropriations.

CONCLUSION

The many and conflicting standards that can be used to evaluate potential financing sources—including distributive equity, which has been the focus of this chapter—confront designers of NHI plans with numerous political constraints. Concern over the level of federal spending argues for off-budget revenue sources, but progressive financing argues for federal general revenues. Access to care argues for elimination of direct patient payments, but expenditure control may argue for their retention. We have come to wonder whether the constraints have become so numerous that a politically acceptable solution no longer exists. Only time will tell whether or not this extreme point has already been reached in the NHI debate, but none of the many proposals considered by Congress has succeeded in achieving whatever delicate balance would have been required for passage. Fifteen years after the fact, the passage of the Medicare and Medicaid programs remains the high-water mark in efforts to collectively finance American health care.

REFERENCES

Andersen, Ronald. 1975. National Survey Trends in Health Service Utilization and Expenditures as a Basis for Social Policy Formulation, Contract No. HSM-110-70-392, Department of Health, Education, and Welfare.

Arrow, Kenneth J. 1963. "Uncertainty and the Welfare Economics of Medical Care." American Economic Review, 53, 5 (December 1963), pp. 941-73.

Battelle Human Affairs Research Centers. 1980. Study to Develop Methods of Encouraging the Growth and Maintenance of Employee Benefit Plans Among Firms with No Such Plans: User's Guide to Data. Prepared for U.S. Department of Labor, Contract No. J-9-P-7-0150. Mimeo. Seattle, March 28, 1980.

Carlson, Michael D. 1974. "The 1972-73 Consumer Expenditure Survey." Monthly Labor Review, 97 (December 1974), pp. 16-23.

Carroll, Marjorie Smith, and Ross H. Arnett, III. 1979. "Private Health Insurance Plans in 1977: Coverage, Enrollment, and Financial Experience." Health Care Financing Review, 1, 2 (Fall 1979), pp. 3-22.

Davis, Karen. 1975. National Health Insurance: Benefits, Costs, and Consequences. Washington, D.C.: Brookings Institution.

Emery, E. David, Stephen H. Long, and John H. Mutti. 1979. "Tax Increases to Finance Social Security and National Health Insurance: A Comparison of Disaggregated Employment Impacts." Unpublished working paper, The Maxwell School, Syracuse University, May 1979.

Enthoven, Alain C. 1980. Health Plan. Reading, Mass.: Addison-Wesley.

Fisher, Charles R. 1980. "Differences by Age Groups in Health Care Spending." Health Care Financing Review, 1, 4 (Spring 1980), pp. 65-90.

Gibson, Robert M. 1979. "National Health Expenditures, 1978." Health Care Financing Review, 1, 1 (Summer 1979), pp. 1-36.

Harris, Jeffrey E. 1980. "Taxing Tar and Nicotine." American Economic Review, 70, 3 (June 1980), pp. 300-11.

Link, Charles R., Stephen H. Long, and Russell F. Settle. 1980. "Cost Sharing, Supplementary Insurance, and Health Services Utilization Among the Medicare Elderly." Health Care Financing Review, 2,2 (Fall 1980), pp. 25-31.

Long, Stephen H., and John L. Palmer. 1982 (forthcoming). "Financing Health Care." In Income-Tested Transfer Programs, edited by Irwin Garfinckel. New York: Academic Press.

Mitchell, Bridger M., and Charles E. Phelps. 1976. "National Health Insurance: Some Costs and Effects of Mandated Employee Coverage." Journal of Political Economy, 84, 3 (May/June 1976), pp. 553-71.

Mitchell, Bridger M., and William B. Schwartz. 1976. "The Financing of National Health Insurance." Science, 192, 4240 (May 14, 1976), pp. 621-36.

Mitchell, Bridger M., and Ronald J. Vogel. 1975. "Health and Taxes: An Assessment of the Medical Deduction." Southern Economic Journal, 41, 4 (April 1975), pp. 660-72.

Moeller, John F. 1973. TRIM Technical Description. Urban Institute Working Paper 718-1.

Pechman, Joseph A., and Benjamin A. Okner. 1974. Who Bears the Tax Burden? Washington, D.C.: Brookings Institution.

Sloan, Frank, Janet Mitchell, and Jerry Cromwell. 1978. "Physician Participation in State Medicaid Programs." Journal of Human Resources, 13 (Supplement 1978), pp. 211-45.

Steuerle, Eugene, and Ronald Hoffman. 1979. "Tax Expenditures for Health Care." National Tax Journal, 32, 2 (June 1979), pp. 101-15.

Sulvetta, Margaret B. 1976. An Analyst's Guide to TRIM—The Transfer Income Model. Urban Institute Working Paper 996-03.

U.S., Department of Commerce, Bureau of the Census. 1978. Microdata from the Survey of Income and Education: Data Access Descriptions. Washington, D.C.: U.S. Government Printing Office.

U.S., Department of Commerce, Bureau of the Census. Technical Documentation for the 1976 Survey of Income and Education Computer Microdata File. Mimeo, undated.

U.S., Department of Health, Education, and Welfare, National Center for Health Statistics. 1978. Personal Out-of-Pocket Health Expenses: United States, 1975, Vital and Health Statistics, Series 10, No. 122, Hyattsville, Md.

U.S., Department of the Treasury, Office of Tax Analysis. 1975. Labor and Capital Shares of Economic Income. Memorandum.

U.S., Office of Management and Budget. 1981. Special Analyses: Budget of the United States Government, Fiscal Year 1981. Washington, D.C.: U.S. Government Printing Office.

U.S., Internal Revenue Service. 1978. Statistics of Income—1975, Individual Income Tax Returns. Washington, D.C.: U.S. Government Printing Office.

Waldman, Saul. 1976. National Health Insurance Proposals: Provisions of Bills Introduced in the 94th Congress as of February 1976. Washington, D.C.: Office of Research and Statistics, Social Security Administration, DHEW Pub. No. (SSA) 76-11920.

Yohalem, Martha. 1977. "Employee Benefit Plans, 1975." Social Security Bulletin, 40, 11 (November 1977), pp. 19-28.

APPENDIX:

TECHNICAL DETAILS ON SIMULATING NHI FINANCING BURDENS WITH MICRODATA

Data

The primary data source on which the tax and premium simulations are performed is the 1976 Survey of Income and Education (SIE). This is a file of 151,170 household interview units, containing the records of 440,815 individuals residing in the 50 states and the District of Columbia (U.S. Department of Commerce 1978). The March questionnaire of the Current Population Survey forms the core of the SIE questionnaire, providing information on labor-force status, work experience, household structure, and demographic characteristics. Also covered by the SIE are more detailed breakdowns of calendar year 1975 income by type, transfer program participation, health insurance coverage, disability conditions, languages spoken, and educational characteristics. When survey case weights are used, the sample represents the total civilian noninstitutionalized population of the United States. These features of the SIE allow the microsimulation of tax burdens according to their appropriate income bases and allow construction of the family income distribution of the U.S. population.

The SIE household interview unit consists of all persons occupying the same residence (house, apartment, or other group of rooms). In some cases this household unit will encompass smaller family groups that are largely economically independent, and it is this economically independent family that serves as the unit for our analysis. Tax and premium burdens, initially allocated to individuals or tax filing units as described below, are ultimately aggregated to the SIE family level.

Microsimulation of Tax and Premium Burdens

NHI financing burdens are simulated, using a version of the Transfer Income Model (TRIM), originally developed by the Urban Institute (Moeller 1973; Sulvetta 1976) and modified by the authors to address special issues in health-care financing. In apportioning taxes and premiums (which may statutorily fall on firms and other nonpersons) to specific individuals or families, incidence assumptions are crucial. We follow a widely accepted approach that presumes perfect competition, price flexibility, and factor mobility (Pechman and Okner 1974, pp. 25–43). Moreover, it is assumed that the only budgetary change taking place is the additional $10 billion in revenues from each NHI financing source; that is, we employ the comparative static methodology common to many microsimulation exercises. This section highlights the TRIM procedure for simulating the burdens attributable to each source.

Payroll Taxes

Payroll taxes are assumed to be ultimately borne by workers — the employee tax borne directly and the employer tax borne in the form of lowered wages. Using appropriate payroll tax rates and tax-base ceilings, calculations are performed for private wage and salary earners, the self-employed, and railroad workers. Those not in railroad or government jobs and who had less than $400 in self-employment income are classified as private wage and salary earners. In this group, the combined social security employer and employee tax rates (.0585 each) are applied to annual gross wages up to the $14,100 taxable base ceiling. Although the Social Security system does not mandate coverage of government employees, about 70 percent of all nonfederal government workers participated in the system through voluntary state and local government buy-ins. A random 70 percent sample of the SIE individuals working for state and local governments, then, were also charged the OASDI/HI payroll taxes. Self-employment income of $400 or less is disregarded. Individuals with self-employment income over $400 and no other earnings are assigned payroll taxes equalling the 1975 self-employment tax rate (.0790) times annual gross earnings up to a $14,100 base ceiling. For individuals with self-employment income over $400 and other earnings, payroll taxes on other earnings are calculated in the usual way, and the self-employment tax rate is applied only to that self-employment income which, when added to the other earnings, does not exceed $14,100. Workers who reported railroad or railway express as the industry of their longest job held in 1975 are assumed to be contributors to railroad retirement. The individual's average monthly salary for months worked last year is calculated, and that amount up to $1175 (the 1975 monthly ceiling on taxable wages) is considered countable income. The contribution amount then equals the employee tax rate (.0585) plus the employer tax rate (.1535), multiplied by monthly countable income times the number of months worked.

Mandated Employer-Employee Premiums

As with payroll taxes, we assume that the entire burden of any mandated insurance premiums falls entirely on employees. There-fore, we charged premium liabilities to all wage and salary workers earning over $2,000 per year. This procedure is a proxy for the plan specified in the text, under which students and employees working less than 25 hours per week would be exempt from participation. In 1975, this plan would have required a premium payment of just over $122 per worker to raise $10 billion in revenue.

Excise Tax on Cigarettes

Data from the 1972-73 Consumer Expenditure Survey (Carlson 1974) were used to calculate the probability that a family made pur-chases of cigarettes during the year. Families were then assigned randomly to smoking and nonsmoking status. CES data were also used to estimate an ordinary least squares regression equation, relating nonzero expenditures on cigarettes to Consumer Unit (CU) income and location and various CU head characteristics such as age, race, education, occupation, and marital status. The estimated re-gression coefficients were then used to impute predicted cigarette expenditures to TRIM-assembled tax filing units assigned as smokers, which in definition closely resemble the Survey's Consumer Units. Our assumptions are that the tax would take the form of an ad valorem tax and that its full burden would fall on smokers.

Federal General Revenues

The federal personal income tax is simulated by the FEDTAX module of TRIM. A complex FEDTAX routine reorganizes SIE house-hold interview units into realistic tax filing units and determines the type of return to be filed (single, joint, or unmarried head of house-hold). FEDTAX then computes adjusted gross income (AGI) by aggre-gating taxable income sources across members of the filing unit. Personal exemptions are assigned, using financial support tests for dependents and tests for additional old age and blindness exemptions. Based upon IRS statistics on actual returns (Internal Revenue Service 1978), a proportion of filing units in each income class is randomly chosen as "itemizers" and assigned the average itemized deduction for itemizers in that income class. The standard deduction formula is applied to all other filing units. Taxes due are determined by cal-culating AGI, less exemptions and deductions, and referring to the appropriate Tax Rate Schedule (X, Y, or Z). For certain filers, this tax liability was reduced by an earned income credit. The federal corporation income tax is assumed to ultimately rest with all owners of financial and real property. Property income is assigned to SIE individuals on the basis of the following items: interest, dividends, rent, self-employment income, and pension income, according to Department of the Treasury (1975) estimates regarding the proportion of each source that represents a return to capital. The bulk of remaining general revenues comes from a variety of taxes, most of which (e.g., federal excise taxes and customs duties) are taxes on consumption goods. These taxes are, therefore, assumed to fall on individuals in proportion to their disposable incomes.

Estimates of Family-Financing Burdens

The above calculations—performed for individuals and personal income tax units as well as families, depending on the particular financing source—are followed by aggregation to the SIE family level. The $10 billion control totals for payroll taxes, premiums, and cigarette excise taxes are then distributed over all families in proportion to their simulated share of, respectively, total payroll tax payments, number of earners, and imputed cigarette expenditures. The $10 billion control total for federal general revenues was broken down into subtotals, reflecting the relative importance of personal income taxes, corporate income taxes, and other taxes in 1975. These subtotals were then distributed over all families in proportion to their simulated shares of, respectively, total personal income tax payments, property income, and disposable income. In effect, the microsimulation results are used as weights for allocating financing burdens.

To summarize the results, we order families into quintiles by total family income (that is, in five groups from the lowest 20 percent to the highest 20 percent). This approach, which is common in the literature on income distribution, avoids putting the results in dollar denominations for a particular year, thereby stating results for relative incomes that remain approximately correct over several years.

5

THE DISTRIBUTIVE IMPACT OF
A MEDICARE CATASTROPHIC BENEFIT

M. Susan Marquis

Medicare was enacted in 1965 to provide basic health insurance to persons 65 and older, who incur higher health-care expenditures yet are less protected by private insurance and have fewer financial resources than other population subgroups. Medicare consists of two insurance plans: the Hospital Insurance program (HI) provides coverage for inpatient hospital care, posthospital days of care in a skilled nursing facility, and posthospital home health visits. Supplementary Medical Insurance (SMI) covers physicians' and certain other practitioners' services, home health visits, and a variety of other medical services such as x-rays and durable supplies.

Although Medicare plays an important role in helping the elderly pay for medical care, the program has been criticized for not meeting the objective of eliminating the financial burden on the aged of obtaining health care. About 3 million aged spend, out-of-pocket, more than 5 percent of their income on medical care each year.[1] Further, the aged comprise a large fraction of all people who have high medical expenditures relative to income. More than 30 percent of all people who spend out-of-pocket in excess of 5 percent of income are aged, yet the aged are only 11 percent of the total population.

The Medicare program requires beneficiaries to share in the cost of hospital and medical care, and there is no limit on the patients' liability. This is one reason the aged may face burdensome

This research was supported by the Health Insurance Study Grant to The Rand Corporation from the U.S. Department of Health and Human Services. I would like to acknowledge useful comments on the research from Robin Barlow, William Birdsall, Edward Gramlich, Kent Marquis, William Neenan, and Joseph Newhouse.

medical costs despite the major role the public pays in financing the health care of the elderly.

Medicare hospital insurance provides up to 90 days of hospital care in a benefit period. The patient is responsible for a deductible in each benefit period and for a copayment during the sixty-first through ninetieth days. (All estimated values presented in this chapter are in 1976 dollars and are based on 1976 expenditures for Medicare covered services, enrollment in 1976, and 1976 benefits. In 1976, the hospital deductible was $104, and the copayment was $26 per day.) An additional 60 days are available as a lifetime reserve that can be used if the patient exhausts the basic 90 covered days. The patient is also responsible for a copayment for each reserve day ($52 in 1976).

Many elderly patients have private insurance or Medicaid to protect them from hospital charges unmet by Medicare. However, 23,000 aged who don't have this additional protection exhaust their 90 days of basic benefits each year and spend $1,000 (1976 dollars) or more out-of-pocket for hospital care.[2] At least 5,000 aged without additional insurance protection have hospital stays exceeding 150 days. These aged exhaust both their basic and reserve benefits and have out-of-pocket liability exceeding $4,000.

Under the SMI plan, the patient is responsible for a deductible of $60 in each calendar year and for 20 percent of charges above the deductible. There is no limit on how much the patient might spend in coinsurance charges. As a result, 1 million aged spend more than 5 percent of their income out-of-pocket for physician care each year.

Various proposals for insuring the catastrophic expenditures of the elderly have been introduced before Congress as part of proposals for national health insurance. This chapter compares the effect of ten prototype catastrophic supplements to the Medicare program on the economic well-being of the aged. The plans are examined for their effect on the distribution of expected real income (that is, before the illness loss is known) and on the redistribution of income once the health loss has occurred. The plans considered vary on two dimensions:

1. The structure of the catastrophic limit: a fixed dollar amount versus an income-related amount.
2. The financing of the catastrophic benefit: increase in the Medicare deductible, the coinsurance, premiums, payroll taxes, or personal income and corporate profits taxes.

A key feature of the Medicare catastrophic plans examined, and of most health insurance, is that payments to the individual depend upon the amount of medical care consumed; that is, the insurance

effectively alters the price of medical care to the consumer. A Medicare catastrophic benefit lowers the price of health care faced by the
aged if they have large medical expenditures and their real income,
in terms of the uses of income, rises. However, the lower own price
of catastrophic care may lead to increased use of health services and,
hence, affect the budgetary costs of the new plan and the burden on
those who share in financing the new Medicare benefits. In the next
section, using the framework of a utility-maximizing consumer, the
price elasticity of demand is shown to be an important determinant
of the net effect.

In the third section, behavioral equations relating demand to
the own price of care are specified and combined with information
about the health-care expenditures of the aged to compare the effect
of the different plans.

The final sections of the chapter present empirical estimates
of the budgetary impact and the distributional effects of the prototype
catastrophic supplements. Under the assumed demand model, the
premium and deductible financed plans result in a net income loss
for the aged. However, under the coinsurance-financed plan, aggregate demand for health care by the aged falls and there is a small
net real income gain. Tax-financed plans result in net-income gains
to beneficiaries, which are a transfer from the nonbeneficiary population. The distribution of income changes among the aged, however,
is not substantially affected by the choice of financing mechanism.
Similarly, the structure of the catastrophic benefit has a surprisingly
small impact on the expected income distribution, partly because of
the sizeable role of government programs in addition to Medicare in
financing the catastrophic health expenditures of the aged poor.

In contrast to the small effect on the expected income distribution, the choice of plan has a substantial effect on the postillness
distribution of income, as shown in the final section. Large positive
transfers accrue at catastrophic health losses, which are approximately equal across income groups under the fixed dollar plan but
favor the aged poor under income-conditioned plans. In lower health
loss states, income losses occur. For tax-, premium-, or deductible-
financed plans, the income losses are shared equally across noncatastrophic illness states. However, under the coinsurance-financed
plans, the income losses increase with the size of the health loss.
The contrast between the variability in real income changes for the
noncatastrophic states and the expected aggregate real income changes
under the different plans illustrates the trade-off in risk spreading
and appropriate incentives that must be made in designing any public
insurance program.

EFFECT ON ECONOMIC WELL-BEING
OF CHANGES IN THE PLAN

In this section, I investigate how changes in the catastrophic limit in the insurance policy affect the economic well-being of a representative individual. The model assumes that the individual maximizes utility, which is a function of health and other goods. The health of the individual is assumed to be subject to random loss, so the individual has an expected utility, taking into account uncertainty about the health loss. The insurance policy is assumed to pay (1 - C) percent of all charges for purchases of medical care up to purchase h* and to pay all of the charges for purchases h* or greater. I wish to examine the gains or losses in expected utility stemming from a decrease in h*.[3] To do so, it is also necessary to consider how the increased catastrophic claims against the insurance policy are to be financed. The financing may be by taxation (assumed in the model below to be a lump sum tax or premium paid by beneficiaries of the insurance program), by a change in the plan coinsurance rate, C, so that the actuarial value of the plan is unchanged, or by a combination of methods.

The model can be represented as follows:[4]

U = utility
ℓ = health loss
H_0 = ex ante level of health
$h(\ell)$ = purchases of medical care given loss, ℓ
$g(h(\ell))$ = function relating medical care purchases to health increases
$H_0 - \ell + g(h(\ell))$ = health consumed given loss, ℓ
$X(\ell)$ = purchases of composite good given loss, ℓ
I = income
P_h = price of medical care
C = coinsurance rate or fraction of the medical bill paid by the patient
h^* = catastrophic limit
T = lump sum tax or premium

Prices and income are measured with the composite good, X, as the numeraire. Purchases of medical care are assumed to restore health via the technological relation represented by the function, g. Utility is a function of health and the composite good:

$$U = U[X(\ell), H_0 - \ell + g(h(\ell))] \tag{1}$$

Once the health loss is known, the consumer chooses the

amount of medical care and the amount of the composite good that maximize utility, subject to the budget constraint. The budget constraint, however, depends upon whether the health loss leads to purchases less than h*, or whether purchases exceed h* so that a part of the purchase is wholly subsidized. Let ℓ^* be the illness loss such that $h(\ell^*) = h^*$. Then the relevant budget lines for loss ℓ are

$$I = X(\ell) + CP_h h(\ell) + T \qquad \text{for } \ell < \ell^*$$
$$I = X(\ell) + CP_h h^* + T \qquad \text{for } \ell \geq \ell^* \tag{2}$$

The first order conditions for maximizing utility, subject to the budget constraint, are:

$$\left.\begin{aligned}
U_{X(\ell)} - \lambda(\ell) &= 0 \\
U_{H(\ell)} g'(h(\ell)) - \lambda(\ell)CP_h &= 0 \\
I - X(\ell) - CP_h h(\ell) - T &= 0
\end{aligned}\right\} \qquad \text{for } \ell < \ell^*$$

$$\left.\begin{aligned}
U_{X(\ell)} - \lambda(\ell) &= 0 \\
U_{H(\ell)} g'(h(\ell)) &= 0 \\
I - X(\ell) - CP_h h^* - T &= 0
\end{aligned}\right\} \qquad \text{for } \ell \geq \ell^* \tag{3}$$

Changes in the insurance contract affect the price of medical care faced by the consumer and alter the system of equations (3) for each illness loss. However, the insurance contract is specified before the illness loss is known. At the beginning of the insurance period the consumer has an expected utility, which takes into account the uncertainty about the health loss and is represented by

$$E(U) = E[U(X(\ell), H_0 - \ell + g(h(\ell))] \tag{4}$$

for which the expectation is over all values of ℓ.

To examine the effect of an exogenous change in h*, C, and T on expected utility, it will be assumed that all goods are produced under conditions of constant costs. [5] Therefore, the individual's money income and the market prices of goods are unaltered by a change in the insurance plan. The mathematics of the solution are somewhat simplified by assuming that there are only two possible states of health loss. Let:

$$s_1 = \text{probability that } \ell = 1$$
$$s_2 = (1 - s_1) = \text{probability that } \ell = 2$$
$$\ell = 1 < \ell^*$$
$$\ell = 2 > \ell^*$$

With two states of health loss, the expected utility defined in equation (4) is rewritten as

$$E(U) = s_1 U[X(1), H_0 - \ell_1 + g(h1))]$$
$$+ s_2 U[X(2), H_0 - \ell_2 + g(h(2))] \tag{5}$$

An exogenous change in C, h*, and T changes expected utility by:

$$dE(U) = s_1 \left[U_{X(1)} \left(\frac{\partial X(1)}{\partial C} dC + \frac{\partial X(1)}{\partial h^*} dh^* + \frac{\partial X(1)}{\partial T} dT \right) \right.$$
$$\left. + U_{H(1)} g'(h(1)) \left(\frac{\partial h(1)}{\partial C} dC + \frac{\partial h(1)}{\partial h^*} dh^* + \frac{\partial h(1)}{\partial T} dT \right) \right]$$
$$+ s_2 \left[U_{X(2)} \left(\frac{\partial X(2)}{\partial C} dC + \frac{\partial X(2)}{\partial h^*} dh^* + \frac{\partial X(2)}{\partial T} dT \right) \right.$$
$$\left. + U_{H(2)} g'(h(2)) \left(\frac{\partial h(2)}{\partial C} dC + \frac{\partial h(2)}{\partial h^*} dh^* + \frac{\partial h(2)}{\partial T} dT \right) \right] \tag{6}$$

Next, totally differentiate the budget constraint (2),

$$dI = 0 = \frac{\partial X(1)}{\partial C} dC + \frac{\partial X(1)}{\partial h^*} dh^* + \frac{\partial X(1)}{\partial T} dT + CP_h \frac{\partial h(1)}{\partial C} dC$$
$$+ CP_h \frac{\partial h(1)}{\partial h^*} dh^* + CP_h \frac{\partial h(1)}{\partial T} dT + P_h h(1) dC + dT \quad \text{if } \ell = 1, \tag{7}$$

$$dI = 0 = \frac{\partial X(2)}{\partial C} dC + \frac{\partial X(2)}{\partial h^*} dh^* + \frac{\partial X(2)}{\partial T} dT + P_h h^* dC$$
$$+ CP_h dh^* + dT \quad \text{if } \ell = 2$$

Substitute conditions (7) and the first order conditions (3) into (6),

$$dE(U) = s_1 \lambda(1)(P_h h(1) dC + dT) - s_2 \lambda(2)(P_h h^* dC + CP_h dh^* + dT) \tag{8}$$

This result is easily understood with the aid of the following definitions:

$$dRI = -s_1 P_h h(1)dC - s_2 P_h h^*dC - s_2 CP_h dh^* - dT \qquad (9a)$$

= the expected real income change,

$$dRI(1) = -P_h h(1)dC - dT \qquad (9b)$$

= the change in real income realized if $\ell = 1$,

$$dRI(2) = -P_h h^*dC - CP_h dh^* - dT \qquad (9c)$$

= the change in real income realized if $\ell = 2$,

$$E(\lambda(\ell)) = s_1 \lambda(1) + s_2 \lambda(2) \qquad (9d)$$

Using these definitions and reworking equation (8) yields:

$$\frac{dE(U)}{E(\lambda(\ell))} = dRI + \frac{s_1\lambda(1)}{E(\lambda(\ell))}[dRI(1) - dRI] + \frac{s_2\lambda(2)}{E(\lambda(\ell))}[dRI(2) - dRI]$$

$$= dRI + \frac{E[\lambda(\ell)(dRI(\ell) - dRI)]}{E(\lambda(\ell))} \qquad (10)$$

The ratio $dE(U)/E(\lambda(\ell))$ measures the change in expected utility in terms of the composite good, X. The first term on the right-hand side of (10) measures the expected real income change resulting from the change in relative prices and from the additional tax. The second term is the covariance of the marginal utility of money with the change in real income. The difference between the change in income in state ℓ, $dRI(\ell)$, and the expected income change, dRI, measures the change in risk for state ℓ. Weighting this term by the marginal utility of income in state ℓ measures the value of the risk reduction in state ℓ. Hence, the covariance of the marginal utility of money with the change in real income may be interpreted as the value of the change in welfare due to changes in risk as the parameters of the insurance policy are modified.

To sign the direction of the real income change and the change in risk for a decrease in h*, the increased premium and/or coinsurance rate needed to finance the lower catastrophic limit need to be determined. For a specific dh*, increases in the actuarial value of the plan are financed by an increase in premium; however, the coinsurance may be increased to offset the effects of a change in h* on the actuarial value of the plan and to reduce the additional tax levy. The actuarial value of the plan, AV, is:

$$AV = s_1[(1 - C)P_h h(1)] + s_2[P_h(h(2) - h^*) + (1 - C)P_h h^*] \qquad (11)$$

Totally differentiate AV (and recall that P_h is assumed to be constant):

$$dAV = s_1 \left[(1 - C)P_h \frac{\partial h(1)}{\partial C} dC + (1 - C)P_h \frac{\partial h(1)}{\partial h^*} dh^* - P_h h(1) dC \right]$$
$$+ s_2 \left[Ph \frac{\partial h(2)}{\partial C} dC + P_h \frac{\partial h(2)}{\partial h^*} dh^* - P_h h^* dC - CP_h dh^* \right]$$
$$(12)$$

Solve for dh* in terms of dC and dT when dAV is set to dT:

$$dh^* = \frac{dT}{D} - \frac{dC}{D} \left[s_1(1 - C)P_h \frac{\partial h(1)}{\partial C} + s_2 P_h \frac{\partial h(2)}{\partial C} \right.$$
$$\left. - s_1 P_h h(1) - s_2 P_h h^* \right]$$
$$(13)$$

where

$$D = s_1(1 - C)P_h \frac{\partial h(1)}{\partial h^*} + s_2 P_h \frac{\partial h(2)}{\partial h^*} - s_2 CP_h$$

First, use result (13) to evaluate the change in real income (equation 9a):

$$dRI = - \frac{dT}{D} \left[s_1(1 - C)P_h \frac{\partial h(1)}{\partial h^*} + s_2 P_h \frac{\partial h(1)}{\partial h^*} \right]$$
$$- \frac{dC}{D} \left[(s_1 P_h h(1) + s_2 P_h h^*) \left(s_1(1-C)P_h \frac{\partial h(1)}{\partial h^*} + s_2 P_h \frac{\partial h(2)}{\partial h^*} \right) \right]$$
$$+ \frac{dC}{D} \left[s_2 CP_h \left(s_1(1 - C)P_h \frac{\partial h(1)}{\partial C} + s_2 P_h \frac{\partial h(2)}{\partial C} \right) \right]$$
$$(14)$$

Notice that D is negative (the demand response to changes in h*, $\partial h(2)/\partial h$, and $\partial h(2)/\partial h^*$ are less than or equal to zero) and dT and dC are both positive for a decrease in h*. The direction of the real income change then depends on the response of demand to each of the insurance parameters. The following observations may be made:

1. If there is no moral hazard, $\frac{\partial h(1)}{\partial C} = \frac{\partial h(2)}{\partial C} = \frac{\partial h(1)}{\partial h^*} = \frac{\partial h(2)}{\partial h^*} = 0$,

   dRI = 0

2. If demand rises in response to the fall in h*, $\frac{\partial h(1)}{\partial h^*} < 0$ and/or

   $\frac{\partial h(2)}{\partial h^*} < 0$, but there is no response to a change in C, dRI < 0

3. If demand falls in response to the increase in C, $\frac{\partial h(1)}{\partial C} < 0$ and/or $\frac{\partial h(2)}{\partial C} < 0$, but there is no response to a change in h*, dRI > 0 if dT = 0, dRI = 0 if dC = 0

Next evaluate how changes in the insurance policy affect utility through changes in risk. From equation (10), the value of the risk change is the covariance $E[\lambda(\ell)(dRI(\ell) - dRI)]$. Substituting explicit expressions for $dRI(\ell)$ and dRI for the two-state world (equation 9) and the expression for dh* in equation (13):

$$E[\lambda(\ell)(dRI(\ell) - dRI)] = s_1 s_2 [\lambda(1) - \lambda(2)] CP_h \frac{dT}{D}$$

$$+ \left[(P_h h^* - P_h h)\left(s_1(1 - C)P_h \frac{\partial h(1)}{\partial h^*} + s_2 P_h \frac{\partial h(2)}{\partial h^*}\right) \right.$$

$$\left. + P_h h(1)CP_h - CP_h\left(s_1(1 - C)P_h \frac{\partial h(1)}{\partial C} + s_2 P_h \frac{\partial h(2)}{\partial C}\right) \right] \times$$

$$(\lambda(1) - \lambda(2))s_1 s_2 \frac{dC}{D} \tag{15}$$

where D is defined in equation (13).

The terms dT/D and dC/D are negative, as discussed previously. To evaluate 15, it is necessary to sign $\lambda(1) - \lambda(2)$ and the expression in brackets. For a risk averter, $\lambda(2) > \lambda(1)$ and, hence, $\lambda(1) - \lambda(2)$ is negative. Arrow (1976) formally proves this proposition. Intuitively, we expect this to be so. An increase in health loss is equivalent to an income loss (Phelps 1973). For a risk averter, the marginal utility of income falls with income. State 2 is a higher health loss state than state 1; hence, state 2 is equivalent to lower income. For a decrease in h* financed wholly by premiums (dC = 0), there are welfare gains from reduced risk.

To evaluate the change in welfare from risk changes for a decrease in h* financed by an increase in C, it remains to sign the expression in brackets in equation (15). The covariance is positive if this term is positive. The bracketed expression depends upon assumptions about demand response. If demand does not change in response to changes in h*, the covariance is positive and there is a gain from decreased risk. However, if changes in h* stimulate demand, the sign of the covariance is ambiguous. It is possible for the required change in coinsurance to be sufficiently large that the additional risk the individual would face in the less hazardous states outweighs the benefits of less risk in the more hazardous state.

To summarize, the effects on the individual's well being of adding a catastrophic insurance benefit cannot be signed a priori. The net effect depends upon the elasticity of demand with respect to changes in the parameters of the insurance plan. If demand is responsive to changes in h*, consumers will increase their purchases of care. However, the value to them of the additional care falls short of the market value of providing the care and, hence, the burden of financing the plan. Thus there is a fall in real income, analogous to the standard result of the welfare analysis of price distortions. If the change in h* is financed by premiums, the fall in income will be compensated, at least in part, by gains from reduced risk. However, risk changes may also lead to a welfare loss if the plan is financed by an increase in the coinsurance rate, a demand response to h*. On the other hand, if demand is responsive to the increased changes for small medical bills but does not respond to the decreased changes for catastrophic bills, the individual will find his real income position improved; in effect, moral hazard falls.

DEMAND RESPONSE MODEL AND ESTIMATION METHODS

The effect on economic well-being of adding a catastrophic benefit was shown to depend critically upon the probability distribution of health losses and the assumed model of demand response. In the conventional model of economic choice, the consumer is able to purchase as many units of a good as he wants at a fixed price. He faces a straight-line budget constraint. However, the Medicare hospital and medical insurance programs contain deductibles and coinsurance rates and thus present the consumer with a price schedule, where the amount paid for a marginal unit of care varies with the total amount purchased. The budget line is kinked. Providing a catastrophic benefit would add another kink in the budget line; the nominal price of care is reduced to zero above the limit.

The one-period model typically adopted to analyze the consumer's behavior when he is confronted by a kinked budget line assumes the consumer can accurately predict which segment of the budget line he will attain. Under the one-period model, the consumer who has catastrophic medical care expenditures is assumed to predict this health state, and so after adding a catastrophic limit, the decision-making price for this consumer is zero.

However, the one-period model does not take into account the uncertainty about health losses during the insurance benefit period. The insurance contract specifies the prices that apply during a fixed time period rather than the episode of illness. At the beginning of the period, the individual may not anticipate catastrophic expenses

and his behavior at the beginning of the period will reflect his expectation about the segment of the kink where he anticipates his health
needs will place him (the expected price of a marginal unit). The
consumer (or the physician acting as his agent) may reevaluate the
probability of exceeding the catastrophic limit at each illness episode
and make consumption decisions on the basis of this assessment. In
this event, health-care purchase decisions are made sequentially
under uncertainty. [6] In making each purchase decision, the effective
price of care depends not only upon the nominal price of the purchase
but also upon the marginal prices at other segments of the price
schedule, weighted by the consumer's assessment of the probability
that he will spend beyond the kinks in the time remaining in the
accounting period.

   To incorporate this model of behavior into the demand response
to catastrophic limits, one would ideally simulate the occurrence of
illness episodes throughout the insurance accounting period. Purchase
decisions for each episode would be determined as a function of the
effective marginal price of a unit of care. However, the data available for analysis provide information on annual total expenditures
for Medicare-covered services rather than expenditures by illness
episode. Assumptions relating the average effective price of care
for all illness episodes during the year to the price schedule are
necessary to estimate the demand response to changes in the price
schedule. Because the limit in the plans to be considered, described
in detail below, is exceeded by a very small proportion of beneficiaries, it will be assumed that the expectation of incurring expenditures equal to the threshold is perceived to be close to zero until it
occurs. That is, persons who do not exceed the catastrophic threshold face an average effective price of care that is unchanged by the
cost-sharing limit in the catastrophic supplement.

   To establish an average effective price of care for those who
do reach the catastrophic range, consider the following simplified
model of illness. Suppose that, on each day of the accounting period,
there is some probability of suffering a noncatastrophic illness and
some additional small probability of suffering a catastrophic illness.
Assuming that illness episodes occur randomly during the year, the
catastrophic illness will occur on average at midyear. Under the
simplified assumptions of this model, the individual who suffers a
catastrophic illness will also suffer, on the average, an equal number
of minor illnesses before and after the severe illness. (Given a low
probability of the major illness, the incidence of two catastrophic
episodes is negligible.) That is, if the individual is observed to reach
the catastrophic threshold, the decision-making price is the coinsurance rate times the gross price for half of the accounting period (and
half of the illness episodes) and zero for the other half. The average

effective price of care is one-half the coinsurance times gross price among those who reach the catastrophic range. This simple model of illness does not allow for changes in the incidence of severity of minor illnesses, given that a catastrophic illness has occurred or for a large number of minor illnesses to be "catastrophic." However, it may serve as a reasonable approximation for the catastrophic plans considered here. The median individual with "catastrophic" expenditures does, in fact, purchase approximately equal quantities of medical services above and below the threshold.

A semilogarithmic relationship between the quantity demanded and the average effective price of care is assumed because it has the desirable property that demand becomes less elastic as the coinsurance rate falls.[7] If the initial policy specifies a constant coinsurance rate, the demands for hospital and medical care under the new policy containing catastrophic limits are:

$$
Q_M = \begin{cases} Q_M^1 e^{\gamma(C_M - C_M^1)} & \text{if } Q_M \leq M^* \\[2mm] Q_M^1 e^{\gamma(\frac{1}{2}C_M - C_M^1)} & \text{if } Q_M > M^* \end{cases} \tag{16a}
$$

$$
Q_H = \begin{cases} Q_H^1 e^{\beta(C_H - C_H^1)} & \text{if } Q_H \leq H^* \\[2mm] Q_H^1 e^{\beta(\frac{1}{2}C_H - C_H^1)} & \text{if } Q_H > H^* \end{cases} \tag{16b}
$$

where

Q_M, Q_H are (nonzero) quantities of medical and hospital care demanded under the new policy[8]

Q_M^1, Q_H^1 are the base-period quantities demanded

C_M, C_H are the coinsurance rates for front end expenditures under the new policy

C_M^1, C_H^1 are the base-period coinsurance rates

$\frac{1}{2}C_M$, $\frac{1}{2}C_H$ are the effective price of care for those with catastrophic expenditures

M^*, H^* are the catastrophic expenditures limits

γ, β are parameters

The market price of care is normalized by one, that is, quantities are measured in expenditure units.

The parameters γ, β indicate the relationship between changes in the effective coinsurance rate and demand. The values given to these parameters are based on the work of other researchers. From data in Newhouse, Phelps, and Schwartz (1974), the coefficient γ is estimated to be -1.31. This yields an elasticity of demand for medical care of -0.26 at the current medical coinsurance rate of 0.2, and at the new effective price of care in the catastrophic range (0.1), the elasticity is -0.13. The own price coefficient for hospital care in equation (16b) is estimated to be -0.453, based on two studies surveyed by Phelps and Newhouse (1974). That is, a one percentage point decrease in the coinsurance rates causes a 0.453 percent decrease in demand.

Cross-price elasticities are assumed to be zero. Hospital and medical care, while substitutes in some respects, are complements in other respects, and the empirical literature contains results that support positive, negative, and zero cross-price effects.[9] In the absence of consistent support for the sign, a zero cross-price elasticity appears to be a reasonable assumption.

The demand equations in (16) are written for a constant base-period coinsurance rate. However, under the current Medicare plans, the own price of care varies with the expenditure level because of the presence of deductibles and the copayment schedule for hospital care. The effective base-period prices are assumed not to depend upon the deductible. For decisions about hospital length of stay, the deductible should have little influence on the perceived marginal price of care because the deductible is almost always exceeded for stays of one night or longer. Although there may be less certainty about exceeding the deductible for medical services, the empirical analysis assumes that the base-period effective price is the coinsurance rate of 0.2, and the deductible does not influence medical purchase decisions.

A base-period nominal price schedule for hospital care is obtained by using an average per day charge for hospital care to describe the Medicare copayment schedule in terms of a set of coinsurance rates that vary with the level of expenditure. The copayment for the sixty-first through ninetieth days translates to a coinsurance of 16 percent; the copayment for reserve days is equivalent to a coinsurance of 32 percent. Although the base period average effective price is related to the entire nominal price schedule, any specification of this relationship is rather arbitrary. The specification to be used measures the average effective price of care as the simple average of the coinsurance on the first 60 days (0 in the base period) and the nominal coinsurance rate for the last unit of care purchased. This assumes no expectation of exceeding subsequent kinks of the schedule. The effect is to scale down the certainty response to a catastrophic limit by approximately half.

If the base-period distribution of hospital and medical expenditures is known, values of Q_M^1 and Q_H^1 can be drawn with the appropriate probabilities and equation (16) can be used to calculate aggregate demand under alternative benefit structures. Expenditure distributions are derived for 48 subgroups of Medicare enrollees: persons eligible for Medicaid benefits in families with low and middle income in 12 income intervals, persons with private supplementary insurance in families in 18 income intervals, and persons without sources of supplementary medical care financing in 18 income subclasses. The procedures used to derive the subgroups expenditure distribution are detailed in Marquis (1979).

The basic approach is as follows. Data on the distribution of expenditures for SMI services for all Medicare enrollees who used services are combined with information about mean differences in expenditures among the subgroups of users and an assumed shape of the distribution to mathematically characterize the subgroup medical expenditure distribution.[10] The lognormal distribution was chosen because other investigators have found that the lognormal fit their data for medical expenditures (Keeler, Relles, and Rolph 1975). The hospital expenditure distributions were derived from data collected by the Medicare claims system on the length of hospital stays and the average per day charge by assuming a lognormal frequency function for nonzero hospital expenditures.[11] However, because no data are available on expenditures by hospitalized individuals by income or sources of supplementary third-party financing, the base-period distributions for the 48 subgroups are taken to be identical. The base-period expenditure distributions are in 1976 dollars.

Each base-period expenditure distribution is associated with a base-period price schedule that reflects not only the Medicare benefit structure but also any supplementary protection. The assumptions used to determine the average effective base-period prices corresponding to the current Medicare provisions were described above. These assumptions give the effective base-period price for beneficiaries who do not have other third-party sources of financing. Medicaid and the private insurance companies are assumed to pay the full 20 percent SMI coinsurance and, hence, the base-period price of medical care for covered persons is zero. Base-period hospital prices for persons with Medicaid or private third-party protection are obtained by assuming that Medicaid and private insurance pay the full Medicare cost-sharing; Medicaid is assumed to pay the full charge for days in excess of reserve days, while a 20 percent coinsurance is used for private insurance.

Given the base-period expenditure distributions, the corresponding base-period price, and the demand equations, the demand response to a catastrophic insurance benefit is then simulated for each of the 48 subgroups, yielding information about average expenditures for users of the service in each group under the new insurance plan. Population sizes in each subgroup and the number of users of services are estimated from the Current Population Reports (U.S. Bureau of the Census, 1975, 1977) and the Current Medicare Survey (see: Peel and Sharf, 1969 and Gornick, 1976) to obtain aggregate changes in expenditure. The increased subsidy cost of the plan is then determined as a function of the insurance plan structure.

BUDGETARY EFFECTS OF PROTOTYPE MEDICARE SUPPLEMENTS

Two catastrophic Medicare benefits are considered. Under both catastrophic benefits, restrictions on the number of covered hospital days of care would be removed, and limits would be placed on cost sharing for hospital care and for medical services. Once the patient has incurred cost sharing[12] equal to the limit, Medicare would pay the costs of all additional services. The first type of benefit establishes a fixed dollar maximum liability. Under the fixed-dollar limit plan, cost sharing for SMI covered services is limited to $250 per year and the limit on cost sharing for hospital care is $600 a year (limits are measured in 1976 dollars).

To account for differences in ability to pay, the second type of benefit adopts an income-related limit for cost sharing: cost sharing in excess of 5 percent of family income per year is used for SMI covered services, and cost sharing exceeding 10 percent of family income per year is used for hospital care. The increased Medicare benefit payments are approximately equal under the fixed limit and the income-tested limit, which facilitates a contrast of the redistributional consequences of the alternative benefit structures.

Five methods of financing each of the plans are considered: premiums, payroll taxes, personal income and corporate profits taxes, an increase in the Medicare deductible, and an increase in the coinsurance. Under the first three methods, additional taxes are raised to finance the increase in the actuarial value of the Medicare plan. Under the latter two methods, the actuarial value of HI and SMI is held constant. Table 5.1 summarizes the ten catastrophic plans.[13]

The budgetary impacts of the plans are summarized in Table 5.2. In addition to the effect on the Medicare budget, changes in the Medicare insurance indirectly impact other government programs that subsidize the medical care purchases of Medicare enrollees.

TABLE 5.1. Medicare Catastrophic Benefit by Financing Method
(estimates in 1976 dollars)

| | Type of Limit | |
| | Fixed Cost-Sharing | Income-Related |
Type of Financing	Limit	Limit
Federal personal income and corporate profits tax	0.58% surtax	0.55% surtax
Payroll tax on 1976 wage base	0.12% tax	0.11% tax
Premium	$3.67/enrollee/ month	$3.47/enrollee/ month
Increase coinsurance		
HI	To 3% (up 3 pts)	To 3.25% (up 3.25 pts)
SMI	To 35% (up 15 pts)	To 32% (up 12 pts)
Increase deductible		
HI	To $180 (up $76)	To $185 (up $81)
SMI	To $150 (up $90)	To $150 (up $90)

Source: Compiled by the author.

The largest of these other programs is Medicaid, under which the
federal government shares with the states in financing the medical
care of persons on welfare and the medically indigent. Medicaid
pays the amount of the Medicare SMI and HI deductible and copayments for an estimated 18.5 percent of the enrollees. Changes in the
Medicare liability of those protected by Medicaid will result in corresponding changes in Medicaid payments. In addition, through buy-in
provisions of the Medicare Act, the SMI premium is paid by states
for persons receiving Medicaid assistance, and increases in the
premiums for SMI or HI will be reflected in the Medicaid budgets.
    Current tax policy also provides some degree of protection
against catastrophic medical expenditures. The medical deduction
provides an insurance plan that pays benefits equal to the marginal
tax rate on out-of-pocket expenses above 3 percent of adjusted gross
income. The deduction of one-half of health insurance premiums
subsidizes the purchase of private health insurance to protect against
large medical expenditures. The Medicare plans will affect the cost
of both these programs: changes in a patient's liability under Medi-

care affects the medical deduction because only out-of-pocket expenditures are deductible; changes in the Medicare premium or in the
amount of supplementary protection purchased will affect the premium
deduction. [14]

Under a premium-financed plan, the net effect of these indirect
changes is very small (see Table 5.2); however, under other tax-
financed plans, decreased Medicaid expenditures and the tax subsidies offset about 25 to 30 percent of the increased Medicare expenditures. Notice that the government expenditures for the ageds' health
care are reduced under plans that are financed by an increase in the
coinsurance rate for medical charges below the catastrophic limit.
Although Medicare payments are unchanged, the expenditures under
the other programs are smaller, in part because of the reduced demand for care and in part because a larger share of Medicaid beneficiaries' health-care costs are shifted to Medicare beneficiaries in
the form of higher copayments.

TABLE 5.2. Increase in Cost to Government for Medicare
Catastrophic Protection by Type of Plan
and Type of Financing
(in 1976 $ million)

Type of SMI Plan and Financing Method	Change in Medicare Program Cost	Change in Other Subsidy Costs*	Change in Total Budgetary Costs
Fixed cost-sharing limit			
Tax-financed	1084	-256	828
Premium-financed	1084	-3	1081
Increase in coinsurance	0	-70	-70
Increase in deductible	0	30	30
Income-related limit			
Tax-financed	1024	-311	713
Premium-financed	1024	-56	968
Increase in coinsurance	0	-172	-177
Increase in deductible	0	-76	-76

*Other subsidy costs include Medicaid and the federal tax
subsidies to medical expenditures and insurance premiums.
Source: Compiled by the author.

TABLE 5.3. Paasche Index of Expected Real Income Gain from Cost-Sharing Limit on Medicare by Type of Limit, Type of Financing, and Family Income (in 1976 $ per person)

Gross Family Income in 1976	Personal Income and Corporate Profits Tax	Payroll Tax	Premium	Coinsurance	Deductible
	Expected Increase with Fixed Cost-Sharing Limit				
$4,500 or less	18	18	-6	2	-6
$4,501-$11,000	20	21	-12	-1	-10
$11,001 or more	17	29	-3	7	-7
All enrollees	18	22	-8	3	-7
	Expected Increase with Income-Related Limit				
$4,500 or less	27	28	4	17	11
$4,501-$11,000	17	19	-13	-2	-16
$11,001 or more	1	10	-19	-17	-31
All enrollees	16	19	-9	1	-11

Source: Compiled by the author.

EXPECTED REAL INCOME GAINS

The effect of these program changes on the expected real income position of the aged and on the distribution of income changes among the aged is shown in Table 5.3. The measure presented is the Paasche index of real income change; it is the index of the change in the price of medical care, net of all subsidies, evaluated at the new quantities consumed, less the burden of the taxes.[15] As is well known, the Paasche Index overstates income gains and understates losses. Evaluating the price changes at the base-period quantities, a Laspeyres Index provides the lower-bound estimate of income gains and, thus, the two indices would bracket the real change. Elsewhere (Marquis 1979), I have presented both indices, and the differences between them are small.

The index of real income change is shown for persons in three income subgroups, which approximately correspond to income tertiles of the aged in 1976. The measure for each income subgroup is the average real income change over all levels of illness loss realized by persons in the subgroup. If the probability distribution of health losses is the same for all individuals within each income group, this measure is the expected real income change for a representative individual in the group.

Under tax-financed plans, beneficiaries are better off; there is a small net redistribution of income to Medicare enrollees from the rest of the population. If the plan is financed by premiums, however, the beneficiaries realize a net loss of income. As shown earlier, premiums paid by enrollees include the market cost of additional health-care purchases whereas the value that beneficiaries derive from these purchases is less than market cost because of the existing large subsidies to medical care.

Note that the beneficiaries' real income gain is positive for the plans financed by a change in the coinsurance. However, real income falls under plans financed by an increase in the deductible. This result is consistent with the earlier derivation and is dependent upon the assumed model of consumer behavior. It was shown that the effect on real income of providing catastrophic protection by increasing the cost sharing for front-end expenditures depends upon the relative size of the demand response to changes in the front-end expenditures and the catastrophic expenditure. If demand is more responsive to the increased front-end expenditure than to the catastrophic limit, real income rises. This is the model adopted for the coinsurance rate change.

On the other hand, it was assumed that an increase in the deductible does not affect behavior. As shown earlier, real income falls under a catastrophic plan financed by increases in the cost sharing for front-end expenditures if the demand responds to the limit but the demand response to the change in cost sharing is zero. The fall in real income under the deductible plans is thus expected on the basis of the theory.

A key feature of the tables is the small impact of the type of catastrophic benefit and the financing method on the distribution of expected income gains among income groups. The fixed-dollar plan favors the high-income enrollees, whereas income gains decrease with income under the income-tested plan. The differences in the two plans are surprisingly small, however, due in part to the sizeable role of other government programs in financing the health care of the aged poor. The method of financing also has little impact on the differences among subgroups in expected real income changes. Differences between the high-income group and other groups are smaller under the fixed-dollar benefit and increased under the income-related benefit if the method of financing is related to income (personal income and corporate profits taxes) or medical expenditures (coinsurance or deductible).

The indices of real income change understate the value of the catastrophic insurance to the extent that the consumer's welfare is increased from reduced risk. Quantifying the welfare gain from the risk avoided requires assumptions about the shape of the utility function. Quite divergent estimates of the value of the reduced risk from a catastrophic benefit are likely, depending upon whether the assumed utility function is characterized by constant or by decreasing risk aversion and the assumed degree of risk aversion. Little empirical research has been directed toward finding a parametric specification of the utility function that is consistent with observed behavior in the presence of uncertainty. If a specification of the utility function is absent, direct estimates of the utility gains from decreased risk will not be made. However, the approximate magnitude of the gain may be inferred from premiums paid for private insurance policies. The loading fees (that is, the premium charges for administration costs and risk bearing) for supplementary hospital policies average about 40 percent, and for companion medical policies the loading fee is about 10 percent.[16] For the enrollee who chooses to supplement the Medicare plan, the value of avoiding the loss he remains exposed to under Medicare is at least as high as the loading fee. However, 67 percent of enrollees do not purchase additional medical care coverage, and 42 percent do not supplement the Medicare hospital plan. For about half of the enrollees, then, the risk premium (expressed as a percentage of the actuarial value of the risk) is less than 10 percent for medical care and 40 percent for hospital care.[17] The observed loading fees can, therefore, be taken as a rough average of the risk premium for all enrollees. However, about 20 percent of

Medicare enrollees also receive Medicaid benefits, and there is no gain to them from shifting their protection from one public program to another. The value of the decreased risk of a catastrophic supplement is, therefore, about 30 percent of the catastrophic liability under the current Medicare benefits (the 80 percent of enrollees without Medicaid times the risk premium of 40 percent), or about $4; the gains in reduced risk from catastrophic medical protection are about 8 percent of the catastrophic liability, or about $1. These estimates suggest that adding gains from reduced risk would not substantially alter the conclusions based on the measure of expected change in real income. [18]

NET REALIZED GAINS FOR DIFFERENT HEALTH LOSSES

Although the choice of catastrophic benefit and the choice of financing have little effect on the expected real income of the aged, the postillness income distribution is substantially affected by these choices. Table 5.4 shows the actual real income changes for different health loss levels. The measures are presented for persons who do not have third-party financing to supplement their Medicare benefits. Those who have purchased additional insurance have averaged income losses or risk over all health loss states by the insurance purchase. Changes in the Medicare subsidy alter the average loss and income in each state of health loss by this average change. (Recall that it has been assumed that the Medicare coinsurance is supplemented to zero.)

This table presents the Paasche Index of realized net real income gains from the two prototype catastrophic plans combined with alternative financing mechanisms. The tax-financed plans are not shown in the tables. The tax-financed plans and the premium-financed plan differ in their average effect because of differences in the share of the burden borne by the beneficiaries. However, the difference between the tax and premium-financed plans is the same for different health losses.

Illness levels are measured by total physician expenditures under the current Medicare benefit provisions. The illness losses represented in the table assume no hospital expenses. Assuming no income elasticity of demand, the total expenditure represents the same illness loss for persons at each income level. The health loss represented by total physician expenditures of $250 has approximately a 25 percent probability of occurring. Under current provisions, only 25 percent of enrollees incur total medical expenditures of $250. The second illness level in Table 5.4 ($1,100 expenditures)

TABLE 5.4. Paasche Index of Realized Net Income Gains from
Medicare Catastrophic Protection by Type of Plan,
Family Income, and Illness Loss—Enrollees
Without Supplementary Insurance
(in 1976 $ per person)

Gross Family Income and Illness Loss	Realized Gain with Fixed Cost–Sharing Limit		
	Premium	Coinsurance Increased	Deductible Increased
$4,500 or less income			
$250 physician charges	−43	−22	−72
$1,100 physician charges	6	25	49
$2,500 physician charges	325	315	368
$4,501–$11,000 income			
$250 physician charges	−39	−20	−69
$1,100 physician charges	−3	22	42
$2,500 physician charges	277	271	316
$11,001 or more income			
$250 physician charges	−36	−21	−72
$1,100 physician charges	12	26	48
$2,500 physician charges	307	316	343
	Realized Gain with Income–Related Limit		
$4,500 or less income			
$250 physician charges	−30	−5	−27
$1,100 physician charges	121	142	161
$2,500 physician charges	437	436	479
$4,501–$11,000 income			
$250 physician charges	−39	−17	−69
$1,100 physician charges	−30	−36	−14
$2,500 physician charges	197	198	244
$11,001 or more income			
$250 physician charges	−37	−15	−70
$1,100 physician charges	−37	−102	−70
$2,500 physician charges	−36	−170	−51

Note: Illness loss is measured as physician charges under the
current Medicare provisions, assuming no hospital expenses are
incurred for the illness.
Source: Compiled by the author.

occurs with 5 percent probability, while the highest loss in the table occurs less than 1.5 percent of the time.

As expected, the tables show a small net income loss realized by persons with minor illnesses but very large income gains for persons with catastrophic illnesses.

The real difference between the two prototypes is clearly seen in this table. For most people, those with a minor illness loss, the two plans have a small nearly equivalent effect. The effect on most people does not vary by income group. However, under the income-related prototype, the gains to high-income persons at large levels of illness loss are much smaller than the gains to low-income persons, whereas the real income changes under the fixed-dollar plans are similar across income groups. This, of course, is the effect the plans were designed to have.

An interesting feature of the tables is a comparison of the effect of different methods of financing the plans on persons who have high, but not "catastrophic" illnesses.[19] For example, comparing the real income change for high-income families from the income-related plan, it can be seen that the loss increases with the level of health loss if the plan is financed by an increase in the co-insurance. Under the other two financing methods, however, the changes in real income across noncatastrophic health loss states is quite constant within income groups. Small differences appear, which reflect the effect of the tax subsidy to medical expenditures.

The greater risk at high noncatastrophic losses under the coinsurance-financed plans relative to the premium or deductible methods of financing contrasts with the earlier comparison of the changes in average real income. Average real income falls under the deductible or premium-financed plans but is unchanged or increased if the catastrophic plan is financed by an increase in coinsurance. This contrast illustrates a basic dilemma in the choice of a public insurance plan. The increase in the coinsurance rate restores incentives in purchase decisions, moral hazard falls, and expected real income under the catastrophic plans increases. Under the premium or deductible plans, however, demand increases in response to the limit and the amount of the premium or deductible required to finance the limit is greater than the expected value of the additional quantities; thus, real income falls. This fall in income is equally shared across noncatastrophic health states. In contrast, under the coinsurance-financed plan there are increasing real income losses in noncatastrophic health states. The expected gains in income and reduced risk for catastrophic illnesses are positive under the coinsurance-financed plan. However, there are risk increases in noncatastrophic states, which increase with the size of the loss. The contrast between the expected gains but unequal changes in risk for the coinsurance plan and the expected, but shared loss, for the other plans illustrates the trade-off between appropriate incentives and risk sharing that must be faced in designing a public insurance plan (Zeckhauser 1970).

NOTES

1. Estimate based on data from the 1971 Health Survey of the Center for Health Administration Studies. The survey is described in Andersen et al. (1972).

2. Estimates are based on expenditure distributions that are described later.

3. This model extends Arrow's (1976) study of the welfare effects of changes in the coinsurance rate by considering a two-parameter insurance policy.

4. The development follows Phelps (1973) and Phelps and Newhouse (1974).

5. Elsewhere, I have estimated the effect of adding a catastrophic Medicare benefit under conditions of inelastic medical care supply. However, the estimated change in the market price of medical care was less than 1 percent and, hence, the impact on economic welfare can be accurately assessed without considering supply response.

6. A model that incorporates sequential behavior in medical purchase decisions has been developed as a dynamic programming problem by Keeler, Newhouse, and Phelps (1977).

7. See Phelps and Newhouse (1974) and Ginsburg and Manheim (1973).

8. The probability of using services is assumed to be independent of the insurance policy.

9. Davis and Russell (1972) find a positive relationship between the price of inpatient hospital care and outpatient hospital visits; Helms, Newhouse, and Phelps (1978) reported that an increase in the own price of physician care increased demand for hospital inpatient services in a welfare population. However, Newhouse and Phelps (1976) find results consistent with the hypothesis that medical care and hospital care are complements. Lewis and Keaines (1970) and Hill and Veney (1970) find the cross-price effect to be zero.

10. Data from the 1969 Current Medicare Survey (Peel and Scharff 1973) and unpublished data from the 1974 Current Medicare Survey were used in deriving the distributions.

11. Based upon unpublished data provided by the Social Security Administration about discharges among beneficiaries in 1973.

12. Cost sharing refers to statutory liability under the Medicare plan and not actual out-of-pocket expenditures.

13. The additional payroll tax estimate assumes an increase in taxes or qualified wages but no change in the maximum wage subject to tax; a uniform percentage increase in the personal income and corporate profits tax rates is assumed. Estimated tax increases are based on total tax receipts in the 1976 and 1977 United States Budget (Office of Management and Budget 1975 and 1976). The estimated increase in the coinsurance assumes that persons with private insurance continue to supplement the Medicare coinsurance to zero (there is no change in the effective price of care). The change in the coinsurance or deductible that will maintain the base-period actuarial value of the plan is obtained by an iterative procedure simulating demand and Medicare benefits under alternative benefit structures that combine various increases in the coinsurance or deductible with the catastrophic limit until the estimated Medicare payments under the new benefit structure equal current payments.

14. The change in tax subsidy due to the medical deduction assumes that the change in the amount deducted is the difference between out-of-pocket expenditures for SMI services (or hospital care) in excess of 3 percent of adjusted gross income under the current benefit structure and those under the new structure. The calculation underestimates the change in the subsidy to the extent that expenditures for other services and by other family members contribute to the "deductible" of 3 percent of family income. On the other hand, all individuals with out-of-pocket expenditures in excess of the "deductible" are assumed to itemize and, on this account, the estimated charge is overstated. Similarly, the premium deduction is assumed to be taken by all persons, which may overstate the charge. However, it neglects the additional insurance premium deduction available to persons with large medical expenses. Details of the estimation of changes in these subsidies is available in Marquis (1979).

15. The assumptions made regarding the incidence of the taxes are that the payroll tax is borne by labor, the personal income tax is borne by the person upon whom it is levied, and the corporation tax is borne by property owners as a whole. Decreases (increases) in Medicaid or the tax subsidies are assumed to result in corresponding decreases (increases) in personal income and corporate profits taxes. Details of the calculations of the tax burdens are in Marquis (1979).

16. Based on data in Mueller and Piro (1976).

17. The observed loading fees may overstate the risk premium because the tax subsidy to insurance purchases, which decreases the effective price the individual pays, is not deducted. On the other

hand, assuming that the marginal value of insurance decreases as the remaining risk decreases, the risk premium for catastrophic coverage relative to the actuarial value of catastrophic expenditures may exceed the loading fee. These two considerations work in opposite directions.

18. However, observed behavior in purchasing insurance may underestimate the value the individual would be willing to pay for reduced risk if decisions are made without information about the true probability of the catastrophic event, the cost of the catastrophic event, or the cost of insurance.

19. "Catastrophic" is defined as the Medicare limit on cost sharing.

REFERENCES

Andersen, Ronald, Rachel McL. Greeley, Joanna Kravits, and Odin W. Anderson. 1972. Health Service Use: National Trends and Variations. DHEW Publication No. (HSM) 73-3004. Washington, D.C.: Government Printing Office.

Arrow, Kenneth. 1976. "Welfare Analysis of Changes in Health Coinsurance Rates." In Richard N. Rosett (ed.), The Role of Health Insurance in the Health Services Sector, pp. 3-23. New York: National Bureau of Economic Research.

Davis, Karen, and Louise B. Russell. 1972. "The Substitution of Hospital Outpatient Care for Inpatient Care." Review of Economics and Statistics, 54, 2 (May 1972), pp. 109-20.

Ginsburg, Paul B., and Larry M. Manheim. 1973. "Insurance, Copayment and Health Services Utilization: A Critical Review." Journal of Economics and Business Bulletin, 25 (Winter 1973), pp. 142-53.

Helms, L. Jay, Joseph P. Newhouse, and Charles E. Phelps. 1978. Copayments and the Demand for Medical Care: The California Medicaid Experience. The Rand Corporation, R-2167-HEW (February 1978).

Hill, D. B., and J. E. Veney. 1970. "Kansas Blue Cross/Blue Shield Outpatient Benefits Experiment." Medical Care, 8 (March/April 1970), pp. 143-58.

Keeler, Emmett B., Joseph P. Newhouse, and Charles E. Phelps.

1977. "Deductibles and the Demand for Medical Services: The Theory of the Consumer Facing a Variable Price Schedule Under Uncertainty." Econometrica, 45, 3 (April 1977), pp. 641-55.

Keeler, Emmett B., Daniel Relles, and John E. Rolph. 1975. The Choice Between Family and Industrial Deductibles in Health Insurance. The Rand Corporation, R-1393 -HEW (October 1975).

Lewis, C. E., and H. Keains. 1970. "Controlling Costs of Medical Care by Expanding Insurance Coverage." New England Journal of Medicine, 282 (June 18, 1970), pp. 1405-12.

Marquis, M. Susan. 1979. The Costs, Financing and Distributional Effects of a Catastrophic Supplement to Medicare. The Rand Corporation, R-2431-HEW (August 1979).

Mueller, Marjorie Smith, and Paula A. Piro. 1976. "Private Health Insurance in 1974: A Review of Coverage, Enrollment, and Financial Experience." Social Security Bulletin, 39, 3, pp. 3-20.

Newhouse, Joseph P., and Charles E. Phelps. 1976. "New Estimates of Price and Income Elasticities of Medical Care Services." In Richard N. Rosett (ed.), The Role of Health Insurance in the Health Services Sector. New York: National Bureau of Economic Research, pp. 261-313.

Newhouse, Joseph P., Charles E. Phelps, and W. B. Schwartz. 1974. "Policy Options and the Impacts of National Health Insurance." New England Journal of Medicine, 290, pp. 1345-59.

Peel, Evelyn, and Jack Scharff. 1973. "Impact of Cost Sharing on Use of Ambulatory Services Under Medicare, 1969." Social Security Bulletin, B6, 10 (October 1973), pp. 3-25.

Phelps, Charles E. 1973. Demand for Health Insurance: A Theoretical and Empirical Investigation. The Rand Corporation, R-1054-OEO (July 1973).

Phelps, Charles E., and Joseph P. Newhouse, 1974. "Coinsurance, The Price of Time, and the Demand for Medical Services." Review of Economics and Statistics, 56, 3 (August 1974), pp. 334-42.

U.S., Office of Management and Budget. 1976. The Budget of the United States Government, Fiscal Year 1977. Washington, D.C.: Government Printing Office.

_____. 1975. The Budget of the United States Government, Fiscal Year 1976. Washington, D.C.: Government Printing Office.

U.S. Bureau of the Census. Current Population Reports, 1975, 1977.

Zeckhauser, Richard. 1970. "Medical Insurance: A Case Study of the Tradeoff Between Risk Spreading and Applied Incentives." Journal of Economic Theory, 2 (March 1970), pp. 10-26.

6

A DOMINANT BUYER
IN A MIXED INDUSTRY:
THE ROLE OF MEDICAID IN
THE LONG-TERM CARE MARKET

Paul J. Gertler
Ralph L. Andreano

The rapid rate of inflation in the health-care sector, and particularly in the nursing home industry, has been well documented. In fact, the price of nursing home care increased 44 percent from 1973 to 1977. Further, total nursing home expenditures have increased an average of 17 percent annually over the last 30 years, from approximately 19 million dollars in 1950 to 17.8 billion dollars in 1979 (U.S., Department of Health and Human Services 1980). Health care regulators have the task of controlling inflation while simultaneously promoting access and maintaining a high standard of quality. This task is complicated because the nursing home industry is comprised of a mixture of 3 types of firms: 61 percent are proprietary, 34 percent are nonprofit, and 5 percent are government run (U.S., Department of Health and Human Services 1980). Each type of home potentially exhibits a different type of behavior and a different reaction to government intervention. Further, the industry has two types of consumers: private pay and government subsidized. The government is the dominant buyer in the market of nursing home services. In 1977, through Medicaid, Medicare, and other smaller programs, the government purchased approximately 62 percent of all nonprofit nursing home services and 60 percent of all proprietary nursing home services (U.S., Department of Health and Human Services 1980). The purpose of this chapter is to analyze how the government's dominant buying power affects profit and nonprofit behavior in terms of price, quality, and access for private-pay and government-subsidized patients. At issue is: what does the government

---

The authors are indebted to Charles Wilson, Henry McMillan, and Richard Clarke for helpful comments. Any remaining errors are the authors' responsibility.

get when it tries to purchase more services by raising the Medicaid (public-pay) reimbursement rate?

In the middle 1960s, the government established the Medicaid subsidization program. Through direct subsidies, the Medicaid program makes health care available to individuals who could not otherwise afford it. The government reimburses a nursing home a fixed amount for the care of each Medicaid patient in two ways: flat-fee and actual cost-of-care based. As would be expected, there is much controversy over the determination of the reimbursement rates. While regulators are concerned about fueling inflation and the total size of the Medicaid expenditure, nursing home administrators have complained that, historically, the rates are too low. They argue that a low reimbursement rate will not allow them to maintain a standard of quality of care that the government insists homes must have. Moreover, they say that low rates force them to limit the number of Medicaid patients they are able to accept and to charge private-pay patients more in order to make up revenue deficiencies.

Previous analytic work on how the Medicaid program affects nursing home behavior is limited. Holahan and Ehamenn (1975) developed a model of supply and demand. They identified the role of Medicaid in increasing demand for nursing home care by heavily subsidizing purchases of care. Scanlon (1980) points out that this creates persistent excess demand and, therefore, is an incentive for expansion of capacity. He uses a discriminating monopolist model to describe equilibrium, given the Medicaid reimbursement rate. Neither model (Scanlon or Holahan and Ehamenn) links the level of quality of care to the reimbursement rate, nor do they consider how changes in the rate affect behavior. Moreover, they do not integrate Certificate of Need (CON) regulations, which aim to restrict the total capacity of each nursing home.

In the second section of this chapter, we develop a model of demand for nursing home care that incorporates a precise notion of quality. An individual chooses to enter a nursing home if the maximum utility derived from independent living is less than the utility from nursing home living and the individual can afford the nursing home option. The lower an individual's health status, the more likely the person is to enter a nursing home. A nursing home's quality is dependent upon the quantity and intensity of services provided to each individual. Since individuals are distributed over income levels and health status, private-pay demand is increasing in quality and decreasing in price. We assume that there are sufficient numbers of Medicaid eligibles such that they could more than fill existing capacity. Currently, nursing homes have an average capacity of 95 percent, and there are long waiting lists for many homes. Consequently, Medicaid demand is perfectly elastic at the prevailing Medicaid reimbursement rate.

The third section of the chapter analyzes the proprietary nursing home. In our model, quality is endogenous, and a CON capacity constraint is imposed. The proprietary nursing home is just a special case of the discriminating monopolist, for which one price is fixed and the other endogenous. The major results of this section concern the question of how the nursing home responds to changes in government behavior. Unless there are large decreases in the marginal valuation of quality, an increase in the Medicaid reimbursement rate will lower quality, decrease the number of private-pay patients, and increase the number of Medicaid patients. Further, the price charged private-pay patients will rise unless there is a large increase in the price elasticity of demand. This follows from the fact that such an increase provides incentives to substitute private-pay patients with public-pay patients. The substitution is achieved by increasing price and lowering quality.

We next consider the nonprofit nursing home. The nonprofit nursing home is assumed to maximize utility over the total number of patients and quality, subject to a zero profit constraint. If the CON constraint is binding, an increase in the Medicaid reimbursement rate will increase quality, increase the number of private-pay patients, and decrease the number of Medicaid patients unless the marginal valuation of quality falls drastically. The whole increase in revenue is used to increase quality because the CON capacity constraint restricts quantity. The increase in quality attracts more private-pay patients. The home then substitutes private pay for Medicaid patients.

In the last section, we consider the welfare aspects of nursing home behavior by comparing the profit and nonprofit solutions to a social optimum, where the social optimum is defined as the solution to the consumer surplus maximization problem. We show that both types of homes set their private-pay price too high. Further, both types of homes deviate from the socially optimal level of quality and relative numbers of private-pay and Medicaid patients. Moreover, we show that adjustments in the Medicaid reimbursement rate do not move us closer to the social optimum in several important variables, such as quality, private-pay price, and the ratio of public- to private-pay patients. The consumer surplus welfare criteria are also used to determine the net change in benefit to private and Medicaid patients from an increase in the Medicaid reimbursement rate. In both cases, we observe that changes in quantity and quality affect patients' net benefits and that the effects do not necessarily move in the same direction. Finally, we show that an increase in the Medicaid reimbursement rate may cause the total cost of the Medicaid program to decrease in the nonprofit world.

THE DEMAND FOR NURSING HOME CARE

Unlike acute care, nursing home care is essentially assistance in the performance of normal living activities. Acute care is aimed at curing illness and helping individuals to recover from incapacitating conditions. Very little curing and rehabilitation occurs in nursing homes. At best, nursing home services restore partial functioning in some areas of activity but generally not enough to allow independent living. In fact, the vast majority of people who enter nursing homes seldom leave the health-care system before death.[1]

Nursing homes provide a fixed package of goods and services to their patients such as food, shelter, nursing care, and social services, all of which could be obtained independently in the private marketplace. The individual then has the choice of purchasing the nursing home package or buying the most pleasing combination of goods and services from the marketplace. Given their budget constraints, elderly individuals with deteriorating health and severely handicapped persons might prefer the nursing home option. Not only are all of their special needs met in one place, but the process of obtaining and consuming goods and services is assisted by nursing home personnel. Consequently, the amount of the individual's own time and effort required to meet daily living needs is reduced in a nursing home setting. For the elderly and handicapped, the increased leisure time may be very important to the quality of their lives.

Another potential gain is that nursing homes specialize in meeting the needs of the elderly and handicapped. The nursing home's social, medical, and other services are geared toward serving these people. Moreover, the nursing home is able to use its expertise and scale to combine these goods and services in a more optimal way than are these types of individuals independently. The nursing home removes administrative, financial, and budgeting responsibilities from the patient, and it is able to make bulk purchases. Further, it has expert medical, social and other personnel who provide specialized services routinely and quickly in emergencies. An individual on his own would have to find, purchase, and arrange the timing of the services by himself or through some community social service agency. Due to imperfections in the marketplace, many of the highly specialized services may not be available; if they are available, they are likely to be quite expensive and not eligible for Medicaid or Medicare reimbursement.

The individual is concerned with the return in terms of meeting personal needs from the nursing home's package of goods and services. A higher quality nursing home provides more services at a greater level of service intensity and combines and processes those services in a more efficient manner than will a lower quality nursing home.

The higher the quality of nursing home care, the greater the return to the individual per unit time and effort.

Individuals will enter nursing homes if they feel the life lived there will be better than if lived independently.[2] The poorer an individual's health, the more likely is entry to a nursing home. As health status declines, the greater the need for the special types of services supplied by nursing homes. These specialized services are likely to cost less in a nursing home than in the marketplace, whereas routine services such as food service and shelter are likely to cost more. Hence, another important factor is the relative price of nursing home life to independent living. Moreover, an individual's income and assets determine if the nursing home option is affordable. The existence of subsidy programs, such as Medicare and Medicaid, mitigate the restrictiveness of this feasibility criterion. Finally, the quality of nursing home care available influences individual decisions. The higher the quality of nursing home care available, the more attractive the nursing home option appears, relative to independent living.

We shall now formalize the above discussion in order to make precise predictions about the demand for nursing home care.[3] We begin by assuming that a typical individual has a utility function defined over an aggregate consumption good and leisure. The consumption good is the embodiment of all basic needs and desires except leisure. Consumption is produced from market goods and effort (time) through a household production function. The individual is assumed to have no labor market possibilities. All per period disposable wealth is unearned and fixed.[4]

Specifically, the individual is assumed to choose the quantities of n market goods and the amount of time used for consumption production so as to solve the following problem:[5]

$$\max_{\substack{G_i, T \\ i=1,\ldots,n}} U[C, L]$$

subject to:

$$C = C[G_1, \ldots, G_n; T] \tag{1}$$

$$L = T^A - T \tag{1.1}$$

$$T^A = h(H) \tag{1.2}$$

$$W = \sum_{i=1}^{n} P_i G_i \tag{1.3}$$

where

> $U(\cdot)$ is the individual's utility function
> C is the aggregate consumption good
> L is leisure
> $C(\cdot)$ is the household production function that produces consumption
> G_i is the quantity of market good i
> T is the quantity of time used in producing C
> L is the quantity of leisure
> T^A is total time available for leisure and consumption
> $h(\cdot)$ is the function that converts the individual's stock of health into available time
> H is the individual's stock of health
> P_i is the price of market good i
> W is the individual's endowment of wealth

The utility function is assumed to be increasing, twice continuously differentiable, and concave in both arguments. The first constraint is the aggregate consumption good production function. We assume that in order to gain utility from raw market goods, one must devote time and effort into processing those goods (for example, cooking food). The consumption production function maps market goods and time into consumption space. It gives the maximum amount of consumption attainable from any combination of market goods and time. We assume that the consumption production function is increasing, twice continuously differentiable, and concave in all arguments. The consumption production function may vary by individual. The weights used to aggregate the market goods depend upon the individual's tastes and preferences. For example, the consumption production function of an individual who prefers tea to coffee will exhibit a higher marginal product for tea relative to coffee, whereas a person who prefers coffee would have the opposite relationship.

The second constraint says that leisure equals the time left over after consumption production. Constraint (1.3) maps the individual's stock of health into total time available. We assume that $h(\cdot)$ is increasing in H. The poorer an individual's health, the more time required for rest and recuperation, implying that there will be less time available for leisure and production consumption. Constraint (1.4) is just the budget constraint.

We can describe the optimal solution to the individual's problem in (1) by the following conditions:

$$\frac{U_C C_{G_i}}{U_C C_{G_j}} = \frac{P_i}{P_j} \qquad \text{for all i and j} \qquad (2.1)$$

$$\frac{U_L}{U_C} = C_T \qquad (2.2)$$

$$\sum_{i=1}^{n} P_i G_i = W \qquad (2.3)$$

where:

$$U_C = \frac{\partial U}{\partial C}, \text{ etc.}$$

Condition (2.1) sets the ratio of the marginal utility of market good i to market good j equal to the ratio of their respective prices. The marginal utility of market good i equals the marginal utility of consumption times the marginal product of good i in producing consumption. Condition (2.2) equates the marginal product of time in the production of consumption to the marginal rate of substitution of leisure for consumption. Finally, condition (2.3) says that the total amount of money spent on all market goods must equal available wealth. [6]

The decision as to how much wealth to spend on each market good is independent of the time allocation question. [7] From (2.1) and (2.3), we see that the amount of wealth spent on good i is a function of the relative marginal products of $G_1, \ldots, G_n$ and their relative prices. The solution is depicted in Figure 6.1, in the two-market-good case. The point (G_1^*, G_2^*) is the point at which the slope of the budget constraint is tangent to the slope of the indifference curve in the market good space and, hence, is the point where utility is maximized conditional on leisure. From (2.2) we see that the optimal amount of leisure depends upon the marginal productivity of time in the production of consumption. This solution is presented in Figure 6.2. Given $(G_1^*, \ldots, G_n^*)$, the more time spent in the production of consumption, the greater the amount of consumption produced. Hence, by choosing a certain amount of leisure, the individual implicitly chooses the consumption level. The optimal amount (C^*, L^*) is given by the tangency of the time budget constraint and the indifference curve in consumption-leisure space. The points $(G_1^*, \ldots, G_n^*)$ and (C^*, L^*) fully describe the values that maximize the individual's problem as expressed in (1). When they are inserted into the utility

FIGURE 6.1

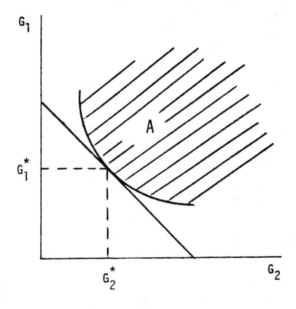

FIGURE 6.2

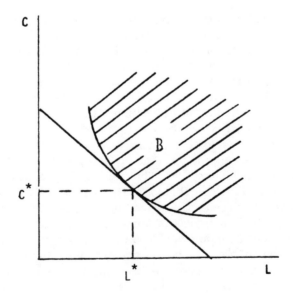

function, we get the maximum attainable utility available to the individual through independent living.

We can, in a similar way, describe the amount of utility the individual would gain from living in a nursing home. The nursing home provides a fixed package of goods and services $(G_1^{NH}, \ldots, G_n^{NH})$. Therefore, the individual problem reduces to choosing the amount of leisure that maximizes utility.

$$\max_T U[C, L] \tag{3}$$

subject to:

$$C = C^{NH}[G_1^{NH}, \ldots, G_n^{NH}; T] \tag{3.1}$$

$$L = T^A - T \tag{3.2}$$

$$P^{NH} \leq W \tag{3.3}$$

Constraint (3.3) is the feasibility requirement that the individual be able to purchase the nursing home package.[8] The consumption production function, $C^{NH}(\cdot)$, under the nursing home option, differs from the one under independent living because of the nursing home's ability to specialize and the assistance by the nursing home's personnel in helping the individual process and consume the market goods.

One nursing home may have higher quality than another because its patients can produce more consumption with the same amount of $G_1, \ldots, G_n$ and T. The consumption production function of the superior quality nursing home will have greater marginal products for some of the market goods because it is better able to exploit its economies of specialization in geriatric medical and social care. Further, the marginal product of time will be higher because the superior nursing home's personnel are better at helping the individual with processing and actual consumption activities. One nursing home may have superior quality because it provides the market goods, $G_1, \ldots, G_n$, in greater quantities, holding constant the consumption production technology.

The solution to (3) is given by (3.3) and

$$\frac{U_L}{U_C} = C_T^{NH} \tag{4}$$

which is similar to (2.2) under the independent living option. The individual spends time in consumption production up to the point where the marginal product of time equals the ratio of the marginal utility of leisure to consumption. From (4) we get T^{NH}. Then from (3.1) and (3.2) we get C^{NH} and L^{NH}.

The individual will enter the nursing home if the maximum utility from the nursing home package exceeds the maximum utility from independent living:[9]

$$X = \begin{cases} 1, \text{ living in nursing home if } U[C^{NH}, L^{NH}] > U[C^*, L^*] \\ \quad \text{and } p^{NH} \leq W \\ \\ 0, \text{ living independently otherwise} \end{cases} \quad (5)$$

Equivalently, the individual will enter a nursing home if (3) gives a solution that is in region A in Figure 6.1 and region B in Figure 6.2, and it is feasible.

The higher the quality of available nursing home services, the greater the probability that an individual would choose to enter a nursing home holding prices constant. The higher the quality of care, the more consumption is returned to the individual per dollar spent. Moreover, the consumption per unit time invested is greater, implying more time available for leisure. Hence, the higher the quality of care available the more likely the nursing home package will be in regions A and B in Figures 6.1 and 6.2, respectively.

Suppose an individual experiences a decline in the level of his health stock. The total time available for leisure and consumption production has diminished. This is analogous to a decline in wealth. Therefore, if both goods are normal, the optimal levels of both leisure and consumption decline. In Figure 6.2, the decline in available time shifts the time budget constraint toward the origin and increases its slope (see Appendix A). The decline in health moves the individual from point E to point F in Figure 6.3, the effect of which is to increase the area of region B in Figure 6.2. Since there are no changes in prices, all nursing home options that were feasible before the change in health are still feasible. Hence, the feasible area of region B has also increased. Moreover, region A in Figure 6.1 has been unaffected. The decline in health increases the probability that a nursing home package exists that is jointly in the feasible regions of A and B. Therefore, a decline in the stock of health increases the probability that an individual will enter a nursing home.

Consider the role of Medicaid. If an individual whose wealth endowment is so low that no nursing home package in regions A and B is feasible and if there is no subsidy, that person will be forced to live independently. However, if the individual's health stock is below

FIGURE 6.3

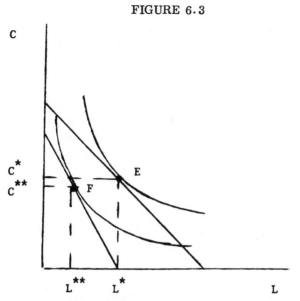

some prespecified level and the income (assets) is below another governmentally prespecified level, then that person is eligible for subsidies from the Medicaid program. Medicaid will pay the difference between the individual's income and the price of nursing home care. The existence of Medicaid makes any nursing home package feasible to eligible individuals. The feasibility requirement, $p^{NH} \leq W$, is no longer binding for Medicaid eligibles. Consequently, for Medicaid eligibles the choice in (5) is only a function of health status and available quantity.

THE PROPRIETARY NURSING HOME

The demand for nursing home services can be decomposed into the demand from Medicaid-subsidized individuals and the demand from private-pay individuals. As was discussed earlier, the private-pay demand is an increasing function of quality and a decreasing function of price. The Medicaid subsidized demand is solely a function of quality. If quality is above a certain point, a Medicaid eligible individual will always choose to enter a nursing home. The government sets minimum quality standards. We shall assume that the standard is set at a point such that Medicaid demand is essentially infinite.[10] Since the government reimburses the nursing home a predetermined amount for the care of each Medicaid patient per day, the number of Medicaid subsidized patients in a nursing home is equal to the number the home is willing to take at that fixed rate.

Nursing homes are not able to expand their scale of operation at will. Increasing the Medicaid reimbursement rate can be shown to be an incentive for nursing homes to expand capacity. Nursing homes were able to respond to this incentive until the mid-1970s when Certificate of Need (CON) regulation was passed into law in many states. Nursing homes then required a Certificate of Need for expansion from government before being able to increase capacity.[11] In essence, CON limits the number of total patients in a nursing home to a fixed amount. Because of excess demand from Medicaid-subsidized patients, we assume that the nursing home operates at full capacity.[12]

The nursing home has four variables with which it maximizes profit. It chooses the number of private-pay patients and the quality of care directly. The price paid by private-pay patients is determined implicitly through the demand function, and the number of Medicaid patients is determined by the CON capacity constraint. Formally, the proprietary nursing home solves the following profit maximization problem:

$$\max_{X, X^m, Q} \Pi(X, X^m, Q; P^m) = PX + P^m X^m - C \qquad (6)$$

subject to:

$$P = P(X, Q) \qquad (6.1)$$

$$C = C(\tilde{X}, Q) \qquad (6.2)$$

$$\tilde{X} = X + X^m \qquad (6.3)$$

$$P^m = \bar{P}^m \qquad (6.4)$$

$$Q \geq \bar{Q} \qquad (6.5)$$

$$\tilde{X} = \bar{X} \qquad (6.6)$$

where:

$\Pi(\cdot)$ is the profit function
$P(\cdot)$ is the inverse demand function
$C(\cdot)$ is the cost function
X is the number of private-pay patients
X^m is the number of Medicaid patients
Q is the level of quality
P is the price charged to the private-pay patients

$\bar{P}^m$ is the Medicaid reimbursement rate
$\tilde{X}$ is the total number of patients in the nursing home
C is the total cost of providing care of quality Q to $\tilde{X}$ patients
Q is the minimum quality level required by the government
$\bar{X}$ is the total number of patients allowed in the home, as specified by the CON regulatory authority

The inverse demand function gives the price X private-pay individuals are willing to pay for nursing home care at quality level Q. It is assumed to be increasing in quality, decreasing in quantity, and twice continuously differentiable in both. The cost function gives the minimum cost of providing care to $\tilde{X}$ total patients at quality level Q. It is assumed to be increasing, twice continuously differentiable, and convex in both quantity and quality. The convexity assumption rules out increasing returns to scale. Constraint (6.3) says that all patients in the nursing home must be private pay or Medicaid.[13] The last three constraints describe the forms of government control over the nursing home. Condition (6.4) says that the Medicaid reimbursement rate is exogenously fixed by the government, (6.5) says that the nursing home must operate at a quality level greater than $\bar{Q}$, and (6.6) says that the nursing home can have, at most, $\bar{X}$ total patients. The behavioral conditions that solve (6) are:

$$P\left(1 - \frac{1}{\eta}\right) = \bar{P}^m \tag{7.1}$$

$$P_Q X = C_Q \tag{7.2}$$

$$X^m = \bar{X} - X \tag{7.3}$$

where

$$\eta = \frac{\partial X}{\partial P} \frac{P}{X}, \text{ the price elasticity of private-pay demand}$$

These profit maximizing conditions have straightforward interpretations. The nursing home admits private-pay patients until marginal revenue from their admission equals the Medicaid reimbursement rate (which is the marginal revenue from Medicaid patient admission), holding quality constant. This is a profit-maximizing condition for a discriminating monopolist. The home chooses a quality level such that the marginal revenue of quality equals the marginal cost of quality, holding the total quantity of patients constant. Since Medicaid demand is perfectly elastic for both price and quality, only the marginal revenues of private-pay patients are important in (7.1)

FIGURE 6.4. The Proprietary Nursing Home Equilibrium

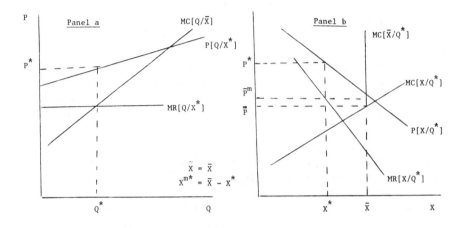

and (7.2). Finally, the home's profit-maximizing number of Medicaid patients is capacity less the number of private-pay patients.

Equilibrium as described in (7) is presented in Figure 6.4. Panel a represents the part of the solution that is in price-quality space. Note that the marginal cost of quality depends on total quantity of patients. Therefore, there are many marginal cost-of-quality curves in price-quality space, one for each level of total quantity. Since the total number of patients is fixed at $\bar{X}$ by the government, the marginal cost-of-quality curve is stationary at $MC(Q/\bar{X})$. Similarly, the private-pay demand curve in price-quality space depends upon private-pay quantity. The greater the private-pay quantity, the higher the demand price at each level of quality. The slope of the marginal revenue-of-quality curve depends only upon the second derivative of the demand function with respect to quality. For the sake of exposition we assume it to be zero, implying a flat marginal revenue-of-quality curve. Given the optimal private-pay quantity X^*, the optimal quality Q^* and equilibrium private-pay price P^* are determined by the intersection of the marginal revenue from private-pay patients and the marginal cost of total quantity curves in panel a (condition 7.2).

Similarly, the part of the equilibrium solution that is in price-quantity space is presented in panel b. Both the marginal cost-of-quantity curve and private-pay demand curve in price-quantity space depend upon the level of quality. The marginal cost-of-quantity curve becomes vertical at $\bar{X}$. Given the optimal level of quality, we can solve for the optimal values of the other variables. The total number of patients in the nursing home $\tilde{X}^*$ is defined exogenously by the CON constraint (condition 7.3). The number of private pay patients, X^*, and the price they pay are given at the intersection of $\bar{P}^m$ and marginal revenue (condition 7.1). The optimal number of Medicaid patients, X^{m*}, is the difference between $\bar{X}^*$ and X^*.

In panel b the private-pay price is higher than the Medicaid reimbursement rate. In fact, the proprietary nursing home will always set the private-pay price higher than the Medicaid reimbursement rate if the elasticity of private-pay demand is not infinite. Moreover, the magnitude of the difference depends on the elasticity of demand. The less elastic is demand, the greater the difference. We can see this in two ways. By rearranging (7.1) we can express private-pay price as a function of the price elasticity of demand and the Medicaid reimbursement rate:

$$P^* = \left(\frac{\eta}{\eta-1}\right) \bar{P}^m \qquad (8)$$

Since $\eta > 1$ (otherwise P^* would be nonpositive), P^* will always be greater than $\bar{P}^m$. The bigger is η, the closer P^* is to $\bar{P}^m$. Second, in panel b of Figure 6.4, P^* is read off the demand curve at the point where $\bar{P}^m$ equals marginal revenue. Since the demand curve lies everywhere above the marginal revenue curve, except when demand is perfectly elastic, P^* will always be greater than $\bar{P}^m$. Further, the steeper the demand curve, the greater the difference. The nursing home's differential pricing, based on elasticity of demand, is just a special case of the discriminating monopolist model.

From (7) it is clear that the optimal values of the choice variables are dependent upon the government's selection of the Medicaid reimbursement rate. Suppose the government increased the Medicaid reimbursement rate. In Appendix B we show formally that an increase in the Medicaid reimbursement rate causes the nursing home to:

1. Decrease the number of private-pay patients.
2. Decrease the quality of care unless P_{QX} is negative and very large.
3. Increase the number of Medicaid patients.

The partial P_Q is the marginal valuation of quality.[14] It tells how much more an individual on the margin is willing to pay for an epsilon more quality. If P_{QX} is negative, then the marginal valuation of quality falls, and the greater the number of nursing home patients. Then, the more patients a nursing home takes, the less the individual on the margin is willing to pay for an epsilon more quality. The term P_{QX} is also the change in P_Q as we move down the demand curve where individuals are ordered by willingness to pay. It is the change

FIGURE 6.5. The Proprietary Nursing Home: Increase in P^m when $P_{QX} = 0$

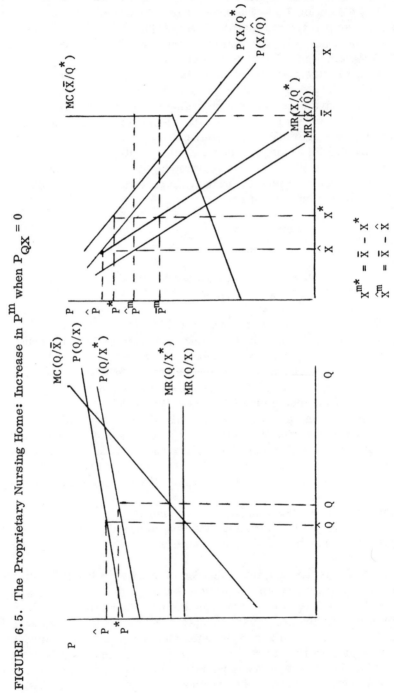

in the slope of the demand curve in price–quality and price–quantity space. Given this definition, we can interpret the qualification on 2. An increase in the Medicaid reimbursement rate will cause the nursing home to decrease quality unless the marginal valuation of quality drastically falls as the number of private-pay patients rises. We will now discuss in depth the differences in three cases; when $P_{QX} = 0$, $P_{QX} > 0$, and $P_{QX} < 0$.

In Figure 6.5 we represent the effect of an increase in the Medicaid reimbursement rate from $\bar{P}^m$ to $\hat{P}^m$, when $P_{QX} = 0$, by movement from the starred values to the capped values. The increase amounts to a rise in the marginal revenue from Medicaid patients. Behavioral condition (7.1) requires that the marginal revenues from both types of patients be equal. Consequently, the home reduces its number of private-pay patients and replaces them with Medicaid patients. The decrease in private-pay patients causes an upward shift in the private-pay demand curve and a downward shift in the marginal revenue curves in price–quality space. Therefore, the home reduces quality until marginal revenue of quality equals marginal cost. The fall in quality means the demand curve in price-quantity space shifts down, resulting in a further substitution of Medicaid for private-pay patients. In the end, the number of private-pay patients has fallen by $X^* - \hat{X}$ patients, while the number of Medicaid patients has increased by an equal amount. Moreover, quality has fallen $Q^* - \hat{Q}$, and price has risen $\hat{P} - P^*$.

When $P_{QX} > 0$, the marginal individual's marginal valuation of quality rises as we move along the demand curve and the demand curve becomes more elastic. This assumption reinforces the reactions of the nursing home to an increase in the Medicaid reimbursement rate. All variables move in the same direction, but now they move in greater magnitudes. This follows because the more elastic the demand curve, the more the values of quantity and quality must fall to raise marginal revenues to equal the Medicaid reimbursement rate and the marginal cost of quality, respectively.

By a similar argument, $P_{QX} < 0$ mitigates the nursing homes' responses to an increase in $\bar{P}^m$ (see Figure 6.6). The demand curve becomes more inelastic as quality and quantity fall. Consequently, the home does not have to adjust its choice variables as far as before to satisfy its first-order conditions.

An increase in the Medicaid reimbursement rate will increase quality if (see Appendix C, 2):

$$-(P_{QX}X + P_Q) > 0 \tag{9}$$

Condition (9) represents the direct effect of the reimbursement-rate

FIGURE 6.6. The Proprietary Nursing Home: Increase in P^m when $P_{QX} < 0$

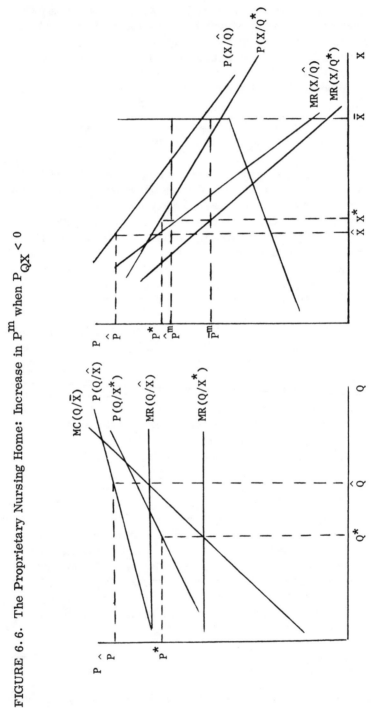

158

increase on quality. The second term is the marginal individual's marginal valuation of quality. It is an income effect and positive by hypothesis. The first term is the substitution of quality-for-quantity effect, and it must be negative and greater than the income effect for quality to rise. If (9) holds, then a decrease in private-pay patients (through, say, a price increase) raises the marginal revenue from quality. The home then increases quality so that marginal cost equals marginal revenue.

The private-pay price increases or decreases in response to an increase in the Medicaid reimbursement rate, depending upon the price elasticity of private-pay demand. From (7.1):

$$P^* = \frac{\eta}{\eta - 1} \bar{P}^m$$

Hence,

$$\frac{dP^*}{d\bar{P}^m} = \frac{2\eta - 1}{(\eta-1)^2}\left[\frac{\partial \eta}{\partial X^*}\frac{\partial X^*}{\partial \bar{P}^m} \frac{\partial \eta}{\partial Q^*}\frac{\partial Q^*}{\partial \bar{P}^m}\right] + \frac{\eta}{\eta - 1}$$

The price elasticity of demand η must be greater than unity; otherwise P^* would be nonpositive. Except under extreme conditions, $\partial X^*/\partial \bar{P}^m$ and $\partial Q^*/\partial \bar{P}^m$ are negative. Therefore, private-pay price increases as the Medicaid reimbursement rate increases if the price elasticity of private-pay demand is nonincreasing in private-pay quantity and quality, or if it is increasing, the increase is small. This amounts to $P_{QX} < 0$ or $P_{QX} > 0$ but small.[15] The slope of the new demand curve must not be smaller than the slope of the pre-Medicaid increase, or if it is smaller, the decrease must not be large.

The final result is that increased reimbursement rate means higher nursing home profits. Suppose the home were to hold constant its number of private-pay patients, Medicaid patients, and quality level. The increased reimbursement rate means higher revenues, while costs are unchanged. The only reason to vary its output mix would be to increase profits. In the most reasonable cases, the home not only enjoys higher revenues but it cuts its costs by decreasing quality. We observe this formally by totally differentiating the maximized profit function and invoking the envelope theorem:

$$\frac{d\Pi}{d\bar{P}^m} = X^{m*}$$

Therefore, profit increases by the number of Medicaid patients in the home.

THE NONPROFIT NURSING HOME

Nonprofit behavior can be characterized by the nursing home maximizing some objective function, subject to a zero profit constraint. We will consider a utility-maximizing nursing home. This model assumes that there exists a utility function that represents the preferences of the nursing home over quantity and quality of care. These homes gain utility from providing high-quality care to as many patients as possible.

As in the profit-maximizing case, the utility maximizer has four choice variables with which it maximizes its objective. It chooses X and Q directly. The private-pay price is determined implicitly through the demand function, and X^m from constraint (6.6). Formally, the utility maxim

$$\max_{X, Q, X^m} U(\tilde{X}, Q) \tag{10}$$

subject to (6.1) through (6.6) and

$$PX + \bar{P}^m X^m - C \geq 0 \tag{10.1}$$

The function $U(\cdot)$ is the nursing home's utility function. We assume it to be twice continuously differentiable and concave in both arguments. From these assumptions, we can infer that quantity and quality have positive but diminishing marginal utilities. Further, the indifference surfaces will be smooth and convex.

The conditions that describe the nonprofit nursing home's optimal behavior are:

$$P\left(1 - \frac{1}{\eta}\right) - \bar{P}^m = 0 \tag{11.1}$$

$$P_Q X - C_Q = -\frac{1}{\lambda} U_Q \tag{11.2}$$

$$(PX + \bar{P}^m X^m)/\bar{X} = C/\bar{X} \tag{11.3}$$

$$X + X^m = \bar{X} \tag{11.4}$$

where λ is the Lagrange multiplier for the nonprofit constraint (10.1). As was true with the profit-maximizing nursing home, the nonprofit home admits private-pay patients until marginal revenue from their admission equals the Medicaid reimbursement rate, holding quality constant. The nonprofit home will choose a quality level

FIGURE 6.7. The Nonprofit Equilibrium

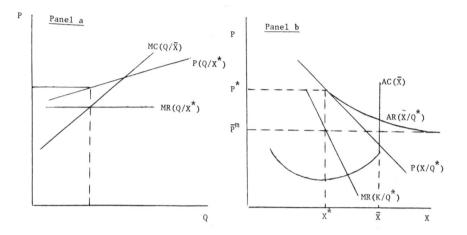

such that the marginal revenue from quality exceeds the marginal cost of quality by the marginal rate of substitution of quality for extra revenue in the nursing home's utility function. Condition (11.3) is the zero-profit constraint that average revenue equals average cost, and condition (11.4) is the CON capacity constraint. The nonprofit solution is pictured in Figure 6.7.

Conditions (11.1) and (11.2) imply that the nonprofit nursing home operates at a higher quality level than does the profit nursing home. The right-hand sides are both equal to zero in the profit case. Since marginal cost exceeds marginal revenue in (11.2) and the cost function is convex, quality must be greater for the nonprofit home, assuming the profit and nonprofit homes face the same $\bar{P}^m$ and $\bar{X}$.

Taking ratios, we can write the first-order conditions as (11.3), (11.4), and:

$$\frac{\Pi_X}{\Pi_Q} = \frac{-0}{U_Q} \tag{12}$$

The nonprofit nursing home maximizes utility by equating the marginal rate of substitution in the profit function to the marginal rate of substitution in the utility function, given profits are zero. The marginal utility of quantity is zero because the CON capacity constraint means that the home cannot admit any more patients and, hence, cannot gain any more utility from more admission.

FIGURE 6.8. Comparison of Profit and Nonprofit Solutions

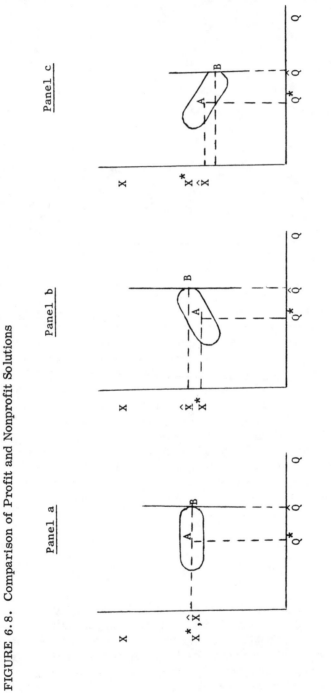

EQUILIBRIUM PROFIT VALUES = $A(X^*/\hat{Q}^*)$
EQUILIBRIUM NONPROFIT VALUES = $B(X,Q)$

Given that P and X^m are determined by the constraints, we can represent the profit function as concentric isoprofit ellipses in R^2 with coordinates X and Q. The third dimension would measure profit. The center of these ellipses is the profit-maximizing solution described in (7). As we move out from the center, each isoprofit sphere represents less and less profit. The nursing home's preferences can be represented in the same space as indifference curves. Since the CON capacity constraint is assumed to be binding, the indifference curves will have infinite slope. Conditions (12) and (11.3) state that the nursing home maximizes utility at the point where the indifference curve is tangent to the zero isoprofit ellipse (see points A in Figure 6.8). This point will be at the farthest point to the right of the ellipse (see points B in Figure 6.8). Consequently, quality is higher in the nonprofit nursing home.

The relative levels of private-pay patients (and therefore Medicaid patients) in profit and nonprofit homes depends on the shape of the zero isoprofit ellipse. If the slope of the long axis is increasing (decreasing), then the nonprofit home will have more (fewer) private-pay patients and fewer (more) Medicaid patients than will the profit home (see panels b and c in Figure 6.8). The slope depends upon whether the price elasticity of demand is increasing or decreasing in quality. If it is increasing (decreasing), then the nonprofit home's higher quality level means, by (11.1), that its price is lower (higher). If the price is high enough to offset the greater quality level in the demand function, then the nonprofit home will care for fewer private-pay patients (see panel b in Figure 6.8); otherwise the number will not be less than in the profit home (see panels a and c in Figure 6.8). Recall that a decreasing price elasticity in quality is equivalent to $P_{QX} < 0$. Hence, nonprofit homes will have higher prices, more private-pay patients, and fewer Medicaid patients if the marginal consumer's marginal valuation of quality falls as we move down the demand curve.

The nonprofit nursing home also sets the private-pay price above the Medicaid reimbursement rate. Rearranging (11.1) yields:

$$P = \frac{\eta}{\eta - 1} \bar{P}^m$$

The more inelastic is private-pay demand, the greater the difference between private-pay price and the Medicaid reimbursement rate. This differential pricing rule, again, is a version of the discriminating monopolist.

Suppose that the government increased the Medicaid reimbursement rate. In Appendix D we show that an increase in the Medicaid reimbursement rate will:

FIGURE 6.9. Nonprofit Nursing Home: Increase in $\bar{P}^m$ to $\bar{\bar{P}}^m$ Equilibrium Values at $\bar{P}^m$ are P^*, Q^*, X^*, X^{m*} Equilibrium Values at $\bar{\bar{P}}^m$ are $\hat{P}$, $\hat{Q}$, $\hat{X}$, $\hat{X}^m$

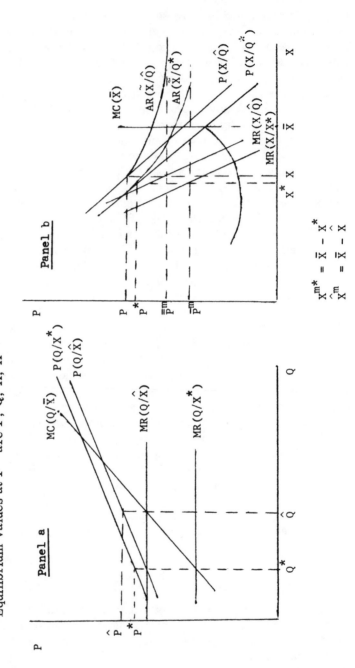

1. Increase the number of private-pay patients unless $P_{ax}X + P_Q > 0$ and large
2. Increase quality unambiguously
3. Decrease the number of Medicaid patients unless $P_{QX}X + P_Q > 0$ and large

When the Medicaid reimbursement rate increases, average revenue increases. Since the nursing home cannot increase quantity, it puts the new revenue into increasing quality. The increase in quality increases private-pay demand, which the nursing home uses to replace Medicaid patients. The increase in quality raises average cost. The nursing home continues to increase quality and, thus, to increase private-pay patients and to decrease Medicaid patients until average revenue from quantity equals average cost of quantity, marginal revenue from private-pay patients equals the Medicaid reimbursement rate, and marginal revenue from quality equals marginal cost of quality less the marginal rate of substitution of quality for revenue in the nursing home's utility function. The resulting equilibrium is presented in Figure 6.9 under the assumption that $P_{QX} = 0$.

The home's responses depend upon the value P_{QX}. When $P_{QX} < 0$, marginal revenues do not rise as fast and potentially decline. Consequently, the home must increase quality and private-pay quantity by even more. In turn, the number of Medicaid patients falls by an even greater amount. Alternatively, when $P_{QX} > 0$, marginal revenues rise quicker, leading to a retardation of the nursing home's responses. Since the home values quality, the home will always increase its value in response to an increased reimbursement rate. Marginal revenue from private-pay patients may then rise so fast that the home might have to reduce private-pay patients in order to satisfy its first order conditions.

Finally, the private-pay price increases or decreases, depending upon the price elasticity of private-pay demand. From (11.1):

$$\frac{dP}{d\bar{P}^m} = \frac{2\eta - 1}{(\eta - 1)^2}\left[\frac{\partial \eta}{\partial X}\frac{dX}{d\bar{P}^m} + \frac{\partial \eta}{\partial Q}\frac{dQ}{d\bar{P}^m}\right] + \frac{\eta}{\eta - 1}$$

Except under extreme conditions, $dX/d\bar{P}^m$ and $dQ/d\bar{P}^m$ are positive. Therefore, if the price elasticity of private-pay demand is nondecreasing in quantity and quality, or slightly increasing, an increase in the Medicaid reimbursement rate will cause a private-pay price increase.

WELFARE

In this section we compare the social optimum to the profit-maximizing and utility-maximizing solutions. The social optimum is taken to be the solution to the consumer-surplus maximization problem. Using the consumer-surplus criteria, we then analyze gains and losses from an increase in the Medicaid reimbursement rate.

We assume that all private-pay individuals are identical, except for health endowments, and have separable utility functions are are linear in wealth. At a given quality level an individual is willing to pay up to his marginal valuation of quality. Integration from zero to Q, less the price paid, yields the individual's consumer surplus. Integrating the individual's consumer surplus over the number of private-pay patients less private-pay price times the number of private-pay patients yields total private-pay consumer surplus. We can write it as:

$$CS = \int_0^X P(V_1 Q)dV - XP(X_1 Q) \tag{13}$$

All Medicaid patients are also assumed to be identical. We assume their utility function to be linear and valued in dollars. Hence, the total Medicaid consumer surplus is:

$$CS^M = bQX^m \tag{14}$$

where b is a Medicaid patient's marginal valuation of quality.

The social optimum is found by solving:

$$\max_{X, Q, X^m} W(X, Q, X^m, \bar{P}^m) = \int_0^X P(V, Q)dV + bQX^m - C$$

subject to (6.1) through (6.6).

The behavioral conditions are:

$$P = \bar{P}^m \tag{15.1}$$

$$\int_0^X P_Q(V, Q)dV + bX^m = C_Q \tag{15.2}$$

By comparing (15.1) to (2.1) and (11.1), we observe a familiar market failure in monopoly situations for both profit and nonprofit homes. They both set their prices above the socially optimal one, by a factor proportional to the price elasticity of demand.

The market failure associated with quality is less obvious. Given X, (15.2) describes the socially optimal level of quality, while (7.2) and (11.2) describe the profit and utility-maximizing levels of quality, respectively. The left side of (15.2) is reexpressed as:

$$\int_0^X P_Q(V, Q)dV + bX^m - XP_Q(X, Q) + \Pi_Q$$

where: Π_Q = the derivative of the profit function with respect to quality

At the profit optimum, $\Pi_Q = 0$. Hence, the profit home will undersupply quality if:

$$\frac{1}{X} \int_0^X P_Q(V, Q)dV + bX^m \frac{1}{X} > P_Q(X, Q)$$

It will oversupply quality if the inequality is reversed. The first term is the average valuation of quality over all private-pay patients. The second term is marginal valuation of quality of all Medicaid patients, and the final term is the private-pay marginal valuation of quality.

A sufficient condition for the profit home to oversupply quality is $P_{QX} \leq 0$. In this case the marginal valuation of quality is always less than the average. When $P_{QX} > 0$, it will depend on the size of $bX^m (1/X)$. The marginal valuation will be greater than the average, but if $bX^m (1/X)$ is greater than the difference, the home will still oversupply quality.

In the nonprofit case (15.2) becomes:

$$\frac{1}{X} \int_0^X P_Q(V, Q)dV + bX^m - XP_Q(X, Q) - \frac{1}{\lambda} U_Q + L_Q = C_Q$$

where L_Q is the first derivative of the Lagrangian associated with the nonprofit's utility maximization problem.

At the utility maximization optimum $L_Q = 0$. The only other new term is the fourth, which is the home's marginal rate of substitution of quality for revenue. Hence, the nonprofit home will undersupply quality if:

$$\frac{1}{X} \int_0^X (P_Q(V, Q)dV + bX^m) > P_Q(X, Q) + \frac{1}{X}\frac{U_Q}{\lambda}$$

It will oversupply quality if the inequality is reversed. The quality market failure occurs in both cases because the home is reacting to marginal signals, whereas the social optimum is based on average values.

When quality is undersupplied, both types of homes care for more Medicaid and fewer private-pay patients than is socially optimal. This follows from the definition of the private-pay demand function, the CON constraint, and a higher than socially optimal private-pay price. When quality is oversupplied, we cannot determine the direction of the deviation.

The consumer surplus framework is also useful for determining the welfare properties of an increase in the Medicaid reimbursement rate. We have already seen the profits in the proprietary case and utility in the nonprofit case rise. The change in private-pay consumer surplus is:

$$\left[\int_0^X P_Q(V, Q)dV - XP_Q(X, Q)\right]\frac{dQ}{d\bar{P}^m} - [P_X(X, Q)X]\frac{dX}{d\bar{P}^m}$$

The first term is the change in surplus due to quality adjustment, and the second term is the change in surplus due to quantity adjustment.

In the profit case, both quantity and quality are likely to decrease. The quantity adjustment term is then negative, whereas the direction of the quality adjustment depends upon the sign of P_{QX}. If $P_{QX} < 0$, the average valuation of quality is less than the marginal and, therefore, the quality adjustment term is also negative. In this case, private-pay surplus increases. When $P_{QX} > 0$, the change in surplus depends upon the relative magnitudes of the quantity and quality adjustments.

In the nonprofit case, quantity and quality are both likely to increase. Therefore, the quantity adjustment term is positive, and if $P_{QX} < 0$, the quality adjustment term is also positive. This leads to an increase in private-pay surplus. Again, when $P_{QX} > 0$, the change in surplus depends upon the relative values of the quantity and quality adjustments.

The change in Medicaid consumer surplus is:

$$[bX^m]\frac{dQ}{d\bar{P}^m} + [bQ]\frac{dX^m}{d\bar{P}^m}$$

The first term is the quality adjustment, and the second is the quantity adjustment. The number of Medicaid patients is likely to increase in the profit case and decrease in the nonprofit case. In the profit case, surplus falls from a decrease in quality but rises from an increase in quantity, while the opposite occurs in the nonprofit home.

Finally, the increased Medicaid reimbursement rate affects the total cost of the Medicaid program. The total cost is:

$$T = \bar{P}^m X^m$$

The change due to an increase in $\bar{P}^m$ is:

$$\frac{dT}{d\bar{P}^m} = X^m + \bar{P}^m \frac{dX^m}{d\bar{P}^m}$$

The first term is the adjustment due to the price change and is always positive. The second term is the adjustment due to a quantity change. In the profit case it is likely positive, meaning the total cost of the Medicaid program rises. In the nonprofit case the quantity adjustment is likely to be negative. Hence, the total cost of the Medicaid program could fall.

CONCLUSIONS

The results of our analysis suggest that government regulators should consider criteria other than subsidizing the nursing home care of financially indigent patients in the setting of the Medicaid reimbursement rates. The government can affect the rate of inflation of nursing home care, the quality of care, and the access of financially indigent individuals to nursing homes by adjusting these reimbursement rates. The usual reimbursement methods, such as flat-fee and cost based, ignore these issues. A reimbursement method that incorporated these tradeoffs would clearly benefit everyone.

A purpose of the Medicaid program is to increase the needys' access to nursing home care. When the government tries to buy more services by increasing the reimbursement rate, it increases access in the profit homes but reduces access in the nonprofit homes. The price of increased access in the profit homes is reduced quality and higher private-pay prices. The reduced access in nonprofit homes is offset by an increase in quality. These factors should be taken into account when determining the optimal reimbursement rate. Some empirical work should be done on the marginal valuation of quality to determine the true direction of the nursing home reactions.

Both profit and nonprofit homes deviate from the social optimum. Again further empirical work needs to be done to determine the direction of the bias. Further, it is not clear that adjustments in the Medicaid rate move as close to the social optimum. In reaction to changes in the Medicaid rate, homes in either quality or quantity move further away from the social optimum. When the government tries to buy more services by increasing its reimbursement rate, private-pay patients' net benefit usually falls, while public-pay patients' net benefit rises or falls, depending upon the relative values of the quality and quantity adjustments in the profit case and vice versa in the nonprofit case. Finally, the total cost of the Medicaid program rises for proprietary nursing homes, while it will decline if the decrease in quality offsets the rise in price in the nonprofit case. Again, empirical work is needed to determine the reaction directions.

APPENDIX A

THE EFFECT OF A DECLINE IN HEALTH ON THE CONSUMPTION-LEISURE DECISION UNDER THE INDEPENDENT LIVING OPTION

A decline in the stock of health is equivalent to a decline in total time available. The Lagrangian corresponding to the problem in (1) is

$$L(G_1, \ldots, G_n; T) = U[C(G_1, \ldots, G_n; T), T^A - T] + \lambda\left(W - \sum_{i=1}^{n} P_i G_i\right)$$

The first order conditions are:

$$L_{G_i} = U_C C_{G_i} - \lambda P_i = 0 \qquad i = 1, \ldots, n$$

$$L_T = U_C C_T - U_L = 0$$

$$L_\lambda = W - \sum_{i=1}^{n} P_i G_i = 0$$

Suppose $i = 1$, then totally differentiating the first order conditions,

$$\begin{bmatrix} L_{GG} & L_{GT} & L_{G\lambda} \\ L_{TG} & L_{TT} & 0 \\ L_{\lambda G} & 0 & 0 \end{bmatrix} \begin{bmatrix} dG \\ dT \\ d\lambda \end{bmatrix} = \begin{bmatrix} L_{GT^A} \\ L_{TT^A} \\ 0 \end{bmatrix} dT^A$$

By Cramer's rule,

$$\frac{dG}{dT^A} = 0$$

$$\frac{dT}{dT^A} = \frac{-1}{|D|} (L_{\lambda G} L_{TT^A} L_{G\lambda})$$

where $|D|$ is the determinant of the coefficient matrix from the total differentiation of the first-order conditions. From the first-order conditions:

$$L_{\lambda G} = -P$$

$$L_{TT^A} = U_{CL} C_T - U_{LL}$$

$$L_{G\lambda} = -P$$

The matrix D is the bordered Hessian matrix for (1). It must be negative semidefinite at the maximum. Hence, $|D|$ must be negative, implying that dT/dT^A has the same sign as L_{TT^A}. Therefore, dT/dT^A is positive if $U_{CL} C_T - U_{LL} \geq 0$. The term U_{LL} is negative by the concavity of $U(\cdot)$, and C_T is positive by hypothesis.

The total time available is analogous to the stock of wealth. A decline in total time available is an increase in the price of time. If both consumption and leisure are normal goods, reduction in total time will be split between reduction in consumption production and reduction in leisure time. Therefore, normality implies L_{TT^A} is positive and, hence, $dT/dT^A \geq 0$.

The decline in health decreases the amount of time spent in consumption production. The right-hand side term in (2.2), C_T, increases because $C(\cdot)$ is concave in T. Since C_T is the slope of the time budget constraint in Figure 6.2, the decline in health will cause that constraint to shift toward the origin and become steeper, as shown in Figure 6.3. Since C_T increased, the left-hand side, U_L/U_C, must also increase. Since $U(\cdot)$ is concave in both L and C, leisure declined more, relative to consumption, as shown in Figure 6.3 by the movement from (C^*, L^*) to (C^{**}, L^{**}).

APPENDIX B

COMPARATIVE STATICS FOR THE
PROPRIETARY NURSING HOME

The nursing home maximizes (6), subject to constraints (6.1) through (6.5), and $\tilde{X} = \bar{X}$. $\bar{X}$ is total allowed capacity by the government under CON regulation. Substituting the constraints into the objective function:

$$\max_{X, Q} \Pi(X, Q_1; P^m) = P(X, Q)X + \bar{P}^m(\bar{X} - X) - C(\bar{X}, Q) \qquad (B.1)$$

The first order conditions are:

$$\Pi_X = P_X X + P - \bar{P}^m = 0 \qquad (B.2)$$

$$\Pi_Q = P_Q X - C_Q = 0 \qquad (B.3)$$

Totally differentiating the first order conditions yields:

$$\begin{bmatrix} \Pi_{XX} & \Pi_{XQ} \\ \\ \Pi_{QX} & \Pi_{QQ} \end{bmatrix} \begin{bmatrix} dX \\ \\ dQ \end{bmatrix} = \begin{bmatrix} \Pi_{X\bar{P}^m} \\ \\ \Pi_{Q\bar{P}^m} \end{bmatrix} d\bar{P}^m \qquad (B.4)$$

1. Applying Cramer's rule to (B.4),

$$\frac{dX}{d\bar{P}^m} = \frac{\Pi_{QQ}}{|D|} \leq 0$$

where $|D|$ is the determinant of the coefficient matrix in (B.4) and the determinant of the Hessian matrix for the maximization problem (B.1). Therefore, $|D| > 0$ when evaluated at the optimum. The term Π_{QQ} is a diagonal element of D and therefore negative.

2. Applying Cramer's rule to (B.4),

$$\frac{dQ}{d\bar{P}^m} = \frac{-1}{|D|} [P_{XQ}X + P_Q]$$

The term P_Q is positive by hypothesis. Therefore, $dQ/d\bar{P}^m$ is negative unless P_{XQ} is negative and large.

3. From the CON constraint and (1),

$$\frac{dX^m}{d\bar{P}^m} = \frac{-dX}{d\bar{P}^m} \geq 0$$

APPENDIX C

COMPARATIVE STATICS FOR THE NONPROFIT NURSING HOME UNDER CON REGULATION

The nursing home maximizes (17), subject to (6.1) through (6.5), (17.1), and $\tilde{X} = \bar{X}$. Substitution of all the constraints except (17.1) into the utility function and (17.1) gives us the following equivalent problem in Lagrangian form:

$$\max_{X, Q, \lambda} \ L(X, Q, \lambda; \bar{P}^m, \bar{X}) = U(\bar{X}, Q) + (P(X, Q)X + \bar{P}^m(\bar{X} - X) - C(\bar{X}, Q)) \quad \text{(C.1)}$$

The first order conditions are:

$$L_X = \lambda[P_X X + P - \bar{P}^m] = 0 \quad \text{(C.2)}$$

$$L_Q = U_Q + \lambda[P_Q X - C_Q] = 0 \quad \text{(C.3)}$$

$$L_\lambda = PX + \bar{P}^m(\bar{X} - X) - C = 0 \quad \text{(C.4)}$$

Total differentiation of the first order conditions yields:

$$\begin{bmatrix} L_{XX} & L_{XQ} & 0 \\ L_{QX} & L_{QQ} & L_Q \\ 0 & L & 0 \end{bmatrix} \begin{bmatrix} dX \\ dQ \\ d\lambda \end{bmatrix} = \begin{bmatrix} \lambda \\ 0 \\ -X^m \end{bmatrix} d\bar{P}^m \quad \text{(C.5)}$$

1. Applying Cramer's rule to (C.5):

$$\frac{dX}{d\bar{P}^m} = \frac{-\lambda}{|D|} (L_{\lambda Q} L_{Q\lambda}) - \frac{X^m}{|D|} (L_{XQ} L_{Q\lambda}) \qquad (C.6)$$

The term $|D|$ is the determinant of the coefficient matrix in (C.4) and (C.5) and is the determinant of the bordered Hessian matrix for the problem in (C.1). Therefore, $|D| \leq 0$ when evaluated at the optimum. From (C.3) and (C.4):

$$L_{\lambda Q} = L_{Q\lambda} = P_Q X - C_Q$$

Since $U_Q \geq 0$, (C.2) implies $L_{\lambda Q} = L_{Q\lambda} \leq 0$. From (C.2):

$$L_{XQ} = \lambda(P_{XQ} X + P_Q)$$

Therefore, $dX/\bar{P}^m \geq 0$ unless $P_{XQ} > 0$ and very large.

2. Applying Cramer's rule to (C.5):

$$\frac{dQ}{d\bar{P}^m} = \frac{-X^m}{|D|} (L_{XX} L_{Q\lambda})$$

The term L_{XX} is a diagonal element of D and, consequently, is nonpositive at the optimum. Therefore, $dQ/d\bar{P}^m \geq 0$.

3. The CON constraint is:

$$\bar{X} = X + X^m$$

Total differentiation yields:

$$\frac{dX^m}{d\bar{P}^m} = \frac{-dX}{d\bar{P}^m}$$

From (1), $dX^m/d\bar{P}^m \leq 0$ unless $P_{XQ} > 0$ and very large.

NOTES

1. For example, in 1976 only 24 percent of nursing home discharges reentered the community. Of these, 31 percent were heavily dependent on daily community living activities (National Center for Health Statistics,1979).
2. The family also has input into this decision, but we refer to the individual as the decision-making entity.
3. The model of demand we develop is static. Ideally, one would like a model that incorporates obvious dynamics. For example, an individual's health stock depreciates over time, but the rate of depreciation can be reduced by investing in medical services. A model of the demand for medical care of this type was developed by Michael Grossman (1972). The purpose of this work is to develop the conditions under which an individual would enter a nursing home in the hope of developing properties of aggregate demand functions. We implicitly assume people are acting optimally over time, a la Grossman. The behavior we are looking at is a discrete choice at a point in time and is, hence, static. The added richness of Grossman's model adds little to our purpose, at a great cost.
4. This assumption characterizes the majority of potential nursing home patients. Eighty-six percent of persons living in nursing homes are over 65 (National Center for Health Statistics, 1979). Only 16.4 of that population participated in the labor force in 1970 (U.S. Bureau of the Census, 1973). Further, it is unlikely that an individual who is considering nursing home care has the physical ability to work.
5. The form of this problem falls out of the household production theory of consumer demand literature (e.g., Lancaster 1971) and the theory of the allocation of time literature (e.g., Becker 1965). The specific model is very similar to the one developed by Scanlon (1980).
6. We could include savings by letting it be the nth good, G_n with $P_n = 1$.
7. This follows from the weak separability of the utility function.
8. For now we will avoid the problem of what the individual would do with leftover wealth if $P^{NH} < W$ by assuming that he cannot use that money for further purchases nor does he gain utility from savings in a nursing home.
9. A similar rule was used by Domencich and McFadden (1975) in the analysis of urban travel demand.
10. Scanlon (1980) tests and accepts the hypothesis that there is excess demand from Medicaid-subsidized patients. Therefore, the perfect elasticity assumption seems reasonable.

Note that this level of quality is the amount that would induce a private-pay patient to enter at zero price. As price increases, the level of quality must also increase for the individual to still choose to enter the nursing home. Therefore, unless the nursing home only wants Medicaid patients, it will set quality above this level.

11. There are questions as to whether CON boards are rubber stamps for nursing home administrators. In this case the constraint would not be binding, implying the model of the previous section is the one at which we should look. The fact that the CON disapproved many expansion proposals suggests that this is not the case.

12. Note 7 applies here, plus the fact that nursing homes in Wisconsin operate, on the average, at 85 to 90 percent capacity, and half have active waiting lists (Wisconsin, Bureau of Health Statistics 1976).

13. This assumption rules out private insurance and Medicare. These types of patients are small in number relative to the types we are concerned with in this chapter (Wisconsin, Bureau of Health Statistics, 1978).

14. Spence (1975) used this terminology in a similar context.

15. Of course, if $\partial X^*/\partial \bar{P}^m \geq 0$ and $\partial Q^*/\partial \bar{P}^m \geq 0$, then the inequalities for these conditions would reverse directions.

REFERENCES

Becker, G. S. 1965. "A Theory of the Allocation of Time." Economic Journal, 75, pp. 493-517.

Domencich, Thomas A., and Daniel McFadden. 1975. Urban Travel Demand: A Behavioral Analysis. Amsterdam: North Holland.

Grossman, Michael. 1972. The Demand for Health: A Theoretical and Empirical Investigation. New York: National Bureau of Economic Research.

Holahan, John, and Christian Ehamenn. 1975. "Public Policy and Utilization of Long Term Institutional Care." Working Paper 975-08. Washington, D.C.: The Urban Institute.

Lancaster, Kelvin. 1971. Consumer Demand: A New Approach. New York: Columbia University Press.

Scanlon, W. J. 1980. "The Market for Nursing Home Care: A Case of an Equilibrium with Excess Demand as a Result of Public Policy." Unpublished Ph.D. dissertation, University of Wisconsin-Madison.

Spence, A. M. 1975. "Monopoly Quality and Regulation." The Bell Journal of Economics, 6(2), pp. 417-29.

U.S., Department of Health and Human Services, Public Health Service, Office of Health Research, Statistics, and Technology. Health, United States, 1980. Washington, D.C.: Government Printing Office.

U.S., National Center for Health Statistics. 1979. "The National Nursing Home Survey: 1977 Summary for the United States." Vital and Health Statistics, Series 13, No. 43 (June). Washington, D.C.: Government Printing Office.

Wisconsin, Bureau of Health Statistics. 1976. Wisconsin Health Facility Statistics, Nursing Homes, 1976. Wisconsin State Division of Health, Madison, Wisconsin.

PART III

Controlling the Cost of Health Care

7

MEDICARE AND HEALTH
SERVICES UTILIZATION

Paul B. Ginsburg
Nancy T. Greenspan
Ronald J. Vogel

In response to rapid increases in federal outlays for Medicare, the degree of cost sharing in the program's benefit structure has been receiving increased attention. The Omnibus Budget Reconciliation Act of 1981 (Public Law 97-35) increased the deductible in both Part A (Hospital Insurance) and Part B (Supplementary Medical Insurance). Additional increases in cost sharing are likely to be debated in 1982.

Changes in Medicare cost sharing raise a number of analytical questions. First, how would utilization of services by the elderly change in response to increased cost sharing? A very extensive literature on determinants of utilization by the general population indicates that additional cost sharing reduces use. On the basis of this literature, it appears that going from full coverage to 25 percent cost sharing, for example, reduces spending on covered services by 15 to 20 percent. (See, for example, Manning et al. 1981.)

In contrast with the extensive literature on the general population, few estimates are available for the elderly population. Prior to Medicare, comparing rates of use between those insured and those uninsured was restricted by lack of data on the specifics of the insurance policies and the likelihood that persons insured were not randomly chosen from the elderly population but selected themselves.

This work was supported by a contract (SSA-PNB-73-218) from the Health Care Financing Administration. Research assistance by Robert Andrew and Dan Roble is acknowledged. Ted Frech provided useful suggestions, and Regina Loewenstein was invaluable in helping us become familiar with the data.

When Medicare became effective in 1966, all persons over 65 received uniform federal insurance coverage. Fortunately, the Social Security Administration had the foresight to take before and after surveys of this population. Analysis of these surveys indicated that Medicare did indeed increase the use of services (Loewenstein 1971). The most significant increase was in short-stay hospital care, for which days of care per aged person rose 25 percent. Increased admission rates and increased length of stay each contributed about half of this increase. Ambulatory care visits did not increase, however.

A second analytical question raised by the debate on cost sharing concerns whose use is affected the most. For example, if cost sharing is increased, will relatively healthy people decrease their utilization by a greater degree than those who are sick? Or will people with low incomes be affected more? In more technical terms, the question is whether a change in insurance coverage alters the structure of the demand for medical care. Are there significant changes in the parameters of the demand relationship beyond the price parameters?

This study examines the question of changes in the structure of demand associated with changes in insurance coverage, focusing specifically on changes in demand associated with Medicare. It employs data from the twin surveys from before and after Medicare mentioned above, using the technique of analysis of covariance on the pooled data set. It concludes that a number of nonprice variables became more important determinants of utilization with the beginning of Medicare.

MODEL AND DATA

The demand model follows those developed by economists in an extensive literature on determinants of the use of health services. The dependent variables are an individual's expenditures on or use of medical services. In addition to an equation for total expenditures, separate equations are estimated for hospital care and physicians' services. Independent variables include price, income, other characteristics of the individual (such as age and health status), location (for example urban versus rural), and medical care resources available in the area. Table 7.1 presents the specific variables and Table 7.2 presents their unweighted means and standard deviations.

The practice of including medical care resources in a demand equation is common, though controversial. Many have shown that when there are more beds per capita in an area, physicians are more likely to hospitalize patients, all other things (including prices) being

TABLE 7.1. Independent Variables

POST	Post-Medicare
SOUTH	Region of residence (1 = South, 0 = Other)
FSIZE	Family size
FINC	Family income (in thousands of dollars)
MALE	Sex (1 = male, 0 = female)
WHITE	Race (1 = white, 0 = all others)
AGE	Age
PRIVINS	Private health insurance (1 = had health insurance, 0 = otherwise)
MARRIED	Marital status (1 = married, 0 = other)
RURAL	Rural-urban residence (1 = rural, 0 = urban)
HEALTH	Number of health conditions present
PCGP	General practitioners per 1,000 physicians
MDCAP	Physicians per 1,000 population
BEDCAP	Hospital beds per 1,000 population
NHBCAP	Nursing home beds per 1,000 population
INDEX H	Hospital cost index = hospital cost per day in the state relative to the national average
INDEX P	Physician fee index = physician fees in census division relative to national average

constant. Some critics concede the empirical point but claim that omitted variables such as time prices are the real explanation, while other critics ascribe results supporting the existence of this relationship to identification problems.

This demand model is estimated with pooled data from two surveys of the elderly population. The first of these twin surveys was taken in 1965, the year before the commencement of Medicare; the second was taken in 1967. While the questionnaires and sampling design were the same, the two samples were drawn independently.[1] A shift dummy denoting whether the observation came from the pre-Medicare or the post-Medicare survey was included in the specification, both independently, and as part of an interaction term with each of the other independent variables. This specification is equivalent to separate regressions on the pre-Medicare and post-Medicare surveys.

TABLE 7.2. Means and Standard Deviations

Variables	Mean	Standard Deviation
Dependent Variables:		
Total expenditures	352.5788	946.5998
Probability of hospital admission	.1744	.3795
Length of stay	8.2463	22.5393
Probability of a physician visit	.7406	.4383
Number of physicians' visits	8.5010	10.5268
Expenditures per physician visit	13.087	31.571
Independent Variables (N = 9,964):		
POST	.4584	.4983
SOUTH	.3187	.4660
FSIZE	2.0510	1.1440
FINC	3.9493	2.3127
MALE	.4565	.4981
WHITE	.9361	.2446
AGE	72.3699	5.6425
PRIVINS	.5788	.4938
MARRIED	.5700	.4951
RURAL	.4913	.4999
HEALTH	2.3673	2.1913
PCGP	314.6530	238.0296
MDCAP	1.2727	.7073
BEDCAP	4.2090	2.0517
NHBCAP	2.9935	2.6830
INDEX (Hospitals)	.9707	.1460
INDEX (Physicians)	.9771	.9792

Dependent Variables

The following describes the dependent variables:

1. Total expenditures (Total medical bills including hospital care, physicians' services, nursing home care, and home health care over the last 12 months; the post-Medicare expenditures are deflated by an index of per capita medical spending so as to be comparable to pre-Medicare spending.)
2. Probability of a hospital admission (A binary variable for whether or not admitted within the past 12 months; this equation was estimated using logit analysis.)

3. Length of stay (The average number of days for a respondent's hospital stays during the past 12 months; respondents without hospital stays were excluded.)
4. Expenditures per hospital day (for those respondents with hospital stays, the bill divided by the number of days, deflated by area hospital cost index)
5. Probability of a physician visit (A binary variable for whether or not the respondent had a physician visit during the past 12 months; this equation was estimated using logit analysis.)
6. Number of visits (for those respondents with visits, the number of visits)
7. Expenditures per physician visit (for those with visits, the total amount of bills divided by the total number of visits, deflated by the average cost per visit for sampled persons in the respondent's primary sampling unit)

Independent Variables

A binary variable (PRIVINS) was used to denote the presence or private insurance. For the total expenditures model, the presence of hospital coverage was interpreted as the presence of private insurance. For the hospital and physician equations, the presence of hospital and medical coverage, respectively, were used to represent the presence of private coverage.

Unfortunately, a binary variable for the presence of insurance coverage fails to represent variation in the comprehensiveness of insurance among policies. We nevertheless chose this specification over an alternative of the ratio of bills paid by insurance to total bills. The latter had the problem of not being defined for those with no medical bills and being partly determined by the extent of medical spending. With the proportion of the elderly with any type of private insurance nearer to the middle of the zero-to-one range than to the extremes, we judged the inadequacies of a binary variable less serious than those from an ex post proportion of the bill paid by insurance.

Family income (FINC), a binary variable for post-Medicare (POST), and an area health price index (INDEXH or INDEXP) complete the list of economic variables.

Demographic variables included AGE, MARRIED, MALE, family size (FSIZE), and WHITE. A health status variable (HEALTH) was included, which was the number of positive responses to a series of 21 questions about the presence of health problems.

Variables referring to the area of residence include RURAL and SOUTH and a series of resource availability variables. The latter, which are for the SMSA or rural county or residence, include short-term hospital beds per capita (BEDCAP), physicians per capita (MDCAP), the proportion of physicians that are general practitioners (PCGP), and nursing home beds per capita (NHBCAP).

RESULTS

Estimation of regressions on the pooled sample showed a change in the structure of demand associated with Medicare. Noneconomic variables thought to reflect the "need" for medical care and resource availability became more important while private insurance tended to become less important. An alternative way of looking at these results is that those persons with greater medical care "needs" or those living in areas with more medical care resources had larger than average increases in medical care use. These results tended to be consistent from equation to equation, although some that were statistically significant in the total expenditures equation were not significant in some of the component equations.

Total Expenditures

During the pre-Medicare period, variables with a statistically significant impact on expenditures included FINC, AGE, PRIVINS, and HEALTH (see Table 7.3). Those with higher family income spent more for medical care, with the elasticity at the mean approximately 0.4. Age was positively associated with medical spending, with an additional year associated with roughly $8 per year (compared with a mean of about $350). Those with private insurance had higher spending by about $96, when all other variables were held constant. Those with more medical problems spent more; an addition of one medical problem increased spending by about $55. Race had a very large effect on spending, although the coefficient was not significant at conventional levels. Being nonwhite was associated with roughly $76 per year less spending; other variables such as income and location held constant.

A number of coefficients had statistically significant shifts in the post-Medicare period. The presence of medical problems increased its role as a determinant of spending. An additional medical condition increased expenditures by $105, post-Medicare, compared to $55, pre-Medicare. An additional year of age increased spending by $17, post-Medicare, compared with $8, pre-Medicare.

Rural areas increased medical care spending under Medicare much less than urban areas. The rural variable had a small and

TABLE 7.3. Total Expenditures

Variables	Pre-Medicare Coefficients	Shift Coefficients
CONSTANT/POST	-.5874+03	-.8079+03
		(257.3849)
SOUTH	-.2005+02	.4022+02
	(30.8986)	(46.2451)
FSIZE	-.3889+02	.1769+02
	(12.5848)	(18.0172)
FINC	.3573+02	-.3257+01
	(6.4644)	(9.2586)
MALE	-.2596+02	.1887+01
	(26.7166)	(39.7561)
WHITE	.7598+02	.3765+02
	(53.1967)	(79.5172)
AGE	.8413+01	.8704+01
	(2.2946)	(3.4134)
PRIVINS	.9564+02	-.2445+02
	(27.1136)	(39.4291)
MARRIED	-.5591+02	.4189+01
	(28.2948)	(41.9151)
RURAL	.1709+02	-.2185+03
	(37.8846)	(52.1843)
HEALTH	.5511+02	.4967+02
	(5.8435)	(8.5161)
PCGP	.6393-02	-.7905-01
	(.0652)	(.0951)
MDCAP	.2771+02	.1492+03
	(27.7786)	(38.9508)
BEDCAP	-.8268+01	.2157+02
	(7.5385)	(11.3717)
NHBCAP	-.1952+01	-.1043+02
	(5.0812)	(7.5217)

Note: Standard errors in parentheses; N = 9,964.

TABLE 7.4. Probability of a Hospital Admission

Variables	Pre–Medicare Coefficients	Shift Coefficients
CONSTANT/POST	-.3389+01 (.6398)	-.5125+00 (.9308)
SOUTH	.4939-01 (.0972)	.1771-01 (.1423)
FSIZE	-.1015+00 (.0405)	.8661-01 (.0552)
FINC	.7372-01 (.0187)	-.9261-02 (.0263)
MALE	.1946+00 (.0813)	-.1319+00 (.1180)
WHITE	.1071+00 (.1739)	-.8133-01 (.2523)
AGE	.9032-02 (.0067)	.1033-01 (.0098)
PRIVINS	.1119-01 (.1312)	.1648+00 (.1764)
MARRIED	-.1991+00 (.0862)	.1652+00 (.1247)
RURAL	-.1929+00 (.1178)	-.3679+00 (.1560)
HEALTH	.1948+00 (.0162)	.5267-01 (.0234)
PCGP	.2982-03 (.0002)	-.3242-03 (.0003)
MDCAP	-.1277+00 (.0971)	.1503+00 (.1362)
BEDCAP	.6711-01 (.0226)	.2212-01 (.0328)
NHBCAP	.7702-02 (.0112)	-.1026-10 (.7795-11)
INDEX H	.2635-03 (.0004)	.2635-03 (.0005)

Note: Standard errors in parentheses; N = 9,964.

insignificant positive coefficient, pre-Medicare, but a large, significant negative coefficient, post-Medicare.

Availability of medical resources became more important with the enactment of Medicare. The elasticity of expenditures with respect to physicians per capita (MDCAP) increased from an insignificant 0.1 to a significant 0.5. Similar, though less powerful, results were obtained for hospital beds (BEDCAP). This variable went from a small, insignificant negative elasticity, pre-Medicare, to a positive (but insignificant) elasticity, post-Medicare. The shift was almost significant at the 5 percent level.

With Medicare, economic variables become less important, but the magnitude of the shifts was small. The coefficients on PRIVINS and FINC both declined, but the shifts were neither large nor statistically significant. Racial differences increased with Medicare, though the shift was not statistically significant.

Hospital Care

Two hospital care equations were estimated: the probability of admissions and the length of stay.[2]

Probability of Admission

Variables affecting the probability of a hospital admission during the pre-Medicare period include family income and size, mental status, sex, health status, and hospital beds per capita (see Table 7.4). Those with high family income were more likely to be admitted. At the mean probability of admission (.17), an additional 1,000 in annual family income increased the probability by .01. Persons who were married or had large families were less likely to be admitted. The presence of medical problems increased the probability of admission substantially. An additional problem increased the probability by .03. More hospital beds increased the probability of admission, with an elasticity of admissions with respect to beds of 0.2.

Only two coefficients shifted by a statistically significant amount. The presence of medical problems become somewhat more important. Residence in a rural area became more important in discouraging hospital admissions, or those living in rural areas increased use less than those living in urban areas.

Those variables that had significant shifts in the total expenditures equation but not in the admissions equation moved in the same direction. AGE, MDCAP, and BEDCAP all had positive shifts, as they did in the total expenditures model.

TABLE 7.5. Length of Stay

Variables	Pre-Medicare Coefficients	Shift Coefficients
CONSTANT/POST	.3748+02	-.2423+02
		(23.6801)
SOUTH	-.7859+01	.4528+01
	(2.4800)	(3.4536)
FSIZE	-.9736+00	-.3354+00
	(1.0056)	(1.2932)
FINC	.2452+00	-.4542+00
	(.4573)	(.6321)
MALE	-.2837+01	.2899+01
	(2.0605)	(2.8317)
WHITE	-.3556+01	.3516+00
	(5.6694)	(7.1642)
AGE	.1723+00	.4278+00
	(.1714)	(.2397)
PRIVINS	-.1651+01	-.2569-01
	(2.3156)	(3.0354)
MARRIED	-.4315+00	-.5323+01
	(2.1724)	(2.9693)
RURAL	.2932+01	-.3510+01
	(2.9696)	(3.7948)
HEALTH	.1874-01	-.3049+00
	(.4336)	(.5849)
PCGP	-.8757-02	.2618-02
	(.0048)	(.0066)
MDCAP	.7927-01	.4633+01
	(2.4849)	(3.2980)
BEDCAP	-.1128+01	.5845+00
	(.5502)	(.7644)
NHBCAP	-.1105+00	-.5717+00
	(.3480)	(.4790)
INDEX H	-.2092-01	-.5816-02
	(.0098)	(.0133)

Note: Standard errors in parentheses; N = 1,599.

Length of Stay

In the pre-Medicare period, the only variables with a statistically significant coefficient were SOUTH and INDEXH, both of which had negative coefficients (see Table 7.5). None of the shift coefficients was statistically significant at the 5 percent level, although AGE came close to meeting this criterion. Those shifts that were significant in the total expenditure equation took on the same sign in this equation, with the exception of HEALTH.

Physicians' Services

Equations estimated for physicians' services were structured in a manner parallel to those for hospital care.

Probability of Visits

The pre-Medicare determinants of the probability of physicians' visits have strong similarities to those for hospital admissions (see Table 7.6). Variables statistically significant in both equations were FINC, FSIZE, and HEALTH. MALE was also significant in both equations but changed sign. Persons with high family income were more likely to have seen the doctor. At the mean probability of a visit (.74), an increment of family size by one person decreased the probability of a visit by .02. An additional medical problem increased the probability of a visit by .08. Males had lower probabilities of seeing a physician, in contrast to higher probabilities of being hospitalized. No other variables were statistically significant.

Changes in the structure of demand were also similar. The presence of medical problems increased in importance. An additional medical problem increased the probability of a visit by .10, post-Medicare, compared with .08, pre-Medicare. The coefficient of SOUTH changed from slightly positive before Medicare to negative after Medicare. While neither coefficient was statistically significant at the 5 percent level, the size of the shift was.

Two shifts in coefficients had different signs than in the probability of admissions equation. BEDCAP had a negative coefficient while PRIVINS had a positive-shift coefficient. The latter result appears to be inconsistent with the others reported for this variable.

Number of Visits

For those persons with some physicians' visits, significant variables in the equation for number of visits during the pre-Medicare survey are FINC, HEALTH, INDEXP, and NHBCAP (see Table 7.7). Persons with high family income tended to have more physicians'

TABLE 7.6. Probability of a Physician Visit

Variables	Pre-Medicare Coefficients	Shift Coefficients
CONSTANT	.6233–01	–.1398+00
	(.6192)	(.9197)
SOUTH	.9088–01	–.2673+00
	(.0819)	(.1245)
FSIZE	–.7932–01	–.9753–02
	(.0329)	(.0468)
FINC	.1465+00	–.2809–01
	(.0176)	(.0254)
MALE	–.4133+00	.3788–02
	(.0701)	(.1059)
WHITE	–.6924–01	.5519–02
	(.1366)	(.2033)
AGE	–.1253–01	.8976–02
	(.0060)	(.0091)
PRIVINS	–.9208–01	.3475+00
	(.1109)	(.1630)
MARRIED	.1301+00	.1166+00
	(.0746)	(.1122)
RURAL	–.6725–01	–.7279–02
	(.0985)	(.1393)
HEALTH	.4251+00	.6816–01
	(.0213)	(.0332)
PCGP	.4453–03	–.1838–03
	(.0002)	(.0002)
MDCAP	.3114–01	–.3811–01
	(.0823)	(.1174)
BEDCAP	.8272–02	–.6558–01
	(.0210)	(.0314)
NHBCAP	.2282–02	.7157–11
	(.0105)	(.7385–11)
INDEX P	.6885–03	–.2821–03
	(.0004)	(.0006)

Note: Standard errors in parentheses; N = 9,964.

192

TABLE 7.7. Number of Physician Visits

Variables	Pre–Medicare Coefficients	Shift Coefficients
CONSTANT/POST	-.2087+01	.1048+02
		(4.6929)
SOUTH	-.7940+00	.3090+00
	(.4153)	(.6150)
FSIZE	-.6894-02	-.1361+00
	(.1684)	(.2456)
FINC	.3839+00	-.3200+00
	(.0836)	(.1192)
MALE	-.4337+00	-.2613+00
	(.3672)	(.5388)
WHITE	-.7921+00	.3376-01
	(.7806)	(1.1411)
AGE	-.2445-01	-.2199-01
	(.0315)	(.0458)
PRIVINS	-.5666-01	-.2972+00
	(.5688)	(.7827)
MARRIED	-.6017+00	.1226+01
	(.3856)	(.5645)
RURAL	-.5937+00	.6891+00
	(.5213)	(.7093)
HEALTH	.1184+01	.4928-01
	(.0796)	(.1142)
PCGP	-.4597-03	.1701-02
	(.0009)	(.0013)
MDCAP	-.1159+00	.8829+00
	(.4259)	(.5929)
BEDCAP	.4894-01	-.2605+00
	(.1086)	(.1624)
NHBCAP	-.1415+00	.1606+00
	(.0680)	(.0993)
INDEX P	.1036-01	-.1020-01
	(.0022)	(.0031)

Note: Standard errors in parentheses; N = 6,904.

TABLE 7.8. Expenditures per Physician Visit

Variables	Pre-Medicare Coefficients	Shift Coefficients
CONSTANT/POST	.1235+01	-.3201+01
		(1.4450)
SOUTH	.2633-01	-.1016+00
	(.1279)	(.1894)
FSIZE	-.9012-01	.4240-04
	(.0519)	(.0756)
FINC	.8106-01	.3789-01
	(.0257)	(.0367)
MALE	.8118-01	.9818-02
	(.1131)	(.1659)
WHITE	.3192+00	.1678+00
	(.2404)	(.3514)
AGE	.4168-02	.3783-01
	(.0097)	(.0141)
PRIVINS	.5137-01	-.5489-01
	(.1752)	(.2410)
MARRIED	-.2374-01	-.1623+00
	(.1187)	(.1738)
RURAL	.1727+00	-.7787+00
	(.1605)	(.2184)
HEALTH	-.2691-01	.4917-01
	(.0245)	(.0352)
PCGP	-.2266-04	-.8856-03
	(.0003)	(.0004)
MDCAP	.7226-02	.1527+00
	(.1311)	(.1826)
BEDCAP	-.1592-01	.4317-01
	(.0334)	(.0500)
NHBCAP	.6755-02	-.8343-01
	(.0209)	(.0306)
INDEX P	-.9273-03	.1148-02
	(.0007)	(.0009)

Note: Standard errors in parentheses; N = 6,904.

194

visits. (They were also more likely to have any visits.) Those in poor health also tended to have more visits. An additional medical problem added 1.2 visits. Persons in areas with more nursing home beds tended to have fewer physicians' visits. SOUTH had a negative coefficient that almost achieved significance at the 5 percent level.

Variables with significant shifts included FINC, MARRIED, and INDEXP. Family income became a less important determinant of visits. Indeed, the shift was almost as large as the pre-Medicare coefficient, so that in the post-Medicare survey, FINC played a very small role as a determinant of the number of visits for those who saw the doctor. Note, however, that FINC was still an important determinant of who saw the doctor. MARRIED had a large positive shift, but since it had a negative coefficient in the pre-Medicare survey, its positive post-Medicare coefficient was not significant. INDEXP had a negative shift, so that residence in a high-fee area no longer had any significant influence on the number of visits. Looked at in another way, high-fee areas exerted a smaller influence on the number of visits.

Expenditures per Physician Visit

This variable combines the extent to which high priced physicians are chosen and the volume of ancillary services per visit, making interpretation somewhat difficult (see Table 7.8).

In the pre-Medicare period, one variable was significant—FINC. Persons with high family incomes tended to spend more per visit than the average in their communities. AGE, which had a positive but insignificant coefficient in the pre-Medicare period had a positive shift, becoming statistically significant in the post-Medicare period. This result is consistent with the pattern in other equations. RURAL had a negative shift, from a positive coefficient, pre-Medicare, to a negative coefficient, post-Medicare, though neither coefficient was statistically significant. Given that the dependent variable was deflated by expenditures per physician visit of all those sampled in the area, interpretation of this shift variable and others referring to area of residence is difficult.

DISCUSSION

The results indicate that economic variables became less important determinants of medical care use among the elderly with the advent of Medicare. Such a result is consistent with economic theory. The presence of a uniform federal insurance benefit reduced net price differences between those with private insurance and those without. Similarly, since Medicare lowered the amount of out-of-pocket outlays necessary to purchase a given array of medical services, income differences would be expected to play a smaller role in determining medical care use.

Variables associated with medical "need" became more important determinants of use of services. In particular, age and health became more important determinants of spending. Such a result is consistent with a decline in the importance of economic factors. With more extensive third-party payment, those with greater "needs" are in a position to have a larger increase in medical services.

Variables associated with availability of medical resources tended to become more important. This is also consistent with the dramatic reduction in economic barriers to the use of medical services. Those areas best endowed with medical resources were able to increase services the most, or relative endowments of medical services became more important when economic determinants became less important. Unfortunately, however, the data available for this study do not enable us to distinguish between short-term and long-term changes in the availability effect. The substantial increase in hospital use undoubtedly strained hospital bed capacity in certain areas for the first few years of Medicare. The results of the BEDCAP variable could simply reflect that those areas with more excess capacity were expanding use the most. This might be expected to disappear within a few years. On the other hand, reduction in economic barriers and immobility of medical resources could cause such an effect to be permanent. Data from 1967 cannot shed light on this question, however.

NOTES

1. For more detailed discussion of the survey, see Loewenstein 1971.
2. Estimation of an equation for hospital expenditures per day was unsuccessful. An F-test for the equation as a whole failed to reject the null hypothesis of no relationship.

REFERENCES

Loewenstein, Regina. 1971. "Early Effects of Medicare on the Health Care of the Aged." Social Security Bulletin, April 1971, pp. 3-20.

Manning, W. G., et al. 1981. "A Two-Part Model of Demand for Medical Care: Preliminary Results from the Health Insurance Study." In Jacques van der Gaag and Mark Perlman (eds.), Health, Economics, and Health Economics. Amsterdam: North Holland.

8

A MODEL OF PHYSICIAN PRICING, OUTPUT, AND HEALTH INSURANCE REIMBURSEMENT: FINDINGS FROM A STUDY OF TWO BLUE SHIELD PLANS' CLAIMS DATA

Donald E. Yett   Richard L. Ernst
William Der   Joel W. Hay

Although sustained high levels of inflation in the health-care sector are virtually a worldwide phenomenon, the problem has been especially pronounced in the United States.

> Between 1969 and 1978, [U.S.] personal health care
> expenditures . . . increased from $57.9 billion to
> $167.9—an average increase of 12.6 percent per year.
> It is estimated that 63 percent of this growth was due to
> price increases. The impact of inflation has been even
> more pronounced for the latter half of this period. Health
> care expenditures increased rapidly immediately follow-
> ing the end of the Economic Stabilization Program in
> 1974—15.3 percent for the 1974-75 period. Price change
> accounted for 80 percent of this increase; and for 1977-
> 78, 68 percent of the growth in personal health care
> expenditures was attributed to price. (Weichert 1980)

Congressional and administration fears of further accelerating these trends are one of the major factors that have long delayed the enactment of some form of national health insurance in the United States, despite widespread agreement that without NHI disadvantaged population groups will continue to have insufficient access to health services in general and high quality services in particular. In this sense, future health-care policy options will depend critically upon

The research was supported by Contract No. 600-76-0/60 from the Health Care Financing Administration, U.S. Department of Health and Human Services. The data for the study were provided by the Blue Cross and Blue Shield Associations.

developing the ability to curb the strong inflationary forces especially characteristic of the U.S. health-care sector. Correspondingly, the major challenge facing health-care policy analysts is to identify feasible and effective intervention strategies through improved understanding of the market processes at work in the health-care sector.

This chapter focuses on the pricing and output decisions of individual physician practices and how these decisions are affected by several important characteristics of private health insurance reimbursement in the United States. A model of physicians' pricing and output behavior is presented and fitted to insured claims data from two Blue Shield Plans. In particular, two major aspects of the market for physicians' services were explored: (1) the nature of physicians' optimizing behavior, and (2) whether physicians' pricing behavior can be characterized as competitive or monopolistic.

Each of these questions has direct and important implications for the goal of identifying cost containment strategies that are both feasible and likely to be effective. For example, the target income theory of physicians' optimizing behavior holds that physicians can and may generate patient demands (or else raise fees) in order to achieve the income targets. If the theory better describes physicians' behavior than profit or utility maximization, controls on fees may restrain charge inflation but, unless they are accompanied by utilization controls, higher "induced" utilization rates may offset their effect on expenditures for physicians' services. If utilization controls are imposed along with fee ceilings, they must be universal. Otherwise, physicians will curtail the supply of services to patients in the controlled lines of business and make up for the lost business by inducing more patient demands in the uncontrolled lines of business. Since the imposition of such controls would be most likely with respect to governmentally financed services, one result would almost certainly be reduced access to care for disadvantaged population groups, and another result would quite likely be lower quality care provided by those practices that decide to remain active in the controlled market (for example, "Medicaid mills").

As serious as are the possible consequences of fee controls if physicians do indeed possess the capability of inducing demand to meet any level they desire, even more alarming are the implications for physician manpower policies. For over a decade the federal government has provided massive subsidies to greatly increase the number of medical school graduates, partly in expectation that some of the increased supply of practitioners would provide primary care services to disadvantaged population groups. If, however, the physicians' services markets are more or less immune to "normal" competitive processes, the unintended result could well turn out to be lower quality care through "over-doctoring" for the bulk of patients who seldom if ever face problems with respect to access to care. In this case drastic curtailment of physician training might be argued for on the grounds that it would prevent excessive fee inflation. Whether we are, in fact, faced with such a scenario depends upon the validity of the target-income hypothesis and its two key elements— the desire to achieve target incomes and the ability to induce (if necessary) sufficient levels of demand to do so.

Even if the target-income hypothesis could be rejected, the question of whether the markets for physicians' services are basically competitive or noncompetitive has major policy importance. If the markets are basically competitive, this implies that physicians are "price takers" rather than "price setters." If that is the case, government fee controls will inevitably mean reduced access to care and/or lower quality services. On the other hand, if the markets for physicians' services are noncompetitive, that is, physicians are to some degree "price setters," fee controls could result in lower expenditures on physicians' services without any contraction of output and corresponding restraints on access to care. For example, a system of controls could be imposed on the prices received by physicians, as in some states' Medicaid programs. In this case the imposition of regulated fees would, if practice demand curves were found to be quite steeply sloped, lead to increased provision of services, not, as might seem to be the case, as a result of "induced" demand, but because practice demand functions would be horizontal at the regulated fee level up to the limit of the available clientele.

PREVIOUS FINDINGS

The empirical evidence concerning physicians' optimizing behavior, pricing policies, and responses to fee screen reimbursement varies both in amount and in quality. Numerous studies of practice behavior have assumed profit maximization or argued that observed relationships between fee levels and proxies for practice costs, market structures, and reimbursement characteristics are consistent with profit maximization.[1] In its original form, the alternative target-income theory proposed two tests against the profit maximization hypothesis: namely, that high physician-population ratios (since they imply relatively few patients per physician and the highest likelihood of incomes below the targets) should be accompanied by: (1) high fee levels, and (2) high utilization rates. Findings on these tests are mixed.[2] Moreover, Reinhardt (1978) has shown that the utilization rate test is logically inconclusive because the neoclassical market model, which postulates profit maximization, may also predict a positive association between physicians per capita and utilization rates. He showed further that the fee level test is inconclusive because, even though the neoclassical model predicts a fall in fee levels as the physician-population ratio increases, the target-income theory does not necessarily predict a rise; that is, physicians may respond to diminishing clienteles by generating demands rather than by raising fees.

Citing "evidence provided by Kimbell [1974] and Kehrer and Knowles [1974]," Yett (1978) offered an alternative explanation to the physician-induced demand hypothesis for the observations of positive association between physician density and per capita utilization and fees. He observed that markups over unit costs were not positively associated with physician density and, therefore, the findings of positive correlations between fees and density were likely due to greater demands for costly quality amenities and to higher factor prices in urban areas with high physician-to-population ratios.[3]

However, perhaps the strongest evidence to date supporting the target-income theory was produced by Holahan and Scanlon (1978), who examined Medicare utilization rates in California during and after caps were imposed on Medicare reasonable fees by the Economic Stabilization Program (ESP). They found that, as the theory hypothesizes, utilization rates rose sharply while the caps were in effect but stabilized or fell afterward when Medicare fees began to rise rapidly. However, Hadley, Holahan, and Scanlon (1978) reported that California physicians' net incomes leveled off during the ESP. They inferred from this that the rise in Medicare outputs was offset by a decline in non-Medicare outputs, which, they argued, indicated that "physicians either did not or were unable to create enough demand to offset the fee restrictions imposed by ESP."

Although it is generally agreed that the structure of the physicians' services markets departs from the competitive norm,[4] there is little hard information to tell how large or small the departure is. Newhouse (1970) claimed that the markets are monopolistic, basing his claim on the finding that fee levels were positively correlated with the number of physicians per capita. Kehrer and Knowles (1974) obtained a similar finding but regarded it as theoretically implausible[5] and suggested that the correlation, as well as other correlations they found between fee levels and proxies for noncompetitive market elements, may have been due to interactions between service quality and market structure. On these grounds they refused to accept or reject the hypothesis of noncompetitive pricing behavior over the competitive norm.[6]

Unlike the data employed in many prior studies of physicians' economic behavior, those provided for this study contained time-series observations on physicians' procedure-specific fees, service outputs, and carrier (Plan) allowances. This made it possible to explore the policy issues with stronger methodologies than the others used to date. Hence, we believe that the findings given here add to the existing knowledge of physicians' economic behavior and furnish new information relevant to the design of policies to contain the costs of physicians' services.

BLUE SHIELD PLAN REIMBURSEMENT CHARACTERISTICS

Each of the two Blue Shield Plans included in this study, hereafter Plans A and C, marketed two types of health insurance contracts: usual-customary-and-reasonable (UCR) and indemnity. Regardless of the type of contract, claims presented to the Plan identify the services produced by the physician and the physician's fee or amount charged for each service. The Plan then sets the maximum amount allowed for each service. In indemnity business, the amount allowed is the lesser of the amount charged and a fixed, scheduled fee that is the same for all physicians. In UCR business the maximum allowed is called the "reasonable fee" and is ordinarily the minimum of the amount charged and the amounts set by one or both of two fee screens.[7]

Blue Shield Plans call the first screen the "usual fee" or Level 1 screen. In Plan A, the Level 1 is the physician's modal charge for a procedure and in Plan C it is the median. The second screen, called the "customary fee" or Level 2 screen, is a percentile. Both Plans A and C set their Level 2 screens at the ninetieth percentile of the Level 1s.[8]

Like Level 1 screens, Level 2 screens are determined from past fee data and are not affected by the physician's current charges. Thus, unless the physician charges less than the screen amounts, the reasonable fee for each procedure is fixed during the current period, and, unless it happens to coincide with the Level 2 screen, it is different for each physician. Plan A updates its screens annually, while Plan C updates semiannually.

The Plan determines the amount paid to the subscriber or physician, based on the amount allowed. Neglecting deductibles, the amount paid in UCR business is a percentage (up to 100) of the allowance, and in indemnity business it is the full amount of the allowance.

The net price of services to patients (or, alternatively, the amount of copayment) depends upon an institutional arrangement offered by some Plans called a physician participation agreement. Plan A offered such an arrangement, but Plan C did not. As in most Blue Shield Plans having participation agreements, a participating physician in Plan A agrees to accept the Plan's allowance for a procedure as payment in full.[9] In return, the physician may be reimbursed by the Plan rather than being paid directly by the patient. However, the agreement applies only to UCR business and not to indemnity claims.[10] Plan A's participation agreement is nominally on an all-or-nothing basis. Physicians who participate are technically required to participate on all claims, and nonparticipating physicians cannot participate on any claims.[11] On participating UCR claims, the net price to patients is, therefore, the amount allowed by the Plan minus the amount the Plan pays. On nonparticipating UCR claims and indemnity claims, the net price is the amount charged by the physician minus the amount paid by the Plan.

Participation status also has an important effect on the physician's average revenue. For nonparticipating physicians, UCR average revenue is the amount charged per unit of output minus bad debt, and the same is true for indemnity average revenue, independent of the physician's participation status. However, for participating physicians, UCR average revenue is the unit amount allowed by the Plan, and the amount charged has no relation to current earnings. In addition, the participating physician behaves like a price taker in the UCR submarket during the current period. This is because the amount allowed is predetermined by the Plan. Under the assumption that physicians are reasonably aware of their allowances, they have extremely little if any pecuniary incentive to charge (and to receive) an average revenue less than the unit allowance,[12] and therefore, average revenue should not exceed the unit allowance level.[13,14]

PHYSICIAN PRACTICE MODEL

The model outlined here employs the physician as the unit of analysis. It utilizes the following assumptions and hypotheses:

1. Demands are segmented between UCR and indemnity services.
2. The practice produces the same service for UCR and indemnity services and has a single-product cost function.
3. The practice's average revenue functions for indemnity and nonparticipating UCR services are downward sloping in amount charged.
4. The practice's average revenue function for UCR participating services is horizontal at the unit allowance level and has a finite length that depends upon the number and utilization rates of UCR patients.
5. The amounts charged for nonparticipating UCR and indemnity services are equal.
6. The practice's optimality condition can be represented by:

$$R' = C' + M \tag{1}$$

R' is total anticipated marginal revenue over the UCR and indemnity submarkets, C' is marginal cost, and M is a markup = 0 if the practice maximizes (expected) profit but $\neq$ 0 otherwise.

In support of these specifications it should be noted that: 1. is based on the usual convention that submarkets can be regarded as segmented if buyer crossover is impossible or minimal. Since patients cannot be covered by both UCR and indemnity contracts from the same Blue Shield Plan, buyer crossover here is confined to subscribers who switch contracts during the year. We believe 2. is a reasonable assumption, although there may be minor variations in service quality or amenities across lines of business. Such minor variations are much less likely to distort the cost function estimates than would a specification that treats the cost of output for one line of business as being unaffected by the volumes of output for other lines of business. The hypothesis, 3., was tested within the model's framework. Estimates of the demand elasticities were used to draw inferences concerning the practice's effective degree of market power. The assumption, 4., is based on the discussion of reimbursement for participating services given in the preceding section. The assumption of a finite (maximum) quantity demanded was motivated by the finding that observed gross incomes from UCR and indemnity services tended to be small.[15] Since the recorded claims represented large portions of Blue Shield business, the finding suggests that the average physician treated relatively few Blue Shield subscribers. Assumption 5. is based on descriptive results from the physician samples. Both on a procedure-specific level and in terms of overall charges per unit of output, there were no significant, systematic differences between UCR and indemnity charges.[16] A definition, 6., characterizes the practice's optimal charge and output decisions, regardless of the type of optimizing behavior.

Let:

p_t^U, p_t^I = amounts charged (gross prices) of UCR and indemnity services, respectively, in year t

A_t^U = amount allowed per unit of output for UCR services in year t

q_t^U, q_t^I = outputs of UCR and indemnity services, respectively, in year t

q_t^S = outputs of services in the non–Blue Shield submarkets in year t

The practice's nonparticipating average revenue, marginal cost, and markup functions were assumed to have the linear forms:

$$q_t^U = a_{10} + a_{11}p_t^U + a_{12}X_t \quad \text{(UCR nonparticipating} \quad (2)$$
$$\text{average revenue)}$$

$$q_t^I = a_{20} + a_{21}p_t^I + a_{22}X_t \quad \text{(indemnity average revenue)} \quad (3)$$

$$C_t' = c_0 + c_1(q_t^U + q_t^I + q_t^S) + c_2 Z_t \quad \text{(marginal cost)} \quad (4)$$

$$M_t = m_0 + m_1 Y_t \quad \text{(markup)} \quad (5)$$

X_t, Z_t, and Y_t are vectors of exogenous variables. No effort was made to incorporate the physician's participation decision into the model. Instead, different submodels were specified for nonparticipating and participating physicians, treating the participation decision as predetermined.[17]

A simplified version of the nonparticipating submodel is illustrated in Figure 8.1. Only two submarkets, the Blue Shield and non-Blue Shield submarkets, are shown, but it will become obvious that the implications apply to the UCR and indemnity submarkets, with minor modifications. The average revenue function for the non-Blue Shield submarket is the line segment AB, and the average revenue function for the combined Blue Shield submarkets is the line segment KD. The associated marginal revenue functions are AC and KE, respectively. The physician's total average revenue function (the horizontal sum of the individual average revenue functions) is AFG, and the associated marginal revenue function is AHIJ. In the figure it is assumed that $M = 0$, so that optimal output is q and the optimal amount charged in all submarkets is p. The outputs allocated to the non-Blue Shield and Blue Shield submarkets are q^1 and q^2, respectively.

To make the model operational, the total Blue Shield inverse average revenue function was defined as:

$$q_t = \bar{B}_0 + \bar{B}_1 p_t + \bar{B}_2 X_t \quad (6)$$

where q_t is the practice's total output, p_t is the amount charged, and $\bar{B}_0$, $\bar{B}_1$, and $\bar{B}_2$ are the sums of coefficients in the practice's individual average revenue functions.[18]

$$p_t = B_0 + B_1 q_t + B_2 X_t, \quad B_0 = -\bar{B}_0/\bar{B}_1, \quad B_1 = 1/\bar{B}_1, \quad B_2 = -\bar{B}_2/\bar{B}_1 \, (7)$$

FIGURE 8.1

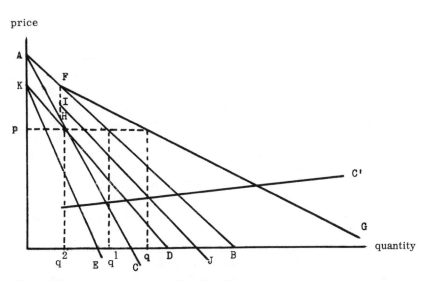

The total marginal revenue function is:

$$R'_t = p_t + B_1 q_t \tag{8}$$

Using this equation, the optimality condition (1), and the expression for marginal cost (4), the optimal charge level and output are given by:

$$p_t = (c_0 + m_0) + (c_1 - B_1)q_t + m_1 Y_t + c_2 Z_t \tag{9}$$

Equations (7) and (9) constitute a two-equation system with two endogenous variables, the average amount charged over all lines of business, p_t, and the physician's total output of services in all lines of business, q_t.

Inasmuch as only the UCR and indemnity outputs were observable, it was necessary to revise the system to make it estimable. The revised form of the nonparticipating submodel is

$$p_t = B_0 + B_1(q_t^U + q_t^I) + B_2 X_t + B_2 q_t^S$$

$$p_t = (c_0 + m_0) + (c_1 - B_1)(q_t^U + q_t^I) + m_1 Y_t + c_2 Z_t + (c_1 - B_1)q_t^S \tag{10}$$

p_t = average amount charged in UCR and indemnity business

$$q_t^U + q_t^I = \text{total output of UCR and indemnity services}$$

The variables p_t and $(q_t^U + q_t^I)$ are endogenous. The terms representing unobservable non-Blue Shield output q_t^S vary with the physician and are absorbed into the variance components in both equations. The variance components technique described below was used in combination with two-stage least squares (TSLS) to estimate the submodel. It should be noted that the markup function cannot be estimated because m_0 cannot be estimated. However, if coefficients on markup variables Y_t are systematically and significantly different from zero, it can be inferred with some justification that practices do not maximize profit. [19]

A simplified version of the submodel for participating physicians is illustrated in Figure 8.2. The physician's average revenue function for indemnity and non-Blue Shield services is AB, and the accompanying marginal revenue function is AC. Again, it is assumed that the amounts charged for indemnity and non-Blue Shield services are the same, so that the average revenue function here is of the general form, AFG, shown in Figure 8.1. The average revenue function for participating UCR services is EF, and the unit allowance level is JF. The total average revenue function is the broken line segment ADEFGH, and the total marginal revenue function is AEFI.

Three possible positions of the marginal revenue function are shown, and for simplicity it is assumed that $M = 0$. If C^{l1} is the practice's marginal revenue function, optimal total output is q^1, the amount EF is allocated to the UCR submarket, the amount $q^1 - EF$ is allocated to the indemnity and non-Blue Shield submarkets, and the optimal amount charged is p^1. If C^{l2} is the marginal cost function, optimal total output is q^3, the amount q^2 is allocated to the indemnity and non-Blue Shield submarkets, $q^3 - q^2$ is produced for the participating UCR submarket, and the optimal amount charged is p^2. In both cases the average revenue in the participating UCR submarket is JE.

Up to this point it has been postulated that the marginal cost function is upward sloping in output. Relatively little is known about physician practice cost functions, but some prior research has shown that practice marginal cost functions may be negatively sloped in output. [20] If the practice's marginal cost function is C^{l3}, it should (except as indicated by Note 20) have a shallower slope than the total marginal revenue function in order for a stable optimum to occur. Also, if the physician is observed to produce any participating UCR services, the amount must be the maximum quantity demanded EF. This is because the second-order optimizing condition cannot be satisfied at any output where C' crosses EF from above. [21]

FIGURE 8.2

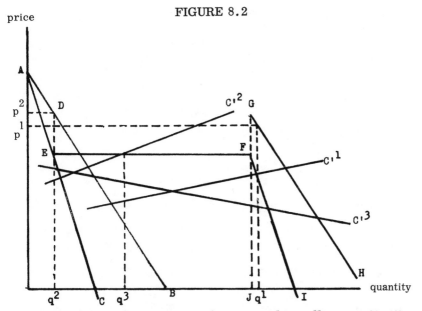

Inasmuch as physicians can be assumed to sell some quantity of indemnity and non-Blue Shield services, the first equation in the participating submodel is the average revenue function for such services:

$$p_t^I = D_0 + D_1 q_t^I + D_2 X_t + D_1 q_t^S \tag{11}$$

Equation (11) and the coefficients D_0, D_1, and D_2 are the counterparts of the corresponding terms in equation (10). The second equation is the optimality condition for indemnity and non-Blue Shield output. The marginal revenue function corresponding to (11) is:

$$R_t' = p_t^I + D_1 q_t^I + D_1 q_t^S$$

and the physician's marginal cost function is again:

$$C_t' = c_0 + c_1 (q_t^I + q_t^U) + c_2 Z_t + c_1 q_t^S$$

These expressions and the optimality condition (1) then give the optimality equation:

$$p_t^I = (c_0 + m_0^{I,S}) + c_1 q_t^U + (c_1 - D_1) q_t^I + m_1^{I,S} Y_t + c_2 Z_t + (c_1 - D_1) q_t^S \tag{12}$$

The superscripts on the markup coefficients refer to the markup on indemnity and non-Blue Shield outputs.

Average and marginal revenues on participating UCR services are just the current period unit allowance, A_t, for such services. Thus, for this segment of the practice's business, the general optimality condition is $C_t' = A_t - M_t^U$, where the superscript refers to UCR business. Writing out this condition and rearranging terms, therefore, gives the third equation in the system:

$$q_t^I + q_t^U = -(c_0 + m_0^U) + (1/c_1)A_t - (m_1^U/c_1)Y_t - (c_2/c_1)Z_t - q_t^S \quad (13)$$

Equations (11) to (13) make up the participating practice submodel. The variables p_t^I, q_t^I, and q_t^U are endogenous. It will be observed that there are three constraints on the coefficients across equations: (1) the coefficients on q_t^I in equations (11) and (12) sum to c_1, (2) the coefficient on A_t in (13) is the reciprocal of the coefficient on q_t^U in (12), and (3) the ratio of the coefficients on Z_t and q_t^U in (12) is the negative of the coefficient on Z_t in (13). The participating submodel was estimated with and without constraint 1. The results shown below apply to estimates using this constraint. It was not possible to include 2. and 3. since the statistical package had no provisions for imposing nonlinear restrictions. However, the relationships in 2. and 3. were employed on the unconstrained estimates to validate the model. The unobserved terms in q_t^S in (11) to (13) were absorbed into the variance components, and the submodel was estimated using the same technique as for the nonparticipating submodel.[22]

The foregoing submodels provide tests of each of the two policy issues discussed at the beginning of this chapter, namely:

1. They furnish the framework for performing two moderately general tests to examine the nature of physicians' optimizing behavior. The first test entails examination of the coefficients on the markup variables Y_t in the optimality conditions. If physicians maximize or approximately maximize profit ($M = 0$), the markup variables should not enter any of these equations significantly. To the extent that they do, it is indicative of optimizing behavior other than profit maximization. The second test involves inclusion of the county physician-population ratio in the vector of exogenous demand variables X_t, appearing in the average revenue functions. Significantly positive signs on the ratio in (11) and in the first

equation in (12) imply that increasing physician density shifts the practice's average revenue function outward. That is, they imply that output of the practice is able to sell increases, given the amount charged, as physician density increases. This type of behavior is compatible with demand generation in order to achieve a target net income. On the other hand, significant coefficients on the markup variables Y_t (indicative of nonprofit maximizing behavior), combined with positive or nonsignificant coefficients on the physician–population ratio, are suggestive of utility maximization rather than pursuit of a target net income.

2. The monopolistic-versus-competitive pricing issue was tested by examining the coefficients on output in the average revenue functions (11) and (10). The more negative are the price elasticities of the average revenue functions (that is, the larger the elasticities are in absolute value), the more competitive the markets can be assumed to be.

DATA AND ESTIMATION OF THE MODEL

The data used in this study were the claims records of 191 participating and 93 nonparticipating physicians in Plan A and 199 physicians in Plan C. The periods of observation were 1973–76 for Plan A and 1975–78 for Plan C. The claims records apply to approximately 60 high utilization medical, surgical, and other procedures and were provided by the Blue Shield Association.

The claims records contain amounts charged and amounts paid by the Plan. They also contain the frequencies with which the procedures were performed and certain additional claims data defined in Table 8.1. To derive a single measure of the physician's output, the procedure frequencies were converted into relative value units (RVUs), using the 1974 California Relative Value Scale. The numbers of RVUs were then aggregated for each physician and year, and mean charges and allowances per RVU were calculated for each physician and year. Finally, measures of RVUs were standardized across specialties in order to generate a common output index for all physicians.

To assure a reasonable degree of stability in the sample composition, only physicians having UCR claims data in all four years of the sample periods and whose participation statuses did not change during the sample period were included. Observations in given years were deleted for physicians having no indemnity claims in those years, so that all valid observations were on physicians having both UCR and indemnity claims. In Plan C the number of physicians meeting the selection criteria was still large, and a 33 percent

TABLE 8.1. List and Definitions of Variables

Variable	Definition
Endogenous and Dependent Variables:	
$CPRVU_t$	Average amount charged per RVU in UCR and indemnity business in year t
$CPRVU2_t$	Average amount charged per RVU in indemnity business in year t
$FIRST.RVU_t$	Total output of RVUs in UCR and indemnity business in year t
$FIRST.RVU1_t$	Total output of RVUs in UCR business in year t
$FIRST.RVU2_t$	Total output of RVUs in indemnity business in year t
Exogenous and Predetermined Variables:	
AGE	Physician's age in 1979
AMASEX	Dummy = 1 if the physician was female
AN	Dummy = 1 if the physician was an anesthesiologist
$APRVU1_t$	Average amount allowed per RVU in UCR business in year t
BORDCERT	Dummy = 1 if the physician was board certified in 1977
$DOCPRCAP_t$	Number of physicians per capita in physician's county in year t
FMG	Dummy = 1 if the physician was a foreign medical graduate
GP	Dummy = 1 if the physician was a general or family practitioner
GROUP	Dummy = 1 if the physician practiced in a group in 1977
GS	Dummy = 1 if the physician was a general surgeon
HOSPEMPL	Dummy = 1 if the physician practiced in a hospital in 1977
$INPAHOSP_t$	Fraction of the physician's RVUs provided in hospitals in year t
$INPERCAP_t$	Per capita income in the physician's county in year t
$LAGPRCLM_t$	Average number of days between claim filing and claim payment in year t (physician specific)
N	Dummy = 1 if the physician was a neurologist
NS	Dummy = 1 if the physician was a neurological surgeon
OBG	Dummy = 1 if the physician was an obstetrician-gynecologist

(continued)

TABLE 8.1 (continued)

Variable	Definition
$OLDRVU_t$	Percentage of physician's RVUs provided to patients aged 65 and older in year t
OMS	Dummy = 1 if the physician had a medical specialty other than and in addition to internal medicine and pediatrics
OPH	Dummy = 1 if the physician was an ophthalmologist
ORS	Dummy = 1 if the physician was an orthopedic surgeon
OSS	Dummy = 1 if the physician had another surgical specialty
OTH_EMPL	Dummy = 1 if the physician practiced in a setting other than solo, arrangement, group, partnership, and hospital in 1977
OTO	Dummy = 1 if the physician was an otolaryngologist
OVER65	Percentage of residents aged 65 and older in physician's county in year t
P	Dummy = 1 if the physician was a psychiatrist
PARTNER	Dummy = 1 if the physician practiced in a partnership in 1977
PD_	Dummy = 1 if the physician was a pediatrician
PCTFEMRV	Percentage of the physician's RVUs provided to female patients
$PRCT\_URB_t$	Percentage of residents in the physician's county living in urban areas in year t
$PCTIND_t$	Fraction of the physician's RVUs provided to indemnity patients
PTH	Dummy = 1 if the physician was a pathologist
R	Dummy = 1 if the physician was a radiologist
SPEC_2ND	Dummy = 1 if physician had a second specialty in 1977
TIME74	Dummy = 1 if the year of observation is 1974
TIME75	Dummy = 1 if the year of observation is 1975
TIME76	Dummy = 1 if the year of observation is 1976
TIME77	Dummy = 1 if the year of observation is 1977
TIME78	Dummy = 1 if the year of observation is 1978
U	Dummy = 1 if the physician is a urologist
$WAGEINDX_t$	Average payroll per employee in physicians' offices in county of practice in year t
$YNGRVU_t$	Percentage of physician's RVUs provided to patients aged 14 and younger in year t

random sample was chosen on which the nonparticipating specification was run.

The physician-specific claims data were merged with additional physician and county data taken from several sources. Physician and practice characteristics, such as specialty, age, sex, board certification status, country of medical graduation, and type of practice were derived from the AMA's 1977 Masterfile of physicians. The county-level data were taken from the 1978 Area Resources File prepared by the Manpower Analysis Branch, Health Resources Administration, DHEW, from the AMA's annual issues of Physician Distribution and Medical Licensure in the U.S., and in the case of the office wage rate proxy (WAGEINDX), from annual issues of the U.S. Bureau of the Census's County Business Patterns.[23]

The variables used in the model are defined in Table 8.1. Three groups of exogenous variables deserve comment:

1. Demand variables (X_t). Excluding the time and specialty dummies, four county-level and nine physician variables were chosen as potential shifting influences on the practice's average revenue function. The first four are county per capita income (INPERCAP), the percentage of the county population aged 65 and older (OVER65), the percentage of the county population living in urban areas (PRCT_URB), and the number of physicians per capita (DOCPRCAP). Justification of the first three of these is standard. The explanation for including the last has been given above.[24] The physician variables are board certification status (BORDCERT), a dummy indicating foreign medical graduation (FMG), the physician's age (AGE), sex (AMASEX), and possession of a subspecialty (SPEC_2ND), and dummies denoting group practice (GROUP), partnership practice (PARTNER), practice in a hospital (HOSPEMPL), and practice in another institutional setting (OTH_EMPL). The deleted mode-of-practice dummy denotes solo practice and practice in expense-sharing arrangements. BORDCERT and FMG are quality proxies. The remaining variables are product differentiation proxies representing quality or other characteristics making the physician attractive to patients as a provider. A final variable, the fraction of the physician's RVUs provided to indemnity subscribers (PCTIND), was included to standardize for the composition of demands facing nonparticipating practices.

2. Cost function variables (Z_t). The standardizing variables specified in the marginal cost function are four measures of the physician's patient mix, the mode-of-practice dummies defined above, the average lag between filing for a claim and Plan payment (LAGPRCLM),[25] and a measure of physicians' office staff wage wage rates in the county of practice (WAGEINDX). The measures

of patient mix are the percentages of the physician's RVUs produced in hospitals (INPAHOSP), for female patients (PCTFEMRV), for patients aged 14 and younger (YNGRVU), and for patients aged 65 and older (OLDRVU).[26]

3. Markup variables (Y_t). The nine physician characteristics listed above were designated as proxies for physicians' tastes that might affect the form of optimizing behavior and the magnitude and overall sign of the markup function. Unfortunately, the markup and cost function variables appear together in the submodel optimality equations, and some or all of the markup variables, especially those denoting mode of practice, may be related to marginal cost. Obviously, this makes it difficult to argue that the values of the markup variable coefficients can be used to draw conclusions as to the type of practice-optimizing behavior. Nevertheless, certain inferences can be made. For example, nonsignificant coefficients on the markup variables suggest that markups do not vary with physicians' tastes (and thus that physicians do not maximize utility), since the alternative theoretical explanation is that the relationships between the markup variables and markups are systematically offset by their relationships with marginal cost. Further, coefficients with signs indicating perverse relationships with marginal cost[27] might be taken as showing that the designated markup variables do, in fact, influence markups rather than marginal cost.

In presenting the physician submodels, it has been shown that the equation systems contain terms in unobservable non-Blue Shield outputs. It was also remarked that, due to the sampling of procedures and editing of the claims records before we received them, portions of the physicians' Blue Shield outputs could not be observed.

Unobservable components of each physician practice are assumed to affect the practice's marginal cost and average revenue functions. Since a random sample of the practices in each Plan are represented in those data, the appropriate model would be a "random effects" or "variance components" model. The effects of the unobservable components of the practices are captured in the estimation process by employing practice-specific dummy variables. The effects of the unobservable outputs (and other unobservable influences on the endogenous variables) were decomposed into two parts, with one part absorbed into the practice dummies and the other part absorbed into time dummies common to all physicians.

When the two-stage least squares estimator is applied, the model is termed a "fixed effects" model.[28] By employing the fixed effects framework, it is assumed that the coefficients on the practice dummies are fixed parameters that are estimated. While the variance components may be more appropriate theoretically, the estimators for the coefficients of the exogenous variables for both a fixed effects model and a variance components model are statistically consistent and asymptotically identical. The fixed effects framework was employed from economic considerations, with respect to computation.

FINDINGS

The estimated submodel for participating physicians [equations (11) to (13)] is shown in Table 8.2. The estimated submodel for nonparticipating physicians [equation (10)] is shown in Table 8.3. Since Plan C does not have physician participation agreements, the first submodel could be estimated only for Plan A. The second was estimated separately for Plans A and C. Seventeen specialties were represented in the data, and 16 specialty dummies were included in the equations. The omitted dummy refers to internal medicine.

Somewhat surprisingly, but consistent with the prior research described above, each of the three estimates of the slopes of marginal cost functions was negative.[29] However, in each case the estimated slope was not significantly different from the estimated slope of the total average revenue function in a neighborhood of equilibrium.[30] Since the marginal revenue functions are always more steeply sloped than the average revenue functions, this means that marginal cost crosses marginal revenue from below, and each of the submodel estimates consequently satisfied the second-order conditions for profit maximization. The possibility that practices maximize profit cannot be ruled out on the basis of negatively sloped marginal cost functions.

Nevertheless, the other results bearing on the type of practice-optimizing behavior are mixed. We argued above that the submodels provide three approaches for determining the nature of optimizing behavior. (1) Nonsignificant coefficients on the markup variables (physician characteristics in the optimality equations), or coefficients whose signs suggest that they capture the influences of marginal cost rather than markups, are generally indicative of profit maximization.[31] Here, the hypothesis is that the markup $M = 0$ and practices maximize profit only if the markup terms enter the optimality equations nonsignificantly, or significantly but with signs indicative of a cost rather than a markup relationship. (2) Systematically significant coefficients on the markup variables that are not plausibly due to relationships with marginal cost tend to imply either utility maximizing or target income-achieving behavior. (3) Systematically significant coefficients on the markup variables coupled with positive and significant coefficients on the physician-population ratio in demand functions suggest target income-achieving behavior. System-

TABLE 8.2. Constrained 2SLS Estimates of Submodel for Participating Physicians: Plan A

Variable	Indemnity/Non–Blue Shield Demand Function (11) Coefficient Estimate	t-ratio	Indemnity/Non–Blue Shield Optimality Equation (12) Coefficient Estimate	t-ratio
INTERCEPT	8.59806	1.50	10.42991	1.91
FIRST.RVU1	—*	—	-.00089[a]	-2.48
FIRST.RVU2	-.00069[b]	-4.13	-.00020	-.52
LAGPRCLM	—	—	-.00488	-.91
AGE	-.06538[a]	-2.11	-.05205	-.72
AMASEX	5.04228[b]	3.15	9.81564[a]	2.14
BORDCERT	-1.86265[b]	-3.11	-4.31906[a]	-2.45
FMG	-2.78944[b]	-3.04	-4.79566	-1.93
SPEC_2ND	-.03365	-.01	1.64744	.62
GROUP	.12597	.31	.30846	.31
PARTNER	-.12562	-.13	.11938	.10
HOSPEMPL	1.38505[a]	1.98	1.10635	.62
OTH_EMPL	-6.05693[a]	-2.56	-10.31772[a]	-2.03
INPAHOSP	—	—	.19688	.19
OLDRVU	—	—	-.84798	-.35
PCTFEMRV	—	—	-.35714	-.52
YNGRVU	—	—	1.06438	.86
DOCPRCAP	186.72515	.23	—	—
INPERCAP	-.00001	-.01	—	—
OVER65	24.72757	.51	—	—
PRCT_URB	-.00321	-1.06	—	—
WAGEINDX	—	—	-.07880	-.88
TIME74	-.01969	-.03	.83734	1.26
TIME75	.00013	.00	1.96720[a]	2.07
TIME76	.19495	.10	3.30388[a]	2.27
PD_	-.98848	-.97	-1.79620	-.44
OMS	-2.46247	-1.76	-4.66268	-1.42
NS	1.12970	1.13	.97268	.30
ORS	.27483	.32	.21621	.08
OTO	2.58503	1.19	1.24306	.32
U	.31301	.25	1.26792	.49
OSS	1.71683	.83	.77132	.21
OBG	.32999	.32	1.78957	.96
OPH	-.37980	-.25	.35953	.10
AN	-1.90470[b]	-3.20	-4.49376	-1.31
P	-.71832	-.61	1.63299	.78
N	-2.26462	-1.82	-4.26038	-1.17
GP	-2.55943	-1.41	-4.18808	-1.12
GS	.88675	.75	.80647	.26
R	4.33940[b]	3.38	10.42507[a]	2.09
Dependent variable	CPRVU2		CPRVU2	
DFE	485		480	
R^2	.45		.13	
F-ratio	2.12		.38	
Prob > F	.0001		1.0000	

(continued)

215

TABLE 8.2 (continued)

Variable	UCR Optimality Equation (13) Coefficient Estimate	t–ratio
INTERCEPT	14223.1^b	3.28
APRVU1	-868.7^a	-2.44
LAGPRCLM	-5.4	-.92
AGE	-78.1	-1.00
AMASEX	7051.2	1.62
BORDCERT	-2766.3	-1.70
FMG	-3212.5	-1.29
SPEC_2ND	4361.6	1.94
GROUP	597.1	.55
PARTNER	422.9	.32
HOSPEMPL	-2689.9	-1.62
OTH_EMPL	-8010.2	-1.67
INPAHOSP	1677.0^a	2.38
OLDRVU	650.2	.25
PCTFEMRV	-115.4	-.15
YNGRVU	1805.2	1.62
WAGEINDX	-91.2	-1.01
TIME74	865.7	1.34
TIME75	1744.2^a	2.08
TIME76	3287.2^b	3.05
PD_	-6013.9	-1.67
OMS	-7809.4^b	-3.86
NS	-4184.7	-1.44
ORS	-4693.9^a	-2.27
OTO	-3860.5	-.99
U	-2666.8	-1.03
OSS	-4448.8	-1.26
OBG	1734.2	.88
OPH	-3889.8	-1.12
AN	-8307.0^b	-5.67
P	-1835.2	-.85
N	-8304.6^b	-4.09
GP	-7761.6^b	-3.11
GS	-3640.5	-1.19
R	11738.2^b	3.61

Dependent variable	FIRST.RVU
DFE	481
R^2	.84
F-ratio	13.00
Prob > F	.0001

*Deleted variables.

[a]Denotes coefficients significant at the 5 percent level (two-tailed tests).

[b]Denotes coefficients significant at the 1 percent level (two-tailed tests).

216

TABLE 8.3. TSLS Estimates of Submodel for Nonparticipating Physicians

Variable	Plan A Coefficient Estimate	Plan A t-ratio	Plan C Coefficient Estimate	Plan C t-ratio
		Demand Equation		
INTERCEPT	9.15877	.41	.38138	.33
FIRST_RVU	-.00009	-.65	-.00019	-1.84
PCTIND	.23948	1.14	.05816	.72
DOCPRCAP	560.53086	.38	473.99365	2.52
INPERCAP	-.00035	-.26	-.00019	-1.82
OVER65	-19.18096	-.26	-54.69584[b]	-2.60
PRCT_URB	-.00156	-.26	.00782[b]	2.58
AGE	-.05700	-.34	-.01388	-.64
AMASEX	—*	—	-.15683	-.48
BORDCERT	2.06766	1.43	.23164	.62
FMG	2.43368	1.93	.41287	1.46
SPEC_2ND	-1.36944	-1.66	.89237	.91
GROUP	-.33608	-.22	-.05387	-.29
PARTNER	-1.12256	-1.63	.07756	.29
HOSPEMPL	-.51319	-.13	.80015[b]	4.06
OTH_EMPL	-1.51410	-.37	.77264	1.41
TIME74	.25618	.43	—	—
TIME75	.60509	1.01	—	—
TIME76	1.10348	.65	.35164[b]	3.61
TIME77	—	—	.62065[b]	4.74
TIME78	—	—	.76834[b]	4.17
PD	-3.28564	-.89	-.96585	-1.86
OMS	-1.95645	-1.19	-1.46871	-1.83
NS	.30695	.12	-1.25925	-1.42
ORS	-1.29523	-.31	-1.13293[b]	-3.37
U	-2.48217	-1.46	-1.11508	-1.44
OSS	.78867	1.88	-2.93311[a]	-1.99
OBG	-1.86470	-.73	-.30798	-.64
OPH	-2.83655	-.87	-.77445[b]	-2.59
AN	-1.09000	-1.51	.24830	1.23
PTH	-1.19291[b]	-4.67	—	—
P	-2.40793	-.78	-1.48063[a]	-2.53
N	-1.87038	-1.03	-.94794	-1.02
GP	-.97898	-.22	-.75565	-1.90
GS	.15003	.34	-.43172	-1.61
R	.25226	.18	-.32367	-1.22
Dependent variable	CPRVU		CPRVU	
DFE	185		495	
R²	.72		.83	
F-ratio	5.05		12.27	
Prob > F	.0001		.0001	

(continued)

217

TABLE 8.3 (continued)

	Plan A		Plan C	
Variable	Coefficient Estimate	t–ratio	Coefficient Estimate	t–ratio

	Optimality Equation			
INTERCEPT	-2.56957	-.56	10.84937	.91
FIRST.RVU	.00001	.30	-.00101	-.74
LAGPRCLM	.00185	1.59	0.00243	-.54
AGE	.06940	.91	-.16637	-.68
AMASEX	—	—	-1.61486	-.64
BORDCERT	.98006	1.43	3.77622	.71
FMG	1.25272^a	1.97	1.27807	.88
SPEC_2ND	-1.72949^b	-3.89	-6.36887	-.65
GROUP	.79487	1.23	.05112	.13
PARTNER	-1.33129^b	-3.28	.51959	.66
HOSPEMPL	2.70100	1.55	1.64657	1.18
OTH_EMPL	1.58136	.88	2.58372	.81
INPAHOSP	-.70461^b	-5.14	.65616	.60
OLDRVU	-.51721	-1.16	—	—
PCTFEMRV	-.16396	-1.08	-.33915	-1.17
YNGRVU	-.35987	-1.78	.38730	1.28
WAGEINDX	.04703	.90	—	—
TIME74	-.24188	-.62	—	—
TIME75	-.07562	-.15	—	—
TIME76	.02015	.03	.49577	1.07
TIME77	—	—	.74808	1.53
TIME78	—	—	.42668^a	2.17
PD_	-.06752	-.04	-4.06071	-.94
OMS	-.69688	-.90	1.16586	.36
NS	2.51946^a	2.19	-5.14524	-.73
ORS	1.70221	.90	-3.55011	-.88
U	-.74977	-.90	-6.38129	-.76
OSS	.62966^a	2.49	-.51475	-.16
OBG	-.47003	-.68	.69887	.42
OPH	.12005	.08	-.28724	-.45
AN	-1.12359	-1.93	.29898	.69
PTH	-1.54708^b	-8.64	—	—
P	-.32184	-.23	-5.96521	-.84
N	-.47316	-.53	-4.61786	-.67
GP	1.53760	1.19	-1.99769	-.83
GS	.79576^b	3.07	-1.37869	-.78
R	-.40494	-.47	1.59124	.50

Dependent variable	CPRVU	CPRVU
DFE	182	494
R^2	.85	.54
F-ratio	10.85	2.86
Prob > F	.0001	.0001

*Deleted variables.
[a]Denotes coefficients significant at the 5 percent level (two-tailed tests).
[b]Denotes coefficients significant at the 1 percent level (two-tailed tests).

atically significant coefficients on the markup variables and nonsignificant or negative coefficients on the physician-population ratio are compatible with utility maximization rather than target income-achieving behavior.

Applying these principles to the Plan A estimates, the results indicate that Plan A physicians were either profit or utility maximizers during the sample period. Three of the eight physician characteristics (FMG, SPEC_2ND, and PARTNER) used as markup variables appeared significantly in the nonparticipating submodel optimality equation for Plan A. And three of the nine characteristics (AMASEX, BORDCERT, and OTH_EMPL) used in the indemnity/non-Blue Shield optimality equation of the participating submodel entered significantly.[32] In addition, there was little consistency among the signs on the markup variable coefficients across equations and little clear indication that the significant coefficients reflect the influences of marginal cost. The results are, therefore, not conclusively consistent with profit maximization. On the other hand, the physician-population ratio did not appear significantly in either of the two submodel demand functions. This argues against the inference that Plan A physicians were target income achievers.

In the estimated (nonparticipating) submodel for Plan C physicians, the markup variables as a group were nonsignificant in the optimality equation. This is necessary but not sufficient evidence for profit maximization. The physician-population ratio entered the submodel demand function positively and significantly. Although one would expect target income achieving to be manifested by significant relationships between markups and physician characteristics (for example, to the degree that income targets vary with these characteristics), it is possible that variations in target income behavior across physicians were captured in the physician dummies. It may also be the case that the intercept term in the markup function, which could not be estimated, was systematically different from zero, even though the other terms in the markup variables were not. In either event, Plan C physicians exhibited behavior consistent in part with the target income hypothesis.

The second issue we sought to explore is the degree of the physician's market power, as revealed by the elasticities of practice average revenue functions. All three slopes of the estimated average revenue functions were negative, but only two of the three (for Plan C, physicians and for Plan A, participating physicians) were significantly negative at the usual levels, using one-sided tests.

Point estimates of the price elasticities of the average revenue functions, evaluated at mean outputs, are:

Plan A participating physicians: -3.01
Plan A nonparticipating physicians: -8.93
Plan C physicians: -12.19

While it is hard to tell how large in absolute value a price elasticity must be to demonstrate the existence of market power, it appears that the sample physicians can broadly be classified as monopolistic competitors. Unfortunately, no prior estimates of similarly specified practice average revenue functions are available with which to compare our estimates. What does seem to be true is that differences in price elasticities exist across physicians in the same Plan and in different Plans. Curiously, the behavior of Plan C physicians was most consistent with the demand generation hypothesis, which presupposes possession of market power, and yet the point elasticity estimates indicated that Plan C physicians faced "more competitive" markets than Plan A physicians.

It is worth observing that the high values of R^2 for most of the submodel equation estimates were largely due to variation explained by the physician dummies; that is, the nonsystematic variation in pricing and output policies among individual physicians was generally much greater than the systematic variation accounted for by the submodel explanatory variables. This, of course, makes it essential to describe the observed behavioral patterns as tendencies rather than as sharply defined characteristics of the sampled physicians' conduct.

CONCLUSION

This chapter has examined two issues concerning government reimbursement policy toward physicians, the nature of physicians' economic motives and the degree of market imperfections, in the context of an econometric model of the practice.

With respect to physicians' economic motives, there are two crucial alternatives: whether physicians are profit or utility maximizers, or whether they are target-income achievers, instead. If the former, then variants of the types of fee controls already in existence can be used to contain expenditures on physicians' services, and continued increases in the supply of physicians will have the same overall effect. If the latter, present policies to restrain fees and to increase physician supplies will tend to produce some combination of increased utilization (if physicians generate demands to maintain their income targets), rising levels of government and private spending on physicians' services, and, perhaps, a lower quality of care due to the possibility of iatrogenic consequences from "over-doctoring." Controls on both government and private utilization rates and limits on physician supplies would have to be imposed to meet the cost containment goals of reimbursement policy.

The findings presented here are somewhat mixed with respect to physicians' economic motivation. In Plan A there was no significant evidence of demand generation by physicians, but there were indications that physicians tend to maximize utility rather than profit. In Plan C the results concerning practice markups were consistent with profit maximization, but there was also evidence of demand generation. At least superficially, these latter two results are conflicting. However, it was not possible to estimate the constant term in the markup function (which measures the difference between marginal revenue and marginal cost at optimal output), and the possibility that Plan C physicians were not profit maximizers, therefore, cannot be ruled out. It is also well known that the appearance of demand generation, that is, outward shifts in practice demand functions with respect to increasing physician density, can be due to patient crossovers from physician-poor to physician-rich areas or to relatively easy access to care in physician-rich areas.

Nevertheless, the likelihood that Plan C physicians were (or were in part) target-income achievers cannot be rejected. What is perhaps more surprising is that Plan A and Plan C physicians appeared to exhibit different forms of optimizing behavior. This may, of course, be the consequence of such factors as differences in market structure that we were unable to observe, systematic differences in the two groups of physicians' medical training and background, or inherent differences in tastes. It does suggest that generalizations concerning the validity of the target-income theory should be made with caution, and that the critics who say that the theory is over-simplified in its present form are probably right. In any event, our findings indicate that the theory does not pervasively apply to physicians' economic behavior and that drastic revisions of current reimbursement policy based on the implications of the theory are premature.

The findings bearing on the degree of physicians' market power were reasonably consistent across plans, although, again, there were some differences between Plan A and Plan C physicians. On the whole, the sampled physicians' average revenue functions can be described as those of monopolistic competitors, downward sloping in price but with moderate to high (in absolute value) price elasticities. Indeed, for one of the three groups of sampled physicians, nonparticipating practitioners in Plan A, the estimated slope of the practice average revenue function was not significantly different from zero. In view of the differences in price elasticities across physician samples, it seems prudent to avoid gross generalizations about the "competitiveness" of physician pricing. Obviously, structural elements such as the ease of entry into local markets, the average size of practices, the prevalence of HMOs, and even the structure of insurance plan copayment can affect the slopes of practice average revenue functions and individual physicians' pricing behavior. But given these qualifications, and pending new evidence, it appears that physician pricing is better described as falling toward the competitive end of the spectrum rather than as characteristic of highly concentrated local markets.

NOTES

1. See, for example, Sloan (1976), Hadley (1978), Sloan and Feldman (1978), Sloan et al. (1978), and Sloan and Steinwald (1978).

2. Positive partial correlations between fee levels and physician-population ratios (supporting the target-income theory) have been found by Newhouse (1970), Huang and Koropecky (1973), Kehrer and Knowles (1974), Newhouse and Phelps (1974, 1976), Redisch et al. (1977), and Kimbell and Barros (1978), but negative partial correlations have been obtained by Steinwald and Sloan (1974), Sloan (1976), and Hadley and Lee (1978). Positive partial correlations between utilization rates and physician-population ratios were reported by Fuchs and Kramer (1972), Newhouse and Phelps (1974, 1976), Holahan (1975), May (1975), Davis and Reynolds (1975), Wennberg and Gittleson (1975), and Fuchs (1978), but negative partial correlations have been found by Kimbell and Barros (1978) and Held and Manheim (1980). And "all studies on physicians' earnings show that, cet. par., physicians located in high physician density areas earn less" [Sloan and Feldman (1978)].

3. Sloan and Feldman (1978) argued that a theoretically acceptable test of the supplier-induced demand hypothesis would require taking into account both differences in "quality amenities" and in the negative marginal utility they presumed is associated with a physician's exercise of the power to induce patient demands. Because of the difficulties inherent in capturing both influences, they concluded that "the reader lacking a vested interest in econometric applications may (perhaps legitimately) question whether economic theory and applied econometrics will ever settle this matter." To the extent that quality amenities and disutility due to demand inducement vary systematically among physician practices, the method of analysis used in this study should come closer to standardizing for these influences than has been the case in previous research.

4. See, for example, Arrow (1963), Rayack (1971), and Sloan and Feldman (1978).

5. One would ordinarily expect fee levels to decline (if tradi-

tional theory applies) as the number of sellers increases, regardless of the level of physician concentration. Somewhat puzzlingly, Newhouse asserted that the decline should occur only if markets are competitive, and, failing to observe the decline, he went on to infer that the markets must be monopolistic. Other authors have taken Newhouse's result more as supporting the target-income theory than as indicative of monopolistic market structure.

6. A few studies have sought to show that variation in fee levels within counties or SMSAs demonstrates noncompetitive pricing behavior. But they do not define meaningful market areas, which may be somewhat smaller than counties, and, even if fee levels were identical within market areas, it would not necessarily imply that markets were competitive. See Sloan and Feldman (1978) for a discussion of these studies.

7. Both Plans included in this study used two fee screens. The actual amount allowed may be higher than the fee screens under special circumstances, such as when the charge can be justified by an unusual complexity of treatment required. "Special circumstance" claims were edited from the data before they were made available to us.

8. Some Plans establish separate geographic areas within their overall markets and calculate a different Level 2 screen for each such area. Plan C follows this practice, but Plan A does not.

9. The amounts of any deductible or coinsurance for which the patient is responsible are thus relative to the amount allowed by the Plan rather than the amount charged by the physician; such copayments are generally collected by the Plan rather than by the physician. In practice, this is not an important feature since Plan A reported that 80 percent of its policies are UCR with no deductible and no coinsurance and the bulk of the remaining 20 percent are indemnity policies.

10. Participation agreements never apply to indemnity business, but they do apply to claims on partial service contracts in Blue Shield Plans having partial service business. Partial service contracts require participating physicians to accept the amount allowed as payment in full for all covered patients with incomes below a specified level. However, neither Plan A nor Plan C offers such contracts to subscribers.

11. Actually, it was found that roughly 10 percent of the Plan A sample physicians submitted both participating and nonparticipating claims, although predominantly one type or the other. The reasons are not pertinent here but are discussed in Yett, Der, Ernst, and Hay (1981). It was decided to classify physicians as participating in any one year if more than 5 percent of their claims in that year were submitted on a participating basis.

12. It could be argued that participating physicians whose UCR clientele was subject to substantial deductibles might charge less than the amounts allowed in order to obtain a desired level of UCR business. However, this would only be important in the highly unlikely event that the physicians wanted to decrease their charges in the current year in order to attract more patients with such insurance coverage.

13. We observed a number of physicians whose recorded charges were equal to their allowances, meaning that their actual charges were equal to or less than the minimum of the Level 1 and Level 2 screens. This could have been due to billing mistakes by physicians, miscoding by the Plans, the failure of the physicians to update their charges over previous years' levels, large amounts of professional courtesy services, or other reasons. The data on these physicians were deleted from the sample because it was not possible to observe the maximum allowances.

14. It is worth noting the parallels between private reimbursement by the Plans and the structure of Medicare and Medicaid reimbursement. As already indicated, Medicare and some states' Medicaid programs use the UCR method, except that: (1) the Medicare Level 1 and Level 2 screens are labeled "customary" and "prevailing," respectively, and (2) the Level 2 screens are seventy-fifth percentiles of the area fee distributions (adjusted downward since 1975 by the Medicare Economic Index formula). Medicaid programs not using the UCR reimbursement system employ a fee schedule system instead. Medicare and Medicaid both utilize an arrangement similar to physician participation called "acceptance of benefit assignment." The arrangement differs from Plan participation agreements in that: (1) accepting assignment under Medicare is on a claim-by-claim basis, and (2) accepting assignment under Medicaid, known as "participating" in the Medicaid program, is mandatory on all Medicaid services.

15. Depending on the Plan, year, and specialty, the mean volumes of recorded business ranged from about $2,000 to $6,000 annually. Assuming that physicians' total gross incomes probably averaged $40,000 or more, the observed Plan business appeared to amount to 5 percent to 15 percent of the total.

16. Similar results have been obtained by Freiberg, Gleeson, and Dolkart (1979) and Hadley (1978). The apparent fact that physicians charge the same fees across lines of business need not imply a lack of profit or income motivation, since the clerical costs of maintaining a two- or multitier billing system may be larger than any profit foregone by charging a single set of fees.

17. For justification of this assumption, see Yett, Der, Ernst, and Hay (1981), p. 17.

18. B_0 is the sum of the intercepts in the individual submarket

functions, B_1 is the sum of coefficients on outputs, and B_2 is the vector sum of coefficients on the components of X_t.

19. This claim needs to be qualified slightly. It is not necessarily true that markups will be the same in all submarkets for any given type of optimizing behavior. Even so, one would suspect that differences in submarket markups due to the failure to optimize separately in each submarket would generally be captured by the markup intercept term m_0. As a result, significant associations between p_t and the Y_t in the optimality condition are still suggestive of other than profit-maximizing behavior.

20. See Ernst and Schwartz (1974). An earlier study by Yett (1967) indicated that unit expense (and hence marginal expense) functions are U-shaped in output, but the upward sloping segment was beyond the range of the observed levels of output.

A downward sloping marginal cost function is not necessarily implausible if practices are not profit maximizers. If psychic costs are monetized and added to observed marginal costs, the slope and curvature of the resulting overall marginal cost function may, of course, be different from the slope and curvature of the observed marginal cost function.

21. As already remarked, it was found that indemnity and UCR charge levels were basically the same for all physicians. Since physicians whose allowances equalled their charges were deleted from the samples, it follows that at least some portion of the indemnity-non-Blue Shield average revenue function lies above the UCR participating average revenue function. This justifies the configuration of average revenue functions illustrated in Figure 8.2.

22. Note that if (as in Figure 8.2 with the marginal cost function at C^{l1}) optimal marginal revenue is less than the UCR allowance, the markup M^U is essentially a residual and should not be significantly related to Y_t.

23. Data on the proxy were not available for 1978, and the proxy was therefore deleted in estimating the model for Plan C.

24. Other county-level variables such as the level of schooling, percentage of minorities, percentage of poor, etc., were considered but abandoned when it was found that virtually all of the county variables were highly correlated pairwise.

25. Strictly speaking, the payment lag, used as a proxy for interest foregone on delayed payments, only affects the marginal costs of participating physicians. On nonparticipating claims, patients bear the costs of delayed payments. However, long payment lags on nonparticipating claims may delay the subscriber's payment to the physician, and for this reason LAGPRCLM was included in the marginal cost function specifications for both participating and nonparticipating physicians.

26. These four variables and LAGPRCLM were constructed from the Plans' claims records.

27. For instance, "perverse" signs are negative and positive signs, respectively, on the quality proxies BORDCERT and FMG.

28. See Mundlak (1978) and Maddala (1971) for discussions of the technique.

29. In the nonparticipating submodel, the slope of the marginal cost function is the sum of the coefficients on FIRST.RVU in the demand and optimality equations. In the participating submodel, it is the coefficient on FIRST.RVU in the indemnity/non-Blue Shield optimality equation (12) and the reciprocal of the coefficient on APRVU1 in the UCR optimality equation (13).

30. In the nonparticipating submodel, the difference between the slopes of the marginal cost and average revenue functions is the coefficient on FIRST.RVU in the optimality equation. In the participating submodel, it was previously remarked that a downward sloping marginal cost function implies that the function cannot intersect the horizontal segment of total marginal revenue function. The difference between the slopes of the marginal cost and marginal revenue functions is, therefore, the coefficient on FIRST.RVU2 in the indemnity/non-Blue Shield optimality equation (12). None of these coefficients was significant at the usual levels.

31. Note from equation (13) that, insofar as they represent influences on marginal cost, the markup variables enter the nonparticipating submodel optimality equation in the form $(c_2/c_1)Z_t$. Thus, since the estimate of c_1 is negative, any element of Z_t that is positively (negatively) related to marginal cost should enter the optimality equation with a positive (negative) sign as long as its dominant influence is on marginal cost. Assuming that one can predict relationships between marginal cost and the physician characteristics, this furnishes a rough way of determining whether the characteristics reflect cost influences or those of markups.

32. None of the nine entered significantly into the optimality equation for UCR services. But as already remarked, downward sloping marginal cost means that optimal output is not determined by UCR marginal revenue and marginal cost. Hence, the difference between UCR marginal revenue and marginal cost is essentially a residual, which, ceteris paribus, should not be related to physicians' tastes.

REFERENCES

Arrow, K. J. 1963. "Uncertainty and the Welfare Economics of Medical Care." American Economic Review, 53 (December 1963), pp. 941-73.

Davis, K., and R. Reynolds. 1975. "Medicare and the Utilization of Health Care Services by the Elderly." Journal of Human Resources, 10 (Summer 1975), pp. 361-77.

Ernst, R. L., and H. J. Schwartz. 1974. "Determinants of the Costs of Physicians' Services." An Original Comparative Economic Analysis of Group Practice and Solo Fee-for-Service Practice— Final Report. Springfield, Va.: National Technical Information Service.

Freiberg, L., S. Gleeson, and D. Dolkart. 1979. "Variations in Physician Pricing: Government Versus Private Insurance." Paper presented at the Western Economic Conference, Las Vegas, Nev., June 19, 1979.

Fuchs, V. R. 1978. "The Supply of Surgeons and the Demand for Operations." Journal of Human Resources, 13 (Supplement, Winter 1978), pp. 35-56.

Fuchs, V. R., and M. J. Kramer. 1972. Determinants of Expenditures for Physicians' Services in the United States, 1948-68. New York: National Bureau of Economic Research.

Hadley, J. 1978. "Physician Participation in Medicaid." Final Report on Contract No. 600-76-0054 with the Social Security Administration, U.S. Department of Health, Education, and Welfare. Washington, D.C.: The Urban Institute.

Hadley, J., J. Holahan, and W. Scanlon. 1978. "Can Fee-for-Service Reimbursement Coexist with Demand Creation?" Washington, D.C.: The Urban Institute.

Hadley, J., and R. Lee. 1978. "Physicians' Price and Output Decisions: Theory and Evidence." Final Report on Contract No. 600-76-0054 with the Social Security Administration, Department of Health, Education, and Welfare. Washington, D.C.: The Urban Institute.

Held, P. J., and L. M. Manheim. 1980. "The Effect of Local Physician Supply on the Treatment of Hypertension in Quebec." The Target Income Hypothesis and Related Issues in Health Manpower Policy, edited by J. M. Hixon. DHEW Publication No. (HRA) 80-27. Washington, D.C.: U.S. Department of Health, Education, and Welfare.

Holahan, J. 1975. "Physician Availability, Medical Care Reimbursement, and the Delivery of Physician Services: Some Evidence
from the Medicaid Program." Journal of Human Resources, 10
(Summer 1975), pp. 378–402.

Holahan, J., and W. Scanlon. 1978. "Price Controls, Physician
Fees, and Physician Incomes from Medicare and Medicaid."
Urban Institute Paper on Health No. 998-5. Washington, D.C.:
The Urban Institute.

Huang, L., and O. Koropecky. 1973. "The Effects of the Medicare
Method of Reimbursement on Physicians' Fees and on Beneficiaries' Utilization." A Report on the Results of the Study of
Methods of Reimbursement for Physicians' Services Under Medicare, prepared by the Health Insurance Benefits Advisory Council.
SS. Publication No. 92-73 (10-73). Washington, D.C.: U.S. Department of Health, Education, and Welfare.

Kehrer, B. H., and J. C. Knowles. 1974. "An Econometric Analysis
of Prices Charged for Medical Services." An Original Comparative Economic Analysis of Group Practice and Solo Fee-for-
Service Practice—Final Report. Springfield, Va.: National Technical Information Service.

Kimbell, L. J. 1974. "Physician Behavior in Scarcity Areas." An
Original Comparative Economic Analysis of Group Practice and
Solo Fee-for-Service Practice—Final Report. Springfield, Va.:
National Technical Information Service.

Kimbell, J. J., and L. L. Barros. 1978. Statistical Hypothesis
Testing of the MAB Health Systems Data Base. Final Report on
Contract No. HRA-231-77-0128 with the U.S. Department of Health,
Education, and Welfare, Health Resources Administration, Bureau
of Health Manpower, Division of Manpower Analysis. Santa Monica,
Calif.: Technology Service Corporation.

Maddala, G. S. 1971. "The Use of Variance Component Models in the
Pooling of Cross Section and Time Series Data." Econometrica,
39 (March 1971), pp. 341-58.

May, J. J. 1975. "Utilization of Health Services and the Availability
of Resources." Equity in Health Services: Empirical Analyses in
Social Policy, edited by R. Andersen et al. Cambridge, Mass.:
Ballinger.

Mundlak, Y. 1978. "On the Pooling of Time Series and Cross Section Data." Econometrica, 46 (January 1978), pp. 69-85.

Newhouse, J. P. 1970. "A Model of Physician Pricing." Southern Economic Journal, 37 (October 1970), pp. 174-83.

Newhouse, J. P., and C. E. Phelps. 1976. "New Estimates of Price and Income Elasticities of Medical Care Services." In The Role of Health Insurance in the Health Services Sector, edited by R. N. Rosett. New York: National Bureau of Economic Research.

Newhouse, J. P., and C. E. Phelps. 1974. "Price and Income Elasticities for Medical Care." In The Economics of Health and Medical Care, edited by M. Perlman. New York: John Wiley & Sons.

Rayack, E. 1971. "The Physicians' Service Industry." In The Structure of American Industry, 4th ed., edited by W. Adams. New York: Macmillan.

Redisch, M., J. Gabel, and M. Blaxall. 1977. "Physician Pricing, Costs, and Income." Paper presented at the Western Economic Association meetings, Anaheim, Calif.

Reinhardt, U. E. 1978. "Comment on 'Competition Among Physicians.'" In Competition in the Health Care Sector, edited by W. Greenberg. Germantown, Md.: Aspen Systems.

Sloan, F. A. 1976. "Physician Fee Inflation: Evidence from the Late 1960s." In The Role of Health Insurance in the Health Services Sector, edited by R. N. Rosett. New York: National Bureau of Economic Research.

Sloan, F. A., and R. Feldman. 1978. "Competition Among Physicians." In Competition in the Health Care Sector, edited by W. Greenberg. Germantown, Md.: Aspen Systems.

Sloan, F. A., J. Cromwell, and J. B. Mitchell. 1978. Private Physicians and Public Programs. Lexington, Mass.: Lexington Books (D. C. Heath).

Sloan, F. A., and B. Steinwald. 1978. "Physician Participation in Health Insurance Plans: Evidence on Blue Shield." Journal of Human Resources, 13 (Spring 1978), pp. 237-63.

Steinwald, B., and F. A. Sloan. 1974. "Determinants of Physicians' Fees." Journal of Business, 47 (October 1974), pp. 493-507.

Weichert, B. G. 1980. "Health Care Expenditures." In Health: United States, 1979, edited by J. J. Feldman, J. C. Kleinman, and L. A. Fingerhut. DHEW Publication No. (PHS) 80-1232. Washington, D.C.: Government Printing Office.

Wennberg, J. E., and A. Gittleson. 1975. "Health Care Delivery in Maine, I: Patterns of Use of Common Surgical Procedures." Journal of the Maine Medical Association, 66 (May 1975), pp. 123-49.

Yett, D. E. 1978. "Comment on 'Competition Among Physicians.'" In Competition in the Health Care Sector, edited by W. Greenberg. Germantown, Md.: Aspen Systems.

Yett, D. E. 1967. "An Evaluation of Alternative Methods of Estimating Physicians' Expenses Relative to Output." Inquiry, 4 (March 1967), pp. 3-27.

Yett, D. E., W. Der, R. L. Ernst, and J. W. Hay. 1981. "Blue Shield Plan Physician Participation." Health Care Financing Review, 2 (Spring 1981), pp. 9-24.

9

THE USE OF MEDICAL SERVICES UNDER PREPAID AND FEE-FOR-SERVICE GROUP PRACTICE

Anne A. Scitovsky

It is by now generally accepted, and there are ample data that bear it out, that prepaid group practice is able to provide quality medical care at lower cost than is generally provided under the fee-for-service system. Data to support this claim show that under prepaid group practice, there is more emphasis on ambulatory care, especially preventive care, and considerably less reliance on hospital care. It is generally argued that this emphasis on ambulatory as against hospital care under prepaid group practice is the result of physicians being at risk for practically all medical care costs of their enrollees and hence, having a financial incentive to keep costs down. It has sometimes been questioned, however, whether the lower costs under prepaid group practice plans are the result of the prepayment feature of such plans or of the group practice form of their organization.

Very little work has been done on this question. However, a study we have recently carried out sheds some light on this subject. In our study, we compare medical care use under two prepaid plans, one of which is the prototype prepaid group practice plan while the other is offered by a large group practice, which, except for a few groups of prepaid enrollees, operates largely on a fee-for-service basis. Thus, our study is in effect a study of medical care delivery under prepaid as against fee-for-service group practice.

This article first appeared in <u>Social Science and Medicine</u> 15C, No. 2, 107-116 (1981); reprinted by permission of Pergamon Press Ltd.

DESCRIPTION OF THE PLANS

The two plans are basic health plans offered by Stanford University, in Palo Alto, California, to its employees and their families. One is a Kaiser plan, under which care is rendered almost exclusively on a prepayment basis by a closed panel group practice of physicians, and hospital care is provided in hospitals owned and operated by the Kaiser system. Kaiser physicians who are partners of the group are remunerated by what in effect amounts to a basic salary, which is supplemented, when there is a surplus in the system, by a bonus that depends largely on the amount of time they worked. In addition, there are a small number of Kaiser physicians who are not partners and who are on salary. The essential difference between physicians in this type of system as compared to fee-for-service physicians is that they have no financial incentive to increase the demand for their services. The Kaiser plan has been available to Stanford employees and their families since the beginning of 1969. There are three Kaiser facilities in close proximity to Stanford University, two of them with large hospital facilities.

Under the other plan, United Medical Clinics/Blue Cross Plan (hereafter referred to as Clinic plan), physician services in and out of the hospital and outpatient ancillary services are provided by the Palo Alto Medical Clinic (PAMC), a multispecialty group practice of about 120 physicians located in the heart of Palo Alto, California. [1] It is predominantly fee-for-service group practice and offers only a few prepaid plans, which between them have accounted for about 15 percent of its gross annual revenue in the years since prepaid plans were offered. PAMC physicians share in the net receipts of the PAMC according to a formula largely, though not exclusively, based on their bookings (i.e., the dollar value of the services they render, excluding that of ancillary services ordered). The PAMC has its own laboratories, radiology and radiotherapy departments, physical therapy department, and other facilities for providing a wide range of ancillary services. It does not operate its own hospital but uses the Stanford University Hospital for patients who need hospital care. Hospital costs under the Clinic plan are covered by a Blue Cross policy incorporated into the plan. Thus, PAMC physicians are not at risk for the hospital costs of Clinic plan members, nor share in savings attributable to low hospital use. Because of this, and because Clinic plan and other prepaid patients constitute such a small percentage of the total PAMC patient population (and, moreover, because PAMC physicians rarely know whether a patient is prepaid or fee-for-service), PAMC physicians are unlikely to feel under any special cost constraints when treating Clinic plan patients and can be assumed to treat them much as they treat their fee-for-service patients. The Clinic plan has been available to Stanford employees since 1965 and in a somewhat different form since the early 1950s.

Benefit provisions under the two plans are very similar. Both provide comprehensive coverage to subscribers and dependents for physician services in and out of the hospital, for outpatient ancillary services, and for hospital services. The Kaiser plan provides somewhat more liberal hospital benefits and considerably more liberal maternity benefits than the Clinic plan and also covers routine eye examinations, which are excluded under the Clinic plan.

The two plans differ, however, in their cost-sharing provisions. While there is no cost sharing under the Kaiser plan except for a token copayment of $1.00 for a physician office visit and $3.50 for a home visit, the Clinic plan has a 25 percent coinsurance provision applying to all physician services in and out of the hospital and to outpatient ancillary services (but not to hospital services). Thus, Clinic plan members have to pay, in addition to their premiums, 25 percent of the scheduled PAMC fee for whatever PAMC service they use, whether it is a physician office visit, a major surgical procedure, or an outpatient laboratory tests. At the time of our study, this translated into a copayment of $3.00 for a routine physician office visit. In addition, Clinic plan premiums are also somewhat higher than those of the Kaiser plan, the difference amounting to about 16 percent at the time of our study. Moreover, since Stanford University contributes the lowest monthly premium of any of its basic health plans toward the cost of the plans for the employee, which happened to be that of the Kaiser plan at the time of our study, a Kaiser plan member without a dependent paid no premium while a Clinic plan member in the same category paid $2.77 a month, and employees with dependents also paid somewhat more for the Clinic than for the Kaiser plan.

STUDY POPULATION AND METHODOLOGY[2]

For the study of the use of physician services under the two plans, we chose as our study population those members covered by the plans the full 12 months, July 1973 through June 1974. This gave us just over 2,000 plan members for each plan. Data on age, sex, and occupation were obtained from Stanford University and the two plans. Data on other member characteristics such as marital status, family income, education of the head of the household, additional insurance coverage, attitudes concerning health care, satisfaction with the plans, health status, regular source of care, and length of plan membership were obtained in a long household interview at the start of the study. We also collected information on out-of-plan use in this interview as well as in three follow-up telephone interviews at intervals of three months. All data on the in-plan use of medical services were coded from the plan members' medical records.

For the study of hospital utilization and the use of ancillary services in ambulatory care, we included all persons who had been covered by the plans at any time between 1 January 1972 and 30 June 1974. This gave us about 7,000 person-years of coverage for each plan. For the majority of this group, the only demographic information we have is age, sex, and occupation of the subscriber since household interviews were held only with the subgroup covered the full 12 months, July 1973 through June 1974. As in the case of the smaller group, all data on in-plan use of medical services were obtained from the plan members' medical records.

The sociodemographic data available for the smaller of the two groups (those covered the full 12 months, July 1973 through June 1974) show some significant differences between Kaiser and Clinic members. The Kaiser group is somewhat younger and ranks lower in family income, occupation, and education of the head of the household than the Clinic group. A smaller percentage of the Kaiser group is covered by Stanford University's major medical insurance (66 percent compared to the Clinic group's 93 percent), but a higher proportion is covered by some other insurance (12 percent compared to 9 percent for the Clinic group). This may be due to two factors: first, that Stanford University employees have to pay for major medical coverage of their dependents, and second, that the Kaiser group may have a slightly higher proportion of two-earner families so that both spouses have insurance coverage through their employers. Kaiser members are somewhat less satisfied with their plan than Clinic members, but the difference is small. Not surprisingly, in view of the longer availability of the Clinic plan, the average length of plan membership is considerably lower for Kaiser members than for Clinic members (3.8 years compared with 10.0 years for Clinic members). The two groups also differ greatly with respect to their regular source of care, a factor that should be kept in mind since we will come back to it later in the chapter. While only 42 percent of Kaiser members reported having a specific plan physician as their regular source of care, 87 percent of Clinic members stated they had a personal physician.[3] The two groups do not differ significantly, however, in their attitudes toward seeking medical care and in their self-assessed health status. About the same proportion of Kaiser as Clinic members (24 percent compared to 22 percent) stated they felt free to consult a physician for minor ills, and 93 percent of Kaiser members and 94 percent of Clinic members reported their health status as either excellent or good.

FINDINGS

Because of the differences in the organization of the providers and in the cost-sharing provisions of the two plans, we expected differences in the patterns of medical care utilization under them. In particular, we hypothesized that there would be:

1. Greater use of ambulatory care under the Kaiser plan (because of the absence of cost-sharing provisions)
2. More patient-initiated and fewer physician-initiated office visits under the Kaiser plan (the first because of the absence of cost sharing, the second because of the lack of incentive under the Kaiser system to generate demand for physician services)
3. Greater use of preventive services under the Kaiser plan (to avoid possible expensive illness in the future)
4. Greater use of outpatient ancillary services under the Clinic plan (since the provision of such services generates income)
5. Lower use of hospital services under the Kaiser plan (because Kaiser physicians are at risk for the costs of such services while Clinic physicians not only are not at risk but can generate income by hospital services, especially surgery)

In the following, we shall take up these points, one by one.

Use of Physician Office Visits

Table 9.1 summarizes our data on physician office services under the two plans. It shows that the mean number of all office visits for the 12-month period, July 1973–June 1974, is almost the same, 2.97 visits for Kaiser members and 3.05 for Clinic members. Not surprisingly in view of the difference in the age composition of the two groups, the Clinic group being somewhat older, the mean number of visits for acute conditions is somewhat higher for Kaiser members than for Clinic members (1.39 compared to 1.23) while the mean number of visits for chronic conditions is somewhat higher for Clinic than for Kaiser members (0.98 compared to 0.90). Kaiser members appear to have more visits for symptoms than do Clinic members (0.26 per member compared to 0.18 for Clinic members), but this may be due to differences in the systems of medical record-keeping in the two organizations. Somewhat surprisingly, Kaiser members have a lower rate of preventive visits than Clinic members (0.42 preventive visits per member compared to 0.66 for Clinic members). We shall discuss preventive services in more detail in a subsequent section.

TABLE 9.1. Mean Number of Physician Office Visits, Kaiser and
Clinic Plan Members (July 1973–June 1974)

	Kaiser	Clinic
Mean number of office visits, all conditions	2.97	3.05
Acute conditions	1.39	1.23
Chronic conditions	0.90	0.98
Symptoms	0.26	0.18
Preventive care	0.42	0.66

Note: Office visits related to an episode of illness involving a
hospitalization have been excluded.

Thus, contrary to our expectations, our data show no marked
difference in the overall volume of ambulatory physician care provided under the prepaid as compared to the fee-for-service group
practice system. In fact, we know from a previous study that the
use of physician services under the Clinic plan has been held down
by a 25 percent coinsurance provision that was introduced in April
1967.[4] Until that time, Clinic members had first-dollar coverage for
all PAMC services. In our study, we compared the use of physician
services in the last full calendar year before the imposition of coinsurance (1966) with use in the first full calendar year after its introduction (1968) and found that the mean number of all physician services
had dropped 24.1 percent and the mean number of physician office
visits 24.9 percent. Moreover, in a follow-up study conducted four
years later,[5] we found that this decline in use was not a temporary
effect but that utilization stayed at the lower level. Thus, in the
absence of coinsurance, the volume of ambulatory care delivered
under the Clinic plan would very probably be higher than that provided
under the Kaiser plan.

However, our current study found some evidence that suggests
that there may be a factor at work under the Kaiser plan that keeps
the use of physician services down. In our analysis of the use of all
physician services, we found that under both plans, members who
have no specific plan physician as a regular source of care use significantly fewer physician services per year than those who have a
regular physician.[6] Holding other member characteristics constant,
Kaiser members who have no specific plan physician use 1.39 fewer
physician services than those with a specific physician; the corresponding figure for Clinic members is 1.05 fewer physician services.

Because, as we mentioned earlier, a much lower proportion of Kaiser than Clinic members had a specific plan physician as regular source of care, the volume of physician services was kept down. Pooling the data for the two plans and using multiple regression analysis, with the number of physician services as the dependent variable and all other member characteristics enumerated above (including plan membership) as independent variables, we found that the small and statistically insignificant difference in the mean number of physician services of members under the two plans (Kaiser members averaged 3.59 services per year, Clinic members 3.83) diminishes still further when all member characteristics except regular source of care are taken into account. When this variable is added, the Kaiser rate becomes 0.48 visits higher than the Clinic rate, which is a statistically significant difference. In other words, if Kaiser and Clinic members had been identical in all characteristics for which we had data, and especially in their physician affiliation rates, Kaiser members would have been higher users of physician services than Clinic members.

While we did not duplicate this analysis for physician office visits, there is no reason to believe that our findings would be different from those for all physician services. Our data thus show that the overall volume of ambulatory physician services is much the same under prepaid as under fee-for-service group practice, that under both plans physician utilization is held down by factors associated with the plans (coinsurance in the case of the Clinic plan, a low physician affiliation rate under the Kaiser plan), that in the absence of these factors physician utilization under both plans would be higher, but that again the rates of use under the two plans would not differ greatly.

Patient-Initiated and Physician-Initiated Visits for Illness

While we did not ask plan members in the household interviews whether a physician visit was initiated by them or by a physician, we coded all data on medical care use by episode of illness and assumed that the initial visit for an episode was patient-initiated while a follow-up visit was physician-initiated. This is obviously an over-simplification, but we believe that the exceptions may cancel out and that, by and large, the assumption holds true.

Our findings are summarized in Table 9.2. Again, our hypothesis about differences in the pattern of use under the two plans is not borne out by our data. While the number of initial visits for illness per plan member is indeed slightly though not significantly higher for Kaiser than for Clinic members—1.55 compared to 1.47—

TABLE 9.2. Initial and Follow-Up Office Visits for Illness, Kaiser and Clinic Plan Members (July 1973–June 1974)

	Kaiser	Clinic
Number of initial office visits for illness		
per member	1.55	1.47
Acute conditions	0.92	0.85
Chronic conditions	0.45	0.50
Symptoms	0.17	0.12
Number of follow-up office visits for illness		
per member	1.00	0.92
Acute conditions	0.47	0.38
Chronic conditions	0.45	0.48
Symptoms	0.08	0.06
Number of follow-up office visits		
per episode of illness	0.65	0.62
Acute conditions	0.51	0.45
Chronic conditions	1.00	0.96
Symptoms	0.49	0.47
Percentage of initial office visits for illness		
with no follow-up visits	68.6	69.5
Acute conditions	72.0	73.9
Chronic conditions	60.7	60.8
Symptoms	70.8	74.7

Note: Office visits related to an episode of illness involving a hospitalization have been excluded.

the number of follow-up visits for illness per member is actually slightly (though again not significantly) higher for Kaiser than for Clinic members—1.00 compared to 0.92. The number of follow-up visits per episode of illness, however, is very similar under the two plans, 0.65 for Kaiser and 0.62 for Clinic members. Similarly, the percentage of all office visits for illness without a follow-up visit is much the same under the two plans—68.6 percent for Kaiser members and 69.5 percent for Clinic members.

Looking at our data by type of condition (i.e., acute, chronic, or symptoms), we find the number of initial and of follow-up visits per member reflect what we would expect from the figures in Table 9.1. Kaiser members have more initial and follow-up visits for acute conditions than do Clinic members (0.92 initial and 0.47 follow-up visits compared to Clinic members' 0.85 initial and 0.38 follow-up visits) while Clinic members have more initial and follow-up visits for chronic conditions (0.50 initial and 0.48 follow-up visits compared to 0.45 initial and 0.45 follow-up visits for Kaiser members). The numbers of follow-up visits per episode of illness by type of condition, however, are not markedly different, although the Kaiser figures are slightly higher than the Clinic figures. As the table shows, the number of follow-up visits for acute conditions is 0.51 for Kaiser and 0.45 for Clinic members; for chronic conditions, the figures are 1.00 for Kaiser and 0.96 for Clinic members, and for symptoms they are 0.49 and 0.47 respectively. There is also little difference between the plans in the percentage of initial office visits without a follow-up visit by type of condition, the Kaiser figures being slightly lower than the Clinic figures for all three types of conditions. Thus, 72.0 percent of initial office visits for acute conditions are without a follow-up visit in the case of Kaiser members as compared with 73.9 percent in the case of Clinic members; for chronic conditions, the percentages are 60.7 percent for Kaiser compared to 60.8 percent for Clinic members, and for symptoms they are 70.8 percent and 74.7 percent, respectively.

To sum up, our study found little evidence of greater use of patient-initiated physician visits under the Kaiser plan and a larger volume of physician-initiated visits under the Clinic plan. If anything, our data show a slightly higher use of follow-up visits and also a somewhat smaller percentage of initial office visits for illness without a follow-up visit under the Kaiser than under the Clinic plan, but the differences are small.

Use of Preventive Services

As was already shown in Table 9.1, while the mean number of all office visits as well as of office visits for acute and for chronic conditions is quite similar under the two plans, the use of preventive services is substantially less under the Kaiser plan, amounting to 0.42 visits per person per year compared to 0.66 under the Clinic plan. This is one of the few relatively large differences in the pattern of medical care use under the two plans and goes counter to our hypothesis that the Kaiser-type prepaid group practice form has special financial incentives to provide preventive care in order to avoid costly care for illness.

The figure for preventive care in Table 9.1 includes all types of preventive services, such as routine physical examinations, gynecological examinations (Pap smears), well-baby care, immunizations, and routine eye examinations. Two of these, routine physical examinations and gynecological examinations, we examined in more detail. In both cases, the Kaiser rate is substantially below the Clinic rate. Our data show that 37 percent of Clinic members and only 26 percent of Kaiser members had one or more routine physical examinations in the 12-month period, July 1973 through June 1974. The Kaiser rates are lower, in most cases significantly so, for all subgroups except members of families with income under $5,000 a year, a very small group. The multivariate analysis (logit) of the data (where we used the log of the probability that a plan member had one or more routine physical examinations during the period as the dependent variable) showed that, as in the case of all physician visits, the absence of a specific plan physician as regular source of care seems to be an important factor in determining the use of this service as well, and that the low physician affiliation rate of Kaiser members explains to a large extent the difference in the Kaiser and Clinic rates of routine physical examinations. When adjustments are made for all member characteristics for which we have data except regular source of care, the difference of 11 percentage points (37 to 26 percent) between the Kaiser and Clinic rates is reduced to 6 percentage points. Adjustment for this factor as well brings the difference between the two rates down to 3 percentage points, a difference which is not statistically significant.

Our findings for gynecological examinations are very similar, the Kaiser rate again being considerably below the Clinic rate. While 47 percent of Clinic plan women aged 17 through 64 years had one or more gynecological examinations in the period, July 1973 to June 1974, only 34 percent of Kaiser plan women had one. Again, the Kaiser rates are lower than the Clinic rates for all subgroups with one exception, that of women aged 17 to 24. Using the same type of multivariate analysis (logit) as in the case of routine physical examinations, we found that when adjustments are made for all member characteristics except regular source of care, the difference between the Kaiser and Clinic rates actually increases slightly. When adjustment is made for regular source of care as well, the difference of 13 percentage points between the Kaiser and Clinic rates (47 to 34 percent) is reduced to 10 percentage points, but the difference between the two rates is still statistically significant.

It is not only somewhat surprising that the Kaiser rates of routine physical and gynecological examinations are lower than the Clinic rates but that both rates are very close to the national rates in the United States, as shown by data from the Health Interview Survey of the National Center for Health Statistics. In fact, the rates of gynecological examinations under both plans are somewhat below the national rates, since national data show that 50 percent of all women aged 17 to 64 years had had a gynecological examination in

1973. National data for routine physical examinations are available only for children under age 17, and they show that 50 percent of this age group had had such an examination in 1973; this compares to 38 percent of Kaiser members and 55 percent of Clinic members in the same age group. The national data are not strictly comparable to ours since they come from household interviews rather than medical records. It is possible that the national data have an upward bias because some respondents, feeling that preventive care is generally regarded as a good thing, may have given what they considered the expected answer. If this is not the explanation for the closeness of the national figures and those for our prepaid plans, some re-examination of preventive care under prepaid group practice may be in order.

Use of Ancillary Services in Ambulatory Care

Tables 9.3 and 9.4 present our data on the use on the principal ancillary services—laboratory tests, X-rays, injections and immunizations, and electrocardiograms (ECGs)—used in ambulatory care. Table 9.3 shows the number of each of these services per physician office visit for all conditions combined and separately for acute conditions, chronic conditions, symptoms, and preventive care. The table also presents the data for all physicians combined and separately for internists and family practitioners and for pediatricians, the principal specialties using ancillary services. Table 9.4 shows the same data, in the same format, in terms of the number of services per episode of care.

To begin with Table 9.3 and the data on laboratory tests for all physicians: PAMC physicians seem to be heavier users of such tests than Kaiser physicians, averaging 2.8 tests per physician office visit compared with 1.8 for Kaiser physicians. As the data by type of care show, however, this difference is due entirely to the greater use of laboratory tests by PAMC physicians in preventive care, where the average number of tests per physician office visit is 8.8 compared to the Kaiser average of 4.7. The explanation for this high use of laboratory tests on the part of PAMC physicians in preventive care may be that during the study period, many physicians sent patients for a general workup to a newly established (and independent from the PAMC) Automated Multiphasic Laboratory (AML), which performed a whole battery of tests (laboratory tests, X-rays, ECGs, hearing tests, eye examinations, etc.) at a cost considerably below the cost at which these tests could have been performed at the PAMC. Excluding preventive care, the use of laboratory tests is much the same for Kaiser and PAMC physicians, 1.2 per physician

TABLE 9.3. Number of Outpatient Laboratory Tests, X-rays, Injections and Immunizations, and ECGs per Physician Office Visit—All Physicians and Selected Specialties—Kaiser and Clinic Members (January 1972–June 1974)

	Laboratory Tests		X-rays		Injections/ Immunizations		ECGs	
	Kaiser	Clinic	Kaiser	Clinic	Kaiser	Clinic	Kaiser	Clinic
All physicians								
Total	1.823	2.826	0.132	0.157	0.219	0.180	0.039	0.046
Total excluding preventive care	1.235	1.089	0.108	0.110	0.182	0.190	0.011	0.013
Acute conditions	0.998	0.693	0.096	0.100	0.065	0.074	0.003	0.002
Chronic conditions	1.306	1.357	0.102	0.112	0.442	0.369	0.016	0.020
Symptoms	2.356	2.418	0.196	0.170	0.038	0.048	0.036	0.048
Preventive care	4.689	8.772	0.248	0.317	0.400	0.146	0.176	0.162
Internal medicine + family practice								
Total	3.018	5.683	0.217	0.300	0.198	0.093	0.093	0.124
Total excluding preventive care	1.845	1.850	0.133	0.162	0.150	0.110	0.022	0.032
Acute conditions	1.505	1.089	0.095	0.146	0.055	0.108	0.007	0.005
Chronic conditions	1.999	2.289	0.147	0.161	0.339	0.130	0.032	0.044
Symptoms	2.743	2.990	0.243	0.224	0.025	0.045	0.057	0.086
Preventive care	11.020	18.131	0.789	0.749	0.525	0.037	0.577	0.424
Pediatrics								
Total	1.399	1.465	0.031	0.059	0.188	0.138	0.002	0.001
Total excluding preventive care	0.893	0.707	0.037	0.073	0.057	0.041	0.002	0.001
Acute conditions	0.698	0.535	0.030	0.070	0.060	0.021	0.001	—
Chronic conditions	1.207	0.852	0.051	0.076	0.048	0.177	0.012	0.008
Symptoms	2.100	3.086	0.078	0.104	0.035	0.005	0.003	—
Preventive care	2.782	3.622	0.016	0.022	0.547	0.416	0.002	0.001

TABLE 9.4. Number of Outpatient Laboratory Tests, X-rays, Injections and Immunizations, and ECGs per Episode of Care—All Physicians and Selected Specialties—Kaiser and Clinic Members (January 1972–June 1974)

	Laboratory Tests		X-rays		Injections/ Immunizations		ECGs	
	Kaiser	Clinic	Kaiser	Clinic	Kaiser	Clinic	Kaiser	Clinic
All physicians								
Total	2.81	4.39	0.20	0.24	0.34	0.28	0.06	0.07
Total excluding preventive care	2.01	1.86	0.18	0.19	0.30	0.33	0.02	0.02
Acute conditions	1.48	1.03	0.14	0.15	0.10	0.11	*	*
Chronic conditions	2.71	2.98	0.21	0.25	0.92	0.81	0.03	0.04
Symptoms	3.46	3.61	0.29	0.25	0.06	0.07	0.05	0.07
Preventive care	5.71	10.35	0.30	0.37	0.49	0.17	0.21	0.19
Internal medicine + family practice								
Total	4.50	8.60	0.32	0.45	0.29	0.14	0.14	0.19
Total excluding preventive care	2.92	3.12	0.21	0.27	0.24	0.19	0.04	0.05
Acute conditions	2.02	1.50	0.13	0.20	0.07	0.15	0.01	0.01
Chronic conditions	4.41	5.18	0.33	0.36	0.75	0.29	0.07	0.01
Symptoms	4.16	4.34	0.37	0.33	0.04	0.07	0.09	0.13
Preventive care	11.71	20.52	0.84	0.85	0.56	0.04	0.61	0.48
Pediatrics								
Total	2.14	2.10	0.05	0.09	0.29	0.20	*	*
Total excluding preventive care	1.34	1.03	0.06	0.11	0.09	0.06	*	*
Acute conditions	1.05	0.75	0.04	0.10	0.09	0.03	*	—†
Chronic conditions	2.18	1.68	0.09	0.15	0.09	0.35	0.02	0.02
Symptoms	2.64	4.05	0.10	0.14	0.04	0.01	*	—
Preventive care	4.44	4.98	0.03	0.03	0.87	0.57	*	*

*Figure less than 0.01.
†Not applicable.

office visit for Kaiser and 1.1 for PAMC physicians. The data for internists and family practitioners show much the same pattern, the PAMC figures for all laboratory tests for all types of care again being higher than the Kaiser figures but almost identical when preventive care is excluded. In the case of pediatricians, the use of laboratory tests is much the same for both groups, even when tests done in connection with preventive care are included, although here too PAMC physicians are somewhat higher users than Kaiser physicians.

The data on the number of x-rays per physician office visit for all physicians show a slightly higher use by PAMC than Kaiser physicians, though the difference is small—0.157 for PAMC and 0.132 for Kaiser physicians. As in the case of laboratory tests, the difference is due largely to the greater use of x-rays by PAMC physicians in preventive care and practically disappears when this type of care is excluded from the figures. However, PAMC internists, family practitioners, and pediatricians are somewhat greater users of x-rays than Kaiser physicians, even when preventive services are excluded. In the case of pediatricians, this may be due to the fact that Clinic plan children tend to be older than Kaiser plan children and that PAMC pediatricians therefore see more trauma patients.

The data on the remaining two types of ancillary services show that Kaiser physicians are somewhat heavier users of injections and immunizations while PAMC physicians use somewhat more ECGs. These differences are likely to be due largely to the different age distributions of the two groups, the Kaiser group having a higher percentage of young children and the Clinic group a higher percentage of older members.

Table 9.4, which presents the same data in terms of the number of different ancillary services per episode of care, shows the same pattern. What emerges from both tables is that there is no major difference in the use of ancillary services in ambulatory care between the two types of group practices. Except for the considerably higher use of laboratory tests in preventive care—which may have been a one-time phenomenon since the AML went out of business shortly after our study ended—and the somewhat higher use of x-rays on the part of PAMC physicians, the fee-for-service group performed very similarly to the prepaid group.

Use of Hospital Services

Perhaps the most surprising finding of our study relates to the use of hospital services. That our hypothesis of lower use under the Kaiser plan is not borne out by the data is shown in Table 9.5, which presents the age-sex adjusted hospital utilization rates under the two

TABLE 9.5. Hospital Utilization by Kaiser and Clinic Plan Members,
January 1972–June 1974: Age-Sex Adjusted
Annualized Rates*

Type of Case	Kaiser	Clinic
Non-maternity		
Number of hospital days per 1,000 person-years	249.8	250.7
Medical	85.9	87.2
Surgical	163.9	163.5
Number of hospital admissions		
per 1,000 person-years	38.2	44.2
Medical	13.2	11.8
Surgical	25.0	32.4
Average length of stay	6.5	5.7
Medical	6.5	7.4
Surgical	6.5	5.0
Surgical procedures		
Number of hospital surgical procedures performed		
on a nonadmission basis, per 1,000 person-years	10.7	5.3
Number of all hospital surgical procedures,		
including admissions and nonadmissions,		
per 1,000 person-years	35.7	37.6
Maternity		
Number of hospital days per 1,000 person-years	66.8	24.6
Number of deliveries per 1,000 person-years	19.0	8.8
Average length of stay	3.5	2.8

*Age-sex adjusted by the direct method to the age-sex distribu-
tion of the combined Kaiser and Clinic plan study population. Percentages may not add up to 100.0 percent because of rounding.

plans. Because the study population for this part of the study consists
of all persons who had been members of the plans at any time (and
for varying lengths of time) between 1 January 1972 and 30 June 1974,
we converted the membership figures into person-years of coverage.[7]
The number of hospital days (excluding maternity) per 1,000
person-years is almost identical under the two plans—249.8 for
Kaiser members, 250.7 for Clinic members. The figures are also
very similar when broken down into medical and surgical hospital

days. Medical hospital days average 85.9 per 1,000 person-years for Kaiser members, 87.2 for Clinic members, while surgical days are 163.9 per 1,000 person-years for Kaiser members and 163.5 for Clinic members.

These figures are low not only when compared to the national figure for the United States, which in 1974 amounted to 912.7 hospital days per 1,000 persons under 65 years of age, but even when compared to the rates under other prepaid group practice plans. A report on hospital utilization under individual and group practice plans of the Federal Employees Health Benefits Program in calendar year 1972, [8] for example, shows that of the 16 prepaid group practice plans offered to these employees, only three had lower hospital utilization rates than our two groups. The rates of the 13 plans with higher use rates ranged from 316.3 days to 590.0 days per 1,000 person-years. The utilization rates of the three exceptions ranged from 171.5 days to 235.7 days per 1,000 person-years. It should be noted, however, that two of these three plans were relatively new plans and may not yet have been fully operating. All the individual practice plans showed a very much greater use of hospital services, the number of days per 1,000 person-years ranging from 383.8 to 754.8.

The hospital admission rate per 1,000 person-years is indeed higher for Clinic than Kaiser members, amounting to 44.2 admissions for Clinic as against 38.2 for Kaiser members. The figures in Table 9.5 show that this difference is due entirely to the higher surgical admission rate of Clinic members, the medical admission rate actually being slightly higher for Kaiser than for Clinic members. The Clinic surgical admission rate is 32.4 admissions per 1,000 person-years compared to the Kaiser rate of 25.0. However, the surgical admission rate is not a very good measure of hospital surgical use under the two plans because under both plans there was also some hospital surgery performed on a nonadmission basis. The rate of this type of hospital surgery was considerably higher for Kaiser members, amounting to 10.7 such procedures per 1,000 person-years compared to 5.3 for Clinic members. As Table 9.5 shows, when these nonadmission hospital surgical procedures are added to the surgical admissions, the total hospital surgical procedure rates under the two plans become almost identical, 35.7 for Kaiser members and 37.6 for Clinic members. [9]

In view of the liberal maternity benefits of the Kaiser plan compared to the rather restricted coverage of maternity care under the Clinic plan, and the higher proportion of women in the childbearing ages among Kaiser members, it is not surprising that maternity days and deliveries per 1,000 person-years are substantially higher under the Kaiser than under the Clinic plan. It is worth noting, however, that the average length of stay for delivery is almost a full day shorter for Clinic than Kaiser patients—2.8 days compared to 3.5 days. This is likely to be due to the fact that Clinic members are reimbursed for only a small part of the costs of a maternity hospital stay (up to $50 at the time of our study) while the Kaiser plan covers such a stay completely.

Our finding that a predominantly fee-for-service group practice can be a conservative user of hospital services has been supported by a recent study of the health maintenance organizations (HMOs) in the Minneapolis-St. Paul area, which came up with much the same findings.[10] The second largest of the seven prepaid plans in this area, MedCenter Health Plan, is offered by a large (about 90 physicians) multispecialty, predominantly fee-for-service group practice similar to the Palo Alto Medical Clinic, the St. Louis Park Medical Center. Although currently its revenue from the prepaid plan amounts to about 40 percent of its gross revenue, hospital use under the plan was low from its very beginning in 1973, amounting to 320 days per 1,000 members in that year. The authors stress that:

> . . . the St. Louis Park Medical Center Instituted no new hospitalization controls on its physicians when it began to accept a portion of its patients as prepaid enrollees in MedCenter. Yet the hospitalization rate for these members has varied little from its initial year and currently is less than the metropolitan and national HMO average (pp. 815-816).

CONCLUSION

To sum up, our study lends some support to the hypothesis that it may be the group practice form of their organization as much as their prepayment feature that enables prepaid group practice to deliver quality medical care at lower cost, and especially with less use of costly hospital services. Our data show that, with few exceptions, the pattern of care under the two plans is very similar: the overall volume of ambulatory care is much the same, so are the rates of initial and follow-up visits for illness, and most important of all, the use of hospital services is almost identical both in terms of number of hospital days and of admissions (if we include surgical procedures performed in the hospital on a nonadmission basis) per 1,000 plan members per year. This last finding is perhaps the most important finding of the study. The few exceptions are minor: the use of preventive services is considerably higher under the Clinic than under the Kaiser plan, and conversely, PAMC physicians are somewhat heavier users of some outpatient ancillary services, notably of laboratory tests connected with preventive care and, to a considerably lesser degree, of x-rays. Perhaps we should add that we even found out-of-plan use of medical services similar under the two plans, members of both plans averaging about 1.6 physician (including paramedic) visits per person per year.

While we were surprised at the similarity of the use of hospital services under the two plans, there are several reasons why group practice as such, even when it is fee-for-service, can be expected to lead to below-average hospital use. For one thing, such an organization (provided it is of sufficient size) has readily available a large array of diagnostic and treatment facilities that in a solo or small group practice setting are available only in a hospital or (at some inconvenience to the patients) in independent laboratories or radiology facilities. For another, there is the constant presence of the group practice physicians' peers. It would probably be quite difficult for a group practice physician to deviate greatly or for any length of time from the pattern of hospital use of the other physicians in the group, or for a group practice surgeon to perform significantly more highly elective surgical procedures, much less to perform dubious ones.

The principal reason, however, may be the group practice's control over the number and specialties of the physicians in the group. In a group practice, the number of physicians and their distribution by field of specialty are planned on the basis of demand for the group's services. By contrast, the number and kinds of physicians who decide to practice in a given community or area are determined by a great many other factors in addition to demand—factors such as the availability of good hospitals, opportunities for further training, the attractiveness of the area and its cultural amenities, good schools, etc. In general, a fee-for-service group practice, like a prepaid group practice, is unlikely to add a surgeon or any other kind of physician to its staff unless its members have more work than they can or are willing to perform. Thus, while physicians in a fee-for-service group practice do not have the financial incentive to hold down costs which prepaid group physicians have, they are much less likely to be faced with the temptation to generate demand for their services than their solo practice colleagues. This explains not only the low use of hospital services we found under the Clinic plan but also our finding that Clinic members had no more follow-up visits for illness than Kaiser members, as we had hypothesized, because Clinic physicians' income, unlike that of Kaiser physicians, is increased the more services they provide. To put all this in very colloquial terms, there are likely to be fewer "hungry" physicians of any specialty, surgeon or otherwise, in a large, well-established fee-for-service group practice than among their solo practitioner colleagues in the community, especially in an area with as high a physician-to-population ratio as the greater San Francisco Bay Area.

Our findings that the pattern of medical care delivery is very similar under fee-for-service and prepaid group practice, even though supported on the matter of hospital use by the MedCenter Health Plan study referred to above, are of course suggestive rather than conclusive. Many questions remain to be answered, most important among them the question of the size of the fee-for-service group practice required to lead to low use of hospital services and possibly also to a low volume of physician-initiated services. Both the PAMC and the St. Louis Park Medical Center, which offers MedCenter Health Plan, are very large multispecialty group practices (of 120 and 90 physicians, respectively). Whether smaller fee-for-service groups would perform similarly remains yet to be explored.

In concluding, there is one further point we would like to make about prepaid group practice. We mentioned that under the Kaiser plan, the low physician affiliation rate of its members had "held down" the use of physician services. (Presumably this in turn leads to lower use of hospital services.) We have speculated elsewhere about possible reasons for this low physician affiliation rate and shall not go into details here.[11] However, one possibility deserves mention, and that is that some individuals and families enroll in the Kaiser plan who are low users in general, and who regard the plan as a protection against possible major illness but do not plan to use it regularly. If this is the case, then it is not the low physician affiliation rate of Kaiser members that holds down utilization, but the large proportion of generally low users that keeps utilization low and explains why so many Kaiser plan members do not trouble to choose a personal plan physician. We do not know whether there is such a self-selectivity on the part of Stanford Kaiser members, and possibly on the part of members of prepaid group practice plans in general since they are all characterized by a low physician affiliation rate. Thus, here too, there is an area that deserves further exploration.

NOTES

1. Three other, much smaller, group practices also participate in the plan. Because of their small number of enrollees, they have been omitted from the study.
2. For the more detailed description of the selection of the study populations, see Scitovsky A. A., Benham, L. and McCall N.

Factors affecting the choice between two prepaid plans. Med. Care 16, 8, 1978.

3. Because the Clinic plan has been available considerably longer than the Kaiser plan, it might be thought that this could be the explanation for the difference in the physician affiliation rates between the two plans. However, when we look at only those Clinic plan members who joined the plan after January 1969—when the Kaiser Plan became available—we find that 79 percent reported having a specific plan physician as regular source of care. Thus the difference, though slightly smaller, persists.

4. Scitovsky A. A. and McCall N. Effect of coinsurance on use of physician services. Soc. Sec. Bull. 35, 6, 1972.

5. Scitovsky A. A. and McCall N. Coinsurance and the demand for physician services: Four years later. Soc. Sec. Bull. 40, 5, 1977.

6. Scitovsky A. A., Benham L. and McCall N. Use of physician services under two prepaid plans. Med. Care 17, 5, 1979. That persons without a regular physician are lower users of physician services is not a novel finding. See, for example, Andersen R. A Behavioral Model of Families' Use of Health Services. Center for Health Administration Studies, University of Chicago, Research Series No. 25. Chicago, IL, 1968. Also, Andersen R., Kravits J. and Anderson O. Equity in Health Services: Empirical Analysis in Social Policy. Ballinger, Cambridge MA, 1975. Unpublished data from the National Center for Health Statistics' Health Interview Survey also show higher use of physician services by persons with a regular physician than by those without such a source of care. Similarly, other studies have also found that enrollees in prepaid group practice plans tend to have a lower percentage of members who have a specific plan physician as regular source of care than enrollees in other types of plans. See for example, Berki S. D., Ashcroft M., Penchansky R. and Fortus R. S. Enrollment choice in a multi-HMO setting: The roles of health risk, financial vulnerability, and access to care. Med. Care 15, 2, 1977.

7. For a more detailed analysis of our findings on the use of hospital services, see Scitovsky A. A. and McCall N. Use of hospital services under two prepaid plans. Med. Care 18, 1, 1980. This article, among other things, examines in detail the mix of surgical procedures under the two plans.

8. U.S. Civil Service Commission. Annual Report of Financial and Statistical Data for Fiscal Year Ended June 1973. U.S. Govt Print. Off. The figures cited above have been calculated from data presented in this report. Since these figures are not adjusted in any way, it should be noted that the unadjusted figures for our two plans are 223.6 hospital days per 1,000 person-years for Kaiser

members and 278.8 days per 1,000 person-years for Clinic
members.

9. The higher rate of nonadmission hospital surgery under the
Kaiser plan is due almost entirely to the greater number of
such procedures as D and C's, therapeutic abortions, other
abortions, biopsies of the cervix or uterus, and vasectomies.
In other respects, the mix of nonadmission surgical procedures
is fairly similar. For details, see Scitovsky A. A. and McCall
N. Use of hospital services under two prepaid plans. Med. Care
18, 1, 1980.

10. Christianson J. B. and McClure W. Competition in the delivery
of medical care. N. Engl. J. Med. 301, 15, 1979.

11. Scitovsky A. A., Benham, L. and McCall N. Use of physician
services under two prepaid plans. Med. Care 17, 5, 1979.

PART IV

Health and Public Policy

10

SOME SOCIOECONOMIC
DETERMINANTS OF MORTALITY

Sherwin Rosen
Paul Taubman

A person's life expectancy depends upon his own genetic endowments and his environment, broadly defined. Since a person's genetic
endowments are fixed, social and life scientists have expressed a
great interest in how changes in certain types of observed environment affect life expectancy.

The different types of environment that affect a person's life
expectancy include: third-party provided health care, health care
provided by oneself or by other family members, work conditions,
and home life conditions. These conditions, in turn, can be related
to variables such as occupation, industry, family income, education,
IQ, marital status, and so forth. There now exist several studies
that relate age-specific death rates to variables such as those listed
above. However, since most of the available studies use aggregate
data, such as a country or a state, it is difficult to disentangle the
separate effects of income, education, occupation, etc.[1]

The major studies that contain extensive data on individuals
and examine age-specific death rates were conducted before the
development of computers with large memories.[2] Analysis, thus,
was generally limited to two-way cross tabs. In this study we will
use a newly developed body of information to estimate more complex
models of age-specific death rates. With such models it is possible,
for example, to explore whether the more educated have lower death
rates because education is a proxy for permanent income, because
the more educated work at different types of jobs, or because the
more educated are better processors of information.

THE MODEL

The general model we have in mind is one in which death occurs
when a person's health level (H) drops below some critical level. H,

itself, is determined by a person's genetic endowments, private and public expenditures on preventive and curative health care, services provided by and support of other family members, knowledge of how to produce healthiness, diet and lifestyle, work, and residential conditions. Such a model is consistent with economists' utility maximizing framework.

The model can be represented as:

$$M = F(H, A, u) \tag{1}$$

$$H = F_1(G, X, A, u_1) \tag{2}$$

where:

M is a zero, one dummy variable for being alive or dead at the end of a time period
H is a person's health stock
A is his age
u is a random variable
G is a person's genetic endowments
X is a vector of observed variables
u_1 is a random variable

To estimate this model it would be ideal to have measures of M, H, X, and A. However, if H is not observed we can substitute (2) into (1) and estimate the effect of X on M.

The model described verbally above is one that contains several difficult to measure Xs. It is still possible to proceed, however, by hypothesizing that observed variables, such as family income, are proxies for or cause difference in, say, the purchase of health care. Of course, there may not be a unique pairing of observed and unobserved variables, which makes it difficult to determine why, for instance, income matters. If, however, some observed variables are better proxies for unobserved variables than others, it is possible to start to sort out the reasons why, for instance, income and education have significant effects.

In the next section, we will indicate the various roles that certain variables could play. Then we will discuss the sample we will use.

OBSERVED AND UNOBSERVED VARIABLES

We have proposed a fairly general health model. The sample used in this paper has relatively limited information on many of the key components in that model. The sample, however, does have the following information: date of death, age, current income, an income history, current occupation, education, marital status, current location, veteran status, and some limited and crude health indices. In a subsequent section, we will relate mortality to these variables. Now, however, we wish to explain the various reasons why specific variables may be related to age specific mortality.

Education can be correlated with mortality because: the more educated have higher incomes to purchase better health care and better living conditions; are more likely to be married and in a stable home environment; work in jobs that expose the individual to fewer health hazards; have more knowledge and are brighter and thus are better able to follow a doctor's advice; and live different life-styles.

Income can be correlated with mortality for the same reasons as education. There are, however, several additional points to consider. First, current income may be affected by poor health, with seriously ill people forced to reduce hours worked. Education, on the other hand, may be a better indicator of permanent income. Second, increased income may lead to life-styles that reduce health. A u-shape may appear for income effects but may not appear for education because of the multiple roles of education or because education only indicates average differences in earnings and not the existing wide extremes. Third, occupationally specific health hazards may be compensated for by extra wages; hence, there would be a positive association between income and mortality.

Marital status can be important because family members can nurse one another. In addition, married persons may live longer than single persons because of reduced strain and because seriously ill people are less likely to marry. In addition to these reasons, married people may live longer than divorced or widowed persons because widows have poor diet and living conditions or because grief affects mortality.

Occupational effects can flow through health hazards and income. Location can reflect climatic differences and differences in the availability of medical care. In addition, variables such as education may vary across locations.

The health measures we have, in part, will be related to mortality for obvious reasons. In addition, these variables may reflect income effects since, for example, ill people who choose not to accept Social Security Disability Payments may be those with high wage rates.

THE CPS-SSA SAMPLE

The March 1973 Current Population Survey (CPS) was a stratified multistage cluster sample of about 45,000 interviewed households containing some 136,000 persons. To be eligible for the CPS, an individual had to be living in one of the 50 states or the District of Columbia. The institutional population was excluded, as were all Armed Forces members except those living off-post and on-post with their families.

As part of the 1973 Exact Match Study, an attempt was made by the Census Bureau to obtain the Social Security numbers of the 101,000 sampled persons 14 years or older. In about 80,000 cases, potentially useable numbers were recorded by the interviewers. An additional 10,000 adults were matched to SSA files using CPS data on name, age, sex, and race.

Available evidence suggests that the matching was done accurately, and the inability to match everyone has not caused the matched subset to differ greatly from the whole CPS.[3]

The total number of deaths per year in the CPS-SSA Exact Match sample is given in Table 10.1. It should be noted that about 400 people in the SSA files were recorded as having died prior to March 1973, though CPS information is recorded for March 1973. This anomaly occurs due to mismatches, CPS and SSA punching and transcription errors, or some women's (legal) use of their deceased husband's Social Security number. We exclude these people from our analysis as well as the few individuals whose dates of death are unknown. The remaining 3,030 physically matched cases who died and the more than 85,000 people alive as of the end of 1977 will constitute our basic study group.

Since the CPS survey was undertaken in March, we would expect recorded 1973 deaths to be about 75 percent of the number in all of 1974. This compares favorably with the 73 percent found in the sample. The total number of deaths in 1975 is a bit higher than in 1976 and more than 10 percent higher than the number in 1974. While the 1976 deviation may be due to sampling variability, we believe that further updating of information will probably raise the 1976 figure; it is more affected than the one for 1975 by exclusion of the institutionalized from the CPS, since some who were not institutionalized in March 1973 became so subsequently. The 1977 figures are obviously incomplete. We have no reason to suspect that the death data already posted are not a random draw of the population of dead people.

In Rosen and Taubman (1979), we examined the breakdown of age-specific death rates by race and sex. We found that blacks have a higher-age specific death rate than whites for each sex for nearly

TABLE 10.1. Annual Number of Deaths in the CPS-SSA
Sample through June 1977

Year of Death	Physical Matches	"Good" Matches
TOTAL	3,445	2,786
Year Unknown	8	6
Before 1973	386	67
1973*	534	479
1974	700	626
1975	815	736
1976	801	697
1977 (part year)	201	181

*There were 20 physical matches for persons who were recorded as dying the first three months of 1973.

Note: In the Exact Match Study, users are provided all the matches obtained plus rules for determining which matches might be considered accurate. The rule employed here is the same as that described in Scheuren and Oh (1975).

all age groups, that death rates rise with age, and that white males have a lower life expectancy than white females.

In that paper we have also compared the CPS-SSA age-specific death rates with those in Vital Statistics. For white males and females under 65, the ratio of the sample of death rate to that of the Vital Statistics is about 70 percent and 50 percent, respectively. In the 65+ age group, 74 percent of white females and 94 percent of white males are recorded, although this comparison is less informative since we are forced to estimate the Vital Statistics rate for this group because the true numbers are not published. This undercount occurs because not all deaths are reported to the Social Security Administration and because, until recently, Social Security only retained reported deaths for people who were in insured status, that is, receiving or entitled to benefits.

Because of the above results, we only studied males, and because of the small number of nonwhites who died in this sample, we will concentrate on whites. For white males, there seems little reason to suspect that the small SSA undercount is correlated with education and most other independent variables to be used in the present study.[4]

RESULTS

To try to test the various explanations, we estimate some linear probability models for white males. We recognize that more costly probit or logit estimating techniques would be preferred; however, some sample logit equations yield estimated effects, calculated at the mean, that are the same to two decimal points as OLS coefficients.

All the equations include the expected number of deaths (and its square) calculated for white males of a given age in 1973 from Vital Statistics for the period 1973 to 1977. Because of the undercounting of deaths, even the expected number-of-deaths variable need not have a coefficient of one when used alone. We use this variable in place of a large number of age-dummy variables to economize on parameters and to facilitate computations.

When only the expected death rate is included, its coefficient is about .70 to .78, which is close to the average actual-to-expected death rates ratio of .75 discussed earlier. Since both the expected death rate and its square are always significant in the analysis, we only present these versions.

Equations for white males 25 to 64 years old in 1973 are given in Table 10.2. As indicated above, both the expected death rate and its square are significantly positive in Equation (1). Since no other variables are used, this suggests that either there are some problems with, for example, age reported in Vital Statistics or in the census (from which death rate denominations are taken).

The results in column (2), in general, support the notion that more highly educated people have lower age-specific death rates, though the coefficients do not follow a monotonic path. Since the average death rate during the 1973-77 period was 2.1 percent for this age group, the nearly 1 percentage point difference between an elementary school person and a college graduate is very large.

The results in column (3) indicate that those in the lowest category have a death rate that is a huge 3.4 percentage points above those in the highest income group.[5] There is also a hint of a u-shaped pattern.

As shown in column (4), married men with spouse present have a death rate about 1.7 percentage points less than those who are divorced. Divorced men, however, do better than widowers. Single individuals have the same death rate as married men, but this may occur because single men have no children to file for dependent benefits and, thus, may be undercounted in the SSA records.

Both education and current family income may be proxies for a person's permanent income level. Thus, it is of interest to observe that, in column (5), both sets of variables retain the qualitative

TABLE 10.2. White Males, 25-64

	(1)	(2)	(3)	(4)	(5)	(6)	(7)	(8)
Years of Education								
0/8		.008			.004	.0021	.0013	.0017
		(2.5)			(1.22)	(.632)	(.389)	(.503)
9/11		.0102			.009	.0085	.0074	.008
		(3.17)			(2.7)	(2.55)	(2.23)	(2.4)
12		.0025			.0024	.0023	.0019	.0022
		(.956)			(.905)	(.866)	(.716)	(.823)
13/15		.0058			.0053	.0053	.0051	.0052
		(1.76)			(1.59)	(1.61)	(1.55)	(1.59)
Family Income								
$0-3,297			.034		.03	.02	.026	.021
			(7.17)		(6.06)	(3.88)	(5.28)	(4.2)
3,298-6,594			.0075		.005	-.00046	.0007	-.0016
			(2.19)		(1.3)	(-.124)	(.184)	(-.44)
6,595-9,892			.0022		.0002	-.002	-.0016	-.0027
			(.787)		(.069)	(-.67)	(-.56)	(-.922)
9,893-13,190			-.001		-.0024	-.0031	-.003	-.0035
			(-.398)		(-.899)	(-1.17)	(-1.21)	(-1.34)
13,191-16,488			-.0026		-.0035	-.0038	-.004	-.0042
			(-.931)		(-1.24)	(-1.37)	(-1.45)	(-1.5)

(continued)

TABLE 10.2 (continued)

	(1)	(2)	(3)	(4)	(5)	(6)	(7)	(8)
Single				-.015 (-2.42)	-.014 (-2.26)	-.013 (-2.18)	-.013 (-2.2)	-.013 (-2.24)
MSP				-.017 (-3.4)	-.013 (-2.46)	-.011 (-2.06)	-.012 (-2.3)	-.011 (-2.21)
MSA				-.0006 (-.068)	.00005 (.0062)	.00071 (.085)	.0006 (.798)	.0004 (.045)
WID				.0196 (1.98)	.019 (1.958)	.0197 (1.99)	.0197 (1.7)	.019 (1.91)
NODIS							-.0463 (.0042)	-.041 (-9.41)
FY/FT						-.015 (-3.26)		-.018 (-4.63)
FY/PT						-.0015 (-.154)		-.0065 (-.707)
PY/FT						-.017 (-3.31)		-.0182 (-4.23)
PY/PT						-.017 (-2.18)		-.0198 (-2.65)
EDR^2	4.68 (4.24)	4.85 (4.38)	4.24 (3.8)	4.56 (4.11)	4.5 (4.0)	4.46 (3.96)	5.013 (4.66)	4.65 (4.13)
EDR	.336 (3.07)	.297 (2.68)	.355 (3.21)	.334 (3.03)	.305 (2.7)	.264 (2.33)	.192 (1.7)	.219 (1.93)

	(1)	(2)	(3)	(4)	(5)	(6)	(7)	(8)
NOWORK						.035 (4.94)		
PTYR						.019 (3.46)		
CONSTANT	.0038 (2.46)	.00014 (.06)	.0021 (.96)	.0199 (3.84)	.0125 (2.17)	.0262 (3.63)	.0599 (8.36)	.071 (9.44)
R^2	.024	.025	.027	.026	.028	.032	.033	.034

Variable Definitions:

Years of Education: 0/8 = 0-8 years of school
9/11 = 9-11 years of school
12 = 12 years of school
13/15 = 13-15 years of school

Family Income: The amounts are the income ranges.

Single = single

MSP = married spouse present

MSA = married spouse absent

WID = widower

NODIS = disability indicator is blank, i.e., no activity

FY/FT = in 1972 work status was full year, full-time

FY/PT = in 1972 work status was full year, part-time

PY/FT = in 1972 work status was part year, full-time

PY/PT = in 1972 work status was part year, part-time

PTYR = reason only part year—ill

NOWORK = reason didn't work—ill

t-statistics are in parentheses.

pattern shown in columns (2) and (3) but that the coefficients of the lowest education and income variables have been reduced somewhat, and elementary school is no longer significant. The coefficients on the marital status variables, however, are not much affected by the inclusion of the income and education variables.

It is possible that the greater death rate for those with the lowest 1973 income occurs because those fatally ill were forced to drop out of the labor market a year or more before they died. Some of those not married may also be in that category because of poor health status. To control for these possibilities, we included two sets of variables in columns (6) to (8). The first relates to the person's work status in 1972, and the second relates to the person's disability status as determined by Social Security. From column (6), we learn that those working in 1972 a full year, full-time, had a 1.5 percentage point lower death rate than those not working for reasons other than poor health. Since the average death rate in the sample in this age group was only 2.1 percent, this is a large difference. In addition, those who indicated that they had not worked at all or part of the year because of ill health had 1.9 and 3.6 percentage points higher death rates than others who had not worked at all. The other status categories have about the same coefficients except those who worked a full year, part-time, and we have no information if this choice was made because of poor health. The disability variable is whether the person had never received disability benefits from Social Security. The coefficient on this variable in columns (7) and (8) is about -.05 and highly significant. Some of the people in this program apparently are quite ill.

When either or both of these health-related variables are included in the equations, the coefficients on the lowest education and income variables drop sharply. We believe that the drop in the income coefficients represent the effect of illness on labor force participation. Since, in our sample, deaths occur up to 5 years after the period to which the work status variables are measured, it seems likely that this causal path is even more important to other studies such as Kitagawa and Hauser (1973), in which death occurs in the four-month period after the 1960 census is studied. The drop in the education coefficient, however, is much more likely to indicate that those with low education have poorer overall health, which causes shorter life expectancy. [6] The stability of the marital status variables suggests that the higher death rates of the nonmarrieds is not because poor health kept them from marrying.

We have tried a number of regional variables, but only one was significant. Living on a farm has a negative effect on death probability. We have also included a set of (current) occupational dummies coded at the 1 digit level, for example, sales persons or operatives. These dummies are not individually or jointly significant.

In equations for white males 65 and over presented in Table 10.3, both the expected death rate and its squares are significant. We remind the reader that, in this age group, the expected death rate is estimated from a semilog trend equation, so that the estimated equation need not follow the actual death rates very well. Indeed, the negative coefficient on the squared variable indicates that the estimated expected death rate series is rising too quickly, which is in accord with the findings of Bayo (1972). This finding is confirmed by another test. In this age group, when we do not include the square of the expected death rate, the coefficient on expected death rate is about .3; however, when we fit the same equation to those 65 to 99, that coefficient rises to 0.8, which is much closer to the ratio of average actual to expected death rate of 1.0. (There are about 60 males who are 100 or more years old.) Since most of the other coefficients in the 65 to 99 equations are about the same as those in the full equation with the EDR and EDR^2 variables, we only present the latter ones.

Equations for white males 65 and over are given in Table 10.3. In column (2), we generally find that the death rates decrease with education. The difference between the college graduates and elementary school students is nearly 7 percentage points, which is a large fraction of the average death rate of about 15 percent.

In column (3) we find that the lowest-income people have the highest death rate. This result may be of more interest for this age group since only about 20 percent of the people are usually in the labor force and since pensions may be related to permanent income.

In column (3) we again find that married men live longer than divorced. However, single men live slightly longer than married men and widowers slightly longer than divorced men.[7]

A comparison of columns (2), (3), and (4) with (5) indicates that the coefficients on the lowest education and income level are not much affected by controlling for more variables. However, some of the other education coefficients are reduced sharply when health is controlled in columns (6) and (7). The coefficient on the marital status variables is affected very little, except for that of the widower.

About 60 percent of this age group had not participated at all in the labor market in 1972. Those who worked had a death rate that was 1.5 to 5.0 percentage points smaller. Those who indicated that they had not worked or only worked part-time because of ill health had excess deaths of 16 and 6 percentage points, respectively.

A person is only eligible for disability payments from Social Security up to the age of 65. After that, the person receives regular old age benefits. The Social Security records indicate the switch in

TABLE 10.3. White Males, 65 and Older

	(1)	(2)	(3)	(4)	(5)	(6)	(7)
Years of Education							
0/8		.067 (3.13)			.055 (2.48)	.051 (2.29)	.048 (2.16)
9/11		.04 (1.55)			.034 (1.33)	.031 (1.22)	.029 (1.15)
12		.067 (2.78)			.061 (2.53)	.057 (2.38)	.056 (2.32)
13/15		.0024 (.077)			-.003 (-.092)	-.007 (-.222)	-.006 (-.208)
Family Income							
$0-3,297			.072 (3.42)		.048 (2.15)	.041 (1.84)	.027 (1.2)
3,298-6,594			.011 (.57)		.0016 (.079)	-.004 (-.198)	-.014 (-.69)
6,595-9,892			-.003 (-.133)		-.008 (-.372)	-.011 (-.522)	-.017 (-.76)
9,893-13,190			.043 (1.70)		.04 (1.56)	.039 (1.53)	.034 (1.32)
13,191-16,488			.007 (.255)		.004 (.14)	.006 (.210)	.0024 (.084)

266

Single				-.114 (-2.51)	-.112 (-2.5)	-.103 (-2.28)	-.10 (-2.23)
MSP				-.105 (-2.7)	-.092 (-2.34)	-.086 (-2.20)	-.083 (-2.12)
MSA				-.053 (-.93)	-.057 (-.99)	-.055 (-.96)	-.052 (-2.12)
WID				-.012 (-.28)	-.011 (-.26)	-.0056 (-.134)	-.0052 (-.91)
NODIS						-.154 (-6.24)	-.0052 (-.13)
FY/FT							-.14 (-5.58)
FY/PT							-.041 (-2.27)
PY/FT							-.037 (-1.57)
PY/PT							-.035 (-1.52)
							-.058 (-2.68)
EDR²	-1.68 (-12.88)	-1.63 (-12.45)	-1.62 (-12.3)	-1.58 (-11.85)	-1.52 (.136)	-1.61 (-11.84)	-1.52 (-10.87)
EDR	1.87 (16.21)	1.83 (15.64)	1.81 (15.44)	1.75 (14.81)	1.7 (14.0)	1.80 (14.82)	1.7 (13.4)
CONSTANT	-.089 (-4.85)	-.135 (-5.26)	-.102 (-4.37)	.022 (.533)	-.038 (-.806)	.09 (1.76)	.118 (2.27)
R²	.059	.062	.063	.066	.071	.078	.080

(continued)

TABLE 10.3 (continued)

Variable Definitions:
Years of Education: 0/8 = 0-8 years of school
                    9/11 = 9-11 years of school
                    12   = 12 years of school
                    13/15 = 13-15 years of school

Family Income: The amounts are the income ranges.

Single = single

MSP   = married spouse present

MSA   = married spouse absent

WID   = widower

NODIS = disability indicator is blank, i.e., no activity

FY/FT = in 1972 work status was full year, full-time

FY/PT = in 1972 work status was full year, part-time

PY/FT = in 1972 work status was part year, full-time

PY/PT = in 1972 work status was part year, part-time

t-statistics are in parentheses.

status at age 65. As shown in column (6), those who never received such disability payments have a 15 percentage point lower death rate. While Parsons (1980) has indicated that the size of the disability benefits has induced people to leave the labor force, many of the individuals apparently have a substantially impaired health status.

In columns (6) and (7), the coefficients on the lowest education and earnings variables fall sharply once we control for the labor force and disability variables. Again this suggests a consequence of low education and poor health and that, even in this age group, terminally ill individuals are forced to reduce their labor force participation and, thus, their earnings.

In these equations, the coefficients of single and married spouse present are reduced a bit, but these coefficients are still significantly negative. The coefficient on widowed is cut in half. This finding suggests that much of the high death rate of widowers is due to prior poor health, which perhaps indicates a common poor environment shared by some married couples. It also suggests that the divorced have not been particularly unable to obtain a spouse because of poor health.

We have tried several other variables in equations for this age group. Of the locational variables, only living on a farm has a significant negative coefficient. We also included variables for being a veteran of the Korean War or earlier time periods, neither of which was significant.

CONCLUSION

At the beginning of this chapter, we listed a number of possible hypotheses that could be used to generate a relationship between age-specific death rates and a variety of variables. Based on the above results, we can begin to assess the various possibilities.

For white males, the negative relationship of education and mortality tends to persist even when we control for current earnings, marital status, and health status. (See the 9/11 group in Table 10.2 and the 0/8 group in Table 10.3.)

This suggests that the effect of education does not flow solely or primarily through income effects, does not reflect a combination of differential marriage patterns and the health benefits of having a wife, and that those who are disabled or not working because of ill health are not found disproportionately in any one education group. Generally, this suggests that differences in life-styles and/or resource allocation associated with education and perhaps with unmeasured intelligence are important.

The pattern of income effects is not clear, though there is a hint of a u-shaped relationship. The sharp reduction on the coefficient of the lowest current income group when health is controlled suggests that poor health leads to lower labor force participation prior to death. However, the coefficient remains positive and significant even when we control for all the other variables. This suggests that either there still are some unmeasured health effects or that low income restricts investment in health care.

For the young men, the marital effects persist even when we control for the other variables, though the advantage of married men drops a bit when we control for education and income. The same general results hold for the older men, though the advantage of widowers over divorced men falls when health is controlled. These suggest that it is not poor health that determines marital status; the reduction in the coefficient for older widowers when health is controlled may indicate some such effect on marital status. However, this coefficient remains significant. Single men tend to do much better than widowers or divorced men. While this may be due to a differential undercount of deaths for young men for whom there are no beneficiaries to inform SSA of their deaths, there is little reason to expect this to be true of older men who draw old age benefits. Thus, it appears that the stress associated with change in marital status is important.

NOTES

1. See Fuchs (1974), Silver (1972), or, for a recent survey, Brenner (1976).
2. Kitagawa and Hauser (1973) studied a sample based on the 1960 census, which was matched to deaths in the following four months. Other studies are summarized in the Technical Consultant Panel samples, obtained by taking information from death certificates used by sending surveys to people such as next of kin listed on the death certificate.
3. See Scheuren and Oh (1975).
4. The one variable that may be correlated is being single. One of the reasons Social Security learns of a person's death is that dependent children file for benefits.
5. The peculiar break-points were chosen to facilitate comparisons with Kitagawa and Hauser (1973). These are given in Rosen and Taubman (1979).
6. Rosen and Taubman (1980) provided some evidence consistent with this idea.
7. Single men are less likely to be undercounted in this age group since they receive old age benefits that stop at death.

REFERENCES

Bayo, F. 1972. "Mortality of the Aged." Transactions of the Society of Actuaries, March 1972, pp. 1-24.

Brenner, H. 1976. Estimating the Social Costs of National Economic Policy: Implications for Mental and Physical Health and Criminal Aggression. Joint Economic Committee, Congress of the United States, Washington, D.C.: Government Printing Office.

Fuchs, V. 1974. "Some Economic Aspects of Mortality in Developed Countries." In M. Perlman (ed.), The Economics of Health and Medical Care. London: Macmillan.

Kitagawa, E., and P. Hauser. 1973. Differential Mortality in the U.S. Cambridge, Mass.: Harvard University Press.

Parsons, D. 1980. "The Decline in Male Labor Force Participation." Journal of Political Economy, 88 (February 1980).

Rosen, S., and P. Taubman. 1979. "Changes in the Impact of Education and Income on Mortality in the U.S." Proceedings of the Social Section of the American Statistical Association.

____. 1980. "Healthiness, Investment in Health Care and Mortality." Technical Consultant Panel to the U.S. National Committee on Vital and Health Statistics, Report on Environmental Health Statistics on Statistics Needed to Ascertain the Effects of the Environment on Health. Mimeo.

Silver, M. 1972. "An Econometric Analysis of Spatial Variations in Mortality by Race and Sex." In V. Fuchs (ed.), Essays in the Economics of Health and Medical Care. New York: NBER and Columbia University Press.

Scheuren, F., and H. L. Oh. 1975. "Fiddling Around with Non Matches and Mismatches." Proceedings of the Social Statistics Section of the American Statistical Association.

11

VARIATIONS IN INFANT
MORTALITY RATES AMONG
COUNTIES OF THE UNITED STATES:
THE ROLES OF PUBLIC POLICIES
AND PROGRAMS

Michael Grossman   Steven Jacobowitz

From 1964 to 1977, the infant mortality rate in the United States declined at an annually compounded rate of 4.4 percent per year. This was an extremely rapid rate of decline, compared with the figure of 0.6 percent per year from 1955 to 1964. The reduction in mortality proceeded at an even faster pace in the 1970s than in the late 1960s (5.2 percent per year from 1971 to 1977 versus 3.8 percent per year from 1964 to 1971).[1]

The period from 1964 to 1977 witnessed the introduction of Medicaid, maternal and infant care projects, federally subsidized

This article first appeared in Demography 18, No. 4, pp. 695-713 (1981); reprinted by permission.

Research for this paper was supported by a grant from the Robert Wood Johnson Foundation to the National Bureau of Economic Research. We are indebted to Gary Becker, Larry Bumpass, Willard Cates, Ann Colle, Joy Dryfoos, Linda Edwards, Victor Fuchs, Louis Garrison, Eugene Lewit, Robert Michael, Charlotte Muller, Cathy Schoen, and two anonymous referees for their comments on an earlier draft. In addition, we would like to thank Joy Dryfoos, Edward Duffy, Jack Hadley, and Letty Wunglueck for providing us with the data to conduct our research. This is a revision of a paper presented at the World Congress on Health Economics, Leiden University, The Netherlands, September 8-11, 1980. A preliminary version of the paper also was presented at a session sponsored by the American Economic Association and the Health Economics Research Organization at the annual meeting of the Allied Social Science Associations, Atlanta, Georgia, December 28-30, 1979. This version contains sources for the extrapolations in Table 11.2 and a detailed description of the assumptions that underlie these extrapolations.

family planning services for low-income women, the legalization of abortion, and the widespread adoption of oral and intrauterine contraceptive techniques. These developments have been pointed to in discussion of the cause of the acceleration in the downward trend in infant mortality (for example, Eisner et al. 1978; Lee et al. 1980), but the question has not been studied in a multivariate context. Moreover, the relative contribution of each factor has not been quantified. The purpose of this study is to estimate the impacts of public policies and programs on infant mortality.

ANALYTICAL FRAMEWORK

Economic models of the family and household production developed by Becker and Lewis (1973) and Willis (1973) provide a fruitful theoretical framework to generate multivariate health outcome functions and to assess the roles of public programs and policies in these functions. Ben-Porath (1973), Ben-Porath and Welch (1976), Williams (1976), and Lewit (1977) have utilized the economic model of the family to study theoretically and empirically the determinants of birth outcomes. Following these authors, we assume that the parents' utility function depends upon their own consumption, the number of births, and the survival probability. Both the number of births and the survival probability are endogenous variables. In particular, the survival probability production function depends upon endogenous inputs of medical care, nutrition, and the own time of the mother. In addition, the production function is affected by the reproductive efficiency of the mother and by other aspects of her efficiency in household production. Given the considerable body of evidence that education raises market and nonmarket productivity, one would expect more educated mothers to be more efficient producers of surviving infants.

The above model calls attention to the important determinants of the survival probability and its complement, the infant mortality rate. In general this set of determinants is similar to that used in multivariate studies of infant mortality with different and less theoretical points of departure (for example, Fuchs 1974; Williams 1974; Brooks 1978; and Gortmaker 1979). Moreover, the model provides a ready structure within which to interpret the effects of public programs and policies on infant mortality.[2] Thus, Medicaid and maternal and infant care (M and I) projects lower the direct and indirect costs[3] of obtaining prenatal and obstetrical care, which should increase the likelihood of a favorable birth outcome and lower infant mortality. Federal subsidization of family planning services, abortion reform, and the diffusion of oral and intrauterine contraceptive techniques (the pill and the IUD) reduce the costs of birth control and increase its availability. Within the context of an economic model of the family, these developments raise the "optimal" survival probability and lower the "optimal" number of births. In addition, they will lower the observed infant mortality rate if less healthy fetuses are less likely to be conceived or more likely to be aborted.[4]

To measure the relative importance of the above factors in the recent U.S. infant mortality experience, we perform a cross-sectional regression analysis of variations in infant mortality rates among counties of the United States in 1971. Our procedure capitalizes on variations in the programs at issue among counties at a moment in time. Thus, it provides a set of impact coefficients to identify the contribution of each program net of basic determinants of infant mortality, such as poverty, schooling levels, and the availability of physicians. After estimating the regression, we apply its coefficients to national trends in the exogenous variables between 1964 and 1977 to "explain" the trend in infant mortality.

Our methodology has a number of desirable properties. It mitigates the multicollinearity problems that almost certainly would arise in a time-series regression analysis for the United States as a whole. Moreover, the state-of-the-art in neonatology, which has changed over time and is difficult to quantify, is constant in the cross section. Finally, with the exception of abortion reform, the programs that we study are aimed at poor persons. Therefore, the appropriate way to measure their impacts is to interact the policy variables with the fraction of births to poor women. We incorporate this insight into our basic regression specification.

The last point is worth explaining in more detail. Let d_{pj} be the infant mortality rate of babies born to poor mothers (infant deaths divided by live births) in the jth county, and let d_{nj} be the infant mortality rate of babies born to nonpoor mothers. As an identity,

$$d_j = k_j d_{pj} + (1 - k_j)d_{nj} \tag{1}$$

where d_j is the observed infant mortality rate, and k_j is the fraction of births to poor mothers. We specify behavioral equations for d_{pj} and d_{nj} as follows:

$$d_{pj} = \alpha_0 + \alpha_1 x_{pj} + \alpha_2 y_{pj} + \alpha_3 w_{pj} + \alpha_4 z_j \tag{2}$$

$$d_{nj} = \beta_0 + \beta_2 y_{nj} + \beta_3 w_{nj} + \beta_4 z_j \tag{3}$$

In these equations, x_{pj} is a vector of policy variables that affects the mortality rate of poor babies alone, such as Medicaid; w_{ij} ($i = p, n$) is a vector of policy variables that affects both groups, such as the group-specific abortion rate (legal abortions per thousand live births); y_{ij} refers to a group-specific vector of basic determinants of infant mortality, such as mother's schooling; and z_j is a vector of variables that has the same value for each group, such as physicians per capita. Since there are no data on income-specific mortality rates at the county level, substitute equations (2) and (3) into equation (1) to obtain

$$d_j = \beta_0 + (\alpha_0 - \beta_0)k_j + \alpha_1 k_j x_{pj} + \alpha_2 k_j y_{pj} + \beta_2(1 - k_j)y_{nj}$$
$$+ \alpha_3 k_j w_{pj} + \beta_3(1 - k_j)w_{nj} + \alpha_4 k_j z_j + \beta_4(1 - k_j)z_j \qquad (4)$$

Equation (4) gives a multiple regression of d_j on eight variables (vectors): k_j, $k_j x_{pj}$, $k_j y_{pj}$, $(1 - k_j)y_{nj}$, $k_j w_{pj}$, $(1 - k_j)w_{nj}$, $k_j z_j$, and $(1 - k_j)z_j$. Attempts to estimate this equation would be plagued by severe problems of multicollinearity and by the absence of income-specific measures of certain variables, such as the legal abortion rate. Therefore, we assume that the income-specific abortion rate (w_{ij}) is proportional to its weighted average ($w_{ij} = r_i w_j$). In addition, we assume that schooling of poor mothers in a given county is proportional to schooling of nonpoor mothers ($y_{pj} = s y_{nj}$). The actual equation that we fit is:

$$d_j = \beta_0 + (\alpha_0 - \beta_0)k_j + \alpha_1 k_j x_{pj} + \delta_2 y_{nj} + \delta_3 w_j + \delta_4 z_j \qquad (5)$$

where δ_2 estimates $\alpha_2 k_j s_p + \beta_2(1 - k_j)$, δ_3 estimates $\alpha_3 k_j r_p + \beta_3(1 - k_j)r_n$, and δ_4 estimates $\alpha_4 k_j + \beta_4(1 - k_j)$. The important point to note is that we employ k_j and the product of k_j and x_{pj} as independent variables in the regression. Thus, we employ a specification that explicitly recognizes that the impact on the observed infant mortality rate of policies aimed at the poor is larger, the larger is the fraction of births to poor mothers ($\partial d_j / \partial x_{pj} = k_j \alpha_1$). Moreover, our specification yields a direct estimate of the impact parameter (α_1).

A more general formulation of the above model can be developed by decomposing the observed infant mortality rate in the jth county into rates associated with a variety of birth characteristics such as mother's age, mother's income, parity, birth weight, and legitimacy status of the birth:

$$d_j = \sum_{i=1}^{m} k_{ij} d_{ij} \qquad (6)$$

In this equation k_{ij} is the fraction of births in the ith category and d_{ij} is the infant mortality rate associated with that category. An example of one such category is an illegitimate, low birth-weight birth to a low-income, teenage mother with no previous live births. The policies that we study can lower the observed infant mortality rate by lowering the fraction of births in high-risk categories (categories where d_{ij} is higher than on average) and by lowering the mortality rate in a given risk category (d_{ij}). Our regression estimates incorporate both effects because we do not control for characteristics such as the percentage of births to teenage mothers, the percentage of illegitimate births, the percentage of fourth and higher-order births, and the percentage of low birth-weight births. We do include the percentage of births to low-income mothers, but as indicated in the section, Empirical Specification, we employ a measure that varies among counties only because the percentage of the population in poverty varies among counties.

Note that some discussions of the probable impacts of abortion reform on infant mortality assume that this public policy operates solely by reducing the percentage of high-risk births, especially the percentage of low birth-weight births (for example, Lee et al. 1980). Yet abortion reform also can lower infant mortality by lowering risk-specific death rates. In particular, more prenatal and perinatal care may be allocated to pregnancies that are not aborted. Indeed, in the context of the economic model of the family outlined above (Becker and Lewis 1973; Willis 1973), it is likely that a reduction in the cost of birth control will have a larger impact on the amount of medical care demanded and, therefore, on the survival probability than will a reduction in the price of care. The reason is that a reduction in the cost of fertility control raises the cost (price) of a birth, while a reduction in the price of medical care lowers the cost of a birth. Although both developments almost certainly will raise the optimal survival probability, a reduction in the cost of fertility control will lower the optimal birth rate, while a reduction in the price of care may increase it. This point should be kept in mind when the effects of abortion reform on infant mortality are compared with the effects of Medicaid coverage of prenatal and perinatal care services.[5]

EMPIRICAL SPECIFICATION

Data and Measurement of Infant Mortality

Our basic data set is the Urban Institute's expanded version of the Area Resource File (ARF). The ARF is a county-based data service, prepared by Applied Management Sciences, Inc., for the

Bureau of Health Professions, Health Resources Administration, U.S. Department of Health and Human Services. It incorporates information from a variety of sources for 3,078 counties in the United States. These counties can also be aggregated into larger geographic areas such as county groups, Standard Metropolitan Statistical Areas, and states. Demographic and socioeconomic characteristics are taken from the 1970 Census of Population. Socioeconomic characteristics of women ages 15 to 49 come from the 1970 Census of Population, Women of Childbearing Age, tape. Deaths by age, race, and sex for the years 1969 through 1976 are obtained from the National Center for Health Statistics (NCHS) mortality tape. Births by race for those years are obtained from the NCHS natality tape. Health manpower and facilities come from the American Medical Association, the American Hospital Association, and other sources. We have added measures pertaining to the policies and programs discussed previously to the ARF from sources indicated in the section, Measurement of Independent Variables.

There are two components of infant mortality: neonatal mortality and postneonatal mortality. Neonatal mortality refers to deaths of infants within the first 27 days of life. Postneonatal mortality refers to deaths of infants between the ages of 28 and 364 days. Neonatal deaths are usually caused by congenital abnormalities, prematurity, and complications of delivery, while postneonatal deaths are usually caused by infectious diseases and accidents.

We limit our empirical analysis to the neonatal mortality rate, defined as neonatal deaths per thousand live births. Since the causes of the two types of infant deaths are dissimilar, socioeconomic variables and social programs are likely to have different effects on each. Specifically, the policy variables that we study are more relevant to neonatal mortality than to postneonatal mortality. For instance, the former is considerably more sensitive to appropriate prenatal and obstetrical care than the latter (Lewit 1977). Another reason for our focus is that the neonatal mortality rate is much larger than the postneonatal mortality rate; it was three times as large in 1971. Consequently, trends in the infant mortality rate are dominated by trends in the neonatal mortality rate. Obviously, one cannot hope to explain trends in the infant mortality rate without being able to explain trends in the neonatal mortality rate.

Separate regressions are fitted for white neonatal mortality and for black neonatal mortality. Black neonatal mortality rates are much higher than white rates. In a nonrace-specific regression, one would enter the percentage of black births to control for race differences. However, this variable would be highly correlated with the percentage of births to low-income women, schooling, and other independent variables. By fitting race-specific regressions, we reduce multicollinearity and allow the coefficients of the independent variables to vary between races. Linear regressions are estimated because a linear specification facilitates the aggregation of the two income-specific mortality rate functions given in the first section into a single equation for the entire population.

We use counties rather than states or Standard Metropolitan Statistical Areas (SMSAs) as the units of observation. SMSAs and states are very large and sometimes heterogeneous. Income, schooling levels, medical resources, and other variables may vary greatly within an SMSA or a state. Since counties are much more homogeneous, these problems are reduced in our research. A weakness with the use of counties is that the small size of some of these areas may mean that people may receive medical care outside the county. Moreover, the small number of births in certain counties may increase the importance of random movements or "noise" in the determination of regression coefficients.

We reduce these problems with county data by including in the regressions only counties with a population of at least 50,000 persons in 1970. A county must also have at least 5,000 blacks for inclusion in the black regressions. There are 679 counties in the white regressions and 359 counties in the black regressions. In addition to selecting large counties, we attenuate random elements by employing a three-year average of the race-specific neonatal mortality rate for the period 1970–72 as the dependent variable and by estimating weighted regressions, where the set of weights is the square root of the race-specific number of births in 1971.

We study neonatal mortality for the period 1970–72 because measures of all independent variables are available for a year in that period, or for 1969. In addition, it provides an ideal time frame to estimate the impact of abortion reform because of substantial cross-sectional variations in the legal abortion rate in that period. Abortion reform proceeded at a rapid pace between 1967 and the middle of 1970. Prior to 1967 all states of the United States had laws that permitted abortion only when it was necessary to preserve a pregnant woman's life. Beginning in 1967 some states started to reform these laws to increase the number of circumstances under which abortions could be performed. The reformed statutes legalized abortions if there was a substantial risk that continuance of the pregnancy would seriously impair the physical or mental health of the woman or that the child resulting from the pregnancy would be born with a serious physical or mental defect, or in cases of pregnancy resulting from rape or incest. By 1970, twelve states had enacted such statutes. Moreover, in 1970 four additional states enacted extremely liberal abortion laws that placed no legal restriction on the reasons for which an abortion may be obtained prior to the viability of the fetus (U.S.,

Center for Disease Control 1971). After the middle of 1970, there were no significant changes in abortion laws until 1973 when the Supreme Court ruled most restrictive state abortion laws unconstitutional. Concurrent with these reforms, the U.S. ratio of legal abortions per thousand live births rose from 4 in 1969 to 180 in 1972 and to 361 in 1977 (U.S., Center for Disease Control 1971, 1972, and 1974; U.S., Bureau of the Census 1980).

Measurement of Independent Variables

Wherever possible, race-specific variables are employed in the regressions. Such variables are denoted with an asterisk. Except for the Medicaid and abortion measures, all variables are county specific. Table 11.A1 in the Appendix contains definitions, means, and standard deviations of the dependent and independent variables in the regressions.

The number of active nonfederal physicians per thousand population (MD) serves as a general proxy for the price and availability of medical care. [6] The roles of the percentage of births to poverty mothers (PB*) and the percentage of women of childbearing ages who had at least a high school education (HSP*) were discussed in the first section. Here we note that there are no direct measures of births to poor women, either at the county or at the national level. Therefore, we estimate the race-specific percentage of births to such women by assuming that the race-specific birth rate of poor women does not vary among counties and that the race-specific birth rate of nonpoor women does not vary among counties. Under these conditions, one can compute race-specific birth rates of poor and nonpoor women by regressing the race-specific birth rate (b_j^*, the ratio of births to women ages 15 to 44) on the race-specific fraction of women in poverty (π_j^*):

$$b_j^* = \gamma_0^* + \gamma_1^* \pi_j^* \tag{7}$$

The regression intercept (γ_0^*) gives the birth rate of nonpoor women, and the sum of γ_0^* and γ_1^* gives the birth rate of poor women. [7]

After fitting the regressions for whites and blacks, we obtain the race-specific percentage of births to poverty women as:

$$PB^* = 100\,[(\gamma_0^* + \gamma_1^*)\pi_j^*/(\gamma_0^* + \gamma_1 \pi_j^*)] \tag{8}$$

It is clear that PB* is a monotonically increasing, although nonlinear, function of the fraction of the population in poverty. Therefore, the regression coefficient of PB* summarizes the impact of poverty on infant mortality. Since poverty and family income are highly correlated, we omit the latter from the regression.[8]

One may question the assumption that the birth rate of poor women is the same in every county, especially since subsidized family planning services and abortion reform are likely to have substantial impacts on birth rates of poor women. Our aim in this chapter, however, is to estimate reduced form, as opposed to structural, effects of public policies on infant mortality (see Note 5). That is, these policies can lower the observed infant mortality rate by lowering the fraction of births in high-risk categories and by lowering the mortality rate associated with a given risk category. Since our aim is to measure both mechanisms, the estimated percentage of births to low-income women, which varies among counties only because the percentage of the population in poverty varies among counties, is a superior variable to the actual percentage of such births, even if the latter were available.[9]

The policy and program measures contain variables pertaining to Medicaid coverage of prenatal and perinatal care services, maternal and infant care (M and I) projects, the use of organized family planning clinics by low-income women in childbearing ages, and abortion reform. In the case of prenatal and obstetrical care services, variations among states in the treatment of first-time pregnancies under Medicaid contribute to substantial variations in the percentage of pregnant low-income women whose medical care is financed by Medicaid. In particular, nineteen states cover no first-time pregnancies because their Aid to Families with Dependent Children (AFDC) programs do not cover "unborn children."[10] The treatment of first-time pregnancies of low-income women under Medicaid by the state in which the county is located is described by three dichotomous variables (MN, MU, MA). MN equals one for counties in states that cover first-time pregnancies only if no husband is present. MU equals one for counties in states that provide coverage if no husband is present or if the husband is present but unemployed and not receiving unemployment insurance. MA equals one for counties in states that provide coverage to all financially eligible women, regardless of the presence or employment status of the husband. The omitted category pertains to counties in states that cover no first-time pregnancies because their AFDC programs do not cover unborn children.[11]

Our measurement of Medicaid is imperfect because its impact on neonatal mortality depends upon the percentage of second- and higher-order births covered and on the quantity and quality of services provided per birth. There are no data on these variables. In preliminary regressions, the average Medicaid payment per adult recipient in AFDC families in the state in which the county is located was included as a proxy for the quantity and quality of services. This variable had a positive and statistically insignificant effect on neonatal mortality. Its inclusion had only minor impacts on the coefficients of the other variables.

The presence of an M and I project in a county in 1971 is denoted by the dichotomous variable MI. A second measure of the impact of M and I projects is given by the number of births in an M and I project in 1971, as a percentage of our estimated births to low-income women in 1971 (PMIB). Both variables are employed because the M and I program is relatively small; there were only 53 projects in 1971. The presence of an M and I project and the number of births in the project were taken from Bureau of Community Health Services (n.d.).

The impact of variations in federal, state, and local subsidization of family planning services is given by the percentage of women ages 15 to 44 with family incomes equal to or less than 150 percent of the poverty level who were served by organized family planning clinics in fiscal 1971 (UP). These clinics are organized by hospitals, state and local health departments, Planned Parenthood, and other agencies such as neighborhood health centers. This variable was taken from a survey conducted by the National Center for Health Statistics and by the technical assistance division of Planned Parenthood, then known as the Center for Family Planning Program Development and now known as the Alan Guttmacher Institute (Center for Family Planning Program Development, 1974). It excludes family planning services delivered to low-income women by private physicians.

Dryfoos (1976) reports that almost all clients of family planning clinics use the pill or the IUD. Therefore, the percentage of low-income women who are served by these clinics is positively related to the percentage of low-income women who select the pill or the IUD as contraceptive techniques. There is no information on the use of these techniques by other women at the county or state level, but it is known that women with at least a high school education are more likely to use them. Therefore, part of the observed effect of schooling in the regressions reflects the impact of the diffusion of the pill and the IUD on neonatal mortality.

The Medicaid, M and I, and family planning variables are interacted with the race-specific percentage of births to women in poverty. Since PB* is a percentage rather than a fraction, the regression coefficients must be multiplied by 100 to obtain the vector of impact parameters (α_1) associated with policies aimed at low-income women [see Equations (2), (4), or (5)].

The role of abortion reform is measured by a three-year average of the legal abortion rate for the period 1970-72 in the state in which the county is located (ARATE). The measure is an average of legal abortions performed on state residents per 1,000 live births to state residents and is derived from information reported by the Center for Disease Control (1971, 1972, and 1974). It is assumed that abortions performed in the first half of a given year affect the neonatal mortality rate in the second half of that year. The computation also takes account of the extremely low legal abortion rates before the second half of 1970 in states that reformed their abortion laws that year. The assumptions required to estimate the abortion rate are somewhat arbitrary.[12] Therefore, in some regressions the rate is replaced by a dichotomous variable that identifies counties in states that reformed their abortion laws by the middle of 1970 (RA).

The final variable in the regressions is a three-year average of the infant mortality rate for the years 1966-68 (M66-68). Theoretically, this is an important variable to include in the analysis because programs such as M and I projects and subsidized family planning clinics for low-income women were designed to service target populations with poor health indicators. Consequently, estimates of their impacts are biased toward zero if the initial level of the mortality rate is omitted from the regression. In the case of abortion reform and liberal treatment of first-time pregnancies under Medicaid, the exclusion of the lagged mortality rate might overstate their contributions to reductions in neonatal mortality. This is because most of the states that reformed their abortion laws by 1970 and enacted generous Medicaid programs were liberal states with relatively large welfare programs and probably lower than average infant mortality rates. In general, the use of the lagged rate as an independent variable controls for unmeasured determinants of infant mortality that are correlated with the included variables.

Given lags between the enactment of the programs at issue and their implementation and given lags between implementation and impacts on neonatal mortality, M66-68 provides an ideal control for the initial level of the mortality rate. Note also that M66-68 is superior to the corresponding race-specific neonatal mortality rate because the overall infant mortality rate was used to identify target populations and identifies the size of welfare programs at least as well as a race- and age-specific rate.[13] Note finally, that, to the extent that the programs at issue had an impact on mortality between 1966 and 1968, we understate their effects. Preliminary regressions (not shown) suggest that this bias is minor. When the lagged mortality rate is excluded from the regressions, the impacts of abortion reform and liberal Medicaid coverage rise in absolute value, while the impacts of family planning and the M and I program decline in absolute value. This is precisely what one would expect if the regressions with M66-68 provide an adequate control for the mortality rate in the period prior to the initial impact date of the programs.

EMPIRICAL RESULTS

Ordinary least-squares regressions of white neonatal mortality rates are contained in Panel A of Table 11.1, and ordinary least-squares regressions of black neonatal mortality rates are contained in Panel B of Table 11.1. For whites, the percentage of births to poor mothers has a positive and statistically significant effect on neonatal mortality, while mother's schooling has an insignificant negative effect. For blacks, the negative schooling effect is significant, but somewhat surprisingly, there is an inverse relationship between the percentage of births to poor black mothers and the neonatal mortality rate. For both races, the coefficient of physicians per capita is positive and not significant. Moreover, the infant mortality rate for the period 1966 to 1968 performs well as a control for the neonatal mortality rate prior to the initiation of the programs at issue and for unmeasured determinants of mortality (see regressions A1, A3, B1, and B3).

Because the poverty variable has the "wrong" sign for blacks, it is excluded in regressions A2, A4, B2, and B4. The main impact of this alternative specification is to increase the absolute value of the schooling effect for whites and to reduce it for blacks. Since the coefficients of the policy variables do not change much when PB* is omitted and since the estimation of separate poverty and schooling effects "taxes" the black data, we stress the results contained in regressions B2 and B4 in the rest of this chapter. For whites, both estimates with and without PB* are used. In part, more specifications are used for whites because trends in white neonatal mortality dominate trends in total neonatal mortality. In particular, white births account for approximately 80 percent of all births at the national level. [14]

Table 11.1 sheds considerable light on the roles of the policy variables in neonatal mortality outcomes. Nineteen of the twenty-eight policy coefficients have the anticipated negative signs in the four white regressions. All fourteen coefficients have the anticipated negative signs in the two relevant black regressions (B2 and B4). The exceptions in the white regressions pertain to the coefficients of the variables that identify liberal coverage of first-time pregnancies under Medicaid (MAXPB*, MUXPB*, MNXPB*). Given the high degree of intercorrelation among the variables in the regression and the imprecise measures used, the preponderance of negative effects is an important and impressive finding.

In terms of statistical significance, the hypothesis that no member of the set of policy variables has a nonzero effect on neonatal mortality always is rejected at the 1 percent level. With respect to the four specific policies, in general, abortion and the use of

TABLE 11.1. Ordinary Least-Squares Regressions of Neonatal Mortality Rates

Independent Variable	Panel A: White Regressions				Panel B: Black Regressions			
	(A1)	(A2)	(A3)	(A4)	(B1)	(B2)	(B3)	(B4)
PB*	.037		.042		-.147		-.133	
	(3.00)		(3.45)		(-4.14)		(-3.83)	
MD	.144	.122	.124	.097	.227	.450	.172	.393
	(1.60)	(1.35)	(1.37)	(1.07)	(1.03)	(2.05)	(0.79)	(1.84)
HSP*	-.015	-.036	-.013	-.037	-.124	-.017	-.137	-.035
	(-1.14)	(-3.13)	(-0.96)	(3.22)	(-2.93)	(-0.49)	(-3.31)	(-1.08)
MAXPB*	.004	.016	-.003	.008	.0004	-.014	-.007	-.010
	(0.39)	(1.83)	(-0.39)	(1.00)	(0.00)	(-0.53)	(-0.31)	(-0.46)
MUXPB*	.003	.010	.004	.012	-.038	-.033	-.041	-.034
	(0.29)	(1.03)	(0.44)	(1.24)	(-1.78)	(-1.51)	(-1.97)	(-1.61)
MNXPB*	-.006	.001	-.002	.007	-.010	-.032	-.010	-.030
	(-0.67)	(0.13)	(-0.21)	(0.77)	(-0.75)	(-2.47)	(-0.73)	(-2.32)
MIXPB*	-.005	-.011	-.008	-.017	-.007	-.003	-.007	-.005
	(-0.36)	(-0.87)	(-0.67)	(-1.37)	(-0.30)	(-0.15)	(-0.34)	(-0.20)
PMIBXPB*	-.022	-.020	-.015	-.011	-.033	-.032	-.037	-.036
	(-1.06)	(-0.98)	(-0.76)	(-0.56)	(-1.19)	(-1.13)	(-1.35)	(-1.31)
UPXPB*	-.001	-.0003	-.001	-.0003	-.0003	-.001	-.0001	-.001
	(-2.99)	(-1.94)	(-2.80)	(-1.58)	(-0.86)	(-2.37)	(-0.34)	(-1.76)
ARATE	-.004	-.005			-.009	-.007		
	(-3.25)	(-3.91)			(-2.25)	(-1.58)		

	(1)	(2)	(3)	(4)	(5)	(6)	(7)	(8)
RA			$-.549$	$-.592$			-1.751	-1.773
			(-3.43)	(-3.69)			(-3.89)	(-3.86)
M66–68	.274	.280	.281	.288	.260	.240	.235	.217
	(12.34)	(12.53)	(12.73)	(13.04)	(3.98)	(3.61)	(3.65)	(3.31)
CONSTANT	7.554	9.400	7.045	9.094	27.184	17.998	27.618	19.238
$\bar{R}^2$	.315	.307	.317	.305	.125	.084	.149	.116
F	29.38	31.05	29.54	30.80	5.64	4.30	6.70	5.68

Note: t-ratios in parentheses. The critical t-ratio at the 5 percent level of significance is 1.64 for a one-tailed test. The eight F-ratios are significant at the 1 percent level.

TABLE 11.2. Contribution of Selected Factors to Reductions in Neonatal Mortality Rates, 1964–77

	Panel A: Whites						Panel B: Nonwhites		
	1964–77		1964–71		1971–77		1964–77	1964–71	1971–77
	Reg. A1	Reg. A2	Reg. A1	Reg. A2	Reg. A1	Reg. A2	Reg. B2	Reg. B2	Reg. B2
Observed reduction in neonatal mortality rate (deaths/thousand live births)	7.5		3.2		4.3		11.8	6.9	4.9
Annually compounded percentage rate of decline in neonatal mortality rate	4.9		3.2		6.9		4.6	4.4	4.9
Contribution of selected factors to observed reduction in neonatal mortality rate									
MD	a	b	a	b	a	c	-0.2	-0.1	-0.1
PB*	0.4	0.6	0.3	0.1	a	c	b	b	b
HSP*	0.2	1.7	0.4	0.1	0.1	0.3	0.3	0.1	0.2
ARATE	1.5	0.2	0.4	0.4	1.1	1.3	2.5	0.6	1.9
UPXPB*	0.6	0.1	0.1	0.1	0.3	0.1	1.4	0.8	0.6
M and I Projects[d]	0.1	-0.2	0.1	a	a	c	0.3	0.3	c
Medicaid[e]	a	a			a	c	0.5	0.5	c
Total explained reduction	2.8	2.4	1.3	0.7	1.5	1.7	4.8	2.2	2.6
Percentage explained	37.3	32.0	40.6	24.7	34.9	39.5	40.7	31.9	53.1

[a] Less than .1 in absolute value.
[b] Variable omitted from regression.
[c] No change in variable.
[d] Combined contribution of MIXPB* and PMIBXPB*.
[e] Combined contribution of MAXPB*, MUXPB*, and MNXPB*.

subsidized family planning services by low-income women have significant impacts, while Medicaid and M and I projects do not. [15] Specifically, for whites the abortion rate (ARATE) achieves significance at all conventional levels in regressions A1 and A2. A similar comment applies to the dichotomous variable that denotes abortion reform by the middle of 1970 (RA) in regressions A3 and A4. For blacks, RA is significant at all levels in regression B4, while ARATE is significant at the 6 percent level, but not at the 5 percent level, in regression B2. For whites, the interaction between the percentage of low-income women who use organized family planning clinics and the percentage of births to low-income women (UPXPB*) is significant at the 5 percent level in the first three regressions and at the 6 percent level in the fourth. For blacks, UPXPB* is significant at the 5 percent level in both regressions.

The significance of the abortion rate is notable because this variable is neither race- nor county-specific and must be computed subject to a number of somewhat arbitrary assumptions (see Note 12). Therefore, it is probably subject to considerable measurement error, which biases its coefficient toward zero. The sizable and significant impacts of the dichotomous variable RA strengthen our confidence in the estimated coefficients of the abortion rate and confirm that the effect for blacks is larger in absolute value than that for whites.

To examine the relative contributions of schooling, poverty, and the public programs to the recent U.S. neonatal mortality experience, we apply the coefficients of regressions A1, A2, and B2 to trends in the exogenous variables between 1964 and 1977. The results of estimating the implied changes in neonatal mortality rates due to selected factors for the period 1964-77 and for the subperiods 1964-71 and 1971-77 are given in Table 11.2. [16] Results for whites and nonwhites are shown because separate time series for blacks are not available.

Since there is little trend in the percentage of families in poverty after 1971 and since the definition of poverty was altered beginning in 1975, the estimates in Table 11.2 assume no change in poverty or in PB* between 1971 and 1977. In these computations, the national levels of the two M and I project measures are zero in 1964 and do not change from 1971 to 1977. The three Medicaid measures are treated in the same manner. This treatment is justified because there were few M and I projects in operation prior to 1967 and almost no trend in the number of projects or the total number of births in projects after 1971 (Bureau of Community Health Services n.d.). The Medicaid program was not enacted until July 1965, and the rules governing coverage of first-time pregnancies under Medicaid did not vary between 1971 and 1977.

Our treatment of Medicaid is somewhat controversial because the percentage of Medicaid-financed births to poor women and the real quantity of medical services per birth may have risen between 1971 and 1977. Although definitive evidence on these matters is lacking, a number of observations can be made. Much of the observed decline over time in the relationship between income and physician visits, which Davis and Reynolds (1976) show was caused by Medicaid, occurred by 1971. The percentage of the poverty population that received Medicaid benefits rose by only 6 percentage points between 1970 and 1974 (Davis and Reynolds 1976; Davis and Schoen 1978). Real Medicaid benefits per recipient show no trend between 1971 and 1977 (Davis and Schoen 1978). The percentage of black mothers who started their prenatal care in the first trimester of pregnancy rose between 1969 and 1975 (Taffel 1978). Except for the last observation, this evidence justifies our treatment of Medicaid. We do, however, examine the sensitivity of the results to an alternative assumption described below.

As shown in Table 11.2, the actual decline in the white neonatal mortality rate between 1964 and 1977 was 7.5 deaths per thousand live births. Regression A1, which incorporates separate poverty and schooling effects, "explains" 2.8 of these deaths or 37 percent of the total reduction. Regression A2, which treats the schooling effect as the joint impact of schooling and poverty, accounts for 2.4 deaths or 32 percent of the total reduction. For nonwhites, the neonatal mortality rate fell by 11.8 deaths per thousand live births between 1964 and 1977. Regression B2 predicts a decline of 4.8 deaths or 41 percent of the observed reduction.

A striking message in Table 11.2 is that the increase in the legal abortion rate is the single most important factor in reductions in both white and nonwhite neonatal mortality rates. Not only does the growth in abortion dominate the other policies, but it also dominates schooling and poverty.[17] For the entire period, the reduction in the white neonatal mortality rate due to abortion, ranges from 1.5 to 1.7 deaths per thousand births. The comparable figure for nonwhites is a whopping 2.5 deaths per thousand births. When the two subperiods are examined separately, abortion makes the largest contribution except for nonwhites in the 1964-71 period. Here it ranks second to the impact of the rise in the use of organized family planning services by low-income women. The extremely large expansion in the abortion rate in the latter period (1971-77) provides a cogent explanation of the acceleration in the percentage rates of decline in both race-specific mortality rates and the acceleration in the absolute rate of change for whites.

The increase in the use of organized family planning services by low-income women is the second most important factor in reductions in nonwhite neonatal mortality for the entire period (1.4 deaths per thousand live births). For whites, the estimate of the contribution of family planning is sensitive to the inclusion in or exclusion from the regression of the percentage of births to poor women. When PB* is included, it dominates all the other factors except for abortion in the entire period and in the two subperiods. Its effect is weaker when PB* is omitted and is no larger than the impact of M and I projects in the earlier subperiod.

There is reason to believe that we understate the impact of the use of all family planning services, as opposed to organized services by low-income women. This is because our measure excludes services delivered by private physicians. National trends in the percentage of low-income women serviced by private physicians contained in the Center for Family Planning Program Development (1974), Dryfoos (1976), and Cutright and Jaffe (1977) suggest that the estimates in Table 11.2 should be multiplied by a factor of 1.6. This adjustment makes family planning a more important contributor to neonatal death rate reductions than M and I projects in the computations based on regression A2. It suggests that the predicted reductions of 1.5 nonwhites deaths per thousand births and between 0.2 and 0.6 white deaths per thousand births due to family planning are conservative lower-bound estimates of the true impact.

M and I projects have small impacts on white neonatal mortality regardless of the regression specification employed. For nonwhites the effect is somewhat more substantial; it amounts to a decline of 0.3 deaths per thousand births for the years during which the projects were expanding. Of course, the impact of M and I projects over the entire period is dominated by the impacts of abortion reform and family planning, in part, because there was no change in the size of these projects between 1971 and 1977. However, suppose that the absolute increase in the size of these projects had been the same in the second subperiod as it was in the first; then their predicted impact on the nonwhite neonatal death rate would amount to 0.6 deaths per thousand births, which still is substantially smaller than the abortion and family planning effects.

Medicaid can be dismissed as a cause of the decline in white neonatal mortality; it predicts either no change or an increase in the white death rate. In the case of nonwhites, Medicaid accounts for a reduction of 0.5 deaths per thousand live births. If the somewhat controversial assumption of no change in the program between 1971 and 1977 is relaxed in the same manner as for M and I projects, we obtain a reduction of 1.0 deaths per thousand births. This is greater than the reduction associated with M and I projects but smaller than the reductions associated with abortion reform and family planning.

To summarize, our results, when combined with information on the use of the pill and the IUD by women of all income classes, provide a coherent explanation of the U.S. neonatal experience from 1964 to 1977. After a period of relative stability, the neonatal mortality rate began to decline following 1964, as a lagged response to the extremely rapid increase in the percentage of women who used the pill and the IUD between 1961 and 1964.[18] The decline was further fueled by the increase in the percentage of low-income women who used subsidized family planning services between 1965 and 1971 and by the dramatic rise in the legal abortion rate between 1969 and 1971. The acceleration in the rate of decline in the mortality rate between 1971 and 1977 was due primarily to the literal explosion of the abortion rate in that period. These conclusions are subject to the qualification that we have no estimates of the impact of the pill and the IUD other than those that we infer through the use of family planning services by low-income women. They also are subject to the qualification that we cannot estimate the contribution of advances in neonatology.

The above findings do not necessarily imply that increases in the quantity of medical care played an unimportant role in the downward trend in neonatal mortality. To be sure, the impacts of Medicaid and M and I projects are smaller than the impacts of abortion reform and family planning. But as indicated previously, this simply may mean that the quantity of medical care per birth is more responsive to a reduction in the cost of fertility control than to a reduction in the price of care.

Our results with respect to the importance of the legalization of abortion in trends in infant mortality differ from those of Bauman and Anderson (1980). Using states of the United States as the units of observation, they find no relationship between changes in the legal abortion rate and changes in the fetal or infant mortality rate. Bauman and Anderson's findings differ from ours for a number of reasons. First, they do not control for other determinants of infant mortality. Second, they do not use race-specific mortality data. Third, they do not examine the impacts of abortion reform on neonatal mortality.

Our results are relevant to current U.S. policy debates with respect to the financing of abortions under Medicaid and with respect to attempts by the Right to Life movement to enact a constitutional amendment that would outlaw abortion except when it is necessary to preserve a pregnant woman's life. Under the Hyde Amendment, which was in effect from June 1977 until February 1980, federal funding of abortions under Medicaid was banned except in cases where the woman's life was in danger. During that period, 28 states refused to pay for "medically necessary" abortions. The other 22 states continued to finance most abortions for Medicaid-eligible women by paying the federal share as well as the state share. As a result, the number of federally financed abortions declined from approximately 250,000 per year before 1976 to less than 3,000 in 1978 (Trussell et al. 1980). Federal funding of abortions resumed temporarily in February 1980, pending a review by the U.S. Supreme Court of a ruling by Federal District Judge John F. Dooling, Jr. that declared the Hyde Amendment unconstitutional. In June 1980, the Supreme Court reversed Judge Dooling's decision and upheld the constitutionality of the Hyde Amendment.

In spite of the Hyde Amendment, the abortion rate continued to rise between 1977 and 1978. In part, this trend reflects the continued diffusion of a relatively new method of birth control. In part, it reflects a substitution of private for federal funds by roughly 80 percent of women who would have been eligible for federal financing in the absence of the amendment (Trussell et al. 1980). One can speculate, however, that the abortion rate would have risen at a more rapid rate between 1977 and 1978 in the absence of the Hyde Amendment. Given the recent Supreme Court ruling, the abortion rate for poor women probably will grow slower than otherwise would be the case and might even fall. According to our findings, this will retard the rate of decline in the neonatal mortality rate of the poor.

Taken at face value, the most striking implication of our study pertains to a constitutional ban on abortions. The current U.S. abortion rate is 400 abortions per thousand live births, while the rate in 1969 was 4 abortions per thousand live births. If a ban reduced the rate to its 1969 level, our regressions predict that the nonwhite neonatal mortality rate would rise by approximately 2.8 deaths per thousand live births or by 19 percent above its 1977 level. The white neonatal mortality rate would rise by approximately 1.8 deaths per thousand live births or by 21 percent above its 1977 level. Yet these estimates must be regarded with caution because they assume that all other factors would remain the same if a ban were enacted. In particular, to the extent that abortion is a substitute for more conventional methods of birth control, the use of these methods would not remain the same.

APPENDIX

TABLE 11.A1. Definitions, Means, and Standard Deviations
of Variables[a]

Variable Name	Definition
NM70-72*	Three-year average neonatal mortality rate for the period 1970-72; deaths of infants less than 28 days old per 1,000 live births ($\mu_w = 12.729$; $\sigma_w = 2.076$; $\mu_b = 21.477$; $\sigma_b = 3.988$)
PB*	Estimated percentage of births to mothers with family incomes less than the poverty level for the period 1969-71 ($\mu_w = 21.324$; $\sigma_w = 8.388$; $\mu_b = 35.188$; $\sigma_b = 11.235$)
HSP*[b]	Percentage of women aged 15 to 49 who had at least a high school education in 1970 ($\mu_w = 21.324$; $\sigma_w = 7.238$; $\mu_b = 44.096$; $\sigma_b = 8.527$)
MD	Active nonfederal physicians per 1,000 population in 1971 ($\mu_w = 1.505$; $\sigma_w = 0.987$; $\mu_b = 1.954$; $\sigma_b = 1.220$)
MAXPB*	Dichotomous variable that equals one if county is in a state that covers all first-time pregnancies to financially elibible women under Medicaid (MA) multiplied by PB* ($\mu_w = 7.892$; $\sigma_w = 10.850$; $\mu_b = 7.104$; $\sigma_b = 12.657$)
MUXPB*	Dichotomous variable that equals one if county is in a state that covers first-time pregnancies under Medicaid only if no husband present or if husband present but unemployed and not receiving unemployment compensation (MU) multiplied by PB* ($\mu_w = 2.810$; $\sigma_w = 7.521$; $\mu_b = 3.857$; $\sigma_b = 10.219$)
MNXPB*	Dichotomous variable that equals one if county is in a state that covers first-time pregnancies under Medicaid only if no husband present (MN) multiplied by PB* ($\mu_w = 2.284$; $\sigma_w = 7.851$; $\mu_b = 7.536$; $\sigma_b = 18.185$)
MIXPB*	Dichotomous variable that equals one if the county had an M and I project in 1971 (MI) multiplied by PB* ($\mu_w = 5.339$; $\sigma_w = 9.390$; $\mu_b = 16.152$; $\sigma_b = 16.577$)

(continued)

TABLE 11.A1 (continued)

Variable Name	Definition
PMIBXPB*	Births in M and I projects in 1971 as a percentage of births to women with low income (PMIB) multiplied by PB* ($\mu_w = 2.174$; $\sigma_w = 5.086$; $\mu_b = 8.470$; $\sigma_b = 12.670$)
UPXPB*	Percentage of women aged 15 to 44 with family income equal to or less than 150 percent of the poverty level who were served by organized family planning clinics in fiscal 1971 (UP) multiplied by PB* ($\mu_w = 639.506$; $\sigma_w = 521.843$; $\mu_b = 1,435.559$; $\sigma_b = 741.955$)
ARATE	Three-year average abortion rate for the period 1970-72 of state in which county is located; legal abortions performed on state residents per 1,000 live births to state residents ($\mu_w = 96.607$; $\sigma_w = 80.497$; $\mu_b = 87.156$; $\sigma_b = 77.518$)
RA	Dichotomous variable that equals one if county is in a state that reformed its abortion law by 1970 ($\mu_w = 0.369$; $\sigma_w = 0.483$; $\mu_b = 0.358$; $\sigma_b = 0.480$)
M66-68	Three-year average infant mortality rate for the period 1966-68, not race or age specific ($\mu_w = 21.517$; $\sigma_w = 3.553$; $\mu_b = 24.380$; $\sigma_b = 3.867$)

[a]Variable names ending in an asterisk (*) indicate variables that are race specific. The symbols μ_w, σ_w, μ_b, and σ_b denote the white mean, the white standard deviation, the black mean, and the black standard deviation, respectively. The white data pertain to 679 counties, while the black data pertain to 359 counties. Means and standard deviations are weighted by the race-specific number of births in 1971.

[b]Variable is available only for whites and nonwhites, as opposed to whites and blacks.

NOTES

1. The above computations are based on data contained in U.S.,
   Bureau of the Census (1980).
2. Descriptive and historical information concerning the programs
   at issue is available in the expanded version of this paper (available on request), and details on abortion reform are provided in
   the section, Empirical Specifications. Briefly, Medicaid, enacted
   in 1965 as Title XIX of the Social Security Act of 1935, is the
   joint federal–state program to finance the medical care services
   of low–income families who are covered by the Aid to Families
   with Dependent Children (AFDC) program. Maternal and infant
   care (M and I) projects originated in the 1963 amendment to
   Title V of the Social Security Act. The amendment provides
   special grants for projects designed to provide adequate prenatal
   and obstetrical care to reduce the incidence of mental retardation
   and other conditions caused by childbearing complications as well
   as to lower infant and maternal mortality. Federal subsidization
   of family planning services for low–income women originated in
   the 1967 amendments to the Social Security Act. Federal efforts
   in this area were expanded by the Family Planning Services and
   Population Research Act of 1970 and by the 1972 amendments to
   the Social Security Act. These subsidies go to family planning
   clinics organized by hospitals, state and local health departments,
   Planned Parenthood, and other agencies, such as M and I projects
   and neighborhood health centers. The diffusion of the pill and the
   IUD did not result from actions by the federal government or by
   states. This development is important for our research, however,
   because it meant that an extremely effective method of birth control could be offered to low–income women by federally subsidized
   family planning clinics.
3. The indirect costs of obtaining a good are generated by the time
   spent traveling, waiting, and obtaining information about the good.
   We use the terms, indirect costs and availability, as synonyms.
4. Eugene Lewit has emphasized to us that theoretically the direction
   of the effects of abortion on fertility and infant mortality may be
   indeterminant. For instance, abortion may substitute for other
   methods of birth control. Moreover, abortion reform may cause
   the birth rate to rise by increasing the level of sexual activity in
   general. In spite of these factors, we feel that the hypothesis that
   abortion reform lowers the infant mortality rates is very plausible.
   In part, this is because we control for the use of family planning
   services in the regression analysis in the section, Empirical
   Results.

5. If abortion reform lowers infant mortality solely by reducing the fraction of high-risk births, a measure of reform such as the legal abortion rate should have no impact on infant mortality in a multiple regression that controls for the percentage of low birth-weight births. This is not the case if the medical care mechanism outlined above also is relevant. Since there is more than one mechanism via which abortion reform and the other policies can affect infant mortality, and since our aim in this paper is to estimate reduced form, as opposed to structural, effect, we omit regressors such as the percentage of low birth-weight births. Another reason for adopting this strategy is that some policy variables may have differential and possibly larger impacts on death rates in high-risk categories. Therefore, a study of the mechanisms via which government policies affect infant mortality should pay careful attention to complicated interactions between the policies and the fraction of high-risk births. Such a study is important, but it is beyond the scope of this chapter.

6. In preliminary regressions, the coefficient of the number of hospital beds per capita was insignificant, and its inclusion had only minor impacts on the coefficients of the other independent variables.

7. The regression equation for whites is:

$$b_j^* = .064 + .169\pi_j^* , \quad \bar{R}^2 = .269, \ n = 679$$
$$(t = 15.90)$$

The regression equation for blacks is:

$$b_j^* = .095 + .059\pi_j^* , \quad \bar{R}^2 = .118, \ n = 359$$
$$(t = 6.98)$$

In each regression, the dependent variable is a three-year average of the birth rate for the period 1969-71. The regressions are weighted by the square root of the race-specific number of women ages 15-44 in 1970. The poverty variable pertains to the fraction of families below the poverty level rather than to the fraction of women ages 15-44. The latter variable is not available on a race-specific basis. Another reason for the use of the fraction of families in poverty is that it facilitates the trend analysis in the section, Empirical Results. The ratios of births per thousand women ages 15-44 implied by the regressions are 233 for poor whites, 64 for nonpoor whites, 154 for poor blacks, and 95 for nonpoor blacks.

8. In regressions not shown in the section, Empirical Results, median family income was included as an independent variable. Its coefficient was not significant.

9. From Equation (5), the reduced form effect of x_{pj} on d_j is:

$$\frac{\partial d_j}{\partial x_{pj}} = (\alpha_0 - \beta_0) \frac{\partial k_j}{\partial x_{pj}} + \alpha_1 k_j + \alpha_1 x_{pj} \frac{\partial k_j}{\partial x_{pj}}$$

Note that

$$k^*_{jp} = \pi^*_j b^*_{jp} / b^*_j$$

where b^*_{jp} is the race-specific birth rate of poor women in the jth county. Clearly, this variable is not held constant in our regressions. Note that reduced form effects also could be estimated by expressing k_j as a function of a set of variables, including the policy measures, in Equation (5). This results in an extremely complicated functional form. Specifically, it includes the level of each policy measure, the square of that measure, and its product with each of the other measures. Such an equation is not tractable from the standpoint of estimation.

10. This list of states includes Arizona, which has no Medicaid program.

11. Our information on the treatment of first-time pregnancies under Medicaid by specific states was obtained from Letty Wunglueck of the Health Care Financing Administration. Note that first-time pregnancies of young mothers who are themselves dependents in AFDC families would be covered under Medicaid in spite of the above provisions. States in one of our three categories, however, cover a larger percentage of first-time pregnancies than other states.

12. Suppose that the neonatal mortality rate (nm_{jt}) and the legal abortion rate (a_{jt}) are measured in half-year intervals. Let the relationship between the two be:

$$nm_{jt} = \beta + \delta a_{jt-1}$$

Aggregate and average this equation over three years (six half-years) to obtain:

$$\overline{nm}_j = \beta + \delta \overline{a}_j \qquad \text{where:}$$

$$\bar{a}_j = \frac{\sum\limits_{t=0}^{5} a_{jt-1}}{6}$$

The neonatal mortality rates pertain to the period from the first half of 1970 (70-1) to the last half of 1972 (72-2). Therefore, ignore the county subscript, and write $\bar{a}$ as:

$$\bar{a} = \frac{a69\text{-}2 + a70\text{-}1 + a70\text{-}2 + a71\text{-}1 + a71\text{-}2 + a72\text{-}1}{6}$$

We have data for a70-2, a71 (the abortion rate during the entire year of 1971), and a72. For states that reformed their abortion laws before 1970, we assume that a69-2 + a70-1 = a70-2, due to the rapid upward trend in the abortion rate during this period. We also assume that the birth rate in the first half of 1971 equaled the birth rate in the second half of 1971, so that a71-1 + a71-2 = 2a71. Finally, we assume a72-1 = a72. Hence, for these states:

$$\bar{a} = (1/3)(a70\text{-}2) + (1/3)(a71) + (1/6)(a72)$$

For states that reformed their laws in the middle of 1970, we assume a69-2 = a70-1 = 0. Hence, given the other two conditions used above,

$$\bar{a} = (1/6)(a70\text{-}2) + (1/3)(a71) + (1/6)(a72)$$

Since the law for New York State has no residency requirements, states near New York are treated in the same manner as New York in the computation of $\bar{a}$.

13. Age- and race-specific infant mortality rates for years prior to 1969 are not available on the Area Resource File.

14. Space limitations prevent us from discussing the effects of poverty, schooling, and physicians in detail and from presenting additional specifications of the basic regressions. Note the following:

(1) The variables PB* and HSP* are highly correlated for whites ($r = -.6$) and for blacks ($r = -.8$). The insignificant regression coefficients of HSP* in regressions A1 and A3 are due in part to multicollinearity. This phenomenon may also contribute to the black results, although the explanation is somewhat more complicated because the simple correlation between the death rate and PB* is negative.

(2) There are few studies of the race-specific impact of poverty on infant mortality. Using a special sample of births and subsequent infant deaths taken by the National Center for Health Statistics, Gortmaker (1979) reports results similar to ours. White babies are more likely to die in poverty families than in nonpoverty families, but this relationship does not hold for black babies.

(3) The unimportance of physicians per capita in our regressions mirrors findings reported by Brooks (1978) in a study of variations in infant mortality rates among SMSAs. The coefficients of other variables are not sensitive to the exclusion of MD. We retain the MD variable because there is almost no trend in it between 1964 and 1977. Hence, its retention does not cloud the forecasts and backcasts that follow.

15. For Medicaid, we always accept the hypothesis that no member of the set given by MAXPB*, MUXPB*, and MNXPB* has a nonzero coefficient at the 5 percent level. For M and I projects, we accept the hypothesis that no member of the set given by MIXPB* and PMIBXPB* has a nonzero coefficient in five of six cases. The exception pertains to regression A4.

16. Note that changes in the lagged mortality rate are not relevant in the forecasts and backcasts in Table 11.2 because the underlying model is not a dynamic one. Rather, the lagged rate serves as a proxy for the initial level, which does not change by definition. In econometric terminology, our model is one with "fixed effects" rather than one with "state dependence."

17. One might argue that we understate the impacts of schooling and poverty by holding constant an average infant mortality rate centered on the year 1967. Although it is reasonable to suppose that changes in the public policies had no impacts until after 1967, this assumption may not be reasonable in the cases of schooling and poverty. This is because the trends in these variables were continuous from 1960 to 1970. To examine the robustness of our conclusion that abortion dominates schooling and poverty, we reestimated the contributions of these variables from regressions that exclude the lagged mortality rate. Although the contribution of schooling rises relative to the contribution in Table 11.2, it is still smaller than that of abortion. Note that if county-level fixed effects that lower mortality are positively correlated with schooling, we overstate the schooling coefficient by excluding the lagged mortality rate.

18. Ryder (1972) reports that in 1961 the percentage of married women under age 35 who used the pill stood at approximately 3 percent. By 1964, it has increased to approximately 16 percent.

REFERENCES

Bauman, Karl E., and Ann E. Anderson. 1980. "Legal Abortions and Trends in Fetal and Infant Mortality Rates in the United States." American Journal of Obstetrics and Gynecology, 136, No. 2 (January 1980), pp. 194-202.

Becker, Gary S., and H. Gregg Lewis. 1973. "On the Interaction between the Quantity and Quality of Children." In New Economic Approaches to Fertility, edited by T. W. Schultz. Proceedings of a conference sponsored by the National Bureau of Economic Research and the Population Council. Journal of Political Economy, 81, No. 2, Part II (March/April 1973), S274-288.

Ben-Porath, Yoram. 1973. "On Child Traits and the Choice of Family Size." The Maurice Falk Institute for Economic Research in Israel Discussion Paper 731 (June 1973).

Ben-Porath, Yoram, and Finis Welch. 1976. "Do Sex Preferences Really Matter?" The Quarterly Journal of Economics, 90, No. 2 (May 1976), pp. 284-307.

Brooks, Charles H. 1978. "Infant Mortality in SMSAs Before Medicaid: Test of a Causal Model." Health Services Research, 13, No. 1 (Spring 1978).

Center for Family Planning Program Development. 1974. Need for Subsidized Family Planning Services: United States, Each State and County, 1971. New York: Planned Parenthood—World Population.

Cutright, Phillips, and Frederick S. Jaffe. 1977. Impact of Family Planning Programs on Fertility: The U.S. Experience. New York: Praeger.

Davis, Karen, and Roger Reynolds. 1976. "The Impact of Medicare and Medicaid on Access to Medical Care." In The Role of Health Insurance in the Health Services Sector, edited by Richard Rosett. New York: Neale Watson Academic Publications, pp. 391-425.

Davis, Karen, and Cathy Schoen. 1978. Health and the War on Poverty. Washington, D.C.: Brookings Institution.

Dryfoos, Joy G. 1976. "The United States National Family Planning Program, 1968-74." Studies in Family Planning, 7, No. 3 (March 1976), pp. 80-92.

Eisner, Victor, et al. 1978. "Improvement in Infant and Perinatal Mortality in the United States, 1965-1973." American Journal of Public Health, 68, No. 4 (April 1978), pp. 359-364.

Fuchs, Victor R. 1974. "Some Economic Aspects of Mortality in Developed Countries." In The Economics of Health and Medical Care, edited by Mark Perlman. London: Macmillan.

Gortmaker, Steven L. 1979. "Poverty and Infant Mortality in the United States." American Sociological Review, 44, No. 2 (April 1979), pp. 280-297.

Lee, Kwang-Sun, et al. 1980. "Neonatal Mortality: An Analysis of the Recent Improvement in the United States." American Journal of Public Health, 70, No. 1 (January 1980), pp. 15-21.

Lewit, Eugene M. 1977. "Experience with Pregnancy, the Demand for Prenatal Care, and the Production of Surviving Infants." Ph.D. dissertation, City University of New York Graduate School.

Ryder, Norman B. 1972. "Time Series of Pill and IUD Use: United States, 1961-1970." Studies in Family Planning, 3, No. 10 (October 1972).

Taffel, Selma. 1978. Prenatal Care in the United States, 1969-1975. U.S. Department of Health, Education, and Welfare, Public Health Service, National Center for Health Statistics, Vital and Health Statistics, Series 21, No. 33 (September 1978).

Trussell, James, et al. 1980. "The Impact of Restricting Medicaid Financing for Abortion." Family Planning Perspectives, 12, No. 3 (May/June 1980), pp. 120-30.

U.S., Bureau of the Census. 1980. Statistical Abstract of the United States, 1979. Washington, D.C.: Government Printing Office.

U.S., Bureau of Community Health Services. n.d. "Maternity and Infant Care Projects—Statistical Summary—Fiscal Years 1969-1976." Department of Health, Education, and Welfare, Public Health Service.

U.S., Center for Disease Control, Public Health Service, Department of Health, Education, and Welfare. 1971, 1972, and 1974. Family Planning Evaluation: Abortion Surveillance Report, 1970-72.

Williams, Anne D. 1976. "Fertility and Reproductive Loss." Ph.D. dissertation, University of Chicago.

Williams, Ronald L. 1974. "Outcome-Based Measurements of Medical Care Output: The Case of Maternal and Infant Health." Ph.D. dissertation, University of California at Santa Barbara.

Willis, Robert. 1973. "A New Approach to the Economic Theory of Fertility Behavior." In New Economic Approaches to Fertility, edited by T. W. Schultz. Proceedings of a conference sponsored by the National Bureau of Economic Research and the Population Council. Journal of Political Economy, 81, No. 2, Part II (March/April 1973), pp. S14-64.

12

IMPLEMENTING
A HEALTH STATUS INDEX IN
A STRUCTURAL HEALTH CARE MODEL

Evelien M. Hooijmans
Wynand P.M.M. van de Ven

In this chapter we develop a structural macromodel of the Dutch health-care system. In this model we explicitly specify a structural relation between the use and the supply of health-care facilities, health and health-determining factors. In explaining various forms of medical consumption, many authors, for example, Feldstein (1967, 1977), Fuchs and Kramer (1972), Rutten (1978), and van der Gaag (1978), use as explanatory variables the supply of health-care facilities (the number of physicians and beds per capita), the distance to these facilities, the price of medical care, the insurance system, and the remuneration system.

Variables indicating morbidity, health, and population characteristics are often only represented by a restricted number of proxy variables, such as the percentage of the population aged 65 years and over, age-sex indexes, the percentage of women or some index of the population density.[1]

In this chapter we try to improve on these models by implementing a health status index that will be endogenous in a structural model of a health-care system. Theoretically, our approach is in the spirit of Robinson and Ferrara (1977); practically our approach looks like the approach of Levine and Yett (1973). We treat our health status index as an unobservable variable. It is an index of the health

This paper forms a part of the Leiden Health Economics Project, directed by Bernard M. S. van Praag. We thank Ralph van den Broek, Jacques van der Gaag, Frank Nauta, and Frans Rutten for their stimulating comments. The research reported in this paper was financed by grants from the Department of Health and from the Sick Fund Council in The Netherlands.

situation in a certain region, as it finds expression in the use of the health-care facilities, the mortality rate, absenteeism because of illness, and so forth, in that region. It is defined as a function of socioeconomic, demographic, and other variables that are presumed to influence health, such as the age-sex structure of the population, the kind of employment, income, environmental pollution, and the percentage of unemployment, plus a disturbance term.

The explicit specification of a health status index appears to have some fruitful applications. By way of example, we illustrate the implementation and estimation of this health index, using Rutten's (1978) model of the Dutch health-care system. In the next section, we briefly describe his model and reestimate it with our data. In the section Health, we present and discuss a structural health-care model including an unobservable health status index, which is only known by its causes and by its (health) indicators. Some of these indicators are the various forms of medical consumption. In the section on results, we present some empirical results and calculate the health status index for each of the 11 provinces of The Netherlands.

RUTTEN'S MODEL OF THE DUTCH HEALTH CARE SYSTEM

Dutch Health-Care System

Before we reestimate Rutten's (1978) model on more recent data,[2] we will briefly formulate the most important features of the Dutch health-care system.

In The Netherlands, we distinguish three levels of care and two types of insurance. Usually one enters the health-care system through a visit to a general practitioner, who provides primary (first level) care and who decides whether the patient needs specialist care.[3] The specialist, in his turn, decides whether the patient has to be treated in an outpatient clinic (second level of care) or admitted to a hospital (third level).

The Dutch health-care sector is partly financed through a public insurance system and partly by private insurance companies. Most of the Dutch families with an annual income below Dfl. 23,200 (1974) are publicly insured against all health-care expenses. In 1974 about 70 percent of the Dutch population was insured in this manner. In the public sector the general practitioner is paid by way of a capitation system, that is, he gets a fixed amount per year for each publicly insured person in his practice, regardless of the amount of care he provides. The specialists' remuneration is partly on a capitation basis (for most of the outpatient care) and partly on a fee-for-service basis (for most of the inpatient care). In the private sector all physicians are paid by the fee-for-service system. While the remuneration of the general practitioner is at the same level for both sectors, a considerable price discrimination exists with respect to specialist care: the fees in the private sector are about three times as high as in public sector. In general, all physicians provide care to both publicly and privately insured persons. Our model deals with medical consumption in the public sector only.

The Model

In this study the medical consumption at the first level of the health-care system (general care) is treated as exogenous.[4] The patient flow from the first to the second level (outpatient specialist care) is approximated by the number of referrals from the general practitioner to the specialist (REF). The consumption within the second level is measured by the number of referrals (REF) plus the number of continuation cards (CON). Although REF and CON don't give the exact policlinical consumption, they are close (and the best available) proxies for it.[5] The patient flow from the second to the third level (inpatient care) is given by the number of admissions in general and university hospitals (ADM). The consumption within the third level is measured by the number of admissions times the mean stay (MS) in general and university hospitals.

As explanatory variables in explaining REF, CON, ADM, and MS in this section, we use variables representing hospital capacity, the availability of outpatient care, supply of physicians, morbidity, distance to the hospital, and the mode of remuneration. In each equation we include the availability of the specific type of care plus the relevant alternative. For example, the number of outpatient working specialists (SPOG) in the REF equation gives the availability of second-level care. The expected mean stay, given the age-sex distribution of the publicly insured (ASIMS) in the MS-equation, is a proxy for morbidity. We will discuss these variables more fully when we present the estimation results.[6]

The complete four equation model reads as follows:

$$REF = f_1(DENSI, PINS, GP, SPOG, SPOU, ASIREF, CONST, \epsilon_1) \qquad (1a)$$

$$CON = f_2(DENSI, PINS, GP, SPOG, SPOU, REF, CONST, \epsilon_2) \qquad (1b)$$

$$ADM = f_3(DENSI, PINS, GP, BED, SPI, NURS, REF, MS, CONST, \epsilon_3) \qquad (1c)$$

$$MS = f_4(DENSI, PINS, GP, BED, SPI, NURS, ASIMS,$$
$$ADM, CONST, \epsilon_4) \tag{1d}$$

where:

REF: The number of referrals to a specialist (all hospitals) per 1,000 publicly insured

CON: The number of continuation cards (excluding specialist care in university hospitals) per referral

ADM: The number of admissions in general and university hospitals per 1,000 publicly insured

MS: The mean stay in general and university hospitals with respect to the publicly insured

DENSI: An index of the population density

PINS: The percentage of the population publicly insured

GP: The number of general practitioners per 1,000 population

SPOG: The number of specialists providing outpatient care in general hospitals per 1,000 population

SPOU: The number of specialists providing outpatient care in university hospitals per 1,000 population

BED: The number of beds in general and university hospitals per 1,000 population

SPI: The number of specialists providing inpatient care in general and university hospitals per 100 beds

NURS: The number of nurses in general and university hospitals per 100 beds

ASIREF: The expected referral rate, based on the age-sex distribution of the publicly insured

ASIMS: The expected mean stay, based on the age-sex distribution of the publicly insured

CONST: A constant term

$\epsilon_1, \epsilon_2, \epsilon_3, \epsilon_4$: Normally distributed disturbances

The main differences between the model used by Rutten and the one presented here are as follows. First, because the hospital admission capacity can be represented by BED, given the mean stay, we assume that a relative increase (or decrease) in MS will influence ADM in the same way that a relative decrease (increase) of the same size in BED will do. Therefore, we estimated the equations (1c) and (1d) under the restrictions that the influences of BED and MS on ADM are of the same magnitude (with opposite signs) and also that the influences of BED and ADM on MS are of the same magnitude (with opposite signs).[7]

Second, we expect both the admission rate and the mean stay to be influenced by hospital characteristics such as hospital facilities, policy of the hospital board, and other commonly omitted factors. Therefore, we assume that the disturbances of equation (1c) and (1d) are correlated.[8] All other correlation coefficients between the disturbances are assumed to be zero.

Estimation Results

We chose a loglinear specification of the model, so the regression coefficients can be interpreted as elasticities. The analysis is based on a cross section of 63 regions covering all of The Netherlands in the year 1974.[9] The full information maximum likelihood estimates are presented in Table 12.1, with t-values in parentheses.

The positive influence of DENSI on outpatient care and its negative effect on inpatient care may reflect the influence of the distance to the specialist. In densely populated regions, patients live relatively close to outpatient care facilities, so they can easily be treated outside the clinic.

The availability of general care is represented by the number of general practitioners per 1,000 population (GP). We see a negative influence on both outpatient and inpatient care, which may be interpreted as a possible substitution of general care for specialist care.

The number of outpatient working specialists in general hospitals (SPOG) has its expected positive influence on outpatient consumption. The negative influence of the number of specialists in university hospitals (SPOU) reflects the fact that referral cards to university hospitals are year cards.[10]

The capacity factor BED has its expected positive influence on clinical consumption. Its influence on the admission rate is greater than on the mean stay. Once a patient has been admitted to a hospital, the length of his treatment depends relatively less on the capacity and more on his illness. The number of nurses per bed (NURS), which may be interpreted as a capacity factor, has a positive influence (+0.17) on the admission rate.

The impact of the number of specialists per bed is significantly negative on both the admission rate and the mean stay. The negative effect on the mean stay suggests that an increase in the number of specialists per bed can increase the turnover rate in hospitals. The negative effect on the admission rate is surprising. However, recalling the differences in the remuneration systems for publicly and privately insured patients, it might be explained in the same way as the negative impact of PINS (the percentage of publicly insured) on the admission rate. In a region with a high number of specialists per bed

TABLE 12.1. Estimation Results[a] of Equations (1a) through (1d)[b]

	REF	CON	ADM	MS
CONST	-1.34 (0.2)	-0.09 (0.1)	5.97 (17.7)	1.80 (1.6)
DENSI	0.10 (3.9)	0.09 (3.6)	-0.03 (5.4)	-0.02 (2.7)
PINS	0.55 (2.7)	0.21 (0.9)	-0.34 (6.2)	-0.22 (3.1)
GP	0.01 (0.0)	-0.26 (1.3)	-0.05 (1.0)	-0.14 (2.1)
SPOG	0.20 (2.6)	0.29 (3.4)		
SPOU	-0.05 (2.0)	-0.11 (4.1)		
BED[c]			0.80 (22.9)	0.57 (6.3)
SPI			-0.11 (4.2)	-0.08 (2.4)
NURS			0.17 (2.7)	0.13 (1.6)
ASIREF	0.81 (0.8)			
ASIMS				1.14 (4.4)
REF		-0.19 (1.3)	0.10 (4.2)	
ADM[c]				-0.57 (6.3)
MS[c]			-0.80 (22.9)	

[a]Elasticities and absolute t-values (in parentheses).

[b]The covariance of the disturbances of the equations of the admission rate and the mean stay is 0.012 (t-value, 4.2), which yields a correlation coefficient of 0.79.

[c]Testing the hypothesis that the coefficients of BED and MS in the ADM equation and the coefficients of BED and ADM in the MS equation are of the same size yields a X^2 of 0.17 with 2 degrees of freedom, so this hypothesis cannot be rejected.

(or with a high percentage of publicly insured), and other things being equal, the specialists have to treat more privately insured patients in order to reach the same level of income as in other regions.[11] This results in fewer admissions of publicly insured patients.

A second interpretation of the negative PINS coefficients in the ADM- and MS-equation is based on capacity differences: "Because hospital capacity is measured as capacity available to all people (both publicly and privately insured) and publicly insured use hospital beds more frequently than privately insured,[12] an increase in the percentage publicly insured in the population will relatively decrease available capacity for publicly insured under ceteris paribus conditions and therefore have a negative effect on consumption." (Rutten 1978, p. 97).

On the average, however, differences in PINS may also partly represent differences in morbidity, that is, regions with a high percentage of publicly insured are, due to socioeconomic and other differences, relatively less healthy. This might explain the positive influence of PINS on REF and CON.

With respect to clinical consumption, we see that the influence of the variable PINS, representing morbidity differences, is more than outweighed by the "remuneration" and "capacity" aspects of PINS. With respect to policlinical medical consumption, we expect those aspects to be of less importance, thus allowing the morbidity differences to dominate. [13]

The coefficients of ASIREF and ASIMS (the expected referral rate and mean stay, given the age-sex structure of the publicly insured) are not significantly different from their expected value, one. The negative influence of REF on CON is as expected because it seems plausible that the amount of care consumed per referred patient will decrease if the number of referred patients increases. The influence of REF on ADM is positive but small.

HEALTH

A crucial point in the preceding section, mentioning criticism of existing macro health models, is the measurement of the population's health status. In accordance with the definition of the World Health Organization (WHO 1948), "Health is a state of complete physical, mental and social well-being and not merely the absence of disease or infirmity," we conclude that health is a multidimensional characteristic and a qualitative variable, which cannot be measured directly (Lerner 1973, pp. 1-3; Brook et al. 1979, p. 6).

Health Status Index and Health Indicators

Although health status cannot be measured directly, many indicators of health are measurable. For instance at an aggregated level, we can use the mortality rate, absenteeism caused by illness, or life expectancy. At an individual level we have blood pressure, cholesterol percentage, prolonged unfitness to work, and so forth. For a comprehensive list of indicators, see Brook et al. (1979) and Levine and Yett (1972, pp. 18-19). The use of health-care facilities is often also considered to be a health indicator.

One of the recommendations of a conference on health status indexes (Tucson, Arizona, 1972) was to make a difference between a health indicator and a health index. The first term is used for rather specific measurements, such as those mentioned above. The latter term should be used for derived measures that combine several health indicators (Berg 1973, p. 253). We might express this as follows:

$$HS = \sum_{i=1}^{m} w_i HI_i + \sum_{j=1}^{n} \tilde{w}_j \tilde{HI}_j \qquad (2a)$$

where:

HS = health status index

HI_i, i = 1, ..., m: use of health care facilities (as a health indicator)

$\tilde{HI}_j$, j = 1, ..., n : other health indicators (for example, mortality rate)

w_i, $\tilde{w}_j$: weight for the i-th, j-th indicator

The health indicators themselves are often explained with the help of relevant explanatory variables, for example, aggregated medical consumption is explained in macro health–care models. In formula:[14]

$$HI_i = \alpha'X + \epsilon_i \qquad i = 1, ..., m \qquad (2b)$$

$$\tilde{HI}_j = \tilde{\alpha}'\tilde{X} + \tilde{\epsilon}_j \qquad j = 1, ..., n \qquad (2c)$$

where:

α, $\tilde{\alpha}$ are vectors of unknown parameters that may be zero

X, $\tilde{X}$ are vectors of relevant explanatory variables

ϵ_i, $\tilde{\epsilon}_j$ are error terms

Some of the problems that arise when using a model as specified above include:

Which weights w_i have to be assigned?
Who determines the weights? (See Berg 1973, pp. 254–255.)
Factors that do not influence health but do have an influence on health–care utilization, HI_i, have in the above presented model an influence on the health status, HS (via HI_i). For instance, an increase in the number of hospital beds might increase health–care consumption. Therefore, if health–care consumption is one of the health indicators, the change in hospital beds would cause a change in HS via HI_i. [Chen (1973) justly warns that this kind of health status index, based on health–care utilization, may be misleading.]

A Structural Health-Care Model

Economists have been engaged in explaining the use of health-care facilities at an aggregate level by means of economic variables (supply, price, income, remuneration, and so forth) and at most a proxy for the regional health status (age-sex index or the percentage of those 65 years and over), without explicitly using "health" as an explanatory variable (Equation 2b). For example, see Feldstein (1967, 1977), Fuchs and Kramer (1972), Rutten (1978), and van der Gaag (1978). Others have been engaged in composing a health status index from various health-care facilities (Equation 2a), without explaining the level of that indicator, for example, Brook et al. (1979). Differences in health-care utilization are poor health indicators since income, insurance, availability, and so forth may have an impact on health utilization without influencing health. However, if we can adequately control for all these variables, it is likely that utilization differences do reflect health differences.

Here we will construct a structural model explaining differences in the level of medical consumption (and other health indicators) between regions while explicitly taking into account the health status of the region.

Our approach is in the spirit of Robinson and Ferrara (1977), who stated, "The approach we take seems new, for we model health as an unobservable link between observable causes and observable effects" (p. 139). After a slight modification, their approach can schematically be presented as follows:

$$HS = \gamma'_1 X_1 + \gamma'_2 X_2 + \epsilon \tag{3a}$$

$$HI_i = \delta_{1i} HS + \beta'_{1i} X_2 + \beta'_{2i} X_3 + \epsilon_i \qquad i = 1, \ldots, m \tag{3b}$$

$$\widetilde{HI}_j = \delta_{2j} HS + \beta'_{3j} X_2 + \beta'_{4j} X_3 + \widetilde{\epsilon}_j \qquad j = 1, \ldots, n \tag{3c}$$

where HS, HI_i, and $\widetilde{HI}_j$ are as mentioned before and

X_1 = a vector of variables, which have a direct influence on HS (and therefore an indirect effect on HI_i and $\widetilde{HI}_j$)

X_2 = a vector of variables, which have a direct influence on HS and both a direct and indirect (via HS) effect on HI_i and $\widetilde{HI}_j$

X_3 = a vector of variables, which only influence HI_i and $\widetilde{HI}_j$ (and not HS)

β_{1i}, β_{2i}, β_{3j}, β_{4j}, γ_1, γ_2, δ_{1i}, δ_{2j} = vectors of unknown parameters, which may be zero

ϵ, ϵ_i, $\widetilde{\epsilon}_j$, $i = 1, \ldots, m$, $j = 1, \ldots, n$ = error terms

X_1 and X_2 may consist of factors that are included in a production function of health (see Grossman 1972), for example, income, education, age-sex, and housing, or other variables such as the kind of employment, environmental pollution, and so forth. The vector X_3 may include health-care facilities, remuneration structure, and so on.[15] In model (3) we explicitly take account of the possibility that income, insurance, and availability of care may influence the health-care utilization without influencing health. However, keeping these variables constant, differences in health-care utilization do reflect differences in health status.

Our approach resembles the approach of Levine and Yett (1973). With the help of factor analysis, they explained approximately 60 health indicators (HI, H̃I) out of 3 factors (HS). Having calculated the factor loading (δ), they calculated the three composed factors (HS) as a function of the indicators (HI, H̃I). They regressed these composed factors (HS) on some socioeconomic variables in order to be able to calculate some "proxy measures for health status" ($\gamma'X$). Our approach, however, differs from theirs in at least two ways.

First, in our equations (3b) and (3c) we explicitly allow for the possibility that, besides the health status, HS, other explanatory variables, included in the vectors X_2 and X_3, may influence HI_i and $\tilde{HI}_i$ (for instance, medical consumption, HI_i, may be influenced by health status, HS, as well as by the supply of facilities).

Secondly we will estimate the parameters of model (3) by means of a full-information maximum-likelihood estimation method, while Levine and Yett estimate δ_1 and δ_2 by factor analysis and γ_1 and γ_2 by a two-stage method.

The health status, HS, as defined by model (3) is an index of the health situation of, for example, the population of a region, as it finds expression in the use of health-care facilities, in the mortality rate, and in other health indicators. HS is a function of socioeconomic, demographic, and other variables, which are assumed to influence health.[16] A random disturbance term is added to represent all variables influencing health that are not present in X_1 or X_2. Because the health status, HS, influences the absolute level of consumption (and not some age-sex adjusted level), it is an index of "absolute" health contrary to "relative" health (for example, for your age you are relatively healthy).

The structural model, as presented in equation (3), has several advantages over the model presented in equation (2). First, model (3) describes the structure of the health-care system, which makes it possible to estimate direct and indirect effects of the explanatory variables separately, while model (2) gives reduced form effects. As an illustration of these possibilities of model (3), we mention the results of van de Ven and van der Gaag (1979), who found evidence that income (an X_2 variable) has both a <u>positive direct</u> effect ($\beta_1 > 0$) and a <u>negative indirect</u> effect via the health status, HS ($\delta_1\gamma_2 < 0$)[17] on medical consumption. Secondly, the value of a health indicator changes as a result of a change in the health status and not the other way around, as in model (2). Thirdly, in model (2) an expansion of the number of beds per capita results, via an increase in medical consumption, in a worsening of the health status, while in model (3) the health status, HS, is not necessarily influenced by an increase of medical supply.

Fourthly, after inserting equation (3a) in (3b), the "reduced form" error terms ($\epsilon_i + \epsilon$) and ($\tilde{\epsilon}_j + \epsilon$) are correlated by the common component ϵ, while in macro health-care models (Equation 2b) these structural characteristics are often not accounted for.

In the next section, we present some empirical results of the use of a health status index, HS, in a macro health-care model by extending the model estimated in the previous section on Rutten's model.

EMPIRICAL RESULTS—A FIRST EXPLORATION

The Model

We define the health status index, HS (Equation 3a) as a function of demographic, socioeconomic, and other variables that are presumed to influence "health." The empirical results presented in this section should be considered as a first exploration because the number of variables influencing health is rather restricted.

An important factor influencing our health status index, HS, is the age-sex structure of the region, which we represent by the following age-sex variables (AS):

AS1: the percentage of publicly insured of 0 years of age
AS2: the percentage of publicly insured with ages 1 through 4
AS3: the percentage of publicly insured with ages 5 through 19
AS4: the percentage of male publicly insured with ages 20 through 39
AS5: the percentage of female publicly insured with ages 20 through 39
AS6: the percentage of publicly insured with ages 40 through 49
AS7: the percentage of publicly insured with ages 50 through 64

The parameter estimates of AS1, ..., AS7 are relative to the omitted age group of 65 years and over. We also include AS1 as an explanatory variable in the inpatient care equations because we expect that the number of births gives an upward shift on clinical consumption, independent of one's "health."

The percentage of the labor force working in <u>agriculture</u> (AGR), is expected to have a positive influence on HS because of a different life-style between urban and rural areas, and because people living in a rural region have more physical exercise on the job and less environmental pollution than people living in an urban region.

In the model in the second section of this chapter, the index of the population density accounts not only for the distance to outpatient health-care facilities, but also for a different "way of life" between urban and rural areas (van der Gaag 1978, p. 67). By introducing into the health status equation the percentage of the labor force working in agriculture, the variable DENSI remains in the consumption equations to account only for the distance to health-care facilities.

Further, we expect the percentage of unemployment in the region (UNEMPL) to have a negative influence on HS because of the stress generated by unemployment itself, by the fear of losing one's job, or even indirectly by the stress experienced by unemployed friends and family members. [van der Gaag and van de Ven (1978) showed that individuals with at least one patient in their family with manifest life problems consumed 10 percent more general practitioner services than those without such a patient in their family.]

In the model in the second section, the percentage of publicly insured in the region (PINS) was introduced to represent some aspects of "remuneration," "capacity," and "morbidity." To account for the morbidity differences among the regions, we now introduce PINS in the HS equation. To account for "remuneration" and "capacity," PINS is only included in the consumption equations of inpatient care and not in those of outpatient care (see also Note 13).

One of the advantages of having defined a health status index in the model is that we can easily expand the model. For instance, it seems very plausible to assume that the allocation of health-care facilities depends upon the needs of a region (indicated by the value of the health status index). Though we cannot take into account some dynamic aspects and though we are missing some relevant specific variables in explaining the regional allocation of health-care supply, we include in our model two health-care supply variables (the number of general practitioners and the number of beds) as endogenous and dependent, among others, on the health status in the region. [18]

We expect the number of general practitioners and beds per 1,000 population in a region to be influenced by the health status of that region, the population density (it is more efficient to place health-care facilities in highly populated regions) and the average income (a widely used variable in explaining the supply of health-care facilities, representing the attractiveness of the region). [19]

We also expect the number of general practitioners per 1,000 population to be influenced by the number of specialists (a general practitioner likes to be situated near outpatient facilities) and by the percentage of the labor force working in agriculture. (In The Netherlands, general practitioners who work in rural regions often have their own pharmacy in addition to their practice. Therefore they may have less time for direct patient care and may prefer to have a smaller practice.)

Our health status index is an index of the health situation in a certain region, as it finds expression in the use of health-care facilities and the mortality rate (MORT) in the region. If the health status of a region is high, both the health-care consumption and the mortality rate in that region will be relatively low.

Health-care consumption is represented by the variables introduced in the second section: the referral rate (REF), the number of continuation cards per 1,000 publicly insured (CON), the admission rate (ADM), and the mean stay (MS).

The complete structural equation model reads as follows:

$$REF = g_1(DENSI, GP, SPOG, SPOU, HS, CONST) \tag{4a}$$

$$CON = g_2(DENSI, GP, SPOG, SPOU, REF, HS, CONST) \tag{4b}$$

$$ADM = g_3(DENSI, PINS, GP, BED, SPI, NURS,\ AS1, REF, MS, HS, CONST) \tag{4c}$$

$$MS = g_4(DENSI, PINS, GP, BED, SPI, NURS,\ AS1, ADM, HS, CONST) \tag{4d}$$

$$MORT = g_5(HS, CONST) \tag{4e}$$

$$HS = g_6(AGR, PINS, AS1, AS2, AS3, AS4, AS5,\ AS6, AS7, UNEMPL, CONST) \tag{4f}$$

$$BED = g_7(DENSI, INC, HS, CONST) \tag{4g}$$

$$GP = g_8(DENSI, SPOG, SPOU, AGR, INC,\ HS, CONST) \tag{4h}$$

where:

MORT: the annual number of deaths per 1,000 population
HS: the unobservable health status of the region
AGR: the percentage of the labor force working in agriculture
AS1: the percentage of publicly insured of 0 years of age
AS2: the percentage of publicly insured with ages 1 to 4
AS3: the percentage of publicly insured with ages 5 to 19
AS4: the percentage of male publicly insured with ages 20 to 39

AS5: the percentage of female publicly insured with ages 20 to 39

AS6: the percentage of publicly insured with ages 40 to 49

AS7: the percentage of publicly insured with ages 50 to 64

UNEMPL: the percentage of unemployment

INC: the average income in a region

For a description of the other variables see the description of the model in the second section. As in that section, we chose a log-linear specification. We imposed the same restrictions on the BED, ADM, and MS coefficients. The error terms in the admission and mean stay equations are assumed to be correlated because of common omitted hospital characteristics.

All other correlation coefficients among the disturbances are assumed to be zero. We assume the error terms to be normally distributed. Furthermore, we assume the exogenous variables to be nonrandom. In order to identify the parameters in the g_6-equation and the coefficients of HS in the equations, $g_1, \ldots, g_5, g_7$ and g_8, we took -1 for the coefficient of HS in the mortality equation, and 0 for the constant in the mortality equation as normalization factors.[20] The structural coefficients of model (4) are estimated with a full information maximum likelihood method by means of the computer program LISREL (Jöreskog 1977 and Jöreskog and Sörbom 1978). Though the structural model (4) has several advantages over model (1), these advantages came at a price. For example, the age consumption profiles for the different forms of medical consumption are the same except for a multiplication factor. What we buy, however, is a health status index. In the last section of this chapter, we will discuss some applications of the structural model with a health status index.

Estimation Results

The estimation results of model (4) are presented in Table 12.2, with t-values in parentheses. The variable HS has only a slight negative influence on the number of referrals per publicly insured (REF) but has an important significant influence on the number of continuation cards per referral card (CON). It appears that differences in the age-sex structure of the population result in only small differences in the number of people referred to the second level of care. Once referred to a specialist, however, the least healthy people (65 years and over) receive the most care. With respect to inpatient care we see that, other things being equal, the hospital admission rate is largely influenced by hospital capacity (BED) and not by the health status of the region. However, once a patient has been admitted the influence of

TABLE 12.2. Estimation Results[a] of Equations (4a) through (4h)[b]

	REF	CON	ADM	MS	MORT	HS	BED	GP
CONST	4.89 (4.6)	3.00 (2.4)	6.05 (15.5)	3.30 (4.0)	0	-16.80 (7.6)	2.85 (1.7)	-3.77 (5.3)
DENSI	0.10 (4.4)	0.06 (2.3)	-0.03 (4.2)	-0.01 (1.8)			0.09 (2.8)	-0.02 (1.3)
PINS			-0.34 (5.7)	-0.32 (4.1)				
GP	-0.09 (0.3)	-0.78 (2.6)	-0.07 (1.0)	-0.35 (3.5)		-0.36 (2.0)		0.03 (0.7)
SPOGC	0.19 (2.4)	0.24 (2.9)						0.02 (1.6)
SPOU	-0.06 (2.2)	-0.11 (4.4)						
BED			0.81 (26.0)	0.45 (4.3)				
SPI			-0.10 (3.9)	-0.05 (1.5)				
NURS			0.15 (2.2)	0.04 (0.5)				
REF		-0.18 (1.4)	0.09 (4.0)					
ADM				-0.45 (4.3)				
MS			-0.81 (26.0)			-0.01 (0.4)		
AGR			0.01 (0.5)	0.02 (1.1)		0.08 (2.8)		0.03 (2.5)
AS1						0.58 (4.6)		
AS2						1.15 (4.9)		
AS3						1.27 (4.0)		
AS4						0.80 (2.3)		
AS5						0.56 (2.9)		
AS6						0.83 (3.2)		
AS7						0.00 (0.1)		
UNEMPL								
HS	-0.16 (0.9)	-0.41 (2.2)	-0.01 (0.3)	-0.41 (4.7)	-1.0		-0.46 (3.7)	-0.46 (8.0)
INC							-0.41 (1.9)	0.09 (1.0)

[a] Elasticities and absolute t-values (in parentheses).

[b] The covariance of the disturbances of the equations of the admission rate and the mean stay is 0.011 (t-value 4.1), which yields a correlation coefficient of 0.74.

316

the capacity decreases and health has a significantly negative influence on the mean stay. In other words, healthier patients show shorter mean stays. Rutten (1978, p. 97) suggested "that the hospital physician focuses his attention on the patients in his own direct care, i.e., those already in hospital. It seems as though medical training and medical ethics urge him to give the best possible care to these patients, without considering that other persons in the community might make a better use of the scarce beds. Doctors' aversion to risk may even reinforce this tendency." Our findings with respect to the influence of health on clinical consumption are in accordance with this hypothesis.

The health status has, as could be expected, a significantly negative influence on the number of beds per 1,000 population. Although in model (4) the influence of BED on the admission rate remains as large as the model (1), its influence on the mean stay dropped from 0.57 to 0.45. The health status also has a significantly negative influence on the number of general practitioners per capita.[21] This might be explained as follows: because of mutually planned weekend services, night services, and so forth, the general practitioners in the Netherlands decide themselves whether or not a new general practitioner is allowed to start a practice in their region. In an area where the health status of the population is relatively low, there are relatively many doctor-patient contacts per capita; this results in a busy practice, which makes the general practitioners inclined to invite a new doctor to their region.

The t-values of the coefficients of the age-sex variables (AS) in the health equation are all significantly positive, indicating (as expected) that the group of 65 years and older is relatively less healthy than the other age groups. Furthermore, our results indicate that regions with a high percentage of publicly insured (PINS) are relatively unhealthy, which may be partly due to socioeconomic differences. Comparing the estimated coefficients in Table 12.1 and Table 12.2, we see that most coefficients remained rather stable after inclusion of the HS-variable (and making BED and GP endogenous). The coefficients of GP in the CON and MS equation are the only exception; they more than doubled after inclusion of HS. This might be explained by the high correlation between GP and the percentage 65 years and older. Both variables have an opposite effect on outpatient and inpatient care: the more aged people, the more medical consumption. Primary health care (GP) is hypothesized to be a substitute for outpatient and inpatient care, that is, the more general practitioners, the less specialized care. Apparently we have succeeded in disentangling the effects of the two variables: the percentage of aged people has, via HS, a positive influence, and the number of GP per capita has, as hypothesized, a strong negative influence on outpatient and inpatient care.

INC has a negative (but not significant) influence on BED and a positive influence on GP. Marshall et al. (1971) also found that an area's affluence alone has little attraction for physicians.

Table 12.3 presents both the direct and indirect components of the elasticity of medical consumption with respect to HS.

The negative direct effect of the health status index on CON (-0.41) is nearly outweighed by the positive indirect effect via GP (+0.39). The large negative direct effect of the health status index on the mean stay (-0.63) results because of the mutually negative relationship between the admission rate and the mean stay, in a large positive indirect effect of the health status index (via the mean stay) on the admission rate ($0.81 \times 0.63 = 0.51$). Due to other indirect effects (via BED and GP), the total reduced form elasticities of the admission rate and the mean stay with respect to the health status index equal 0.00 and -0.45, respectively. Using the coefficients in the HS equation, we are able to calculate the direct and indirect components of the reduced form elasticities of medical consumption with respect to the explanatory variables in the HS equation. Table 12.4 presents the ceteris paribus effects of an increase of the percentage of aged people (65 years and older) and a simultaneous decrease of the age group, 5 to 19 years of age.[22] The same results are also presented when estimating model (4) with the supply variables BED and GP exogenous (as in model 1).

In explaining the admission rate without explicitly defining a health status variable, many authors (Feldstein 1967, Rutten et al. 1975, and Posthuma and van der Zee 1978) estimated a negative elasticity of the admission rate with respect to the percentage of aged

TABLE 12.3. Direct and Indirect Components of the Elasticity of REF, CON, ADM, and MS with Respect to HS

	REF	CON	ADM	MS
Indirect via REF		-0.13	-0.02	+0.01
Indirect via ADM				+0.01
Indirect via MS			+0.51	
Indirect via BED			-0.33	-0.06
Indirect via GP	+0.04	+0.39	-0.15	+0.23
Direct	-0.16	-0.41	-0.02	-0.63
Total reduced form elasticity	-0.11	-0.15	-0.00	-0.45

TABLE 12.4. Components of Reduced Form Elasticities of ADM and MS with Respect to the Percentage of Publicly Insured, Aged 65 Years and Older

| | Model (4) but with Supply Exogenous | | Model (4) | |
	ADM	MS	ADM	MS
Indirect via REF	0.01	−0.00	+0.01	−0.01
Indirect via ADM		−0.01		−0.01
Indirect via MS	−0.28		−0.28	
Indirect via BED			+0.18	+0.03
Indirect via GP			+0.08	−0.13
Direct	0.01	0.35	+0.01	+0.35
Total reduced form elasticity	−0.26	0.33	+0.00	+0.23

Note: These elasticities give the ceteris paribus effect of an increase of the percentage of aged people (65 years and older) and a simultaneous decrease of the age group, 5 to 19 years old. (See Note 22.)

people. Feldstein (1967, pp. 278–279) explained this phenomenon as follows: "Older persons are hospitalized very much more frequently than the rest of the population. But the mean stay increases even more rapidly with age. Older persons therefore occupy so many more bed days that the overall admission rate for the population must decrease." Looking now at the elasticity of ADM with respect to the percentage of publicly insured aged 65 years and older while keeping supply exogenous (Table 12.4), we see that the reduced form elasticity of ADM (-0.26) indeed is mainly determined by the indirect effect via MS (-0.28). This example illustrates an advantage of using a health status index.

Considering the overall number of patient days and the age-sex structure of the publicly insured in 1974, we would expect an increase of 0.24 percent in the number of patient days when the number of publicly insured of 65 years and older increases by 1 percent (reducing the number of publicly insured of 5 to 19 years of age).[23] The results presented in Table 12.4 indicate that the model with supply endogenous is more realistic than the model with supply exogenous. Keeping the supply variables exogenous, we find that a 1 percent increase in the percentage of aged people would result in a 0.07 percent increase in the number of patient days (-0.26 + 0.33), while after making the number of beds and general practitioners <u>endogenous</u>, a more realistic elasticity of 0.23 (0.00 + 0.23) is estimated.

In the next section we will discuss the interpretation of the health status index and calculate its value for the 11 provinces in The Netherlands.

INTERPRETATION OF THE HEALTH STATUS INDEX

Mathematical Implications

The health status index, as defined in this chapter, is a function of socioeconomic, demographic, and other characteristics and is assumed to influence both the use of health-care facilities and other health indicators (such as mortality).

This health status index is determined except for a multiplication factor (it must be given a "dimension") and an additive term (its "base" must be fixed). To make this clear we take as an example the following simplified model:[24]

$$\ln \text{MORT} = \alpha_0 + \beta_0 \ln \text{HS} + \epsilon_1$$
$$\ln \text{REF} = \alpha_1 + \beta_1 \ln \text{HS} + \epsilon_2 \qquad (1)$$
$$\ln \text{HS} = \alpha_2 + \gamma \ln \text{AGR} + \epsilon_3$$

Substitution for HS yields:

$$\ln \text{MORT} = c_1 + c_3 \ln \text{AGR} + \tilde{\epsilon}_1$$
$$\ln \text{REF} = c_2 + c_4 \ln \text{AGR} + \tilde{\epsilon}_2 \qquad (2)$$

with:

$$\alpha_0 + \beta_0 \alpha_2 = c_1$$
$$\alpha_1 + \beta_1 \alpha_2 = c_2$$
$$\beta_0 \gamma = c_3 \qquad (3)$$
$$\beta_1 \gamma = c_4$$

Because MORT, REF, and AGR can be observed, we can make an estimate of c_1, c_2, c_3, and c_4.

Equation (3) can be rewritten in the following way:

$$\gamma = c_3/\beta_0$$

$$\beta_1 = \beta_0 c_4/c_3$$

$$\alpha_2 = (c_1 - \alpha_0)/\beta_0 \tag{4}$$

$$\alpha_2 = c_2 - \frac{c_4}{c_3}(c_1 - \alpha_0)$$

The four equations constituting system (4) can be solved only if two of the six unknown parameters (α_0, α_1, α_2, β_0, β_1, γ) are fixed. As normalization, we chose $\alpha_0 = 0$ and $\beta_0 = -1$.

$\alpha_0 = 0$ implies ln MORT $= \beta_0$ ln HS, that is, the zero point of ln HS is equal to the zero point of ln MORT.

$\beta_0 = -1$ implies ln MORT $= \alpha_0 -$ ln HS; the dimension of ln HS is equal to the dimension of MORT.

From (4) it can be concluded that γ, the coefficient of the exogenous variable in the HS equation, is determined except for a multiplicative factor (β_0). If there are more exogenous variables in the HS equation, it can easily be seen that the coefficients of all these variables are determined except for the same multiplicative factor. Thus, the influences of the exogenous variables on the health status index HS can mutually be compared. For instance, a 1 percent increase in the percentage of the publicly insured of 5 to 19 years old (AS3) results in a $-1.15 \times \beta_0$ percent increase in HS, and a 1 percent increase in the percentage of publicly insured (PINS) results in a $0.36 \times \beta_0$ percent increase in HS.[25] This implies that the influence of an increase of AS3 is three times as large as an increase of PINS, independent of the choice of α_0 and β_0.

From (4) it can also be concluded that β_1, the coefficient of the health status index HS in the REF equation, is determined except for the multiplicative factor β_0. If there are more equations in which the health status index HS is included, it can easily be seen that the coefficient of the health status index in all these equations is determined except for the same multiplicative factor, β_0. Thus, the influences of the health status index in different equations can be compared with one another. For instance, the influence of HS on CON is equal to the influence of HS on MS, independent of the choice of α_0 and β_0 (both coefficients equal -0.41; see Table 12.2).

In this simplified example, we can calculate the health status index HS* for any selected value of α_0 and β_0 as follows: ln HS* = $\alpha_2 + \gamma$ ln AGR. Because ln HS* is determined except for a multiplicative factor and a constant term, the absolute value of HS* is dependent of the choice of α_0 and β_0, but the order of the health status index over the regions is independent of the choice of α_0 and β_0. If for some

TABLE 12.5. The Contributions of the Exogenous Variables to the Health Status Index

Province	$-0.36 \times$ ln PINS	$-0.01 \times$ ln AGR	$0.08 \times$ ln AS1	$0.58 \times$ ln AS2	$1.15 \times$ ln AS3	$1.27 \times$ ln AS4	$0.80 \times$ ln AS5	$0.56 \times$ ln AS6	$0.83 \times$ ln AS7	$0.00 \times$ ln UNEMPL	Ranking of HS*
Noord–Brabant	0.02	0.01	0.02	0.08	0.20	0.18	0.11	0.08	0.00	0.00	1
Utrecht	0.07	0.01	0.02	0.08	0.13	0.13	0.12	0.03	0.07	0.00	2
Limburg	0.00	0.01	0.00	0.00	0.20	0.14	0.08	0.11	0.10	0.00	3
Gelderland	0.03	0.00	0.02	0.10	0.15	0.12	0.10	0.05	0.05	0.00	4
Drente	0.03	0.00	0.03	0.15	0.21	0.04	0.04	0.06	0.05	0.00	5
Overijssel	0.01	0.00	0.04	0.10	0.19	0.08	0.04	0.07	0.08	0.00	6
Zuid–Holland	0.04	0.01	0.02	0.01	0.02	0.09	0.09	0.05	0.16	0.00	7
Noord–Holland	0.04	0.01	0.01	0.00	0.00	0.11	0.10	0.05	0.16	0.00	8
Groningen	0.02	0.00	0.02	0.08	0.05	0.03	0.05	0.04	0.16	0.00	9
Friesland	0.02	0.00	0.03	0.15	0.16	0.0	0.00	0.00	0.07	0.00	10
Zeeland	0.04	0.00	0.02	0.08	0.07	0.01	0.04	0.02	0.13	0.00	11

Note: Deviations from the minimum values per column.

chosen value α_0 and β_0, region 1 is "healthier" than region 2, this remains so, independent of α_0 and β_0.[26]

Empirical Results

As an illustration, we calculate in this section the health status index (using the estimates, presented in Table 12.2) for each of the 11 provinces of The Netherlands.

As mentioned before, our health status index is defined as a function of the percentage of publicly insured of the population (PINS), the percentage of the labor force working in agriculture (AGR), the age-sex structure of the publicly insured (AS), and the percentage unemployed (UNEMPL), plus a disturbance term. The influence of these variables on the health status index and the influence of the health status index on the use of health-care facilities, the mortality rate, the number of beds, and the number of general practitioners are estimated in the previous section. The results indicate that a region with a high percentage of aged persons is relatively "less healthy," and therefore has a relatively high referral rate, a relatively high mortality rate, and relatively many general practitioners.

Using now the estimated coefficients presented in Table 12.2, we can calculate the health status HS* for each of the 11 provinces of The Netherlands as follows:[27]

$$\ln HS^* = -16.80 - 0.36 \ln PINS - 0.01 \ln AGR$$
$$+ 0.08 \ln AS1 + 0.58 \ln AS2 + 1.15 \ln AS3$$
$$+ 1.27 \ln AS4 + 0.80 \ln AS5 + 0.56 \ln AS6$$
$$+ 0.83 \ln AS7 + 0.00 \ln UNEMPL$$

The results are given in Table 12.5.

The absolute value of the health status index is dependent on the choice of the multiplicative factor ("dimension") and the additive term ("base"), but the order of the health status index over the provinces is independent of this choice. For all provinces, the contributions of the exogenous variables to the health status index are given in Table 12.5 as deviations from the minimum. The last column of Table 12.5 gives the ranking of the health status index per province: 1 is the "healthiest," 2 the next "healthiest," and so on. From Table 12.5, it can be seen that Groningen, Friesland, and Zeeland are the less "healthy." These three provinces have a high percentage of aged people. Noord-Brabant and Utrecht are the "healthiest" primarily because of a high percentage of people in the age group, 5 to 39 years old (AS3 and AS4) and, in the case of Utrecht, a low percentage of publicly insured (PINS).

CONCLUSION AND DISCUSSION

In this study we implemented a health status index in a structural health-care model. This unobservable, regional health status index is a function of socioeconomic, demographic, and other regional characteristics, and it is assumed to influence both the use of health-care facilities and other health indicators, such as mortality.

Because the number of variables we used was rather restrictive, the estimation results of the model are primarily an illustration of the potential of a structural health-care model in which a health status index is included. Nevertheless, the parameter estimates can be well interpreted, and the results are encouraging. The health status has a significantly negative influence on medical consumption and on the supply of health-care facilities. Capacity remains the most important variable to explain clinical consumption.

The explicit specification of a health status variable has some fruitful applications. Having estimated the model, it is possible to calculate the value of the health status index for each region and to order the regions according to this health status. This might assist in the allocation of health-care resources or in assigning budgets to regions. Furthermore, if one knows the influence of some variables, such as the percentage of unemployment, road safety, or environmental pollution on health, and if one knows the costs of changing these variables, it is possible to compare the costs of increasing health in different ways (cost effectiveness), as well as to compare the costs of an increase in health with the costs of less medical consumption, as a result of that better health (cost benefit).

As we have already mentioned, because of the restricted number of variables the first empirical results, as presented in this chapter, should primarily be considered as explorative. At the moment we are expanding our data base with more health indicators (for example, absenteeism because of illness, the percentage of disabled people, and so forth), with other relevant explanatory variables (for example, environmental pollution), and with data for more recent years. In this way, it might be possible to expand the health status from a simple index to a vector of health components (according to the multidimensional character of health).

Another expansion then might be to take into account some dynamic aspects, such as taking health-care supply as a function of the health situation some years ago, or making the health status a function of the medical consumption in the past.

TABLE 12.A. Mean Values and Standard Deviations

Variable	Mean Value	Standard Deviation
REF	354.11	73.17
CON	445.46	127.51
ADM	108.69	14.97
MS	16.58	1.45
DENSI	13.62	11.82
PINS	67.01	6.13
GP	0.33	0.04
SPOG	0.35	0.10
SPOU	0.07	0.08
BED	5.26	1.05
SPI	8.43	1.79
NURS	62.85	4.93
ASIREF	325.90	7.65
ASIMS	16.54	0.64
AS1	1.30	0.33
AS2	6.88	1.02
AS3	25.64	2.27
AS4	15.74	1.20
AS5	15.56	1.18
AS6	9.85	0.66
AS7	13.28	1.85
MORT	79.23	15.64
UNEMPL	3.29	1.65
AGR	6.19	4.97
INC	5,046.06	637.25

Note: Information about the construction of the regions is available from the authors.

Sources: The National Information System of Sickness Funds (Landelijk Informatiesysteem Ziekenfondsen), the Department of Health and Environmental Protection, and the Central Bureau of Statistics.

NOTES

1. This index serves at the same time as a proxy for, among others, the attainability of the health-care facilities and for life-style (urban/rural life).
2. In this study we use data from 1974. Rutten's (1978) estimations were based on data from 1973. For a comparison of the estimation results for the years 1974, 1975, and 1976, see Hooijmans (1981).
3. Of course, in case of an emergency, it is possible to enter a higher level of medical care directly.
4. For an analysis of the demand for primary health care in the Dutch health-care system, see van der Gaag and van de Ven (1978).
5. Per referral card, the specialist working in a general hospital gets a fixed amount of money for a one-month treatment (nonclinical) of the patient. A continuation card is a bill (written by the specialist) for a one-month continuation of the treatment within one year. In university hospitals no continuation cards exist; per referral card, the specialist working in a university hospital gets a fixed amount of money for a one-year treatment (nonclinical). For continuation of specialist treatment after one year, the general practitioner has to write a new referral card.
6. For a rationale of introducing these explanatory variables, see Rutten (1978) and Hooijmans (1981).
7. Rutten estimated them without these restrictions and found coefficients of 0.95 and -0.92 in the ADM equation and of 0.46 and -0.34 in the MS equation.
8. Rutten (1978) assumed the covariance matrix to be diagonal.
9. In Appendix Table 12.A1, the mean values and standard deviations of the variables are given.
10. See Note 5.
11. Rutten (1978, p. 188) found a positive influence of the number of inpatient working specialists on the admission rate of privately insured patients.
12. Rutten (1978, pp. 179-183) found 46 percent more patient days per insured in the group of the publicly insured than in that of the privately insured. Similar results were found by a Departmental Commission (1979).
13. The difference between the public and private sectors in remuneration level for general practitioners and for outpatient working specialists is just a fraction of the difference in remuneration level for inpatient working specialists. Moreover, the difference in medical consumption between publicly and privately insured at the level of the general practitioner is only about 15 percent,

whereas the difference at the clinical level is about 50 percent (see van de Ven et al. 1980). In addition, the capacity constraints at the first and second levels of care are not so "hard" as at the clinical level.

14. For simplicity, we assume that each HI_i ($\widetilde{HI}_j$) depends only on exogenous variables, including recursive or simultaneous relations; however, this would not affect the tenor of our arguments.

15. For the estimation of a model like model (3) based on individual data, see van de Ven and van der Gaag (1979) and Wolfe and van der Gaag (1981).

16. One of these variables might be the use of medical facilities. However: "no evidence was found in the literature to indicate whether increases in use of medical services by general populations in developed countries would produce changes in any dimension of health" (Brook et al. 1979, p. 53) and "variation in the consumption of physicians' services does not seem to have any significant effect on health, as measured by either the crude death rate or the infant mortality rate" (Fuchs and Kramer 1972, p. 39).

17. This is the result of a positive (direct) effect ($\gamma_2 > 0$) of income on health (better life-style, hygiene, attitude toward health, and so on) and a negative effect ($\delta_1 < 0$) of health on medical consumption.

18. We did not make the number of specialists endogenous because of difficulties in the measurement of this variable.

19. We did not introduce this variable in our health equation because it represents the average income of the total population (publicly + privately insured), and we analyzed medical consumption in the public sector only.

20. Our health status HS is determined except for a multiplication factor (it must be given a "dimension") and an additive term (its "base" must be fixed). For more details about this normalization, see the next section.

21. Many authors have already pointed to the high correlation between the number of general practitioners per capita and the percentage of the population aged 65 years and older (for example, Rutten 1977, p. 9, Rutten et al. 1975, p. 86, Lave et al. 1977, and Joroff and Navarro 1971).

22. The elasticities presented in Table 12.4 are derived from the elasticities with respect to AS3 (5 to 19 years old) while accounting for the different size of the age groups (a 1 percent increase in AS3 causes, keeping all other variables the same, a 2.07 decrease in the number of publicly insured people aged 65 years and older).

23. The total number of patient days of publicly insured in 1974 was 18,875,506. For the age groups 5 to 19 and 65 years and older, this figure was 1,804,199 and 5,439,186, respectively. These groups form 25.4 percent and 12.0 percent of all publicly insured.
24. With MORT, REF, AGR, and HS as previously defined.
25. Using the results of Table 12.2.
26. $\ln HS^* = (1/\beta_0)(c_1 - \alpha_0 + c_3 \ln AGR)$ with c_1 and c_3 known constants.
27. For the mean values of each variable per province, see the Appendix.

REFERENCES

Berg, R. L. 1973. Health Status Indexes: Proceedings of a Conference Conducted by Health Services Research. Tucson, Arizona, October 1-4, 1972. Chicago: Hospital Research and Educational Trust.

Brook, R. H., J. E. Ware, Jr., A. Davies-Avery, A. L. Stewart, C. A. Donald, W. H. Rogers, K. N. Williams, and S. A. Johnston. 1979. "Overview of Adult Health Status Measures Fielded in Rand's Health Insurance Study." Supplement to Medical Care, 17:7.

Chen, M. K. 1973. "The G Index for Program Priority." In R. L. Berg (ed.), Health Status Indexes: Proceedings of a Conference Conducted by Health Services Research. Tucson, Arizona, October 1-4, 1972. Chicago: Hospital Research and Educational Trust, pp. 28-35.

Departmental Commission. 1979. "Consumption Differences Publicly and Privately Insured: Differences in Consumption of Inpatient Care by Privately and Publicly Insured." (Verschillen in consumptie van intramurale gezondheidszorg door ziekenfonds—en particulier verzekerden; verslag van de werkgroep consumptie-verschillen ziekenfonds—en particulier verzekerden, aangeboden aan de staatssecretaris van Volksgezondheid en Milieuhygiëne). Mimeographed, Leidschendam.

Feldstein, M. S. 1967. Economic Analysis for Health Service Efficiency. Amsterdam: North-Holland.

Feldstein, M. S. 1977. "Quality Change and the Demand for Hospital Care." Econometrica, 45:7, pp. 1681-1702.

Fuchs, V. R., and M. J. Kramer. 1972. Determinants of Expenditures for Physicians' Services in the United States, 1948-68. New York: National Bureau of Economic Research.

Grossman, M. 1972. The Demand for Health: A Theoretical and Empirical Investigation. New York: Columbia University Press.

Hooijmans, E. M. 1981. "Estimation of a Model of the Dutch Health Care System: 1974, 1975, 1976." (Schattingen van een model van de Nederlandse gezondheidszorg over de jaren 1974, 1975 en 1976). Leiden: Center for Research in Public Economics.

Jöreskog, K. G. 1977. "Structural Equation Models in the Social Sciences: Specification, Estimation and Testing." In P. R. Krishaiah (ed.), Applications of Statistics. Amsterdam: North-Holland.

Jöreskog, K. G., and D. Sörbom. 1978. LISREL-IV. Estimation of Linear Structural Equation Systems by Maximum Likelihood Methods. Chicago: International Educational Services.

Joroff, S., and V. Navarro. 1971. "Medical Manpower: a Multivariate Analysis of the Distribution of Physicians in Urban United States." Medical Care, 9:5, pp. 428-37.

Lave, J. R., L. B. Lave, and S. Leinhardt. 1977. "Medical Manpower Models: Need, Demand and Supply." In L. E. Weeks and H. J. Berman (eds.), Economics in Health Care. Germantown, Md.: Aspen Systems Corporation, pp. 77-105.

Lerner, M. 1973. "Conceptualization of Health and Social Well-Being." In R. L. Berg (ed.), Health Status Indexes: Proceedings of a Conference Conducted by Health Services Research. Tucson, Arizona, October 1-4, 1972. Chicago: Hospital Research and Educational Trust, pp. 1-7.

Levine, D. S., and D. E. Yett. 1973. "A Method for Constructing Proxy Measures of Health Status." In R. L. Berg (ed.), Health Status Indexes: Proceedings of a Conference Conducted by Health Services Research. Tucson, Arizona, October 1-4, 1972. Chicago: Hospital Research and Educational Trust, pp. 12-23.

Marshall, C. L., et al. 1971. "Principal Components Analysis of the Distribution of Physicians, Dentists and Osteopaths in a Midwestern State." American Journal of Public Health, 61: 8, pp. 1556-64.

Posthuma, B. H., and J. van der Zee. 1978. "Tussen eerste en tweede echelon (Between the First and Second Level of Health Care)." Medisch Contact, 33, pp. 245-50.

Robinson, P. M., and M. C. Ferrara. 1977. "The Estimation of a Model for an Unobservable Variable with Endogenous Causes." In D. J. Aigner and A. S. Goldberger (eds.), Latent Variables in Socio-economic Models. Amsterdam: North-Holland, pp. 131-42.

Rutten, F. F. H. 1978. "The Use of Health Care Facilities in The Netherlands: An Econometric Analysis." Dissertation. Leiden: Center for Research in Public Economics.

Rutten, F. F. H., J. van der Gaag, and B. M. S. van Praag. 1975. Het ziekenhuis in de gezondheidszorg (The Hospital in the Health Care Sector). Leiden: Stenfert Kroese.

Rutten, F. F. H. 1977. "Extramurale specialistische hulp in de ziekenfondssector; een ekonometrische analyse van tarief I en II (Outpatient Care in the Public Sector)," Report 77.01. Leiden: Center for Research in Public Economics.

van der Gaag, J., and W. P. M. M. van de Ven. 1978. "The Demand for Primary Health Care." Medical Care, 16:4, pp. 299-312.

van der Gaag, J. 1978. "An Econometric Analysis of the Dutch Health Care System." Dissertation. Leiden: Center for Research in Public Economics.

van de Ven, W. P. M. M., and J. van der Gaag. 1979. "Health as an Unobservable: A MIMIC-Model for Health-Care Demand," Report 79.15. Leiden: Center for Research in Public Economics.

van de Ven, W. P. M. M., F. A. Nauta, R. C. J. A. van Vliet, and F. F. H. Rutten. 1980. "Inventarisatie en achtergronden van de consumptieverschillen tussen ziekenfonds en particulier verzekerden." Gezondheid en Samenleving, 1, pp. 224-54.

Wolfe, B., and J. van der Gaag. 1981. "A New Health Status Index for Children." In J. van der Gaag and M. Perlman, Health, Economics and Health Economics. Amsterdam: North Holland, Contributions to Economic Analysis.

World Health Organization. 1948. Constitution, Basic Document, Geneva, p. 2.

PART V

Selected Issues

13

THE QUANTITY AND
QUALITY OF HOSPITAL LABOR

Ronald B. Conners

The productivity of hospital labor is affected not only by the quantity of labor employed in hospitals but also by the quality of labor employed. In this chapter I will measure changes in the quantity and quality of the U.S. hospital labor force over the period from 1950 to 1976 and compare the resulting indices with similar characteristics for the U.S. labor force. The results show that quantity changes are far more important than quality changes in measuring total hospital labor input, even when monopolistic or monopsonistic exploitation is assumed.

QUANTITY AND QUALITY INDICES

An index of labor input for the U.S. hospital labor force that incorporates changes in the quantity of labor can be determined from:

$$\frac{T_t}{T_0} = \frac{N_t}{N_0} \cdot \frac{H_t}{H_0}$$

where 0 and t are subscripts denoting the base period and the current period. T is an index of total hours worked per week. N is an index of the number of employees, and H is an index of the average number of hours worked per week. This method, a man-hours approach,

This article first appeared in Social Science and Medicine 15C, No. 2, 99-106 (1981); reprinted by permission of Pergamon Press Ltd.

The author is grateful to David Schwartzman for comments and suggestions. Financial support from the Pharmaceutical Manufacturer's Association is acknowledged.

permits the labor quantity index to be corrected for changes in the work week. The index of total weekly hours (T_t/T_0) is expected to increase over time because the expected work week decline should not be sufficient to offset the anticipated rise in the number of hospital workers (N_t/N_0).

The quality of labor can be estimated by measuring changes in the education and experience of the hospital labor force. A correction for ability is made because not all improvements in education lead directly to increases in output. These measures of quality can be combined with the measures of quantity to develop an overall index of labor input. This expression is:

$$\frac{L_t}{L_0} = \frac{T_t}{T_0} \cdot \frac{A_t}{A_0} \cdot \frac{E_t}{E_0}$$

where T is defined as above. A is an index of the age–sex composition of total weekly hours, E is an index of education corrected for ability, and L is the final index of labor input developed both for hospitals and the entire economy. The educational index, following the method of Schwartzman[1-3] is calculated as:

$$\frac{E_t}{E_0} = 1 + a \left[\frac{\sum n_{it} w_i}{\sum n_{i0} w_i} - 1 \right]$$

where a is a correction for ability generally set equal to 0.4, n_i is the number of workers in educational group i, and w_i is the average hourly wage rate of workers with an educational level of i. The summation is performed over all levels of education from 0 to 20 years. The average hourly wage rate is used as a weight to permit addition of workers with different levels of education by converting each educational group from units of workers to units of dollars. This is a critical assumption that will be discussed later. The experience index is developed by partitioning the labor force by sex and developing a distribution of hours of workers by age as follows:

$$\frac{A_t}{A_0} = 1 + \frac{\sum_{jk} m_{jkt} w_{jk}}{\sum_{jk} m_{jk0} w_{jk}}$$

In this equation, m_{jk} is the number of hours of workers with an age level of j partitioned into k groups, male and female. As before, w_{jk} is the average hourly wage rate of male and female workers with an age level of j. This procedure corrects the quantity index of total hours worked per week (T_t/T_0) for changes in the quality of the labor force working those hours.

EMPIRICAL RESULTS

Data

Employees of hospitals are measured in full-time equivalent employees on September 30th of the specified year and include both full-time and part-time personnel. Volunteers, private duty nurses, research personnel funded by extramural grants, interns, and residents are excluded. Attending physicians not on the payroll of the hospital but using hospital facilities are also excluded.

Average weekly hours are taken from the Industrial Characteristics Report of the censuses of 1950, 1960, and 1970.[4-6] In these reports, hours worked are determined for hospital workers who are 14 and over and who were at work in the week preceding the census. Hours worked excludes time off and overtime. A worker who is sick or on vacation is not included in the sample universe.

Weekly hours are estimated from census data based on a definition of hospital, which differs from the AHA definition of hospitals. The census definition of hospital uses the Standard Industrial Classification (SIC) system which, in 1972, defined hospitals as:

> . . . establishments primarily engaged in providing
> diagnostic services, extensive medical treatment including
> surgical services, and other hospital services as well as
> continuous nursing services. These establishments have
> an organized medical staff, inpatient beds, and equipment
> and facilities to provide complete health care.[7]

The general definition of hospitals used in the 1972 SIC revision further subdivides hospitals into 4-digit categories of general medical and surgical hospitals, psychiatric hospitals, and specialty hospitals. Specialty hospitals include children's, chronic disease, ENT, geriatric, other specialty, maternity, orthopedic, and tuberculosis hospitals.[7] The finer subdivision available in the 1972 revision was not available in the 1967 revision, but the definition of hospitals was the same.

The American Hospital Association defines community hospital as "nonfederal short term general and other special hospitals, excluding hospital units of institutions, whose facilities and services are

TABLE 13.1. Comparison of U.S. Bureau of Census and
American Hospital Association Measures
of Hospital Employees: 1950-1970

Year	Bureau of Census Occupation by Industry Data	AHA Data	Percent Difference
1950	983,820	1,058,000	+7.54
1960	1,691,578	1,598,000	−5.53
1970	2,680,066	2,537,000	−5.34

Source: U.S. Bureau of the Census, Occupation by
Industry, 1950, 1960, and 1970; and Hospital Statistics,
1976.

available to the public."[8] Before 1972 institutional hospital units were
included in the definition.

The SIC hospital definition makes no distinction between short
and long lengths of stay, while the AHA definition makes a distinction
between hospitals with average lengths of stay above and below 30
days. The agency or group controlling the hospital is not considered
in the SIC definition. It includes hospitals that are federally controlled
as well as hospital units of institutions and psychiatric hospitals.

A comparison of the Occupation by Industry data, which are
based on the SIC definition of hospital, with the AHA data on employees is shown in Table 13.1. In 1950 the AHA employee data were
7.5 percent higher than the Occupation by Industry data. In 1960 and
1970 the Occupation by Industry data were 5.5 percent higher than the
AHA data. The Bureau of Census and AHA data discussed here are
for all U.S. hospitals, not just community hospitals.

With these definitional differences in mind, it is assumed that
the average number of hours worked, developed from the census data,
can be applied to the AHA employee data to calculate total weekly
hours (T_t/T_0). It is also assumed that the census data on average
weekly hours can be applied to either U.S. hospital employees or
U.S. community hospital employees. There is no reason why hours
worked by employees in U.S. hospitals should differ from hours
worked by employees of U.S. community hospitals.

Years of schooling completed is taken as the measure of the
education of hospital workers and is determined in 1960 for persons
aged 5 and over and in 1970 for persons aged 3 and over. It includes

persons who not only completed that particular year but those who attended but did not complete the next highest year. [9] The category 0-4 includes kindergarten, grades 1-4, and never attended, while the category 17+ includes college 5 and college 6 or more.

One element in the measurement of labor input in hospitals is a correction for changes in the demographic composition of the hospital labor force. An hour worked by a male aged 25-29 may be valued differently than an hour worked by a male aged over 65. To develop such an index, the procedure of Denison[10] was followed and it was assumed that the average hourly wage is proportional to the marginal product of labor. This means that if the male aged over 65 earns one-half what the male aged 25-29 earns, then the male aged 25-29 years of age contributed double the labor input of males aged over 65.

The weights are calculated from an analysis of the 1 percent Public Use Sample in which all persons reported as having current employment in hospitals, who were also at work and had a positive income, were cross-classified by age, sex, and years of education. Average hourly earnings were calculated by dividing yearly annual earnings by yearly hours worked, where yearly hours worked was the product of weeks worked in 1959 and hours worked per week in 1960. In addition to taking the average wage rate from the Public Use Sample, the same source for the age-sex distribution and years of schooling completed was used. Details of the computations are available from the author.

The Quantity of Hospital Labor

The first step in the development of the overall labor index for the hospital sector is the index of quantity (N_t/N_0). The number of employees of U.S. hospitals from 1950 to 1976, measured in full-time equivalents, is shown in column 1 of Table 13.2A. The same data are shown converted to index number form in column 2. The data for U.S. community hospitals are shown in column 3, and in index number form in column 4. The index of employees of U.S. hospitals grew at an average annual growth rate of 4.23 percent from 1950 to 1976, while the index of employees of U.S. community hospitals grew at an average annual growth rate of 5.22 percent, almost 1 percent higher.

We next examine an index of average weekly hours worked, H_t/H_0. There has been a general decline in the work week over the post-war period so a correction must be applied. To derive a measure of total hours worked per week (T_t/T_0), the index of employees is multiplied by an index of average weekly hours worked by hospital workers. The data on average weekly hours worked by hospital workers

TABLE 13.2A. Labor Input in U.S. Community Hospitals: 1950-1976

Year	Employees of U.S. Hospitals (thousands) (1)	Index of Employees of U.S. Hospitals (2)	Employees of U.S. Community Hospitals (thousands) (3)	Index of Employees of U.S. Community Hospitals (N_t/N_0) (4)	Index of Average Weekly Hours (H_t/H_0) (5)
1950	1,058	66.21	662	61.30	106.68
1951	1,075	67.27	648	60.00	106.01
1952	1,119	70.03	674	62.41	105.34
1953	1,169	73.15	719	66.57	104.68
1954	1,246	77.97	777	71.94	104.01
1955	1,301	81.41	826	76.48	103.34
1956	1,375	86.05	878	81.30	102.67
1957	1,401	87.67	926	85.74	102.00
1958	1,465	91.68	984	91.11	101.34
1959	1,520	95.12	1,031	95.46	100.67
1960	1,598	100.00	1,080	100.00	100.00
1961	1,696	106.13	1,149	106.39	99.67

1962	1,763	110.33	1,207	111.76	99.33
1963	1,840	115.14	1,277	118.24	99.00
1964	1,887	118.09	1,333	123.43	98.66
1965	1,952	122.15	1,386	128.33	98.33
1966	2,106	131.79	1,532	141.85	98.00
1967	2,203	137.86	1,619	149.91	97.66
1968	2,309	144.49	1,717	158.98	97.33
1969	2,426	151.81	1,824	168.89	96.99
1970	2,537	158.76	1,929	178.61	96.66
1971	2,589	162.02	1,999	185.09	96.33
1972	2,671	167.15	2,056	190.37	95.99
1973	2,769	173.28	2,149	198.98	95.66
1974	2,919	182.67	2,289	211.94	95.32
1975	3,023	189.17	2,399	222.13	94.99
1976	3,108	194.49	2,483	229.91	94.66

Source: Derived from AHA employee data and 1960 and 1970 Public Use Samples. Column 2 is column 1 converted to index number form. Column 4 is column 3 converted to index number form.

339

TABLE 13.2B. Labor Input in U.S. Community Hospitals: 1950–1976

Year	Index of Total Weekly Hours in U.S. Community Hospitals (T_t/T_0) (6)	Index of Age-Sex Composition of Total Hours Worked (A_t/A_0) (7)	Index of Amount of Education, Based on Employees (8)	Index of Amount of Education, Based on Total Hours (9)	Index of Amount of Education Based on Total Hours, Corrected for Ability (E_t/E_0) (10)	Index of Labor Input for U.S. Community Hospitals (L_t/L_0) (11)
1950	65.39	100.00	97.24	97.39	98.43	64.36
1951	63.61	100.00	97.51	97.65	98.59	62.71
1952	65.74	100.00	97.79	97.91	98.75	64.92
1953	69.69	100.00	98.07	98.17	98.90	68.92
1954	74.82	100.00	98.34	98.43	99.06	74.12
1955	79.03	100.00	98.62	98.70	99.22	78.41
1956	83.47	100.00	98.90	98.96	99.38	82.95
1957	87.45	100.00	99.17	99.22	99.53	87.04
1958	92.33	100.00	99.45	99.48	99.69	92.04
1959	96.10	100.00	99.72	99.74	99.84	95.95
1960	100.00	100.00	100.00	100.00	100.00	100.00
1961	106.04	100.00	100.28	100.26	100.16	106.21

1962	111.01	100.00	100.55	100.52	100.34	111.39
1963	117.06	100.00	100.83	100.78	100.47	117.61
1964	121.78	100.00	101.10	101.04	100.62	122.54
1965	126.19	100.00	101.38	101.31	100.79	127.19
1966	139.01	100.00	101.66	101.57	100.94	140.32
1967	146.40	100.00	101.93	101.83	101.10	148.01
1968	154.74	100.00	102.21	102.09	101.25	156.67
1969	163.81	100.00	102.48	102.35	101.41	166.12
1970	172.64	100.00	102.76	102.61	101.57	175.35
1971	178.30	100.00	103.04	102.87	101.72	181.37
1972	182.74	100.00	103.31	103.13	101.88	186.18
1973	190.34	100.00	103.59	103.39	102.03	194.20
1974	202.02	100.00	103.86	103.65	102.19	206.44
1975	211.00	100.00	104.14	103.92	102.35	215.96
1976	217.63	100.00	104.42	104.18	102.51	223.09

Source: Derived from AHA employees data and 1960 and 1970 1% Public Use Samples. Column 6 is the product of column 4 and 5. Column 11 is the product of columns 6, 7, and 10.

TABLE 13.3. Hospital Employees Classified by Weekly
Hours Worked: 1950, 1960, and 1970

Hours Worked	1950	1960	1970
1–14	11,970	76,066	117,983
15–29	51,960	129,158	285,795
30–34		48,437	110,300
35–39	16,860	50,106	129,277
40	357,990	979,741	1,580,096
41–48	373,290	237,123	208,836
49–59	54,960	55,956	74,433
60 and over	55,230	69,045	82,389
Total workers	949,410	1,645,632	2,589,109
Average hours	41.5	38.9	37.6

Source: Derived from U.S. Bureau of the Census,
Industrial Characteristics, 1950, 1960, and 1970.

are shown in Table 13.3 and exhibit the expected steady decline in
the length of the work week from 1950 to 1970. The index of weekly
hours worked by hospital employees (H_t/H_0) is developed by using
linear interpolation to estimate the missing years and is shown in
column 5 of Table 13.2A. The work week of hospital workers has
been changing at an average annual rate of -0.46 percent per year
from 1950 to 1976.

The indices of employees and average weekly hours are multiplied to obtain the index of total weekly hours (T_t/T_0), shown in
column 6 of Table 13.2B. The index is developed for community hospital employees and shows an average annual growth rate of 4.73
percent over the period from 1950 to 1976. This index is the basic
measure of the quantity of labor employed in the hospital sector.

The Hourly Wage Rate of Hospital Workers

Throughout this chapter it is assumed that the wage rate is
proportional to the marginal product of labor. It is this assumption
that allows the combination of different types of labor. For example,
it allows hours of male workers aged 40–44 to be added to the hours

of males aged 55-59 by converting each quantity measure to a value measure. It is expected that a male aged 40–44 is more productive than a male aged 20-24 because the older male has more experience. It is assumed that the average hourly wage rate expresses this improved productivity. The same is true of males or females with differing levels of education. The wage rate, cross-classified by age, sex, and education, captures improvements that may be expected from the labor force as its social and demographic characteristics shift.

These hourly wage rates are used to develop both the experience and the educational index. The weights that will be used to combine hours worked by employees of differing age and sex are shown in Table 13.4. There is no noticeable change in the distribution of hourly wages by age for females from 1960 to 1970. Male hourly wage rates have changed slightly from 1960 to 1970. In particular, there has been an overall increase from 1960 to 1970 in the average hourly

TABLE 13.4. Index of Average Hourly Earnings of
Hospital Employees by Sex and Age
in 1960 and 1970

Age	1960		1970	
	Males	Females	Males	Females
14–19	71	61	61	60
20–24	79	83	80	84
25–29	93	96	107	97
30–34	120	95	127	92
35–39	145	96	161	93
40–44	140	92	161	90
45–49	146	93	154	91
50–54	146	90	145	90
55–59	124	89	130	86
60–64	130	88	137	88
65+	118	86	128	92
Total	123	90	130	89

Source: Derived from the 1960 and 1970 1% Public Use Sample. Expressed as a percentage of the average hourly earnings of all hospital employees in 1960 and 1970.

wage rate for all male hospital employees, with the changes distributed across all ages. Since females contribute such a disproportionate share of the total hospital labor force, small changes in the male wage rates will not have an appreciable effect on the results. Consequently, the 1960 average hourly wage rates will be used as weights.

The Age–Sex Composition of Hospital Workers

Changes in the age–sex composition of the hospital labor force are taken as a measure of the experience of that labor force. The index is calculated by multiplying the proportion of average annual hours worked by age and sex in both 1960 and 1970 times the index of average hourly wages in 1960 (Table 13.4) and converting the result to index number form with the base year set at 1960. Linear interpolation is used to estimate the index value in the missing years.

The distribution of annual hours by age and sex is shown in Table 13.5. The table is remarkable because over 70 percent of all hours worked in this industry are worked by females and the trend

TABLE 13.5. Percent Distribution of Annual Hours Worked by Hospital Employees by Age and Sex in 1960 and 1970

Age	1960		1970	
	Males	Females	Males	Females
14–19	0.59	2.34	0.87	2.15
20–24	2.62	8.49	2.57	11.42
25–29	4.34	7.84	3.93	8.39
30–34	4.20	7.44	3.45	6.63
35–39	3.80	7.50	2.53	6.79
40–44	3.23	8.34	2.44	8.12
45–49	3.01	8.47	2.96	8.45
50–54	2.75	8.13	2.75	8.02
60–64	1.97	3.79	1.75	4.34
65+	1.32	2.05	1.02	1.98
Total	29.94	70.06	26.59	73.41

Source: Derived from the 1960 and 1970 1% Public Use Sample.

from 1960 to 1970 has been toward even more female hours. The proportion of hours worked by males in 1970 has shown a decline in almost every age category while there has been substantial growth in hours worked by females from 20 to 29 years of age.

The calculation of A_t/A_0, using 1960 wage rates as weights, shows no change in the age-sex index from 1960 to 1970. In 1970, the index fell to 99.98 from the 1960 base value of 100.00. Changes in the age-sex composition of the hospital labor force had no effect on labor input from 1960 to 1970. This compares favorably with the results of Denison who found a slight decrease in his index.[11]

Data on total hours worked by hospital employees disaggregated by age and sex are not available for other years. Since there has been such a small change from 1960 to 1970 in the index, the age-sex index is taken to be 100.00 over the study period. This discussion uses a distribution of annual hours worked by hospital employees distributed by age-sex class. This is equivalent to the assumption that the index of age-sex composition of total annual hours worked would be the same as the index of total weekly hours worked, were such an index of hospital workers available.

The Education of Hospital Workers

In this section, changes in the education of hospital workers are discussed, another component of the quality index. To estimate E_t/E_0, years of schooling completed is used as the main variable. The input of labor is expected to increase as the labor force becomes better educated. In this study, education is measured in terms of the number of school years completed and is based on the census definitions. The shift in the number of school years completed by hospital employees overtime needs to be examined and then combined in some way, so that we may develop an index of the changing quality of hospital labor input caused by changes in education.

The standard method for combining workers of different educational levels is to assume that the workers are paid proportional to their marginal products and weight each worker of different educational background by his average hourly wage rate. This requires a table of hourly wage rates by number of school years completed and is shown in Table 13.6. This is similar to the assumption we made in the calculation of the index of age-sex composition. The index of average hourly earnings by sex and years of school completed is then multiplied by the distribution of years of schooling completed by hospital employees (Table 13.7) to yield an index of education based on employees. A similar index using the distribution of annual hours worked by hospital employees of different sex and years of schooling

TABLE 13.6. Index of Average Hourly Earnings by Sex
and Years of School Completed,
1960 and 1970

Years of School Completed	1960		1970	
	Males	Females	Males	Females
0–4	72	55	80	73
5–8	97	64	79	61
9–11	101	71	90	67
12	102	77	91	70
13–15	111	89	104	84
16	131	104	128	102
17–20	171	125	191	125

Source: Derived from the 1960 and 1970 1% Public
Use Sample. Expressed as a percentage of the average
hourly earnings of all hospital employees in 1960 and 1970.

TABLE 13.7. Percent Distribution of Annual Hours
Worked by Hospital Employees by Sex and
Years of School Completed: 1960 and 1970

Years of School Completed	1960		1970	
	Males	Females	Males	Females
0–4	0.54	0.48	0.20	0.31
5–8	2.62	2.81	1.32	1.70
9–11	7.24	14.22	4.17	9.27
12	1.98	4.78	1.56	4.60
13–15	8.53	31.89	9.20	38.41
16	1.12	4.18	1.41	5.19
17–20	7.91	11.70	8.73	13.94
Total	29.94	70.06	26.59	73.41

Source: Derived from the 1960 and 1970 1% Public
Use Sample.

completed as the quantity measure is also developed and shown in column 9 of Table 13.2B as an index of education based on total hours. There is no important difference between these two indices. Both assume that all of the increase in education results in an improvement in the quality of labor. A more realistic assumption is to assume that only some portion of the increase in education is captured as an improvement in the quality of the labor force. We follow the methods of Denison[11] and Schwartzman[1] in assuming that 60 percent of the difference in hourly wage rate is the result of changes in education and 40 percent is the result of changes in ability. It does not matter if employees or total weekly hours distributed by sex and years of schooling are used to compute the index, since the choice has no effect.

The education index, in addition to incorporating any changes in years of schooling completed, should also include the effect of any changes in the length of the school year and any systematic changes in the pattern of attendance since both of these have the effect of altering the definition of school years completed. Of the two effects, the length of the school term is not as important as the reduction in days missed. According to Denison[10] from 1950 to 1968 there was a 0.5 percent increase in the length of the school term and a 3.4 percent increase in the number of days attended by each pupil enrolled. Since both of these measures are so small, it is concluded that changes in the length of the school year and absenteeism do not change the meaning of the number of school years completed over the period studied.

The index of the amount of education of hospital workers, corrected for ability is shown in column 10 of Table 13.2B. Over the study period this index grew at an average annual growth rate of 0.16 percent.

The Input of Hospital Labor

The final index of labor input, L_t/L_0, is the product of the indices of quantity and quality and is shown in column 11 of Table 13.2B. The labor input index for hospital workers shows an average annual growth rate of 4.90 percent from 1950 to 1976. Of this growth rate of 4.90 percent, 4.73 percentage points are due to changes in the quantity of hospital labor used and 0.16 points are due to improvements in the quality of labor achieved through more education. Experience, measured by age-sex changes among hospital workers, did not have an effect on the overall input of hospital labor.

MONOPOLISTIC OR MONOPSONISTIC EXPLOITATION

Suppose monopolistic or monopsonistic exploitation exists. If it does, the marginal product of labor may be above the actual wage rate and a critical assumption of this study will have been violated. If hospital workers have a wage rate below that of other industries, it may be a true reflection of their productivity or it may imply that workers in the hospital industry are not paid according to the value of their marginal product. Consequently, it will be useful to examine the possible effects of this circumstance.

The quantity portion of the index of hospital labor will not be affected by changes in the marginal productivity assumption; the impact will be on the quality indices where the weights used in the computations may be incorrect. This does not imply that the quantity of labor is what it would be if imperfect competition did not exist.

There is evidence that health workers had earnings substantially below the average for all industries in 1959, and further evidence that the differentials were much less by 1969. [12] Health workers, in a study by Fuchs, are defined in such a way as to include hospital workers.

In 1960, the average hourly wage rate of all hospital workers is estimated at $1.68 per hour, with males earning $2.06 and females earning $1.52. Fuchs estimates hospital workers, excluding self-employed workers and workers with 18 years or more of schooling, have an average hourly wage of $1.59 in 1959. [12] Since he excluded high-income workers, his estimate may understate the true wage rate for all hospital workers regardless of educational level. In an unrelated paper, Fuchs estimates that all nonagricultural employees have an hourly wage rate of $2.50 in 1959, with males earning $2.79 and females earning $1.70. [13] These wage rates are substantially above the hourly wages of hospital workers.

Using the 1960 economy-wide weights developed by Fuchs, the indices for experience and education can be recalculated. The total input of hospital labor, using the Fuchs study weights, grows at an annual average rate of 4.63 percent. Of this growth rate, 4.73 percentage points are due to growth of labor quantity, -0.27 points are due to increases in the experience of the labor force, and 0.17 points are due to increases in the education of hospital workers. The effect of substituting Fuchs' economy-wide weights for those used in this chapter is to reduce slightly the growth rate of labor input. The main effect is on the importance of experience in increasing the labor input of hospitals. Using this chapter's weights, experience had no effect on hospital labor input. Using Fuchs' weights, the experience of the labor force declines, and this reduces overall labor input but the reduction is small.

COMPARISON WITH OCCUPATION BY
INDUSTRY DATA

Additional evidence in support of the conclusion that changes in
the quality of the hospital labor force are not a significant factor in
increasing hospital labor input is suggested in the U.S. Bureau of
the Census data on Occupation by Industry. The number of employees
in all U.S. hospitals, as reported in the census, and the occupation
of hospital employees by major census occupational categories are
shown in Table 13.8. This table assumes that there have been only
minor changes in the definitions of the major categories of workers
from 1950 to 1970 and that any changes that have occurred have been
solely due to shifts within the individual categories and not across
categories.

This table shows three large categories of hospital workers:
professional and technical workers, service workers, and clerical
workers. From 1950 to 1970 there has been substantial growth in
total employees but the numbers of professional and technical workers fell rapidly as clerical workers and services workers increased.
This particular shift of worker mix is a move away from more educated employees and toward employees with lower education and is
consistent with previous finding that changes in the quality of hospital
labor due to improved education is not a substantial factor in increasing hospital labor input.

COMPARISON WITH THE U.S. LABOR FORCE

Edward Denison has developed indices of labor input for the
U.S. economy that include the same study period. This will allow a
comparison of the characteristics of the hospital labor force with the
same characteristics for the U.S. labor force.

The labor input indices for nonresidential businesses from 1950
to 1976 are shown in Table 13.9. The index of total employment grew
at an annual rate of 1.18 percent compared to 5.22 percent for employees of U.S. community hospitals.

Average weekly hours changed at a rate of -0.52 percent per year
in the whole economy compared with -0.46 percent in the hospital
sector. The rate of decline in the working week is essentially the
same in the hospital industry as in the economy. The result of the
decline in the working week and the increase in the employment index
is that total weekly hours grew 0.65 percent per year in the U.S.
economy. This contrasts with a growth rate of 4.73 percent in total
weekly hours in the hospital sector; a growth rate that is seven times
greater than that in the economy.

TABLE 13.8. Occupation and Percentage Distribution of Employees of U.S. Hospitals: 1950–1970

Occupation	Employees			Percent		
	1950	1960	1970	1950	1960	1970
Professional, technical	437,460	679,326	987,003	44.5	40.2	36.8
Managers, officials	15,330	28,918	65,844	1.6	1.7	2.5
Clerical	89,430	193,297	404,842	9.1	11.4	15.1
Sales	1,020	1,232	4,040	0.1	0.1	0.2
Craftsmen, foremen	31,890	53,432	57,575	3.2	3.2	2.2
Operatives	40,560	53,926	65,196	4.1	3.2	2.4
Service workers	356,910	650,830	1,077,778	36.3	38.5	40.2
Laborers	9,090	8,862	17,788	0.9	0.5	0.7
Not reported	2,130	21,755	—	0.2	1.3	—
Total	983,820	1,691,578	2,680,066	100.0	100.0	100.0

Source: U.S. Bureau of the Census, Occupations by Industry, 1950, 1960, 1970.

The Denison index of age-sex composition of the labor force is based on an underlying distribution of total weekly hours worked classified by age and sex. Denison's index grew by -0.24 percent per year. This paper's hospital sector age-sex index does not change over the study period. There are two points to be made here. First, hospitals have a higher proportion of female employees when compared to the entire economy and this proportion grew over the study period. Second, the economy has a lower proportion of female employees but this group is growing more rapidly than the hospital group. This explains, in part, why the index of age-sex composition of all workers is below that of hospital workers.

The educational index of hospital workers grew much more slowly than the corresponding index for all workers. The economy-wide index grew at an average annual rate of 0.68 percent from 1950 to 1976 compared to 0.15 percent for the educational index of hospital workers. This is a rather surprising result to the extent that hospitals are often thought of as centers of advanced technology and knowledge, with the resulting expectation of high rates of growth of education. This may be true of segments of the hospital labor force but is not a general characteristic of hospital labor.

Denison estimates the effect of changes in efficiency caused by changes in hours and considers these indices to change the input of labor. These estimates are not incorporated in recomputations of Denison's estimates since the main interest lies in comparing the U.S. index with the hospital sector and comparable indices are unavailable. Table 13.9, which shows Denison's estimates, excludes the efficiency indices and has been recalculated on a base year of 1960.

CONCLUSION

For the overall economy, improvements in quality of labor due to more education more than offset declines in the quality of the labor force due to experience. The net result was that quality improvements had the effect of substantially increasing the overall labor input to the economy. The economy-wide labor input index grew 1.10 percent over the study period. Of this growth rate, 0.65 points are due to increases in the quantity of labor, 0.68 points are due to increases in the education of labor, and -0.24 percentage points are due to declining experience in the labor force measured by changes in its age-sex composition. The labor input index in the health sector grew 4.90 percent. As mentioned above, 4.73 points are due to changes in the quantity of hospital labor, and 0.16 points are due to improved

TABLE 13.9. Labor Input in Nonresidential Businesses: 1950–1976

Year	Employment	Average Weekly Hours	Total Weekly Hours	Age-sex Composition of Total Hours	Education Corrected for Ability	Labor Input
1950	93.98	104.91	98.58	100.30	93.99	92.93
1951	97.74	104.87	102.47	100.49	94.33	97.13
1952	98.82	104.40	103.15	100.68	105.65	109.72
1953	100.25	103.78	104.02	100.87	95.37	100.07
1954	97.29	102.74	99.94	101.22	96.16	97.27
1955	99.41	102.74	102.37	100.90	96.56	99.74
1956	101.42	102.34	103.78	100.43	97.06	101.16
1957	101.19	100.81	102.00	100.36	97.69	100.00
1958	97.32	99.97	97.28	100.59	98.74	96.62
1959	99.65	100.62	100.27	100.34	99.31	99.92
1960	100.00	100.00	100.00	100.00	100.00	100.00
1961	99.16	99.43	98.57	100.00	100.82	99.47
1962	100.62	99.64	100.25	99.86	101.29	101.40

Year						
1963	101.18	99.54	100.71	99.94	101.73	102.39
1964	102.90	99.38	102.24	99.50	102.20	103.97
1965	105.97	99.59	105.52	98.83	102.83	107.24
1966	109.66	98.58	108.08	98.14	103.38	109.65
1967	111.22	97.00	107.86	98.13	104.10	110.18
1968	113.63	96.54	109.69	97.88	104.78	112.50
1969	117.06	95.92	112.29	97.15	105.37	114.95
1970	116.47	94.47	110.02	96.98	106.14	113.25
1971	116.11	94.09	109.24	96.81	107.07	113.25
1972	119.45	94.14	112.42	95.98	107.83	116.35
1973	125.07	93.67	117.14	95.17	108.72	121.20
1974	127.11	92.42	117.46	94.60	109.81	122.02
1975	123.36	91.56	112.93	95.05	111.04	119.19
1976	127.47	91.50	116.62	94.31	112.24	123.45

Source: Derived from Table 3-1, with deletions, of Denison, Edward F., Accounting for Slower Economic Growth, p. 29, 1979.

quality caused by increased education. Thus, quantity changes are far more important than quality changes in the hospital sector.

Low growth rates in experience and education among hospital workers are related to the unique structure of the hospital labor force. This sector is characterized by a work force that is predominantly female and one in which female workers have substantially lower than average wage rates compared with males. Female wage rates in this sector do not change as age increases, but male wage rates increase as age increases and then decline. Because of these characteristics, a shift toward female workers who are better educated or older does not have as much of an effect as similar changes among male workers. Dual labor market theory may prove to be appropriate to describe the structure of this unique labor market.

NOTES

1. Schwartzman D. The contribution of education to the quality of labor. Am. Econ. Rev. 58, 508, 1968.
2. Schwartzman D. The decline of service in retail trade. Study No. 48. Bureau of Economic and Business Research, Washington State University, Pullman, Washington, 1971.
3. Denison Edward F. The contribution of education to the quality of labor: comment. Am. Econ. Rev. 59, 935, 1969.
4. U.S. Bureau of the Census, U.S. Census of Population: 1950, Vol. IV. Special Reports Part 1, Chapter D. Industrial Characteristics. U.S. Bureau of the Census, Washington D.C., 1955.
5. U.S. Bureau of the Census. U.S. Census of Population: 1960. Subject Reports—Industrial Characteristics. Final Report PC(2)-7F, U.S. Bureau of the Census, Washington, D.C., 1967.
6. U.S. Bureau of the Census. U.S. Census of Population: 1970. Subject Reports—Industrial Characteristics. Final Report PC(2)-7B, U.S. Bureau of the Census, Washington D.C., 1973.
7. U.S. Government Printing Office. Standard Industrial Classification Manual, 1972. U.S. Government Printing Office, Washington D.C., 1972.
8. American Hospital Association. Hospital Statistics. American Hospital Association, Chicago, 1975.
9. U.S. Bureau of the Census. Public Use Samples of Basic Records from the 1960 Census. U.S. Bureau of the Census, Washington D.C., 1975.
10. Denison Edward F. Accounting for United States economic growth: 1924-1969. The Brookings Institution, Washington D.C., 1974.
11. Denison Edward F. The Sources of Economic Growth in the United States. Committee for Economic Development, New York, 1962.

12. Fuchs Victor R. The earnings of allied health personnel—are health workers underpaid? Occasional Papers of the National Bureau of Economic Research 3, pp. 408–432, 1970.
13. Fuchs Victor R. Differentials in hourly earnings by region and city size. 1959. Occasional Paper 101. New York National Bureau of Economic Research, 1967.

14

THE UNION IMPACT ON WAGE DIFFERENTIALS WITHIN AND AMONG HOSPITALS

Catherine McLaughlin

Wage-setting practices used to determine both occupational wage differentials within a hospital (internal wage structure) and wage differentials for a specific occupation across hospitals (external wage structure) have changed over the past two decades. Hospitals in the early 1960s had quite fluid internal and external wage structures, allowing relative wages for occupations to vary from year to year. During the 1960s and 1970s hospitals changed from this wage-setting approach to a more structured wage-setting policy concerned with internal wage ties among jobs and with external wage relationships among hospitals.[1] During this time period there were changes in both state and federal labor laws that permitted collective bargaining by hospital workers.[2] It is the premise of this chapter that the resulting emergence of hospital unionism was a major factor influencing hospitals to alter their wage-setting policies and that this change in policy affected both the internal and the external wage structures.

Standard economic analysis places wage determination in a market context, with wages a function of the firm's derived demand for labor and the labor supply conditions it faces. However, these market equilibrium wages may be only a starting point for actual wage setting.

According to institutional labor economics,[3] these market forces determine a range of possible wages but leave a margin of choice within which employers and unions make decisions to establish

I would like to thank Glen G. Cain and Richard U. Miller for their comments on an earlier version of this study. I would also like to thank Albert E. Schwenk of the Bureau of Labor Statistics for providing much of the data.

or eliminate certain wage differentials. The agreed upon wage differentials are thought to be associated with custom and tradition and with the internal politics of the union. The final individual wage rate is, therefore, determined not only by its relevant product and labor market forces but also by various management and union policies.

Such management policies would include changing an occupational wage in response to the threat of unionization, either from within the hospital or from other hospitals in the area. Union policies in general concern securing what the workers perceive as equal pay for jobs of equal skill or difficulty and a system of wage differentials that in some sense reflects the relative worth of the jobs in the firm (Douty 1963, p. 226).

The key question addressed in this chapter, therefore, is whether the recent growth of hospital unionism has indeed altered either the external or the internal wage structure. More specifically, the empirical question is whether the dispersion of wages for an occupation across hospitals or the dispersion of wages across occupations within a hospital has changed significantly in response to the change in hospital unionism.

The internal wage structure will be dealt with first, giving the market and institutional forces that affect this structure and then presenting the analysis of the union impact. A similar treatment of the external wage structure follows. The specific empirical questions raised are: (1) Has unionism affected the variance of mean occupational wages across occupations within a hospital? (our measure of the internal wage structure); and (2) Has unionism affected the variance of mean hospital wages for an occupation across hospitals within an SMSA? (our measure of the external wage structure).

Due to data limitations, it was not possible to control for all of the factors that could affect either of these variances. This data limitation is particularly strong for the intrahospital variance analysis in which the only hospital-specific explanatory variable available is the degree of unionization. In addition, both the regression results and the analysis of the particular data used have enabled the identification of some errors in model specification.[4]

Finally, an issue discussed but not dealt with in this study is that unionization may not be an exogenous variable in the variance of wage model. For the purpose of this study, individual hospital unionization and the level of hospital unionization in an SMSA will be treated as exogenous. It may be, however, that the variance in wage rates, in part, determines unionization. For example, the existence of a wide range of occupational wages within a hospital, which the workers perceive as inequitable, may actually influence the workers to unionize. Similarly, a wide range of wage rates for a particular occupation among hospitals in an SMSA may encourage unionization of that occupation. The estimation of a single equation model in which the variance of wages is regressed on unionization may, therefore, result in a biased estimate of the union influence.

Because of the above problems, the results of this study should be treated as exploratory. The results do indicate that unions have had a consistent, but weak, wage rate standardization effect on the external wage structure, that is, the interhospital variance of wages decreases as hospital unionization increases. The results of the internal wage structure estimation do not present a consistent picture of how unions are affecting the intrahospital variance of occupational wages. In some cases, the variance of wages was greater in unionized hospitals and, in some cases, it was smaller.

INTERNAL WAGE STRUCTURE

The wage rates established for the individual jobs in a firm are tied into a more or less stable internal structure primarily by two factors: internal human capital formation and equity wage comparisons among workers. With respect to the first factor, when upper level jobs are filled from within the firm, workers invest in on-the-job training to prepare themselves for promotion, and employers invest in screening information about the workers' qualifications for promotion consideration. Wage differentials between these feeder jobs and the upper-level jobs make mobility desirable and encourage on-the-job training investment.

Thus, the job structure, in terms of the mobility between jobs, of a firm influences the internal wage structure, that is, the wage differentials between jobs. More explicitly, with respect to the role of human capital formation, the position of the feeder jobs in the promotion ladder, the openness of upper-level jobs to the external market (the extent to which these jobs are filled from outside the firm), and the amount of on-the-job training determine the wage relationships.[5]

Internal standards of job comparison may also affect occupational wage differentials. Internal job-content comparison by the workers, as a basis for relative wage determination, is essentially an equity concept dealing with the relationship of pay to a worker's "input," as measured by his perception of his efforts and responsibilities. Wage differentials will be perceived as inequitable if a worker believes that other workers are receiving more pay in relation to their input than he is.

This comparison of job content and wage rates is stronger among some jobs than others. A group of jobs within which internal comparison is most significant is often called a "job cluster." Dunlop

(1957, p. 129) defines a job cluster as a group of jobs within a firm "linked together by (1) technology, (2) the administrative organization of the production process, . . ., or (3) social custom." In general, close association of workers in cluster-type jobs accompanies comparison of job content and wage rates.

Thus, a firm's job structure is thought to affect the internal wage structure through human capital formation and worker-perceived wage equity comparisons. This structure of relative wage rates becomes customary, and dissatisfaction may arise when wage relationships are changed. Bishop (1974, p. 1) states, however, that in the 1950s and early 1960s hospitals did not have these fixed internal wage structures. With the exception of direct patient-care jobs (RNs, LPNs, and nursing aides), relative wages for occupations varied from year to year in response to changing external market conditions. A possible explanation for this lack of an institutionally rigid wage structure is the nature of the hospital internal labor market.

Most hospital jobs, both those requiring little skill and those requiring health sector specific skills, are in effect "dead end" jobs. According to one researcher, the hospital occupational "structure itself is a mosaic of job clusters so compartmentalized by licensing, training and custom that movement by personnel between them is difficult, if not impossible" (Miller 1980, p. 378).[6]

When upper-level, highly skilled jobs are filled from the external labor market rather than from within the firm, and there is little or no upward mobility for other jobs, the role of human capital formation in the establishment of internal occupational wage differentials is minimal. There is no incentive to establish wage differentials to encourage on-the-job training or screening.

According to Doeringer (1973) and Bishop (1974), there was a move toward less flexible hospital wage structures in the 1960s. While there has been no change in the mobility of hospital workers and thus in the role played by human capital formation, there has apparently been a change in the workers' attitudes toward their jobs and toward equitable wage-rate differentials. What was once seen as a service to the community is now considered "just another job" (Bishop, p. 59). Changes in the job and wage expectations of minority workers and women may have enhanced this new perspective. In addition, the growth of unionization (not necessarily separate from the changed expectations) of both the highly skilled and low-skilled workers has altered the environment in which hospitals make wage decisions.

There are several ways in which unions influence the internal wage structure. These include direct bargaining on occupational wage rates and the processing of grievances involving alleged inequities in wage rates for particular jobs.[7] Even in the absence of a union, the threat of unionism due to worker dissatisfaction over perceived wage inequities may lead to a change in internal wage differentials.

There have been several studies of hospital unions that reflect the role of unions in determining the internal wage structure. In a study of a union of nonprofessional health personnel in New York City, Doeringer (1973) found that the union did negotiate over occupational wage differentials as well as individual occupational wages. A pattern emerged of first negotiating overall wage increases for the nonprofessional occupations and then adding provisions for a sliding scale of wage increases for all workers that favored the lower paid workers. The effect of these negotiations was to raise the lower tail of the wage distribution more rapidly than the average.

Solomon (1980) conducted more than 100 personal interviews with hospital administrators, labor leaders, and important third parties in 12 SMSAs. The interviewees suggested that unions had tended to compress the internal wage structures in their SMSAs by raising the wages of the lowest paid workers.

Using wage data gathered from 1970 to 1977 from approximately 100 hospitals in each year, Sloan and Steinwald (1980) also found evidence of a compression of the internal wage structure, that is, of low-wage hospital workers making relative wage gains. As they point out, this compression could reflect several changes in the low-skill and higher-skill labor markets, only one of which was collective bargaining activity concentrated in low-skill occupations.

Methodology

In most cases, analysis of changes in internal wage structures involves comparing wage rates for a set of jobs in a firm at one point in time to the same set of wage rates at other dates or by examining the percentage change in those rates. Several techniques have been employed for this comparison. Perhaps the most common technique is to compare wage-rate ratios between two occupations or occupational groups at two points in time.[8] Inferences about the stability and shifting of the internal wage structures are drawn from these figures.

There are two major limitations to this ratio-comparison method. First, the researcher is restricted to looking at wage differentials between only two groupings. The bulk of institutional labor economics literature discusses the interdependence of potentially all job wage rates in a firm. Second, this comparison only indicates if there has been a change in the relative wage rates; it sheds no information on what forces contributed to the change in the ratios.

Sloan and Steinwald (1980, p. 113) used another method to test whether, on the average, hospital internal wage structures had changed from 1970 to 1977 in a national sample of hospitals. Using mean wages for 53 hospital occupations, they computed Pearson product-moment and Spearman rank-order correlation coefficients between the 1972 minimum real wage level for each occupation and the corresponding real wage change between 1970 and 1977. The resulting correlation coefficients, -.26 and -.56, imply that there was a compression of the internal wage structure between 1970 and 1977, with low-wage occupations being granted relatively higher wage increases than high-wage occupations.[9]

The advantage of this method over the more common wage-ratio analysis is that the researcher is not limited to comparisons between only two wage rates but rather, can include as many wage rates as deemed appropriate. As with the wage-ratio method, however, no multivariate analysis is feasible by which one can determine why the structure changed. As Sloan and Steinwald point out, this wage compression from 1970 to 1977 could reflect a number of developments, for example, changing labor market conditions for low-skilled and/or high-skilled workers, increases in the real minimum wage, or a greater degree of union activity in low-wage occupations.

Recently, Freeman (1980a) analyzed the effect of union wage practices on wage dispersion within establishments. To capture this wage dispersion, he used the standard deviation of the natural log of earnings. This measure is one of several measures of inequality.[10] The use of such a measure of inequality enables the researcher to include as many wage rates as desired and to summarize a distribution of wages into one single measure. As such, the variation in the distribution of wages over many years, or the variation in many distributions at one point in time, can be analyzed.

Using multiple regression analysis, we can identify factors that could alter the internal wage structure, including unionization. Specifically, the conceptual equation is:

$$V(W^i) = \sum_{k=1}^{n} a_k X_k^i + bU^i + e^i \tag{1}$$

where i denotes the hospital; $V(W)^i$ is the variance of the natural log of mean occupational wages in hospital i; X^i is a vector of product market and labor market characteristics that could alter the internal wage structure, or $V(W)$; U^i is the degree of unionization in hospital i; and e^i is the stochastic disturbance term.

As is the case with several other measures of wage inequality (for example, variance of wages, the coefficient of variation, the Gini coefficient), the variance of the natural log of wages, $V(W)$, takes all units into account, is sensitive to relative wage changes on one side of the mean and those that cross the mean, is sensitive to equal dollar additions to each wage, and is not sensitive to equal across-the-board percentage changes.

Contrary to the variance or the coefficient of variation, this measure weights changes at the lower end of the distribution more heavily than at the upper end. In other words, wage increases for low-wage workers will result in a larger change in V(W) than comparable absolute wage increases for high-wage workers. If, as indicated by Doeringer (1973) and Sloan and Steinwald (1980), low-wage hospital workers have made relative wage gains, the V(W) will overstate the compression of the wage structure relative to other measures of wage dispersion.

Ideally, to measure the impact of unions on the internal wage structure, we would like to be able to compare the internal wage structure in hospital i when there is no unionization to that when there is unionization. Unfortunately, this kind of data is not available. What we can compare is the wage structure (as measured by V(W)) in a hospital in which some or all of the occupations are covered by a collective bargaining agreement to the wage structure in another hospital in which none of the occupations is covered. As indicated earlier, there are factors other than unionization that could cause the internal wage structure of the two hospitals to differ. These factors should be considered in order to isolate the union impact.

For one thing, the two hospitals may not be producing the same "product." Hospital i may be a large teaching hospital with more specialized facilities and services that require more highly skilled and more highly paid professional workers than are required by hospital j. In this case, with the top end of the distribution more highly paid, the V(W) in hospital i will be greater than that in hospital j, ceteris paribus.

In addition, hospital job structures may vary according to hospital size. Bishop (1974) found that, in general, small hospitals in Boston had different job structures and, therefore, different internal wage structures than did large hospitals. The differences were due, for the most part, to differing products and production processes. In the larger hospitals, skilled workers (for example, RNs, technologists) were divided into specialized departments, with more workers employed to carry out any given task, and with each department relatively self-contained. Skilled workers in smaller hospitals participated in a more integrated production process, facilitating the existence of job content and wage comparisons. We would expect the internal wage structure for skilled workers of smaller hospitals, therefore, to reflect this equity comparison.

The job structure, and therefore the wage structure, for unskilled and semiskilled workers also varied according to hospital size. In general, departments in larger hospitals exhibit more worker mobility for low-skill occupations. Both lateral and upward mobility within the hospital job structure allows comparison of job content and may lead to the establishment of wage differentials that reflect the workers' perception of equity. In addition, there may be wage differentials to encourage human capital formation. The V(W) for low-skill workers in larger hospitals may therefore be different from the V(W) for these workers in smaller hospitals.

Finally, if hospital i and hospital j are in different SMSAs, the wages for certain occupations could differ in response to differing market forces. For example, hospital i could be facing a local shortage of RNs. Unless there is perfect mobility between cities, this shortage would result in hospital i paying a higher real wage for RNs than hospital j. Other things being equal, since RNs are at the upper end of the wage distribution, $V(W^i)$ will be greater than $V(W^j)$.

Unfortunately, the data necessary to control for differences in an individual hospital's product or production process are not available. Nor are data available on relevant labor market conditions in the various cities that are included in this analysis. The second omission presents a less serious problem than the first. A dummy variable for each SMSA can be included that will control for varying market conditions. Because the dummy variable controls for any SMSA-specific factors that could alter the internal wage structures of hospitals in the SMSA, we do not know what market forces are affecting the V(W).

Lack of data concerning individual hospital characteristics poses a more serious problem. If any of the characteristics thought to influence the V(W) are correlated with unionization, our measure of the union impact is biased. If, for example, larger hospitals have a larger V(W) and are also more likely to be unionized,[11] then we will have a biased estimate of the union impact. The direction of the bias depends upon both the direction of the impact of the omitted variable on the V(W) and the direction of the correlation between the omitted variable and unionization.

Data

The data gathered for the 1972 and 1975 BLS Industry Wage Survey: Hospitals were the source of both the wage and the union data. Data for approximately 300 private hospitals and 50 state and local government hospitals in 21 SMSAs in 1972 and in 23 SMSAs in 1975 were used. Although individual hospital data are kept confidential, the variance of ln wages for professionals, nonprofessionals, and all occupations in each individual hospital was made available (Table 14.1). In addition, information was given on whether the

TABLE 14.1. Means and (Standard Deviations) of
Individual Hospital Data

| | Private | | | |
| | 1972 | | 1975 | |
	Professional	Nonprofessional	Professional	Nonprofessional
V(W)	.014	.016	.012	.012
	(.013)	(.019)	(.010)	(.008)
UMAJ	.066[a]	.258	.171	.269
UMIN	.130	.105	.107	.130
% Union[b]	9.8	17.2	15.2	23.5
. . . .				
	Government			
V(W)	.014	.015	.011	.013
	(.013)	(.011)	(.010)	(.008)
UMAJ	.250	.474	.333	.490
UMIN	.267	.079	.111	.057
% Union	25.9	36.7	27.0	38.0

[a]For example, in 1972, 6.6 percent of hospitals had a majority of professionals covered.

[b]Average percent of workers covered by a collective bargaining agreement.

Source: Unpublished BLS data.

majority or the minority of workers in each occupational group was covered by a collective bargaining agreement in each hospital. Any information concerning characteristics of the hospital other than whether it was a private, or a state or local government hospital, and the identification of the SMSA was unavailable. All hospitals included are short-term, general service hospitals.

The variance of ln wages was calculated for professional workers, nonprofessional workers, and for all hospital workers. Specifically:

$$V(W_i) = \sum_{j=1}^{n} (\ln W_i - \ln W_i^j)^2 / n \tag{2}$$

where i denotes the hospital; j denotes the occupation; n is the number of occupations included in the occupational group (n varies from 3 to 4 for professionals, 5 to 4 for nonprofessionals, and 8 for all workers); W_i is the average wage for the occupational group in hospital i; and W_i^j is the average for occupation j in hospital i.

In the case of professionals, the three occupations included in 1972 were RNs, medical technologists, and x-ray technologists. Five occupations were included in the nonprofessional group: ward clerks, licensed practical nurses (LPNs), nursing aides, kitchen helpers, and cleaners. In 1975, BLS changed the classification of LPNs to professionals, so that four occupations were included in the professional group and four in the nonprofessional group. Occupational classifications by the BLS staff were based on a uniform set of job descriptions in an attempt to control for interhospital and interarea variations in job titles. Hopefully, this will reduce any variation in wages due to differing hospital job definitions.

When considering the V(W) for professionals, only hospitals with data for all three (or, in 1975, four) professional occupations were included. In this way, the V(W) we are using is based on a consistent set of occupations across all hospitals. The same procedure was used for nonprofessionals and when all eight occupations were combined. Therefore, the sample size varies according to the group being considered.

These particular professional and nonprofessional groupings are necessary, due to the nature of the unionization data gathered by BLS. BLS does not record the percent of workers in each occupation covered by a collective bargaining agreement. Rather, it records whether the majority or minority of professional and of nonprofessional workers in each hospital are covered.

Model Specification

For purposes of estimation, the internal wage structure equation, measuring the union impact on the V(W) of professionals and of nonprofessionals, will be specified as:

$$V(W_{ij}) = a_0 + b_1 UMAJ_{ij} + b_2 UMIN_{ij} + \sum_{k=1}^{n} B_k SMSA_k + e \qquad (3)$$

where:

i denotes the hospital

j denotes the occupational group, either professional or nonprofessional

k denotes the SMSA, 21 in 1972 and 23 in 1975

$V(W_{ij})$ = the variance of the natural log of mean occupational wages for the j-th occupational group in the i-th hospital

$UMAJ_{ij}$ = one if the majority of workers in the j-th occupational group in the i-th hospital are covered by a collective bargaining agreement; 0 otherwise

$UMIN_{ij}$ = one if a minority are covered by a collective bargaining agreement; 0 otherwise

$SMSA_k$ = one if the i-th hospital is in the k-th SMSA; 0 otherwise

A second model will be estimated to capture any spillover effect within a hospital, that is, whether unionization of the other occupational group has an effect on the variance in ln wages of the group in question. If professionals are unionized, for example, the hospital administrator may alter the wage differentials of nonprofessionals to forestall unionization of nonprofessionals due to worker-perceived wage inequities.

$$V(W_{ij}) = a_0 + b_1 UMAJ_{ij} + b_2 UMIN_{ij} + b_3 UOTH_j + \sum_{k=1}^{n} B_k SMSA_k + e \tag{4}$$

where $UOTH_j$ is the percent of employees in the other occupational group in the j-th hospital covered by a collective bargaining agreement.

The final specification is for estimating the union impact on the hospital's overall wage structure. In this case, the mean occupational wages for all eight occupations considered are used to calculate the V(W).

$$V(W_i) = a_0 + b_1 UP_i + b_2 UNP_i + \sum_{k=1}^{n} B_k SMSA_k + e \tag{5}$$

where UP_i is the percent of professional workers in the i-th hospital covered by a collective bargaining agreement, and UNP_i is the percent of nonprofessionals covered. To compute UP and UNP, we assigned a value of 0 unionization to those hospitals where no workers in the appropriate occupational group were covered by a collective bargaining agreement, a value of 25 percent if a minority were covered, and a value of 75 percent if a majority were covered. In this way, we approximate the percentage of workers actually covered in each hospital.

Private and state and local government hospitals will be treated separately. Bishop (1974, p. 166) reported that government hospitals do not participate in local private hospital wage setting. State hospital employees are paid on the basis of state pay grades applied to all state employees. Local government hospital employees are often paid according to the municipal civil service structure. As such, government hospitals are not as free to respond to the local market conditions for hospital labor.

Using BLS Industry Wage Survey: Hospitals data for 1963, 1966, and 1972, Bishop presents ratios of average wages for government and private hospitals. Although these ratios (government wage/ private wage) are always greater than one, the differences are much greater for the less skilled workers. Government hospitals paid an average of 22 to 37 percent more than private hospitals for these low-skill workers (p. 179). Thus, the V(W) in government hospitals would tend to be different from the V(W) of private hospitals, independent of any other effect.

The first analysis deals with the union impact on the V(W) for the i-th occupational group when either the majority or the minority of these workers are covered by a collective bargaining agreement (Equation 3). If Bishop (1974) is correct in stating that unionization was a primary factor in changing what had been fluid hospital wage structures, with wage differentials established according to external market forces and/or personal evaluation, an obvious avenue for union activity would be to obtain more uniform wage structures based on job evaluations. Employees would be conscious of what they perceive to be appropriate wage differentials based on job content comparisons, not based on market influences.

Unfortunately, we do not know whether the "preunion" wage differentials were perceived to be inequitable because occupations differing in skill and difficulty were being paid the same wage or because occupations of the same skill and difficulty were being paid different wages. As such, we do not know, a priori, whether union changes in the internal wage structure will lead to an increase or a decrease in the V(W).

As noted earlier, an additional problem with this analysis is that of causation. If we observe that unionized hospitals have a lower V(W), for example, we are assuming that one of the effects of unionization has been to narrow wage differentials. It may be, however, that a larger V(W) reflects a job structure with mobility and occupational differentiation. In this case, wage differentials respond to human capital formation, not inequity, and there may be no demand for unionism. We will still observe a negative relationship between unionization and the V(W), but not because of the impact of unionization.

According to most hospital labor market researchers, hospitals in general are characterized by little or no mobility in both professional and nonprofessional occupational groups. We have no way of controlling, however, for the possible case of a large hospital in which there is mobility and a system of accepted wage differentials. In fact, it is possible that workers in such a hospital have unionized, not in order to change what they perceive to be inequitable wage differentials, but in order to increase all wage levels. If the union succeeds in obtaining equal percentage increases for all occupational wages, there will be no change in the $V(W)$ and no observed relationship between unionization and the internal wage structure.

As is clear from the above discussion, several hypotheses can be made about the effect of majority coverage on the $V(W)$. We have little basis on which to make a priori statements on which conclusions to expect. To our knowledge, the only empirical work dealing with the union impact on hospital internal wage structures is that of Bishop, who limited her analysis to Boston, and that of Doeringer, who limited his analysis to New York City. Although both found that unions had the effect of compressing the internal wage structure, that is, decreasing the $V(W)$, extrapolation from these two local markets is tenuous.

The ability to predict the impact of minority coverage is similarly hampered. A collective bargaining agreement covers all workers within the bargaining unit. Therefore, if only a minority of professional or nonprofessional workers are covered, the covered unit is a subset of our occupational group, for example, only kitchen helpers in the nonprofessional group. As such, we expect members of this unit to bargain for relative wage increases. This wage gain will lead to an increase in the $V(W)$ if the unit is composed of workers at the upper end of the wage distribution and to a decrease in the $V(W)$ if the unit is composed of the lower-wage workers.

To complicate matters, if management fears that the other uncovered workers will unionize in response to a worsening of their relative position, management may pass on these wage gains to all workers in the occupational group. If this spillover occurs, the union impact will be to shift up the entire wage distribution, leaving the internal wage structure unchanged. Clearly, without more information as to the identity of the bargaining unit, no prediction about the union impact of minority coverage can be made.

If collective bargaining has been an influence in creating more uniform wage structures, then hospital administrators developing such a structure in response to union demands of one occupational group may be more likely to extend such standards to other workers than would be an administrator with no unionism. The addition of

UOTH in Equation 4 provides an estimate of any such spillover effect within a hospital.

The usage of the V(W) across all eight occupations in the hospital permits us to test whether professional unions have had a different impact on the internal wage structure from that of nonprofessional unions. Two hypotheses regarding the estimation of Equation 5 are made.

First, to the extent that the unions of RNs and technical workers behave like traditional craft unions, we would expect them to try to widen the wage structure by raising the relative wages of the professional workers. Because these more highly skilled workers are at the top of the wage distribution, the effect of these relative wage increases will be to increase the V(W). If there exists the threat of nonprofessional unionization, or if nonprofessionals in that hospital are already unionized, then the professional unions may be limited to maintaining their position as management grants equal percentage increases to the nonprofessionals.

Second, the effect of nonprofessional unionization in hospital i will be to narrow or maintain the V(W) in that hospital. The hypothesized effect of narrowing the internal wage structure stems in part from the empirical results of Doeringer (1973) and Sloan and Steinwald (1980), in which low-wage workers received relative wage gains, thus compressing the internal wage structure. Again, the threat of unionization, in this case by professionals, may lead to a spillover of any wage increases and, therefore, a perpetuation of interoccupational wage differentials.

In all three models, Equations 3, 4, and 5, SMSA dummy variables are included to control for any SMSA-specific factors that could influence the internal wage structures of the hospitals in that SMSA.

Results

The models specified above were estimated for approximately 300 private hospitals and for approximately 50 state and local government hospitals in 1972 and 1975. Cross-section regression analysis allows us to compare internal wage structures, that is, the V(W) of different hospitals under varying unionization situations. All of the results should be interpreted with caution, given the potential bias present, due to the omission of any hospital-specific factors that could alter the V(W) and that are correlated with unionism.

The results of the nonprofessional and professional regressions are shown in Tables 14.2 through 14.5. In general, unionization does not have a statistically significant impact on the V(W). Having the majority of workers in private hospitals covered by a collective

TABLE 14.2. Results of Internal Wage Structure Regressions

| | Private, Nonprofessionals | |
| | Model | |
	1	2

Dependent variable: Variance of ln wages

Independent variables:	1972, N = 267, Mean value V(W) = 0.156	
CONSTANT	.0085	.0077
	(.0068)	(.0068)
UMAJ	.0032	.0017
	(.0034)	(.0036)
UMIN	.0038	.0034
	(.0042)	(.0034)
UP		.0098
		(.0088)
SMSA dummies	Sig.	Sig.
$\bar{R}^2$	.084	.081
S.E.E.	.0179	.0179

	1975, N = 297, Mean value V(W) = .0126	
CONSTANT	.0071[a]	.0072[a]
	(.0019)	(.0019)
UMAJ	−.0006	.0002
	(.0010)	(.0010)
UMIN	.0019[b]	.0026[c]
	(.0012)	(.0012)
UP		−.0038[c]
		(.0019)
SMSA dummies	Sig.	Sig.
$\bar{R}^2$	.527	.532
S.E.E.	.0056	.0056

[a]Significant at .01 level.
[b]Significant at .10 level.
[c]Significant at .05 level.
Source: Unpublished BLS data.

TABLE 14.3. Results of Internal Wage Structure Regressions

	Private, Professionals	
	Model	
	1	2

Dependent variable: Variance of ln wages

Independent variables: 1972, N = 331, Mean value V(W) = .0140

	1	2
CONSTANT	.0070[a]	.0071[a]
	(.0040)	(.0040)
UMAJ	.0047	.0053
	(.0033)	(.0036)
UMIN	.0025	.0029
	(.0024)	(.0026)
UNP		−.0014
		(.0037)
SMSA dummies	Sig.	Sig.
$\bar{R}^2$	.152	.150
S.E.E.	.0119	.0119

1975, N = 345, Mean value V(W) = .0117

	1	2
CONSTANT	.0041[a]	.0040
	(.0024)	(.0024)
UMAJ	.0014	.0011
	(.0017)	(.0020)
UMIN	.0031[a]	.0029
	(.0016)	(.0017)
UNP		.0006
		(.0020)
SMSA dummies	Sig.	Sig.
$\bar{R}^2$	.338	.337
S.E.E.	.0084	.0084

[a]Significant at .10 level.
Source: Unpublished BLS data.

TABLE 14.4. Results of Internal Wage Structure Regressions

| | Government, Nonprofessionals | |
| | Model | |
	1	2
Dependent variable: Variance of ln wages		
Independent variables:	1972, N = 40, Mean value V(W) = .0147	
CONSTANT	.0065	.0060
	(.0058)	(.0054)
UMAJ	-.00001	.0086
	(.0038)	(.0054)
UMIN	-.0027	-.0017
	(.0050)	(.0047)
UP		-.0188[a]
		(.0091)
SMSA dummies	Sig.	Sig.
$\bar{R}^2$	.650	.700
S.E.E.	.0064	.0059
	1975, N = 56, Mean value V(W) = .0129	
CONSTANT	.0036	.0063
	(.0103)	(.0099)
UMAJ	.0038	.0080[b]
	(.0027)	(.0032)
UMIN	.0096	.0069
	(.0082)	(.0079)
UP		-.0110[a]
		(.0052)
SMSA dummies	Sig.	Sig.
$\bar{R}^2$	.286	.352
S.E.E.	.0063	.0060

[a] Significant at .05 level.
[b] Significant at .01 level.
Source: Unpublished BLS data.

TABLE 14.5. Results of Internal Wage Structure Regressions

| | Government, Professionals | |
| | Model | |
	1	2
Dependent variable: Variance of ln wages		
Independent variables:	1972, N = 63, Mean value V(W) = .0140	
CONSTANT	.0068	.0054
	(.0055)	(.0055)
UMAJ	-.0106[a]	-.0172[b]
	(.0052)	(.0066)
UMIN	-.0047	-.0092[c]
	(.0041)	(.0050)
UNP		.0115
		(.0072)
SMSA dummies	Sig.	Sig.
$\bar{R}^2$	.446	.467
S.E.E.	.0093	.0092
	1975, N = 73, Mean value V(W) = .0116	
CONSTANT	.0056	.0051
	(.0065)	(.0067)
UMAJ	.0026	.0012
	(.0034)	(.0051)
UMIN	-.0038	-.0048
	(.0041)	(.0049)
UNP		.0021
		(.0060)
SMSA dummies	Sig.	Sig.
$\bar{R}^2$	.276	.263
S.E.E.	.0087	.0088

[a]Significant at .05 level.
[b]Significant at .01 level.
[c]Significant at .10 level.
Source: Unpublished BLS data.

bargaining agreement, whether professional or nonprofessional, did not significantly alter that group's V(W) (see Tables 14.2 and 14.3); neither did having the minority covered in 1972. In 1975, however, coverage of the minority of both professional and nonprofessional workers significantly increased the V(W); that is, relative wage gains received by the covered workers widened the wage structure. As explained earlier, this result may indicate that the subgroup covered was one of the higher paid occupations in the group. Given what we know about the ranking of the average wages of the two occupational groups, a reasonable conclusion stemming from these results is that medical technologists and ward clerks and/or nursing aides were the occupations achieving relative wage gains. [12]

Coverage of the majority of the workers in government hospitals was also usually an insignificant factor. Coverage of the majority of professionals in 1972 (see Table 14.5) had a significant negative impact on the V(W). The coverage of the majority of nonprofessionals in 1975 (see Table 14.4), however, had a statistically significant positive effect when controlling for the strong negative effect that professional unionization had on the nonprofessional V(W). Instead of compressing the wage structure, unionization increased the nonprofessional wage differentials. Potentially, the "preunion" wage structure was considered inequitable because jobs of unequal skill and difficulty were being paid the same wage; thus, the impact of unionism was to establish wage differentials among nonprofessional occupations.

In terms of our measure of a spillover effect, UOTH, nonprofessional unionization never had a significant impact on the variance of professional wages. In three out of four cases, however, the presence of professional unionism did have a narrowing effect on the V(W) of nonprofessionals.

The results of Model 3, the union impact on a hospital's overall internal wage structure, are presented in Table 14.6. The results are not always consistent with our expectations. Nonprofessional unions had no significant impact on the overall V(W) in private hospitals. This result implies either that nonprofessional unions in private hospitals had no impact on wages or that nonprofessional wage gains spilled over to professionals. Given results of an earlier study, in which unionization had a significant positive impact on the average nonprofessional wage, the second interpretation is more likely. [13]

The unionization of professionals in private hospitals had no significant impact on the overall V(W) in 1975 but had the predicted significant positive impact in 1972. The estimated effect in 1972 implies that professionals gain in relative wages due to unionization. [14]

The results are quite different in the government hospitals. Neither professional nor nonprofessional unions significantly altered

TABLE 14.6. Results of Internal Wage Structure Regressions

	All Occupations, Model 3	
	Private	Government

Dependent variable: Variance of ln wages

Independent variables:

1972	N = 233, Mean value V(W) = .0638	N = 37, Mean value V(W) = .0565
CONSTANT	.0430 (.0073)	.0451[a] (.0127)
UP	.0243[a] (.0080)	-.0364 (.0258)
UNP	.0017 (.0060)	.0133 (.0224)
SMSA dummies	Sig.	Sig.
$\bar{R}^2$	.553	.477
S.E.E.	.0161	.0162
1975	N = 265, Mean value V(W) = .0567	N = 49, Mean value V(W) = .0585
CONSTANT	.0382[a] (.0048)	.0352[b] (.0149)
UP	-.0024 (.0045)	-.0526[a] (.0135)
UNP	-.0017 (.0032)	.0270[b] (.0110)
SMSA dummies	Sig.	Sig.
$\bar{R}^2$	.727	.602
S.E.E.	.0123	.0147

[a]Significant at .01 level.
[b]Significant at .05 level.
Source: Unpublished BLS data.

the V(W) in 1972. In 1975, however, the impact of professional union-ization was significantly positive. Both results are contrary to hy-pothesized impacts.

In most cases, at least half of the SMSA dummy variables were significant in explaining the variation in V(W). The SMSA dummy variables capture all SMSA-specific effects; therefore, any interpretation of these results is limited. Review of these SMSA variables revealed that, in SMSAs with a below average degree of hospital unionization overall, the coefficient was positive and significant; in SMSAs with an above average degree of hospital unionization, the coefficient was negative and insignificant. The persistence of the above pattern suggests that market forces in SMSAs with relatively low hospital unionization tended to increase the V(W). A fruitful extension of this analysis, therefore, would be to include a measure of SMSA hospital unionization and other variables, controlling for market forces that could influence the V(W) of individual hospitals, in place of the SMSA dummy variables. Examples of market forces that would lead to an increase in the V(W) are: a shortage of RNs and high unemployment of low-skilled workers.

EXTERNAL WAGE STRUCTURE

Firms participating in a common product market face similar product demand, derived demand for labor, and labor supply conditions. As such, these product and labor market considerations encourage the formation of an interfirm (external) wage structure. Dunlop (1957, p. 131) proposed the concept of a "wage contour," defined as a stable group of firms, "so linked together by (1) similarity of product markets, (2) resort to similar sources for a labor force, or (3) common labor-market organization (custom) that they have common wage-making characteristics." In his view, the first of these linkages appears to be the crucial one, with competition in the product market equalizing the wage rates of key jobs in the firm's job cluster.

Hildebrand (1963, p. 275) extends Dunlop's notion of a wage contour to include what he calls "union-oriented" jobs. These jobs differ from the "market-oriented" jobs discussed by Dunlop, whose wage rates are sensitive to changes in the product market. The wages of union-oriented jobs are determined by unionism and collective bargaining, not by the market. "Through its effective monopoly of skill, the union achieves both both job standardization and effective enforcement of a non-competitive and generally uniform single rate in the area" (Hildebrand, p. 276).

Ross (1957) also included the notion of union influence in interfirm wage determination:

> . . . external forces in the market determine the rough contours of the external wage structure, but they are ordinarily loose enough to leave a margin of choice. Within

this margin employers and unions make their decision as
to desired relationships—to establish or eliminate a differential, to abandon or follow a leader, and so on.

Ross (1948) called the firms participating in this external wage structure the "orbit of coercive comparison." Wage comparisons between
firms in an orbit of coercive comparison are important to the employer avoiding "getting out of line" with the wages he sets for certain
jobs and to the workers interested in being paid a wage comparable
to what others in similar positions are getting. According to Ross,
the union role in seeking "equal pay for equal work" (as defined by
a union determination of similar jobs or job titles, usually without
regard to productivity characteristics of the individual workers) is
far more important in the formation of an orbit of comparison than
either the product or labor market characteristics.

Several researchers have reported instances of the role of the
union in establishing an interhospital external wage structure.
Doeringer (1973) discusses a master agreement with the Association
of Private Hospitals in New York City in 1965, which established an
occupational wage structure with standard minimum rates for all
member hospitals.

According to Bishop (1974), Boston hospitals responded to
pressure from the Massachusetts Nurses Association in the early
1960s by designing uniform wage changes for RNs in order to minimize perceived inequities among Boston nurses. During the same
time period, many Boston hospitals imposed an established minimum
rate for unskilled workers to reduce the potential for worker dissatisfaction due to inequities and, thus, to forestall unionization.

As an illustration of the existence of orbits of coercive comparison in hospital labor relations, Miller (1980) cites the master
agreement between union Local 1199 and the New York City League
of Voluntary Hospitals. The settlements reached in this agreement
became a "benchmark for the union in its bargaining with some sixty
other New York metropolitan health-care institutions" (p. 413). The
settlements also influenced the nonunion hospitals, as they responded
to the threat of being unionized themselves.

The hospital and union representatives interviewed by Solomon
(1980) indicated that multiemployer collective bargaining tended to
standardize nominal wage rates across hospitals in a city. They also
pointed out, however, that it is possible for hospitals to alter the
amount of experience credit given to a new employee and thereby to
offer a higher entry wage when recruiting workers, a form of wage
drift. Interviewees also indicated that individual collective bargaining
has narrowed variation among hospitals because of threat effects.

Methodology

As noted before, external wage comparisons can play an important role in individual hospital wage determinations. We are interested in what impact unions have had on the external wage structure, for example, the system of wage differentials for specific occupations between hospitals. If we had a time-series of wages for a group of hospitals in what Dunlop called a wage contour, or Ross, an orbit of coercive comparison, we could regress individual wage rates on a unionization variable and, controlling for other factors, estimate the impact of unionization on wage variation. Instead, data for several wage contours, or orbits, at a point in time under varying degrees of unionization (in this case, a wage contour or orbit of coercive comparison is made up of the hospitals in an SMSA) are available.

Equity comparison, in the sense of "equal pay for equal work," has been mentioned as playing an important role in individual hospital wage determinations. Several measures of wage equality can be considered measures of equity when equity is defined as the equal treatment of equals and all units in the distribution are considered equal. As before, the measure of wage equality used is the variance of the natural log of wages.

In this case, the V(W) captures the distribution of mean wage rates for an occupation across all hospitals in an SMSA. To the extent that the average worker in each occupation in each hospital is of equal ability, the V(W) should reflect the union's equity comparisons. Referring to Equation (1) in estimating the union impact on the external wage structure, i denotes the SMSA; $V(W^i)$ is the variance of the natural log of mean occupational wages in the i-th SMSA; X^i is a vector of other factors that could alter the V(W); U^i is the degree of unionization in the i-th SMSA; and e^i is the stochastic disturbance term.

It is necessary to control for factors other than unionization that could lead to hospitals in SMSA i having a different V(W), or external wage structure, than those in SMSA j. The specification of these variables is really a two-step process. Essentially, we need to know what factors would cause the V(W) to be different from zero and then control for the fact that those factors may be present in SMSA i but not in SMSA j.

If there were no labor market imperfections, that is, immobility and imperfect information of market conditions on both the sides of the buyer and the seller, homogeneous labor, and homogeneous products, then there should be no variation in wage rates for a given hospital occupation. Although we have no knowledge of varying labor market "imperfections," we do know that it is possible to have heterogeneous labor and "products" among hospitals. Hospitals vary according to the availability of specialized facilities and services. In general, larger hospitals tend to have more specialized facilities and services, requiring more highly trained and, therefore, more highly paid personnel. Teaching hospitals also tend to offer more specialized facilities and services and, as such, hire more highly skilled personnel.

In her interviews with hospital administrators, Bishop (1974) found that wage contour groups, or orbits, were established based on geographical location (urban versus suburban), teaching orientation, size, and ownership (voluntary nonprofit, private for-profit, and government). Essentially, any factor that could differentiate the product, the quality of labor demanded, or the type of labor supplied,[15] defines the contour and, thus, the variation in wage rates among hospitals.

Data

The same individual hospital data were used for the computation of the V(W) for each SMSA and were used to capture the external wage structure:

$$V(W_i) = \sum_{j=1}^{n} (\ln W_i - \ln W_i^j)^2 / n \qquad (6)$$

i denotes either RNs, professionals, or nonprofessionals;[16] n is the number of hospitals in the SMSA; W_i is the average wage for the i-th occupational group in the SMSA; and W_i^j is the average wage for the i-th occupational group in the j-th hospital.

The average wage rate for each occupational group within a hospital (W_i^j) was computed by applying fixed occupational weights to the average wage rate of each occupation in the occupational group. Weighting each occupation according to the national distribution controls for potential differences in wage variation between SMSAs that are due to different occupational distributions. The average wage rate for an occupational group in an SMSA (W_i) was computed by assigning each W_i^j a weight of one.

Several independent variables were included. The unionization measure for each occupational group was constructed by assigning a value of 0 to those hospitals where no workers in that group were covered by a collective bargaining agreement, a value of 25 percent to those where a minority were covered, and a value of 75 percent to those where a majority were covered. These percentages were then multiplied times the number of employees in that hospital in the appropriate occupational group to yield an approximation of the percent of workers in the SMSA covered by a collective bargaining agreement.

Due to confidentiality requirements, the identity of individual hospitals is unknown. Therefore, it is not possible to control for certain factors that could influence the average wage rate paid by a hospital and, thus, the V(W) in an SMSA. One such factor that cannot be included is hospital location. Bishop (1974) found that location (urban versus suburban) had the strongest and most consistent effect in determining the wage contour.

We can construct SMSA variables, however, to control for the fact that SMSAs could have different mixes of hospital "type," where the different measures of type are thought to influence the V(W). Specifically, measures of the homogeneity of the SMSA hospital market are included. These measures are: hospital size, skill mix, and medical school affiliation.

The variance in the natural log of bed size (the number of beds in a hospital) was used to control for differences in hospital size. A small variance indicates a group of hospitals in the SMSA that are similar, regarding size. The variance in the natural log of the number of salaried personnel was used to control for differences in skill mix. Again, a smaller variance indicates a more homogeneous labor force. Data for both of these measures came from the AHA Guide to the Health Care Field, 1975. This guide gives the number of beds and the number of salaried personnel for all health-care institutions that are members of the AHA. For the construction of these two variables, data for private, short-term general service hospitals in each of the SMSAs were recorded.

The AHA Guide was also the source of data for the third variable. The Guide indicates whether each hospital is affiliated with a medical school. We computed the percent of salaried personnel in each SMSA working in a hospital with a medical school affiliation. Either a high or a low percent of workers in teaching hospitals would represent homogeneity among hospitals. In order to make this variable useful in controlling for differences in mix of hospital type, we utilized the fact that the percent of workers (p) is the probability that a worker is employed by a teaching hospital and is, therefore, the mean of the dummy variable (one if teaching, 0 otherwise) with a Bernoulli probability distribution. The variance of the dummy variable, therefore, is $p(1 - p)$. The variance takes on its maximum value if p equals 0.5 (potentially representing two separate wage contours), and its minimum value if p is either very small or very large (representing a set of hospitals homogeneous in teaching orientation).

Summary statistics for these variables are found in Table 14.7.

TABLE 14.7. Means and (Standard Deviations) of SMSA
Level Variables Used in External Wage
Structure Estimations

	1972	1975
$V(W)$[a]		
RNs	.0024	.0026
	(.0017)	(.0023)
Professionals	.0023	.0025
	(.0016)	(.0020)
Nonprofessionals	.0040	.0044
	(.0035)	(.0026)
UNION[b]		
Professionals	.100	.146
	(.156)	(.223)
Nonprofessionals	.164	.224
	(.182)	(.214)
BED[c]	.637	.655
	(.186)	(.194)
PERS[d]	.857	.882
	(.319)	(.326)
TEACH[e]	.207	.208
	(.046)	(.045)

[a]The variance of the natural log of mean occupational wages.

[b]The percent of hospital workers in the SMSA who
are covered by a collective bargaining agreement.

[c]The variance of the natural log of the number of
hospital beds.

[d]The variance of the natural log of the number of
salaried personnel.

[e]The index of similarity in teaching orientation.

Sources: V(W) and UNION computed from unpublished data gathered for the BLS Industry Wage Survey:
Hospitals. BED, PERS, and TEACH calculated from AHA
Guide to the Health Care Field, 1975; data for private,
short-term general service hospitals in each of the SMSAs
was used.

Model Specification

The impact of unionization on the V(W) of RNs, professionals, and nonprofessionals was estimated using cross-section regression analysis for private hospitals in over 20 SMSAs in 1972 and 1975. The estimation equation was specified as:

$$V(W_{ij}) = a_0 + b_1 UNION_{ij} + b_2 BED_j + b_3 PERS_j + b_4 TEACH_j + e \qquad (7)$$

where

i denotes the occupational group

j denotes the SMSA

$V(W_{ij})$ = the variance of the natural log of wages for the i-th occupational group in the j-th SMSA

$UNION_{ij}$ = the percent of workers in the i-th occupational group in the j-th SMSA, covered by a collective bargaining agreement

BED_j = the variance of the natural log of the number of hospital beds in the j-th SMSA

$PERS_j$ = the variance of the natural log of the number of salaried hospital personnel in the j-th SMSA

$TEACH_j$ = the index of similarity in teaching orientation among hospitals in the j-th SMSA

A second model will also be estimated, in which a refinement of the measure of unionization and its influence will be included:

$$V(W_{ij}) = a_0 + b_1 UNION_{ij} + b_2 BED_j + b_3 PERS_j + b_4 TEACH_j + b_5 ME_j + e$$
$$\qquad (5)$$

ME_j is a dummy variable indicating the presence of multiemployer bargaining in the SMSA. There are four multihospital bargaining situations in our particular sample: Minneapolis–St. Paul, New York City, San Francisco–Oakland, and Seattle.[17] This variable enables us to test the impact of centralized bargaining versus individual hospital bargaining on the uniformity of wage settlements.

It is hypothesized that, as the percent of hospital workers covered by a collective bargaining agreement increases, the variance of ln wages will decrease. This compression of the external wage structure is expected to come from two factors: the direct union effect, and the indirect "spillover" effect. As mentioned before, a major goal of a union is standardizing the wage rates paid by unionized hospitals within the orbit of coercive comparison. Therefore, a narrowing of the V(W) among unionized hospitals is expected. The larger the extent of unionized hospitals within an SMSA, the stronger the compression effect. In addition, wage rates in nonunion hospitals are expected to readjust to the union wage rate in an attempt to ward off unionization, due to worker-perceived wage rate inequities. The strength of this threat effect is hypothesized to vary directly with the extent of unionization.

Even without the spillover effects, a low level of SMSA unionization concentrated in hospitals that paid lower-than-average wage rates prior to unionization would lead to a narrowing of the external wage structure. However, a low level of unionization concentrated in hospitals that had already paid above average wage rates could lead to a widening of wage variation among hospitals if there was no spillover of these wage gains to nonunion hospitals. Unfortunately, there is no way for us to control for the "preunion" position of the hospitals in the wage contour.

The variance in ln beds, ln personnel, and teaching commitment are all measures of homogeneity. There is an expected positive relationship between homogeneity and uniform wage rates. These variables are included primarily as controls for possible differences between SMSAs in terms of the mix of hospital types.

As was discussed earlier, hospital administrators tend to look at other hospitals of similar size in forming wage contours. The smaller the variance in ln beds, the more homogeneous the market and, therefore, the smaller the V(W). It is also the case that a smaller variance of ln beds tends to be associated with a more competitive market (many firms of a similar size). A larger variance of ln beds would indicate a market composed of a few large firms and a few small firms.

Both employers and unions are expected to favor standard wage rates in a competitive market. The employer would not be able to pay more than the competitive wage rate in the long run. From the union perspective, if employers cannot be differentiated to permit price discrimination, "taking wages out of competition" through a single rate is a common strategy. Thus, we would expect a smaller variance in ln beds to be associated with a smaller variance in ln wages because of competitive forces.

Having controlled for variation in hospital bed size, the variance of ln personnel should represent different mixes of labor skills. Hospitals with relatively more personnel are able to hire a range of skill levels within each occupational group, promoting specialization of task. For example, they could hire RNs specifically trained for intensive care units, burn units, and so forth. As such we would expect a wider range of wage rates, reflecting the different internal wage structures.

Results

The results of estimating the models described above are shown in Tables 14.8 through 14.10. A major limitation of this data set is the small sample size. The small number of observations makes it difficult to get statistically significant results. This small sample problem could explain the result that, although always in the predicted direction, the union impact on the external wage structure is not often statistically significant.

In the case of RNs and professionals, once other factors that determine the V(W) are controlled, the degree of unionization has only a small compression effect. The degree of unionization does have a significant compression effect on the nonprofessional V(W) in both 1972 and 1975. This union effect decreases and becomes statistically insignificant, however, when the multihospital bargaining variable (ME = one if there is a multihospital bargaining unit) is included.

The inclusion of the multihospital bargaining variable has a very different effect in the case of RNs and professionals. In these groups, the union effect increases when ME is included. The SMSAs with consolidated bargaining have a significantly higher V(W), however, than SMSAs with individual bargaining or with no unionism. Rather than leading to wage uniformity, formal consolidated bargaining may be accompanied by a form of "wage drift." As mentioned earlier, Solomon (1980) found indication of this wage drift in his hospital interviews. Nonetheless, the result that multiemployer bargaining increases the V(W) does not appear reasonable.

Of the three variables controlling for mix of hospital types, the variance of ln beds had the strongest and most consistent effect. The negative effect is contrary to our expectations, however. As mentioned in Note 4, in hindsight, we realize that SMSA population size should have been included as a control variable. The omission of SMSA size potentially leads to a bias in the coefficient on the variance of ln beds.

There is a strong negative correlation between the variance of ln beds and SMSA size.[18] Review of the AHA Guide reveals that larger SMSAs tend to have a wide range of hospital sizes, with many small, medium, and large hospitals. Smaller SMSAs have a few larger hospitals and a few small hospitals and, therefore, a higher variance of ln beds. It is possible that, in the larger SMSAs, there are several wage contours differing by hospital type and location. The cost of obtaining information and of consolidation may lead to location being a more important determinant of the hospitals included in a contour.

In the smaller SMSAs, however, there may be only one wage contour encompassing the large and the small hospitals. The cost of obtaining information and of consolidation is much lower for both employers and workers than in a large SMSA.

TABLE 14.8. Results of External Wage Structure Estimations, RNs

| | 1972 | | 1975 | |
| | Model | | Model | |
	1	2	1	2
Dependent variable: Variance of ln wages				
Independent variables:				
CONSTANT	$.0060^a$	$.0060^a$	$.0053^b$	$.0044^b$
	(.0024)	(.0025)	(.0027)	(.0024)
UNION	-.0031	-.0031	-.0019	$-.0097^c$
	(.0024)	(.0048)	(.0020)	(.0037)
BED	$-.0082^a$	$-.0082^a$	$-.0099^a$	$-.0094^a$
	(.0038)	(.0039)	(.0046)	(.0041)
PERS	.0031	.0031	$.0048^b$	$.0048^b$
	(.0022)	(.0023)	(.0028)	(.0028)
TEACH	-.0036	-.0036	-.0007	.0037
	(.0084)	(.0089)	(.0100)	(.0090)
ME		.0000		$.0051^a$
		(.0018)		(.0021)
$\bar{R}^2$	.110	.051	.041	.242
S.E.E.	.0016	.0016	.0020	.0018
N	21	21	23	23
Mean value of V(W)		.0024		.0026

[a]Significant at .05 level.
[b]Significant at .10 level.
[c]Significant at .01 level.
Sources: V(W) and UNION computed from unpublished data gathered for the BLS Industry Wage Survey: Hospitals. BED, PERS, and TEACH calculated from AHA Guide to the Health Care Field, 1975; data for private, short-term general service hospitals in each of the SMSAs was used.

TABLE 14.9. Results of External Wage Structure Estimation, Professionals

	1972 Model		1975 Model	
	1	2	1	2

Dependent variable: Variance of ln wages

Independent variables:

CONSTANT	$.0061^a$	$.0060^b$	$.0058^b$	$.0050^c$
	(.0021)	(.0024)	(.0027)	(.0025)
UNION	-.0026	-.0031	-.0017	$-.0097^b$
	(.0023)	(.0045)	(.0020)	(.0039)
BED	$-.0076^b$	$-.0075^c$	-.0056	-.0050
	(.0036)	(.0038)	(.0047)	(.0042)
PERS	.0023	.0022	.0021	.0020
	(.0022)	(.0022)	(.0028)	(.0025)
TEACH	-.0033	-.0031	-.0062	-.0025
	(.0081)	(.0085)	(.0100)	(.0092)
ME		.0002		$.0052^b$
		(.0017)		(.0022)
$\bar{R}^2$	.120	.063	-.068	.142
S.E.E.	.0016	.0016	.0020	.0018
N	21	21	23	23
Mean value of V(W)		.0023		.0025

[a] Significant at .01 level.
[b] Significant at .05 level.
[c] Significant at .10 level.
Sources: V(W) and UNION computed from unpublished data gathered for the BLS Industry Wage Survey: Hospitals. BED, PERS, and TEACH calculated from AHA Guide to the Health Care Field, 1975; data for private, short-term general service hospitals in each of the SMSAs was used.

TABLE 14.10. Results of External Wage Structure Estimation, Nonprofessionals

	1972 Model		1975 Model	
	1	2	1	2

Dependent variable: Variance of ln wages

Independent variables:

CONSTANT	$.0112^a$	$.0110^a$	$.0117^b$	$.0113^b$
	(.0044)	(.0046)	(.0037)	(.0038)
UNION	$-.0066^c$	$-.0050$	$-.0051^c$	$-.0037$
	(.0037)	(.0052)	(.0026)	(.0034)
BED	$-.0166^a$	$-.0170^a$	$-.0105^c$	$-.0109^c$
	(.0068)	(.0070)	(.0057)	(.0058)
PERS	.0030	.0034	.0039	.0042
	(.0040)	(.0042)	(.0034)	(.0035)
TEACH	.0092	.0096	$-.0134$	$-.0122$
	(.0149)	(.0153)	(.0122)	(.0125)
ME		$-.0010$		$-.0012$
		(.0024)		(.0018)
$\bar{R}^2$	.337	.302	.109	.079
S.E.E.	.0029	.0030	.0024	.0025
N	21	21	23	23
Mean value of V(W)	.0040		.0044	

[a] Significant at .05 level.
[b] Significant at .01 level.
[c] Significant at .10 level.

Sources: V(W) and UNION computed from unpublished data gathered for the BLS Industry Wage Survey: Hospitals. BED, PERS, and TEACH calculated from AHA Guide to the Health Care Field, 1975; data for private, short-term general service hospitals in each of the SMSAs was used.

Thus, we may have a situation in which the omitted variable, SMSA size, is positively correlated with the V(W) and negatively correlated with the included variable, the variance of ln beds. It is possible, under these circumstances, for the biased estimate of the variance of ln beds coefficient to be of the opposite sign from the "true" value. An obvious avenue for future research is the inclusion of SMSA size.

Although very small, the effect of skill mix, as measured by the variance of ln personnel, was positive, as predicted. Teaching involvement does not appear to be a significant factor in determining the V(W).

CONCLUSIONS

It has been suggested that unions influence both the internal and the external wage structures. This influence comes about primarily through job and wage comparisons made by workers. Worker-perceived inequities, in terms of unequal pay for jobs of similar skill and difficulty or in terms of occupational wage differentials that do not reflect the relative skill and difficulty of the occupations, are thought to be eliminated either through collective bargaining or through the threat of unionization. As pointed out, several researchers have looked into the role that hospital unions have had in changing the internal and external wage structures of hospitals.

Using unpublished 1972 and 1975 BLS data, the variance of mean occupational wages within each hospital (internal wage structure) and the variance of mean wages for an occupational group across all hospitals in an SMSA (external wage structure) were calculated. These variances were then regressed on measures of unionization and other control variables to analyze the impact of hospital unions on the internal and external wage structures.

The results do not present a consistent picture of how unions are affecting the internal wage structure. The estimated impact was rarely statistically significant. In the cases in which the impact was significant, the impact was sometimes positive and sometimes negative.

Unions apparently have had a weak wage-rate standardization impact on the external wage structure. The impact of unionization on the variance of mean wages in an SMSA for each occupational group was negative but not often statistically significant. Without controlling for multiemployer bargaining, the union impact was significant only for nonprofessionals. With controls for multiemployer bargaining, the union impact was significantly negative for both RNs and professionals in 1975.

The relatively small size of the effect of unionization can be the result of several factors. One, unions may not have been successful in standardizing wage rates across hospitals. Second, we have a small sample size. And, finally, those hospitals in SMSAs in which there exists a large variation in wage rates may be more likely to become unionized due to worker-perceived inequities. Thus, unionization is not exogenous as specified, rather it may be endogenous, in part determined by the existing external wage structure. The most important determinant of wage uniformity in SMSAs, however, was the variance of ln beds. It was suggested that this variable may actually be capturing the effect of SMSA size on the V(W).

Bishop (1974) suggests that "changes in hospital wage setting practices were responsible at least in part for the hospital wage increases of the last decade" (p. 206) in the United States. This suggestion stems in part from her observation that, in Boston hospitals, pressure from unions, or the threat of unionization, to move toward both external and internal wage equity results in wages being adjusted up to more equitable relations, never downward. Our results, using national data, do not indicate that unions have played a significant role in these adjustments.

It should be noted that these results are exploratory in nature. Individual hospital data limitations prevented the inclusion of product and labor market factors, which could influence the intrahospital variance of mean occupational wages, and prevented the inclusion of personal worker characteristics that could influence the interhospital variance of wages.

NOTES

1. See Bishop (1974) for a case study of these changes.
2. See Miller (1980).
3. For discussions concerning the internal wage structure, see Livernash (1957), Douty (1963), and Hildebrand (1963); for the external wage structure, see Ross (1948) and (1957), and Dunlop (1957).
4. For example, SMSA population size should have been included as a control variable in the external wage structure equation. Apparently, the size of the SMSA defines both the size of the market and the homogeneity of hospital size and influences the variation in wage rates due to the presence of more people and, therefore, more diversification of skill. Consequently, the estimate of the influence of hospital homogeneity is biased.
5. See Doeringer and Piore (1971) for an extended treatment of this perspective.

6. Bishop (1974), Metzer and Pointer (1972), and Denton (1976) all discuss the lack of both lateral and upward mobility in hospitals.

7. For a review of these influences, see Douty (1963), Hildebrand (1963), and Freeman (1980b).

8. See Livernash (1957) and Bishop (1974) for examples of studies using this technique.

9. Sloan and Steinwald point out that this interpretation is subject to regression fallacy but that they rejected this possibility. Unfortunately, they do not give the reader an explanation of this decision.

10. See Atkinson (1970) and Berne (1978) for a discussion of several measures of income inequality and their properties.

11. According to a 1976 AHA survey, as reported in Frenzen (1978), 12 percent of small (6-99 beds) hospitals had one or more collective bargaining agreements, 26 percent of moderate (100-399) size had one or more, and 50 percent of large (400 or more) hospitals had one or more.

12. According to calculations by McLaughlin (1980), using BLS Industry Wage Survey: Hospitals, the average wage for medical technologists was $4.54 in 1972 and $5.79 in 1975, versus $3.93 and $5.11 for x-ray technologists, and $4.50 and $5.62 for registered nurses.

13. See Cain et al. (1981) for estimates of the union impact on average wages. Using the BLS data from which these V(W) were calculated, they estimated a large positive spillover effect in 1975, from nonprofessional unionization to the average professional wage.

14. Cain et al. found that in 1972, unionization had a significant positive effect on the average professional wage and that professional unionization had a significant negative impact on the average nonprofessional wage. These results would agree with the conclusion that professional unions were able to make relative wage gains in 1972.

15. For example, hospital administrators indicated to Bishop that in suburban hospitals there was a higher proportion of married RN job applicants looking for part-time work. In urban teaching hospitals, most of the RN job applicants were young RNs seeking professional advancements and prestige (p. 30).

16. In the case of professionals, the three occupations included in 1972 were RNs, medical technologists, and x-ray technologists. Five occupations were included in the nonprofessional group: ward clerks, licensed practical nurses (LPNs), nursing aides, kitchen helpers, and cleaners. In 1975, BLS changed the classification of LPNs to professionals, so that four occupations were included in the professional group and four in the nonprofessional group.

17. This information was obtained in Solomon (1980).

18. The correlation was -.423 in 1972 and -.473 in 1975, both significantly different from 0 at the .03 level.

REFERENCES

American Hospital Association. Guide to the Health Care Field. Chicago, 1975.

Atkinson, A. B. 1970. "On the Measurement of Inequality." Journal of Economic Theory, 2, pp. 244-63.

Berne, Robert. 1978. "Alternative Equity and Equality Measures: Does the Measure Make a Difference." From Selected Papers in School Finance: 1978, DHEW, pp. 1-56.

Bishop, Christine E. 1974. "Hospital Wage Structure in the Greater Boston Labor Market." Unpublished Ph.D. dissertation, Harvard University.

Cain, Glen G., Brian E. Becker, Catherine G. McLaughlin, and Albert E. Schwenk. 1981. "The Effect of Unions on Wages in Hospitals." In Research in Labor Economics, edited by Ronald G. Ehrenberg. Greenwich, Conn.: JAI Press.

Denton, David R. 1976. "The Union Movement in American Hospitals: 1847-1976." Unpublished Ph.D. dissertation, Boston University.

Doeringer, Peter B. 1973. "Explorations in Low Pay, Collective Bargaining, and Economic Mobility." Unpublished mimeograph. Cambridge, Mass.

_____ and Michael Piore. 1971. Internal Labor Markets and Manpower Analysis. Lexington, Mass.: D. C. Heath.

Douty, H. M. 1963. "The Impact of Trade Unionism on Internal Wage Structures." In Internal Wage Structure, edited by J. L. Meij, pp. 222-59. Amsterdam: North-Holland.

Dunlop, John T. 1957. "The Task of Contemporary Wage Theory." In New Concepts of Wage Determination, edited by George W. Taylor and Frank C. Pierson, pp. 117-39. New York: McGraw-Hill.

Freeman, Richard B. 1980a. "Union Wage Practices and Wage Dispersion within Establishments." Unpublished manuscript, Harvard University.

____. 1980b. "Unionism and the Dispersion of Wages." Industrial and Labor Relations Review, 34, pp. 3-23.

Frenzen, Paul D. 1978. "Survey Update: Unionization Activities." Hospital: The Journal of the American Hospital Association, 52, p. 94.

Hildebrand, George H. 1963. "External Influences and the Determination of the Internal Wage Structure." In Internal Wage Structure, edited by J. L. Meij, pp. 260-99. Amsterdam: North-Holland.

Livernash, E. Robert. 1957. "The Internal Wage Structure." In New Concepts of Wage Determination, edited by George W. Taylor and Frank C. Pierson, pp. 140-72. New York: McGraw-Hill.

McLaughlin, Catherine G. 1980. "The Impact of Unions on Hospital Wages." Unpublished Ph.D. dissertation, University of Wisconsin-Madison.

Metzer, Norman, and Dennis D. Pointer. 1972. Labor Management Practices in the Health Services Industry: Theory and Practice. Washington, D.C.: Science and Health Publications.

Miller, Richard U. 1980. "Hospitals." In Collective Bargaining: Contemporary American Experience, edited by G. G. Somers, pp. 373-434. Madison, Wis.: Industrial Relations Research Association Series.

Ross, Arthur M. 1957. "The External Wage Structure." In New Concepts in Wage Determination, edited by George W. Taylor and Frank C. Pierson. New York: McGraw-Hill.

____. 1948. Trade Union Wage Policy. Berkeley: University of California Press.

Sloan, Frank, and Bruce Steinwald. 1980. Hospital Labor Markets. Lexington, Mass.: D. C. Heath.

Solomon, Norman A. 1980. "The Emergence of Multiple Employer Bargaining in the Nonprofit Hospital Sector: An Exploratory Analysis." Unpublished Ph.D. dissertation, University of Wisconsin-Madison.

U.S. Bureau of Labor Statistics. "Industry Wage Survey." Bulletin 1829, 1972, and Bulletin 1949, 1975.

15

PRIVATE FUNDING FOR MEDICAL RESEARCH: THE PERFORMANCE OF NONPROFIT CHARITIES

Susan Feigenbaum

As an increasing share of this nation's resources is devoted to the health-care needs of its population, there has been growing interest in the relative efficiency of alternative institutions as providers of this care.[1] However, little of this increased scrutiny of the health-care sector has been directed toward the performance of institutions that support medical research activities,[2] despite the fact that medical research expenditures grew more than twice as fast as overall health expenditures during the period, 1950 to 1978.[3]

This chapter presents evidence on the performance of one type of institution involved in the provision of medical research activities—the nonprofit, or voluntary, medical research charity. During the decade of the seventies, the share of national health research support attributable to these organizations declined significantly due to a rapid expansion in government support for biomedical research (see Appendix); however, with the advent of federal budget cuts, the eighties promises to see renewed interest in the role of nonprofit charities as alternative providers of medical research funding.

The first part of this study presents a model of nonprofit firm (charity) behavior and its predictions concerning the relationship between nonprofit market structure and the activities of nonprofit firms. We examine the impact of firm age, size, membership in joint collection agencies (such as the United Way), and degree of market competition on the allocation of revenues by medical research charities to administration, fund raising, and, finally, medical research projects.

The author gratefully acknowledges research support from the Haynes Foundation and the Center for the Study of Law Structures. Burton Weisbrod and Ross Eckert provided helpful comments on earlier drafts of this chapter.

The second part discusses two approaches to defining nonprofit markets and uses both of these methods to delineate the medical research charity industry. Utilizing this industry definition and firm data from two independent sources, we present an overview of the structure of the medical research charity industry—firm size and age distributions and degree of competition for donations nationally and in selected communities. The third part of the chapter utilizes this evidence to estimate the parameters of various industry structure–performance relationships implied by our theory of nonprofit firm behavior. An econometric analysis of both cross-section and time-series financial data for a sample of medical research charities sheds light on the significance of various firm characteristics in explaining variations in the expenditure patterns of medical research charities. Evidence pertaining to one specific policy question, whether joint charity collection agencies improve or retard the flow-through of charity dollars to medical research by restraining competitive fund-raising activities of member organizations,[4] will also be presented.

A MODEL OF NONPROFIT FIRM (CHARITY) BEHAVIOR

In order to understand the behavior of organizations operating within the nonprofit sector,[5] it is necessary to consider both the rationale for nonprofit regulation (the demand for nonprofit outputs) and the response of firms to this zero-profit constraint[6] (the supply of nonprofit outputs). Our model of nonprofit firm behavior incorporates both of these aspects in its attempt to describe the decision-making process of a wide variety of nonprofit organizations, including hospitals, legal and health clinics, and medical research charities. This theory of nonprofit regulation and firm behavior focuses on a situation where information is not uniformly distributed across producers and consumers but, rather, where producers face lower costs in ascertaining the quality of goods and services than do their consumers. In such a situation, we say that there exists asymmetry in information.

Earlier analyses of the impact of asymmetric information on the workings of the market (Akerlof 1970) have argued that when many grades of a good or service exist, and when consumers cannot discriminate among them prior to purchase, high quality goods will be competed out of the market by goods of the lowest quality. However, when consumers can ascertain the quality of a product through purchase and subsequent consumption/experience of the good,[7] mechanisms such as brand name capital, producer liability, and product guarantees allow consumers to act before their purchase as if they had satisfactory information about product quality. More specifically, consumer demand for a good will reflect the quality level that producers promise rather than some expected level of quality in the market (thereby allowing higher quality goods and services to successfully compete) because these mechanisms will impose costs on the producer if consumers find, after purchase, that quality promises were fraudulent. [8]

In our analysis of nonprofit markets, we suggest that there is consumer uncertainty about quality not only before but after the purchase of nonprofit outputs, and it is this asymmetry in information after purchase that can lead to either suboptimal quality or fraud. [9] When purchase of a product does not by itself confer adequate information about quality and when the cost of supplemental information to assume that quality promises are truthful is high (relative to the value of the good to the consumer), consumers will be forced to either adopt the same demand schedule for every (undiscernible) grade of output in the market or "trust" producer quality promises and risk the possibility of fraud.

Asymmetric information after purchase is characteristic of goods and services provided by much of the nonprofit sector. The collective consumption, third-party transaction, and/or option-demand attributes of these outputs mean that purchase and subsequent experience will not convey the usual information about product quality, leaving consumers to face high information costs even after they have made their purchases. Charities engage in third-party transactions for which the recipient of the charity differs from the purchaser of the redistribution service (the donor); in the case of medical research charities, there are also collective consumption- and option-demand aspects, since these organizations support research that satisfies collective option demands for medical technology in the event of future illness. Here, the usual sources of consumer information after purchase—inspection, consumption, and control—are lacking to the degree that it is costly for the purchaser (donor) to communicate with the recipient (the medical researcher) and/or exercise the option provided by the service.

Since consumers find it costly to discriminate between high- and low-quality charities (we might define such "quality" in terms of the amount of funds redistributed to the charity's purported recipients[10]), they can either donate to charities indiscriminately or "trust" the promises of specific charity collectors. An alternative to this dilemma is to employ a "monitor" who can detect and/or limit fraud in these markets. Often the government is cast in this monitoring role and, as such, utilizes various types of producer regulation to assure consumers that the quality of a good or service will be maximized for any given price (revenue) level. [11] For charities that engage in redistributional activities we might translate this objective into the maximization of revenue flowing to recipients per dollar of contribution.

One means of government regulation, nonprofit financial regulation, attempts to minimize the degree to which producers can increase their private utility at the expense of higher output quality by severely limiting the ways in which this utility can be acquired. These regulations prohibit the disbursement of reported profits, limit compensation for factors of production to reasonable (market) returns, and require "arms-length" interaction between nonprofit organizations and affiliated for-profit enterprises. Because the government can institute firm reporting requirements and exercise its subpoena powers to overcome a firm's monopoly over production information such as its financial accounts, consumers expect that nonprofit regulation will be successful in constraining producers to satisfy their quality promises. If the Internal Revenue Service (I.R.S.) is successful in restricting firm expenditures to their minimum efficient level (through the monitoring of firm financial accounts) and can ensure that all net income is spent on the tax-exempt purpose of the firm, then it will force producers to maximize the quality of firm output for any given revenue level. Thus, we suggest that consumers perceive a lower expected loss from believing the quality promises of nonprofit organizations because such firms are subject to government financial regulation. As a result, producers benefit from the award of nonprofit status by appearing more trustworthy to consumers; we can view this award of nonprofit status as an investment in the "trust capital" of the firm.

In reality, the effectiveness of financial regulation depends upon the government's ability to restrain the disbursement of reported profits and to monitor transactions according to a standard of "reasonableness." Unless the government can ascertain the true opportunity cost of factors required to supply a product or service of a given quality, producers will still be able to trade off quality for profits and to appropriate at least a portion of these profits through expense-preference behavior.[12]

Our model of nonprofit firm behavior assumes that nonprofit decision-makers engage in an "optimal" level of fraud,[13] reducing product or service quality as much as is possible without detection by either the consumer or the government regulator, thereby lowering firm production costs while continuing to face the same demand schedule for their services. The resulting gap between the minimum cost of producing at the quality level promised to the consumer (and reflected in the revenue schedule facing the firm) and the minimum cost of producing the actual output of the firm provides the nonprofit producer with a "discretionary budget,"[14] to be allocated to nonproduction activities. We define:

discretionary budget = $C(Q;0;\psi) - C(Q;\alpha;\psi)$

where:

α is an index of consumer information costs about product quality,
defined to increase as these costs increase $(0 \le \alpha \le 1)$

ψ is an index of the stringency of government regulation, defined to
increase as regulation becomes more stringent $(0 \le \psi \le 1)$[15]

For any given level of output or service demanded (Q), a non-profit producer's discretionary budget will increase as consumer information costs (α) increase and decrease as I.R.S. regulation becomes more stringent (that is, as ψ increases). However, the size of the producer's discretionary budget may increase or decrease with demand (Q), depending on whether consumer information or stringency of regulation varies with the size of the firm.[16]

We suggest that the discretionary budget of the nonprofit decision-maker will be spent not only on expense preference activities, which yield pecuniary and nonpecuniary returns, but on marketing activities (fund raising in the case of charities) that generate a given level of demand for their services. These marketing activities become the primary form of competition among nonprofit firms because neither price nor quality competition is feasible in markets where consumers cannot evaluate product quality at low cost.[17] As a result, competitive activities in the nonprofit sector take the form of marketing techniques, including solicitation, advertising, and public relations campaigns. These activities lower the cost to individuals of making purchases (for example, donating money for redistribution to medical researchers) by identifying the providers of specific goods and services (advertising) and bringing the firm to the consumer (solicitation). They may also increase the degree to which consumers trust one producer versus another to fulfill quality promises, by conveying a sense of establishment and familiarity. Thus, marketing costs can be viewed as investments in trust capital for the firm, which supplement the trust capital provided by I.R.S. nonprofit status.

While every nonprofit organization faces a marketing cost schedule that dictates the expenditure required to generate any given level of demand, this schedule need not be the same across firms, even for those producing within the same nonprofit market. In fact, this schedule will vary across firms in the same nonprofit industry according to: (1) the amount of previous firm investment in trust capital (reputation), and (2) the relative efficiency of a firm in marketing its services and producing any given level of trust capital. This relative efficiency may stem either from monopoly control over a specific selling technique or from lower input costs into the marketing process. The first source of marketing efficiency is exemplified by the monopoly that United Way has on employer withholding arrangements, while the second is typified by reduced advertising charges for nonprofit firms that the media decide serve in the "public interest."

Given the constraints placed on nonprofit firm behavior by consumer information, I.R.S. regulation, and the presence of competition, we can view the nonprofit entrepreneur's decision as two separable processes: first, the producer maximizes the real profits of the organization, and, second, he appropriates these profits by expense preference behavior.[18] We denote this two-step decision process as:

$$\text{Maximize } R(Q) - C(Q;\alpha;\psi) - M(Q;CMP) \qquad (1)$$
$$Q$$

$$\underset{x_1, \ldots, x_n; S}{\text{Maximize } U(x_1, x_2, \ldots, x_n; S)} \qquad (2)$$

subject to:

$$\sum p_i x_i \leq R(Q) - C(Q;\alpha;\psi) - M(Q;CMP)$$

where:

$R(Q)$ is the gross revenue function of the organization, specified to be a positive function of output; this revenue schedule will depend upon consumer demand for the firm's services at its promised (not actual) quality level.

$C(Q;\alpha;\psi)$ is the schedule of minimum production costs for the firm's actual output (rather than the possibly higher quality output promised to consumers); it is specified to be a positive function of output and the stringency of regulation (ψ) and a negative function of consumer information costs (α).

$M(Q;CMP)$ is the firm's marketing cost function, representing competition costs incurred by the nonprofit firm in order to maintain any given level of demand (holding assumed quality constant); it is specified to increase with the level of demand generated and with the level of competition in the market.

x_i is an activity, good, or service that generates nonpecuniary returns to the nonprofit decision maker.[19]

p_i is the opportunity cost of x_i in terms of foregone real profits of the firm.

S is salary per unit time for the nonprofit decision-maker.

As long as nonprofit decision-makers receive pecuniary and nonpecuniary returns that exceed their opportunity costs, entry into the nonprofit sector will occur.[20] This entry will reduce the real profits of nonprofit firms by shifting up their marketing schedules, $M(\cdot)$. However, this competition will not eliminate inframarginal rents accruing to firms with superior production and/or marketing schedules: in long-run equilibrium, only the marginal firm will spend all of its profits in excess of a normal return on marketing activities. Thus, increases in competition cause the nonprofit producer to spend an increasing portion of his discretionary budget on competitive activities rather than on activities that increase his personal utility.

An important implication of our theory of nonprofit behavior is that the amount of firm revenue devoted to the tax-exempt purpose of the organization $[C(Q;\alpha;\psi)]$ is not directly affected by the degree of market competition. Hence, increased competition for revenues will result in greater firm expenditures on output quality only if such expenditures can be used as a marketing tool to improve a firm's public image or to increase its visibility (by attracting favorable publicity). In such a situation, the marketing expenditures of the organization—$M(Q;CMP)$—would serve to augment the allocation of revenues to output quality mandated by consumer information and government scrutiny. If, for example, philanthropies can use recipients of charity dollars to promote the organization's reputation, then increased competition for donations may have a significant impact on the level of benefits accruing to such recipients. In such situations where competition improves upon output quality, policy-makers will be able to promote efficiency in nonprofit markets by concentrating either on policies that increase nonprofit market competition or on information-generating activities, depending on the relative cost of each approach.

Implications for the Performance of Medical Research Charities

Our theory of nonprofit regulation and firm behavior suggests that the proportion of medical research charity revenues spent on the actual "production" of medical research—$C(Q;\alpha;\psi)/R(Q)$—will be dictated by the degree of consumer information on the charity's allocation of its donations and by the stringency of I.R.S. financial regulation. These determinants of research allocations may vary even across charities competing in the same market if, for example, they vary with the size of the organization.

Revenues retained by the charity, which are not allocated to medical research, constitute a discretionary budget for the charity's decision-makers. This budget will be devoted to both marketing (fundraising) activities and expense preference activities that yield utility to the charity's directors. The degree to which this discretionary budget is allocated to fund raising versus expense preference activities will vary directly with the intensity of intramarket competition for funds. Furthermore, we might expect that the extent to which marginal increases in the discretionary budget are devoted to fund raising versus expense preference activities will depend on the size of the firm; this would the case if there were economies of scale exhibited by the marketing cost schedule ($[\partial^2 M(\cdot)]/\partial Q^2 < 0$). These economies of scale may stem from the fixed costs required to establish a reputation or gain consumer loyalty (acquisitions of trust capital). If such economies in marketing do indeed exist within certain ranges of firm size, then the proportion of medical research charity revenues allocated to fundraising expenditures would vary with the size of the organization.

Additional variation in the fund-raising expenditures of charities of similar size will result from differences in current levels of trust capital (reputation) and in fund-raising efficiency. One index of a charity's accumulated trust capital might be its age, which reflects the degree of establishment of the organization. If the reputation of a charity is closely linked to this degree of establishment, then our model predicts that the proportion of charity revenues devoted to fundraising activities will decrease as charities grow older.[21]

Differences in input costs and monopoly control over specific selling techniques will also cause fund-raising costs to vary across charities of similar size. The United Way, for example, provides its members with superior marketing techniques by sharing its monopoly on employee withholding arrangements. It has been argued (Fisher 1977) that members of joint collection agencies benefit from economies of scale in fund raising realized by the "umbrella" organization. Members may also benefit when potential competitors for donations belong to the same umbrella organization; this organization may coordinate competitive activities and enforce cartel restrictions on the amount of resources devoted by charities to such competition. Smith (1977) notes that "member organizations have been willing to relinquish virtually all public fundraising campaigns of their own in order to participate in the United Way campaigns in various localities." Thus, there is more than one reason to expect that membership in an umbrella marketing organization will increase the relative fund-raising efficiency of medical research charities. We would predict, therefore, that charities belonging to joint fund-raising agencies devote less of their revenue to marketing than do nonmembers of similar size.

Since our model of nonprofit firm behavior postulates that both marketing and expense preference activities are financed out of the nonprofit decision-maker's discretionary budget, it implies that a decrease in the amount of revenue spent on fund raising will be accompanied by an increase in expenditures on expense preference activities. Thus, if members of umbrella organizations incur lower fund-raising costs than nonmembers, they should spend proportionately more on expense preference activities. Their expenditures on medical research should be no different than nonmembers of similar size, unless the umbrella organization itself acts as a monitor of the quality of its members' services.

STRUCTURE OF THE MEDICAL RESEARCH CHARITY INDUSTRY

In order to test whether such structural variables as firm size, age, membership in an umbrella organization, and market competition for funds have an impact upon medical research charity revenue allocations, we must first define the medical research charity "industry" and identify organizations that act in direct competition with one another. One alternative is to define the industry to include all tax-exempt firms that identify medical research funding as their primary activity on annual financial statements filed with the I. R. S. [22] Such organizations are indeed "nonprofit" in that they are subject to profit distribution constraints. Given this definition of the industry, the local medical research charity, regardless of national affiliation, becomes the relevant unit of analysis. Such an approach is desirable if we believe that, as in the case of hospitals, medical research charities act within the confines of specific geographic markets. Alternatively, we can define the medical research charity industry to include firms that have been designated as national voluntary health philanthropies by the National Information Bureau (NIB), a monitor of philanthropic activities. This approach aggregates the local and national activities of charities and considers this aggregate organization as the relevant unit of analysis. In situations in which firm interaction takes place on a national rather than a local level, this latter definition of the industry would appear to be preferable. [23]

Since the appropriateness of each of these definitions of the medical research charity industry hinges crucially on assumptions about the relevant geographic market for medical research charities, we will examine both I. R. S. –designated local charities and NIB-designated national philanthropies, independently, in an effort to shed light on industry structure and performance. Our analysis of local market activity will be limited to charities in seven major metropolitan areas—Chicago, Dallas, New York, Philadelphia, St. Louis, Los Angeles, and San Francisco.

The Size Distribution of Medical Research Charities

During the 1970s, local medical research charity activities were dominated by a small proportion of firms that accounted for a large share of industry revenues and assets. In Table 15.1, we see that in the 7 geographic markets (from 1974 to 1977), approximately 90 percent of total medical research charity revenues accrued to the 10 to 12 percent of local organizations with over 1.5 million dollars in annual revenues. While this degree of concentration remained relatively constant over the 4-year period, total and average revenue of firms in these markets exhibited significant variability during the same period. After realizing increases in both total and average firm revenues between 1974 and 1976, the industry suffered a significant decline in its overall size and average firm size (a decline of 58 percent and 34 percent, respectively) in 1977.[24] If we look at the distribution of assets[25] for the same firms (see Table 15.2), we find that these assets are even more highly concentrated than industry revenues: approximately 5 to 6 percent of local charities (those with at least $5 million in assets) accounted for 80 to 90 percent of total assets reported for the 7 local markets in 1974-77. As in the case of industry revenues, the degree of concentration of assets changed only slightly between 1974 and 1977, despite first an increase and then a significant decrease in total and average firm assets. The issues of firm market shares and industry concentration will be considered again when we examine the extent of competition in these local markets.

In terms of real dollars, the decline in the local medical research charity industry and the average size of local charities between 1974 and 1977 has been dramatic.[26] The 40 percent decline in total nominal revenues and assets between 1974 and 1977 translates into a 54 percent decline in real dollars, while the 2 percent increase in average firm revenues and virtually constant average firm assets correspond to an approximate 20 percent decline in average firm purchasing power.

In contrast to the above trends in average firm size for local charities, Table 15.3 indicates that national medical research charities reporting to the NIB enjoyed constant growth in their nominal revenues between 1974 and 1978. These national organizations, with annual revenues ranging from $224,000 (Parkinson's Disease Foundation)

TABLE 15.1. Local Medical Research Charities and Their Total Reported Revenues, by Revenue Class (Aggregated over 7 SMSAs, 1974-77)

Total Revenue (in current dollars)	1974		1975		1976		1977	
	(percentage of firms, percentage of revenues)							
Under $10,000[a]	14.4	0.1	9.5	0.0	4.0	0.0	0.0	0.0
$10,000-24,999	17.4	0.2	15.5	0.1	15.5	0.1	17.6	0.2
$25,000-49,999	11.1	0.2	12.8	0.2	13.8	0.2	14.8	0.3
$50,000-99,999	11.9	0.5	12.9	0.4	14.2	0.4	12.6	0.6
$100,000-249,999	16.1	1.5	17.0	1.1	16.8	1.0	19.5	1.9
$250,000-749,999	13.6	3.5	14.8	2.8	16.7	2.9	16.3	4.2
$750,000-1,499,999	4.9	3.1	5.2	2.4	5.8	2.4	7.4	4.5
$1,500,000 and over	10.6	90.9	12.3	93.0	13.2	93.0	11.8	88.3
Total revenue	$1,777,000,000		$2,274,000,000		$2,506,000,000		$1,044,000,000	
Average revenue	1,688,000		2,366,000		2,578,000		1,715,000	
Standard deviation	9,075,091		11,960,000		13,010,000		11,490,000	
Number of firms reporting[b]	1053		961		972		609	

[a]Beginning in 1977, firms with less than $10,000 receipts were not required to file I.R.S. financial statements.

[b]The number of firms reporting may vary in the following tables due to the omission of firms with missing tax return entries for the statistics in question.

Source: Compiled by the author.

TABLE 15.2. Local Medical Research Charities and Their Total Reported Assets, by Asset Class
(Aggregated over 7 SMSAs, 1974-77)

Total Assets (in current dollars)	1974		1975		1976		1977	
	(percentage of firms, percentage of assets)							
Under $10,000	24.1	0.0	20.2	0.0	15.3	0.0	13.3	0.0
$10,000-49,999	24.4	0.4	24.3	0.2	24.3	0.2	22.7	0.3
$50,000-99,999	13.0	0.5	13.5	0.4	13.2	0.3	11.4	0.4
$100,000-249,999	13.2	1.2	12.5	0.8	15.9	0.9	18.6	1.3
$250,000-499,999	8.5	1.5	8.9	1.2	9.3	1.2	10.9	2.2
$500,000-999,999	5.2	1.8	6.5	1.7	6.6	1.6	8.2	2.9
$1,000,000-1,999,999	3.4	2.4	4.1	2.2	4.7	2.3	5.6	4.0
$2,000,000-4,999,999	2.9	4.8	3.3	4.3	4.0	4.4	5.1	8.2
$5,000,000-9,999,999	1.6	5.6	1.9	5.4	1.9	5.0	2.0	7.6
$10,000,000-49,999,999	2.8	30.7	3.5	27.2	3.5	26.7	1.6	18.5
$50,000,000 and over	0.9	51.1	1.3	56.6	1.3	57.4	0.6	54.6
Total assets	$2,105,438,000		$2,511,584,300		$2,781,263,100		$1,205,559,000	
Average assets	1,993,786		2,632,688		2,876,177		1,986,094	
Standard deviation	12,977,903		15,390,069		16,883,039		16,997,196	
Number of firms reporting	1056		954		967		607	

Source: Compiled by the author.

TABLE 15.3. National Medical Research Charity Revenues
(Largest Organizations, 1974-78)

	1974	1978
	(in thousands of current dollars)	
American Cancer Society	108,135	139,745
American Heart Association	67,548	86,993
National Foundation (March of Dimes)	50,825	68,490
American Lung Association	45,268	50,984
United Cerebral Palsy Associations	33,540	76,201
Muscular Dystrophy Association	27,614	68,502
National Multiple Sclerosis Society	13,762	26,061
Arthritis Foundation	12,280	19,903
Leukemia Society of America	7,531	10,824
Cystic Fibrosis Foundation	7,009	11,317
American Foundation for the Blind	6,024	8,689
American Diabetes Association	5,156	11,250
National Kidney Foundation	4,570	7,778
Damon Runyon-Walter Winchell Cancer Fund	2,412	2,587
Juvenile Diabetes Foundation	504	2,725

Source: National Information Bureau, Wise Giving Bulletin, 1976-80.

to over $139 million (American Cancer Society) in 1978, realized between 7 and 440 percent increases in annual nominal revenues from 1974 to 1978. In general, the smaller national organizations enjoyed significantly greater growth in nominal revenues than did the largest national charities; in fact, in terms of real dollars, several of the largest organizations suffered a decline in annual receipts between 1974 and 1978.

Competition in the Medical Research Charity Industry

Just as the extent of competition affects firm behavior in the for-profit sector, so, we have argued above, does the degree of competition influence nonprofit organization behavior. In order to assess the extent of intraindustry competition, two measures—the four-firm concentration ratio and the Herfindahl Index—have been relied upon

TABLE 15.4. Medical Research Charity Industry Four-Firm
Concentration Ratios, by SMSA (1974-77)

SMSA	1974	1975	1976	1977
(1) Chicago	41.81	40.73	41.41	63.77
(2) Dallas-Ft. Worth	81.54	78.89	80.42	83.91
(3) New York	37.77	38.74	35.73	52.14
(4) Philadelphia	82.94	80.85	80.05	92.19
(5) St. Louis	59.34	61.51	61.81	67.19
(6) Los Angeles	69.91	65.26	49.97	67.82
(7) San Francisco	84.87	87.16	88.22	81.70

Source: Compiled by the author.

extensively in for-profit industry studies.[27] If these measures are accurate indicators of competition among medical research charities for donations, we can evaluate the degree of market competition from the disaggregated size (revenue) distribution of charities in each of the seven markets.

In Table 15.4 we present the four-firm concentration ratio[28] for each of the local markets; this measure of competition exhibited a simple correlation of 0.91 with the Herfindahl Index, calculated from the same data. As we can see from these concentration ratios, competition among local charities varied significantly across geographic markets between 1974 and 1977. Charities in New York and Chicago appear to have faced consistently stiffer competition for funds than their counterparts in Dallas and Philadelphia from 1974 to 1977. According to our model of nonprofit firm behavior, this evidence would lead us to expect that, ceteris paribus, medical research charities in the latter geographic markets spend a greater proportion of their discretionary budgets on expense preference (versus marketing) activities than do charities in New York or Chicago. Over time, we see that the relative degree of competition in the local markets varied substantially; however, in all but two of the markets, competition decreased from the beginning to the end of the period. If we compare the time trend in concentration for national medical research charities reporting to the NIB, we find that the largest four organizations' share of the national market declined slightly during the same period (from 58 percent in 1974 to 56 percent in 1977). If the level of competition had remained relatively constant during the period, then our model of charity behavior would predict that the share of firm discretionary budgets

allocated to expense preference versus marketing activities also would
have remained relatively constant over time.

Age Distribution of Medical Research Charities

Whereas the size distribution of medical research charities
sheds light on industry concentration and, perhaps, on the extent of
intraindustry competition for funds, the age distribution of these
firms reveals the longevity of the industry and its stability with respect to the entry and exit of firms. This aspect of the structure of
the industry is particularly important because it reflects: (1) the degree of entry into the market, which affects existing firms' marketing
expenditures, and (2) the amount of trust capital already accumulated
by organizations in the market. Table 15.5 presents the age distribution of charities in the 7 local markets for the years 1974-77. While
average firm age increased significantly during the period (from 13.2
to 14.8 years), the 1.6-year increase in average age over the 4 years
implies a rate of entry and exit sufficient to partially offset the aging
of existing firms. National medical research charities exhibited a

TABLE 15.5. Age Distribution of Local Medical Research Charities,
Aggregated over 7 SMSAs (1974-77)

Age (in years)	1974	1975	1976	1977
		(percentage of firms)		
Under 5	24.3	21.5	19.1	17.1
5-9	25.8	25.3	25.1	22.5
10-14	13.9	15.9	17.8	22.0
15-19	8.4	8.8	9.6	10.3
20-24	8.5	8.7	6.7	7.9
25-29	8.5	7.7	8.2	7.4
30-34	5.4	5.9	6.5	5.7
35-39	3.4	3.4	3.8	3.4
40 and over	1.8	2.8	3.2	3.7
Average age	13.2	13.9	14.5	14.8
Number of firms reporting	1226	1161	1238	813

Source: Compiled by the author.

significantly higher average age (34.1 years in 1977) than local charities, reflecting a longer period of "establishment" in national versus
local charity markets.

MARKET STRUCTURE AND THE PERFORMANCE
OF MEDICAL RESEARCH CHARITIES

According to our model of charity behavior, consumer information costs and the stringency of financial regulation will dictate the
amount of medical research charity dollars actually allocated to medical research. While we can assume that these determinants are constant across geographic markets, we have already noted that they may
vary across firms in the same market (if, for example, they vary with
firm size). Variations in the degree of competition across markets
will, we predict, primarily affect the expense-preference, marketing
trade-off for firms in each market. Furthermore, we have suggested
that such firm characteristics as size, age, and membership in an
umbrella fund-raising organization will affect this trade-off, for
organizations competing within the same market.

In order to estimate the parameters of these proposed structure-
performance relationships, we have utilized nonprofit firm-level information provided by I.R.S. and NIB annual financial reports (for
local and national medical research charities, respectively), the only
sources of nonprofit firm-level data.[29] Regrettably, I.R.S. information on firm expenditures is imperfect and omits such potentially important information as whether an organization receives funding from
joint fund-raising groups. Hence, membership in an umbrella organization, hypothesized to be an important determinant of a charity's
expense-preference, marketing trade-off, must be omitted from our
empirical analysis of local charity performance. As long as this membership is uncorrelated with the remaining variables used to explain
performance, we will still get an unbiased picture of the impact of
these latter variables on charity activities. The audited reports of
national charities reporting to the NIB are generally more detailed
than their I.R.S. counterparts in terms of financial data and information on joint fund-raising activities. Cross-sectional and time-
series observations on these national organizations are available for
1972-78, while observations on local medical research charities are
limited to 1974-77.

Equation Models and Predictions

We will utilize three basic expenditure share equations[30] to
represent our proposed structure-performance relationships for the
medical research charity industry:

$$\frac{\text{ADMNC}}{\text{FMREV}} = \beta_0 + \beta_1 \text{FMAGE} + \beta_2 \text{FMREV} + \beta_3 \text{UMMEM}$$
$$+ \beta_4 \text{COMPL} + \beta_5 \text{COMPH} + \epsilon \tag{1}$$

$$\frac{\text{FNDRS}}{\text{FMREV}} = \ell_0 + \ell_1 \text{FMAGE} + \ell_2 \text{FMREV} + \ell_3 \text{UMMEM}$$
$$+ \ell_4 \text{COMPL} + \ell_5 \text{COMPH} + \nu \tag{2}$$

$$\frac{\text{RSRCH}}{\text{FMREV}} = \lambda_0 + \lambda_1 \text{FMAGE} + \lambda_2 \text{FMREV} + \lambda_3 \text{UMMEM}$$
$$+ \lambda_4 \text{COMPL} + \lambda_5 \text{COMPH} + \xi \tag{3}$$

where:

ADMNC	=	firm administrative costs in thousands of real 74 dollars[31]
FNDRS	=	firm fund-raising costs in thousands of real 74 dollars
RSRCH	=	firm allocations to medical research in thousands of real 74 dollars
FMAGE	=	firm age (based on year of establishment or year of tax-exempt status award)
FMREV	=	total firm revenues in thousands of real 74 dollars
UMMEM	=	dummy variable, equaling one if firm belongs to umbrella organization; zero otherwise[32]
COMPL	=	dummy variable, equaling one if firm competes in market with low degree of competition (concentration ratio $\geq .75$);[33] zero otherwise
COMPH	=	dummy variable, equaling one if firm competes in market with high degree of competition (concentration ratio $\leq .45$); zero otherwise
ϵ, ν, ξ	=	error terms; $E(\epsilon) = E(\nu) = E(\xi) = 0$

Our theory of charity behavior predicts that:

$$\beta_1, \beta_2, \beta_3, \beta_4, \ell_5, \lambda_2 > 0 \qquad \beta_5, \ell_1, \ell_2, \ell_3, \ell_4 < 0 \qquad \lambda_4 \leq 0 \quad \lambda_5 \geq 0$$

Estimation Procedures and Results

Each of the above equations was estimated separately for each year included in the two data sets[35] and pooled over the entire period. At a 5 percent significance level, we could not reject the hypothesis that the parameters of each equation remained constant over time, irrespective of which data set was used in the estimation.

Table 15.6 presents estimates of the parameters of the administrative cost equation, derived from NIB and I.R.S. firm-level data

TABLE 15.6. Determinants of Medical Research Charity Administrative (Expense-Preference) Expenditures

NIB Data

$$\frac{ADMNC}{FMREV} = 0.0425 + 0.0008^a\ FMAGE + 0.0000008\ FMREV$$
$$\phantom{\frac{ADMNC}{FMREV} = 0.0425 +}\ (2.159)\ (0.516)$$

$$+ 0.0171^a\ UMMEM \qquad\qquad N = 62$$
$$\ (1.972)$$

- -

IRS Data

$$\frac{ADMNC}{FMREV} = 0.5895 + 0.0039^b\ FMAGE + 0.0000014^b\ FMREV$$
$$\phantom{\frac{ADMNC}{FMREV} = 0.5895 +}\ (3.961)\ (5.990)$$

$$+ 0.0779^a\ COMPL - 0.2074^b\ COMPH \qquad N = 1,529$$
$$\ (2.078)\ (-6.512)$$

t-statistics in parentheses.
[a]Significant at the 5 percent level.
[b]Significant at the 1 percent level.

pooled over time.[36] As we predicted, the proportion of firm revenues allocated to administrative expenditures is positively related to the size[37] of the charity (reflecting, according to our theory, economies of scale in marketing), although this relationship is statistically significant only for the local I.R.S. charities. Degree of market competition also appears to be a significant determinant of administrative expenditures of local medical research charities; charities in highly competitive markets spend, on the average, over 20 percent less of their revenues on administration than do their counterparts in less competitive areas. Perhaps most revealing is the result forthcoming from the NIB data that medical research charities that belong to umbrella fund-raising organizations spend an average of 2 percent more of their total revenues on administrative activities than do nonmembers. Finally, firm age (our proxy for the level of firm trust capital) has, as predicted, a positive and statistically significant effect on administrative expenditures for both local and national medical research charities.

When we consider another aspect of charity performance, expenditures on fund raising, we find that, as predicted, the share of revenues allocated to such expenditures by local medical research charities decreases significantly with increases in firm age (see Table 15.7). Furthermore, competition for funds has the predicted positive effect on fund-raising costs for local charity organizations, resulting in almost a 10 percent increase in revenues devoted to fund raising in highly competitive markets. However, our local charity estimates yield only weak support for the existence of economies of scale in fund raising, given the insignificant negative relationship between the fund-raising expenditure share and firm revenue. In contrast, our national charity estimates show that firm size has the predicted negative, statistically significant, effect on fund-raising expenditures for medical research charities reporting to the NIB. These estimates also indicate that, contrary to our model's prediction, firm age has a _positive_, statistically significant, effect on the fund-raising activities of these national organizations. Since these charities are substantially older and more established than the average local charity (and exhibit less variation in age), it is possible that our estimates reflect inefficiencies in fund raising that set in during the latter part of a charity's life cycle. Finally, as expected, we find that

TABLE 15.7. Determinants of Medical Research Charity Fund-raising Expenditures

---

NIB Data

$$\frac{FNDRS}{FMREV} = 0.1491 + \underset{(6.109)}{0.0019^a} \ FMAGE \ \underset{(-10.139)}{-0.0000014^a} \ FMREV$$

$$\underset{(-4.406)}{- \ 0.0453^a} \ UMMEM \qquad\qquad N = 101$$

- -

IRS Data

$$\frac{FNDRS}{FMREV} = 0.4206 - \underset{(-11.095)}{0.0071^a} \ FMAGE \ \underset{(-0.228)}{- \ 0.0000003} \ FMREV$$

$$\underset{(-1.755)}{- \ 0.0685} \ COMPL + \underset{(2.766)}{0.0983^a} \ COMPH \qquad N = 739$$

---

t-statistics in parentheses.
[a]Significant at the 1 percent level.

TABLE 15.8. Determinants of Medical Research Expenditures

NIB Data

$$\frac{\text{RSRCH}}{\text{FMREV}} = 0.2649 - 0.0033^{b} \text{ FMAGE} + 0.0000017^{b} \text{ FMREV}$$
$$(-4.263) \qquad\qquad (4.613)$$

$$- 0.0561^{a} \text{ UMMEM} \qquad\qquad N = 111$$
$$(-2.365)$$

- -

IRS Data

$$\frac{\text{RSRCH}}{\text{FMREV}} = 0.7070 - 0.0078^{b} \text{ FMAGE} + 0.0000017^{b} \text{ FMREV}$$
$$(-9.076) \qquad\qquad (7.099)$$

$$- 0.0824 \text{ COMPL} + 0.1664^{b} \text{ COMPH} \qquad N = 2,883$$
$$(-1.921) \qquad\qquad (4.396)$$

---

t-statistics in parentheses.
[a]Significant at the 5 percent level.
[b]Significant at the 1 percent level.

members of joint fund-raising agencies spend an average of 4 percent less on internal fund-raising activities than do nonmembers of similar size.

Perhaps the most important measure of charity performance is the amount of donations allocated to the purported recipients of the charity. Table 15.8 presents parameter estimates of the impact of firm size, age, and membership in a joint fund-raising agency on the allocations of a medical research charity to research projects. For both national and local charities, we find that the share of revenues devoted to research expenditures increases significantly with firm size. Our theory would suggest that it is within these higher revenue ranges that increasing consumer and I.R.S. scrutiny is given to charities' budget appropriations, thereby increasing the flow-through of funds to research. According to our estimates, firm age has a significantly negative effect on the research allocations of the organization, perhaps reflecting the increased possibilities for discretionary spending afforded by increased consumer and I.R.S. trust of established charities. Furthermore, our results indicate that research appropriations of charities decrease with membership in joint fund-raising organizations; the estimates reveal that members of such umbrella groups spend an average of 5 percent less on research projects than do nonmembers of similar size. Finally, what may be the most important result for policy-makers is the significant impact of market competition on the research allocations of local charities, particularly when such competition is keen. This result suggests that public policy aimed at enhancing competition in the nonprofit market may, indeed, increase the efficiency of nonprofit organizations that engage in the distribution of private medical research support.

CONCLUSION

This study represents what may be the first attempt to analyze variations in intraindustry firm performance where the industry under consideration is nonprofit. While the focus of this work has been on medical research charities, which play an important role in the private financing of medical research activities in the United States, a similar framework of analysis can be extended to organizations in other nonprofit industries (for example, the environmental protection, health clinic, and aid to the poor industries).

Our model of nonprofit charity performance focuses on such market conditions as consumer information costs, stringency of government regulation, and degree of competition, along with such firm characteristics as age, size, and membership in "umbrella" fund-raising agencies, in order to explain the fund raising, administration, and research allocations of medical research charities. The empirical results, which are generally consistent with our theoretical predictions, reveal that participation in joint fund-raising activities increases the administrative expenditures and decreases the research allocations of medical research charities. In addition, our estimates indicate that there exist economies of scale in fund-raising activities and that these economies of scale are at least partially offset by increased expenditures on administrative activities. Firm age, representing the degree of firm establishment, also appears to be a significant determinant of both research and fund-raising allocations of local and national medical research charities, although the direction of its effect on fund raising differs between the local and national firms. Most importantly, our results indicate that market competition does, indeed, affect the flow-through of donations to medical research projects. This conclusion suggests that antitrust legislation and other public policies aimed at enhancing market competition may have a positive effect on the performance of nonprofit providers of medical research funding.

This chapter has explored the implications forthcoming from a model of nonprofit charity behavior, which characterizes the organization's decision-maker as an expense-preferring, private-utility maximizer. As we grapple with the issue of how to most efficiently provide health-care services for our citizenry, we must investigate in further detail both the motivations and the performance of nonprofit institutions, such as medical research charities. At a time when all levels of government are facing increasing fiscal constraints, these institutions must be viewed as real alternatives to public provision of medical care and research support.

APPENDIX

Funding for Health Research and Development, according to Source of Funds: Selected Years, 1960-79
(millions of dollars)

| Year | Total Funding | Government | | Industry* | Nonprofit Organizations |
		Federal	State and Local		
1960	884	448	44	253	139
1969	2,785	1,674	144	754	213
1970	2,846	1,667	169	795	215
1971	3,167	1,877	197	860	233
1972	3,527	2,147	228	925	227
1973	3,735	2,225	245	1,033	232
1974	4,431	2,754	254	1,171	252
1975	4,689	2,833	286	1,306	264
1976	5,086	3,068	312	1,439	267
1977	5,599	3,396	338	1,592	273
1978	6,254	3,811	386	1,775	282
1979	7,047	4,321	415	2,026	285

*Primarily drug research and development.
Source: U.S. Department of Health, Education, and Welfare, Health, United States, 1980.

NOTES

1. See, for example, Clarkson (1972), Newhouse (1970), and Schweitzer and Rafferty (1976).
2. This is not to say that economists have totally ignored the allocation of resources to medical research activities. See, for example, Weisbrod (1971).
3. Medical research expenditures grew from $120 million in 1950 to over $4.3 billion in 1978. During the same period, total health-care expenditures increased from $12.7 to $192.4 billion.
4. It has been suggested that joint charity collection agencies such as the United Way may, in fact, violate antitrust law by restraining competition. See New York Times (1978).
5. For a detailed presentation of this model of nonprofit regulation and firm behavior, see Feigenbaum (1980).
6. In reality, nonprofit firms are subject only to a zero distributed profit constraint; the making of profits that remain within the firm is not prohibited.
7. These goods would correspond to "experience" goods discussed in Philip Nelson (1970).
8. This conclusion is valid only if consumers face low transactions costs in claiming compensation for fraudulent quality promises.
9. These outputs would correspond to "credence" goods discussed in Darby and Karni (1973).
10. Obviously, defining that the "quality" of charity output in terms of the proportion of charity revenues that flow through to purported recipients is a simplistic approach to a difficult quality measurement problem. The "quality" of the recipient is quite likely an important factor in assessing the quality of the income redistribution service. Charities may incur higher screening costs in selecting higher quality recipients and may, therefore, have a lower proportion of revenue flow-through than charities that indiscriminately allocate funds. However, as long as the degree of screening is uncorrelated with the independent variables that we introduce to explain degree of charity flow-through, our estimates of the impact of such variables on the quality of charity services will remain unbiased.
11. The government is not the only monitor that has been utilized to prevent fraud; producers have suggested that self-policing mechanisms and licensure can also limit fraud in the market. See Arrow (1963) for a discussion of the relationship between physician licensure and asymmetric information.
12. The expense-preference (managerial discretion) model of for-profit firm behavior has been explored by Alchian and Kessel (1962) and Williamson (1963).

13. See Darby and Karni (1973) for an analysis of the "optimal" level of false information about product quality given to consumers by producers.

14. While a discretionary budget arises in for-profit firms because owners are "separated" from managers by high information and monitoring costs, such a budget arises in nonprofit firms because consumers (donors) face high costs in monitoring managerial activity.

15. More precisely, we define $\alpha = 1 - p^*$, where p^* is the probability with which consumers can ensure that their quality demands are satisfied, given their optimal investment in information. ψ is defined to be the ratio of the minimum cost of production of a good of a given quality to the maximum expenditure ("fraud level") allowed by I.R.S. regulators (due to their imperfect information on firm costs). This may be thought of as the regulators' margin of "reasonableness" in evaluating nonprofit firm expenditures.

16. Consumer information costs about medical research charities will decrease with the size of donation $[(\partial\alpha/\partial Q) < 0]$ if, for example, large donations result in tangible output, such as a medical laboratory named for the donor. The quality of this kind of output will be more easily assessed than the quality of allocations to medical research projects. The stringency of I.R.S. regulation will, within certain ranges, vary directly with a charity's size $[(\partial\psi/\partial Q) > 0]$ simply because of the existence of a minimum gross receipts reporting requirement.

17. Consumers must be able to either hold quality constant and seek a lower price or hold price constant and seek a higher quality. Both activities are precluded by their inability to assess product quality in the first place.

18. The two-step decision process presented is similar to the model of managerial discretion developed by Migue and Belanger (1974).

19. Since the nonprofit decision maker's well-being may increase with job tenure (security), he may opt to reinvest some of his budget in the organization. For a discussion of the relationship between expense preference behavior and job tenure, see De Alessi (1974).

20. This assumes no barriers to entry into the nonprofit market. Even though the I.R.S. must award tax-exempt status, this is not a serious barrier to entry; only 6 percent of all tax-exempt applications were denied nonprofit status in 1977.

21. See Grimes (1977) for his discussion and empirical study of variability in fund raising across nonprofit organizations. Organization size and age are cited as two primary factors contributing to differences in firm fund raising efficiency.

22. The I.R.S. requires all but religious tax-exempt organizations to file annual financial statements as long as their annual gross receipts are greater than $10,000 ($5,000 prior to 1977). These organizations must choose from a list of three-digit activity codes to indicate their primary tax-exempt purpose. Thus, we have the basis for a "nonprofit industrial classification."

23. That medical research charities interact on a national level is supported by the prevalence of nationally sponsored fund-raising campaigns and the national characteristic of a charity's reputation.

24. The decline in average firm size between 1976 and 1977 occurred despite the fact that the minimum gross receipts filing requirement increased during the same period. The exclusion of a greater number of "fringe" firms in 1977 should, ceteris paribus, increase the average firm size of reporting firms and cause the percentages in all revenue classes to increase, due to the omission of the lowest revenue class.

25. The value of these (year-end) assets represents ledger value. Except for some security holdings, these figures are unlikely to reflect current market value of the charity's assets.

26. To convert from current to real dollars, we have utilized the personal consumption-expenditures deflator. For a discussion of which deflator is appropriate for private philanthropy expenditures, see Nelson (1977). The deflator used here leads to a more conservative growth rate for charity revenues than do the CPI and GNP deflators.

27. For an excellent review of various oligopoly theories and their relationship to measures of concentration, see Weiss (1974).

28. These concentration ratios have been adjusted to reflect the existence of "fringe" tax-exempt firms, with less than $5,000 gross receipts ($10,000 in 1977), that are not required to file annual financial returns.

29. For the local medical research charities, the I.R.S. financial reports include entries for "expenses attributable to gross income" (including director and employee compensation), "disbursements for purposes for which exempt" and "expenses attributable to gross contributions." We have utilized these data to proxy administrative (expense preference), research, and fund-raising expenditures, respectively.

30. Despite the appearance of firm revenue on both sides of the expenditure share equations, our parameter estimates will be unbiased as long as variation in the shares is due to variation in the numerator. This precludes, for example, reporting error in firm revenue. Note also that our three expenditure shares do not necessarily sum to one because the firm can save revenue and

improve upon its net worth or dissave its previously accumulated assets; hence, our three equations are linearly independent of each other. Accumulation of wealth may be viewed as a discretionary activity that enhances the job security of the nonprofit decision-maker (see De Alessi 1974).

31. See Edwards (1977) and Williamson (1963) for a discussion of the relationship between administrative and staff expenditures and expense preference activities.

32. Since information on membership in umbrella organizations is only available in the NIB data set, the variable UMMEM is excluded from models estimated with I.R.S. data.

33. Weiss (1974) and Bain (1951) discuss the "threshold" effect of increasing concentration on performance in the market. We have chosen 0.45 and 0.75 as our "thresholds" of (four-firm) concentration because they demarcate clear breaks in the degree of concentration in the 7 local markets during 1974–77. We have omitted competition variables from our models estimated with NIB data, since these national organizations are assumed to compete in the same market and, therefore, face the same degree of competition.

34. If consumer information and the stringency of government regulation increase with the size of the charity, then we would expect that $\lambda_2 > 0$. We would also predict that $\lambda_4 < 0$ and $\lambda_5 > 0$ if research expenditures can be used as a marketing tool by charities (see p. 399).

35. We utilized a generalized least squares procedure to estimate each equation in order to correct for heteroskedasticity in the error terms. Using a Goldfield-Quandt test procedure, we found that these error terms were inversely related to the size of the charity (in both the NIB and I.R.S. data). Therefore, all observations were weighted by a function of firm size prior to estimation of the models. While expenditure share equations are typically estimated in Seemingly Unrelated Zellner equation systems, such a procedure improves the efficiency of the parameter estimates only if the independent variables vary across equations.

36. Since our estimates are derived from a weighted least squares procedure, the traditional measure of overall explanation, R^2, is no longer applicable (it is no longer bounded by zero and one); therefore, it has been omitted from our reported estimates of the expenditure share equation parameters.

37. Our estimates did not change significantly when we replaced firm revenue by firm contributions.

REFERENCES

Akerlof, George. 1970. "The Market for Lemons." Quarterly Journal of Economics, 84 (August 1970), pp. 488-500.

Alchian, Armen, and Reuben Kessel. 1962. "Competition, Monopoly, and the Pursuit of Money." In Aspects of Labor Economics. Princeton, N.J.: Princeton University Press.

Arrow, Kenneth. 1963. "Uncertainty and the Welfare Economics of Medical Care." American Economic Review, 53 (December 1963), pp. 941-73.

Bain, Joseph. 1951. "The Relation of Profit Rate and Industry Concentration: American Manufacturing, 1936-1940." Quarterly Journal of Economics, 65 (August 1951), pp. 293-324.

Clarkson, Kenneth. 1972. "Some Implications of Property Rights in Hospital Management." Journal of Law and Economics, 15 (October 1972), 363-84.

Darby, Michael, and Edi Karni. 1973. "Free Competition and the Optimal Amount of Fraud." Journal of Law and Economics, 16 (April 1973), pp. 67-78.

De Alessi, Louis. 1974. "Managerial Tenure Under Private and Government Ownership in the Electric Power Industry." Journal of Political Economy, 82 (May/June 1974), pp. 645-53.

Edwards, Franklin. 1977. "Managerial Objectives in Regulated Industries: Expense-Preference Behavior in Banking." Journal of Political Economy, 85 (February 1977), pp. 147-62.

Feigenbaum, Susan. 1980. "A Theory of Non-Profit Regulation and Firm Behavior." Ph.D. dissertation, University of Wisconsin-Madison.

Fisher, Franklin. 1977. "On Donor Sovereignty and United Charities." American Economic Review, 67 (September 1977), pp. 632-38.

Grimes, Arthur. 1977. "The Fund-Raising Percent as a Quantitative Standard for Regulation of Public Charities." In Research Papers Sponsored by the Commission on Private Philanthropy and Public Needs. U.S. Department of the Treasury. Washington, D.C.: Government Printing Office.

Migue, Jean-Luc, and Gerard Belanger. 1974. "Toward a General Theory of Managerial Discretion." Public Choice, 17 (Spring 1974), pp. 27–48.

Nelson, Philip. 1970. "Information and Consumer Behavior." Journal of Political Economy, 78 (March 1970), pp. 311–29.

Nelson, Ralph. 1977. "Private Giving in the American Economy, 1960–72." In Research Papers Sponsored by the Commission on Private Philanthropy and Public Needs. U.S. Department of the Treasury. Washington, D.C.: Government Printing Office.

New York Times. 1978. "United Way Accused of Monopoly in Fight over Charitable Funds" (April 3, 1978).

Newhouse, Joseph. 1970. "Toward a Theory of Non-Profit Institutions: An Economic Model of a Hospital." American Economic Review, 60 (March 1970), pp. 64–73.

Schweitzer, Stuart, and John Rafferty. 1976. "Variations in Hospital Product: A Comparative Analysis of Proprietary and Voluntary Hospitals." Inquiry, 13 (June 1976), pp. 158–66.

Smith, David Horton. 1977. "The Role of United Way in Philanthropy." In Research Papers Sponsored by the Commission on Private Philanthropy and Public Needs. U.S. Department of the Treasury. Washington, D.C.: Government Printing Office.

Weisbrod, Burton. 1971. "Costs and Benefits of Medical Research: A Case Study of Poliomyelitis." Journal of Political Economy, 79 (June 1971), pp. 527–44.

Weiss, Leonard. 1974. "The Concentration-Profits Relationship and Antitrust." In Industrial Concentration: The New Learning, Harvey Goldschmit et al. (eds.), pp. 184–232. Boston: Little, Brown & Co.

Williamson, Oliver. 1963. "Managerial Discretion and Business Behavior." American Economic Review, 53 (December 1963), pp. 1032–57.

ABOUT THE EDITORS

JACQUES VAN DER GAAG was Research Associate, Institute for Research on Poverty, University of Wisconsin-Madison while preparing this volume. Before that, he was affiliated with the Center for Research in Public Economics at Leiden University, the Netherlands. Dr. van der Gaag organized the World Congress on Health Economics (1980) and is editor of the congress proceedings Health, Economics, and Health Economics with Mark Perlman (North Holland, 1981). He is the author of more than 25 articles and reviews that have been published in both Dutch and English. He is presently an economist for the World Bank in Washington, D.C. He continues to conduct research in health economics and policy and has emerged as a world-recognized authority.

WILLIAM B. NEENAN is Professor of Economics and Dean, College of Arts and Sciences, at Boston College. Previously, he was a Professor of Economics and of Social Work at the University of Michigan. Dean Neenan is the author or editor of 6 books and over 30 journal articles and reviews. His books include Urban Public Economics (Wadsworth) and Financing the Metropolis (Praeger). He continues to conduct research in the area of public policy.

THEODORE TSUKAHARA, JR. is Manager, Venture Development, ARCO Chemical Company, a division of the Atlantic Richfield Company. He was a tenured Associate Professor of Economics at Pomona College and Claremont Graduate School prior to joining Atlantic Richfield in 1976. He has been Manager, Planning & Analysis for ARCO Medical Products Company, a previously owned pacemaker operation. He is the author of 2 monographs and over 15 articles and reviews. His writing includes "Economic Considerations in Genetic Screening Programs for Tay-Sachs Disease." He was in the original group of post-doctoral fellows at the Hastings Center. He continues to do research in applied economics with emphasis on energy and health care.